Early Mississippi Records

Volume #5

Issaquena *and* Sharkey Counties

- 1868-1906 -

Compiled by:
Katherine Clements Branton
&
Alice Wade

Southern Historical Press, inc.
Greenville, South Carolina

This volume was reproduced
from a personal copy located in
the Publishers private library

Please direct all correspondence and book orders to:
SOUTHERN HISTORICAL PRESS, Inc.
1071 Park West Blvd.
Greenville, SC   29611

Originally printed Leland, MS 1986
ISBN #978-1-63914-327-6
Printed in the United States of America

TABLE OF CONTENTS
E M R
SHARKEY & ISSAQUENA COUNTIES
VOL.5

GLOSSARY--ii-iii
ISSAQUENA COUNTY RECORDS:
   PACKET GLEANINGS #121-#203; 1870-1906----------1-18
   SONS OF CONF.VET.APPLICATION PAPERS-------------19-21
   M.E.CHURCH-MARRIAGE,DEATH,BAPTISMS-1877-1901----22-24
SHARKEY COUNTY RECORDS:
   MAPS-County Hwy.-Delta Farm Land for sale 1919-24a-203
   PICTURE--24b
   PROBATE & CC RECORDS-1876-1900-------------------25-48
   WILL BOOK "A"-1877-1902--------------------------49-52
   MARRIAGE BOOK I-1876-1880------------------------53-68
   DEER CREEK PILOT EXCERPTS-1891-1892--------------69-84
   DEER CREEK PILOT EXCERPTS-1899-1900-------------85-106
   UNION CHURCH,MARRIAGES,DEATHS,BAPT.1868-1899---107-109
   CENSUS 1880------------------------------------110-136
CEMETERIES-ISSAQUENA CO.
   HEATH-SMITH------------------------------------137-138
   GRACE--138
   FITLER---138
CEMETERIES-SHARKEY CO.
   VICKLAND---------------------------------------139-145
   STRAIGHT BAYOU---------------------------------146-148
   COOK FAMILY, AT RICHEY-----------------------------148
   ANGUILLA---------------------------------------149-159
   KELLY FAMILY,AT ROLLING FORK-----------------------160
   SPANISH FORT---------------------------------------160
   CARY---161
   HARVEY FAMILY--------------------------------------161
   MOUNDS AT ROLLING FORK-------------------------162-183
INDEX--184-202

GLOSSARY OF LEGAL TERMS AS TAKEN FROM "THE POCKET DICTIONARY OF LEGAL WORDS" BY JOHN J.KASAIAN,EDITED BY DOUGLES B.OLIVER,J.D.-A layman's guide to legalese.

ABSTRACT:The essence or summary

AFFIDAVIT:A written statment witnessed by an authorized officer of the court and made under oath.

ATTACHMENT:The lawfulseizure(of property)by the court during a lawsuit in order to secure the property until controversy is resolved,so that the plaintiff can have recourse against it. If the defendant lives outside the state or territory where the court has jurisdiction, his property within jurisdiction of the court will be seized,and if he does not appear in court, the court gives the authority to dispose of the property to the plaintiff.

CHATTEL:A piece of property other than land or a building; personal property,including an animal.

COMPLAINANT:A party who files a complaint.

CONVEYANCE:The transference of title or property(usually real property) from one party to another.

CROSS COMPLAINT,(Bill of);A counter claim;a charge or claim by a defendant against the plaintiff.

DECREE:An announcement of a court's decision and the legal remedy to correct the situation.

DEED OF TRUST:(D/T)Definition taken from The Reshaping of Plantation Society by Michael Wayne-P.78;A Deed of Trust is identical to a mortgage, with the exception that the property in question is deeded to a third party for a nominal sum rather than to the lender. Should the debt not be paid, the third party is empowered to sell the prop. at public auction and give the proceeds from the sale to the lender.

DEMUR:A formal objection

DEPOSITION:Sworn testimony,in writing,taken from a witness outside of court.

EQUITY:A form of justice based on what is fair & just,as opposed to strict adherence to the written law.

FEMME SOLE:An unmarried female

FEMME COVERT:A married female.

FIERI FACIAS:Acourt order commanding a Sheriff to seize the property of a debtor in order to pay off a debt.

GUARDIAN:A person appointed by the court to care for and manage the affairs of someone who is considered unable to care for his own affairs.

GUARDIAN ad litem:A guardian appointed by the court to represent an infant and to defend him or her,or bring action to court on their behalf.

INJUNCTION:An order by a judge that a person perform or refrain from performing certain acts.

INSOLVENT:A person without the means to pay his debts.

INSTRUMENT:A formal legal document such as a deed or bond

INTESTATE:Dying without leaving a valid will.

LIEN:A claim upon,or a right to retain possession of, property of another as security for some debt owed by the person owning the property.

NON-CUPATIVE WILL;Oral,before witnesses,who may later reduce the words to writing for court approval.

OLIGRAPHIC WILL:Hand written,dated,signed,saying"this is my last will & testament".Does not have to be witnessed but handwriting must be proven in court.

QUIT CLAIM:The name given an agreement by which one party gives whatever rights he had in prop. to another.

SEQUESTER:(2)To place property that is under dispute into hands of a 3rd party to hold until question of ownership is settled.

SURETY:A person who agrees to be responsible for the obligation of another should those obligations not be met.

GLOSSARY(cont.) & ABBREVIATIONS

TESTATORS:Some one who makes or has made a will.

ABBREVIATIONS:
A/C or a/c-annual account of Adm.for an Est.
ADM.-Administrator-ADMX.-female administrator
AFFI.-Affidavit
APPR.-Appraisal
B.or BD.-bond
B.of COMPLT.-bill of complaint.
CITZ.-citizen
CH.-child or children
DECD.-deceased
DISCP.-discription
DEPO-deposition
EST.-Estate
EXEC.-executor-EXEX.-executrix
GUARD.-guardian
INJ.-injunction
INTEST. -intestate
INV.-inventory, as of an Est.
LET.ADM.-Letters of administration
OBIT.-obituary
ORIG.-original
PET.-petition
PERS.-personal
PROP.-property
RES.-residence
SEC.-security as on bond.
SUR.-surety as on bond.
TEST.-testate
WIT.-witness
W.O.W.-Woodman of the World
x-his mark,can't read or write

ABBREVIATIONS OF NAMES:

Chas.-Charles
Jas.-James
Jos.-Joseph
Jno.-John
Edw.-Edward
Fred.-Frederick
Chris.-Christopher
Alex.-Alexander
Wm.-William
Eliz.-Elizabeth
Marg.-Margaret
Geo.-George
Thos.-Thomas
Rich.-Richard
Sam'l-Samuel
Robt.-Robert
Gert.-Gertrude
Wash.-Washington

ISSAQUENA COUNTY PACKET GLEANINGS
PROBATE DRAWER #101-121
Est.means Estate Probate

#101: Est.of ELENA H.NELSON(EMMA),minor heir of SAMUEL NELSON decd.
17 Oct.1883.**PET.OF GUARDIANSHIP:** by LULU L.NELSON-Oct.23,1883-step-
mother of Emma H.-15 years old.Certi.copy dated same day.**A/C's**
to 1891 when guard.discharged.**INTERESTING VOUCHERS:** Oct.1884-Tuition
to Va.Female Institute(Mrs.Gen.F.E.B. Stuart-Principal)also for
1885.Vou.No.7-Emma's signed in Arcadia,Ms.(Arcadia Pltn)Sept.25-
1885 and Dec.26,1886 for Mrs. M.B.Burns and Emma to Dallas.
Order allowing compromise of certain claims by heirs of JAMES
NELSON(son of Sam'l.and EUNICE NELSON);MRS.J.KING MCNEELY,MRS.TRIB-
BLE(Dau.and heirs of Richard Pettway)to the Arcadia Pltn. Sum
of $1,400 Appropriated to HOWARD J., EMMA H.AND SAM'L.NELSON JR.
for ed.and support Oct.1885.Wards own an interest in said Arca-
dia Pltn. on river in Issa.Co.,some of which has fallen in Ms.River
but new lands opened and new houses need to be built for tennants-
order by court to Guard.to erect 3 new houses 1886
LULU pet. to rent Arcadia Pltn for 3 years Apr.1886.
DOCUMENT Oct.1885; Heirs of EUNICE R.NELSON:Sam'l, Tom,James Nelson,
MRS.EMMA NELSON HOOD,MISS MAMIE NELSON AND THE PETTWAY CHILDREN
OF A DAU.UNNAMED. Eunice owned Arcadia;LAND DESCP. Parts of
Sec.4,T9,R9W; all of Sec.8,same T&R;Lots 7&8 Sec.6,T10,R9-Part of
Sec.7,T10,R9W-which in 1878 sold for taxes to JACK HAYS-and was
sold to Lulu Nelson Feb.1881- in Jan.1884 she deeded to HOWARD J.
NELSON-son of Lulu(2nd wife)and Samuel Nelson-and Emma H. and
Sam'l Jr.and Wm.P.Nelson Ch.of Sam'l Nelson by 1st wife Eunice-
an undivided 4/5 int.in Arcadia Pltn.All heirs of Mrs.Eunice Nelson
quit claimed land to children except aboved named heirs & they
dispute Lulu's claim--compromise by settling for $1,400 to them.
THOS. NELSON, of Madison Co.Ms.appot.Guard.of WM.P.NELSON
O.C.SMITHART Manager of Arcadia Pltn.
ALSO INC.IN PKT. Est.of EUNICE R.NELSON-Sam'l Nelson(son) Adm.Bond
oath and Pet.filed July 19,1872. States Eunice died 1 Feb.1867
intestate at Arcadia Pltn.

#102: SAMUEL NELSON-app.Guardian of his and Eunice R.Nelson's
children to Adm.inheritance from G.Father Thomas Nelson.Filed
12 Apr.1852.Ch.NATHAN THOMAS, JOHN W.,SAMUEL,JAMES, FRANCES S.
EUNICE ANN, EMMA. He is also Guard. of MARY L.S.NELSON, minor
heir of HIS BRO.THOMAS C.NELSON,DR. OF HINDS CO.(See p.4 V.II
EMR-p.7 V.II for additional Info.
SEPERATE PKT. concerns WILLIE P.NELSON-includes a letter to Judge
of Probate by N.T.NELSON-rather a sad letter-
"One year after death of my late bro.Sam Nelson's first wife,
June 5,1871-he(Sam) brought his youngest child Wille P. to my
house in Greenville with request my wife and I take him and raise
him as a member of our family---etc)Letter dated 2-3-1884 Canton
Ms. where they now live and he is protesting to the Judge, because
Willie's Stepmother Lulu Nelson is trying for Guard.of Willie.
Willie was 13 in Feb.1883

#103;EST.OF SAMUEL NELSON Jr. (acutally III.)Minor,age 13 Dec.1883
Guard.bond and Pet.by stepmother Lulu L.Nelson.Nov.1891 Lulu
is discharged-Sam of Age.
Jan.1,1890- Mrs. Emma Nelson Wilman of Dallas,Tex.releases Lulu,

ISSA.CO.PKT.GLEANINGS
PROBATE DRAWER #101-121

Cont.#103-J.W. Alexander-Manager Arcadia 1886. Samuel Jr.and Howard are in school-Christian Bros.-St.Louis 1887

#104;Est.of Howard J.Nelson-age 9 minor heir of Sam Nelson Decd. Guard.Lulu L.Nelson Mother-Lett.of Guard.23 Oct.1883

#105:EST.OF ORVILLE MEACHAM-Adm. HENRY L.MAYER, Duvall's Landing, Ms. 15 acres growing cotton-no death date-possibly late 1883 no heirs-no claims to Est. One debt claim dated Sept.19,1883 by SAMUEL MATHEWS for $3.00 for making coffin. MARY LEAH PLTN. Dismissed 7 May 1907

#106;EST. OF S.B.KEEP(Should be **COL.H.V.KEEP, EST**)SALLY B.KEEP,wife and Adm. Jan.1884, A/C's '83 to '89 from New.York.Settled Dec.189 **WILL OF HENRY V.KEEP**-handwriting,sworn to by FRANK W. ANDERSON- "I this day bequeath all my real est.and personal prop. to my wife Mrs. S.B.Keep and my 3 sons now living-towit: H.V.KEEP, O.H.KEEP. CHAS.KEEP."New York,Dec.5,1878-Wit.THOS.J.BOLTON JR. H.V.Keep decd.on GLEN ANNIE PLTN.21 Nov.1883.
DAU. Annie Lum Keep Smith of Orange N.J.(of first wife Caroline M.)paid $1,000 by S.B.Keep--verbal request of hus.-not in will. **Guar.pet.of H.V.Keep on death of wife Caroline M.**for Annie Lum Keep 3 Jan.1866--states wife Caroline decd.Mar.10,1859,leaving Est.worth $40,000-"Glen Annie Pltn: 857 acr. In debt $18,000. Petitions for sale of part of land-contains 432 acr.States Mrs. ANN LUM & MRS.MARY HARRIS of Warren Co.Ms, only relatives of minor Annie Lum Keep-but there are no Co-heirs .20 Apr.1866
2nd wife of H.V.Keep was SALLIE B.COLLINS
PKT.ALSO CONTAINS EST.OF J.R.HARRIS-Inventory of prop. -some moved to Attala Co.Ms. 25 Nov.1862--some left with Mrs. Harris in Issa.
Description of Glen Annie Pltn.that was sold;Lot 1,2,3 Sec.1,T12 R13W-234 ac. S½ of SW1/4 Sec.31, S½of SW1/4,Sec.32-allcontain 432 ac. All in Issaq.Co.Ms.

#107-108-together-ANNIE C. & SARAH GREEN-minor heirs of OSCAR P. GREEN .Sarah E.-12 in May 1884-Annie C.10-same date
Guard.pet.by LUCY A GREEN-mother. E.STOCKNER,bondsman.Pet.of discharge of Guard and Bond.-Apr.1892 shows there was no prop. to account for in court. Document to prove the land was in Lucy A.Green's name are tax receipts and deeds of trust. Also land description.
INC.IN PKT.-5 pieces of RANDALL G. HIGGINS EST.Index says PKT.#13 His will and related Doc.are filed in Drawer H-L-abstracted in Vol.II EMR p.22.New information--Will being contested by Widow SARA E.HIGGINS &(ANNIE STANTON written in ink over typewritten paper by next best friend Sam Stanton) on grounds R.G.Higgins was not of sound mind 19 July 1889.SAM STANTON is father of minor ANNIE-her mother is FANNIE(no relationship stated)of Adams Co.Ms. Bill of complaint by DILLIE F.MAURY vs Sarah E.Higgins & Joel G.Higgins Adm.of R.G.Higgins, Est. gives R.G.Higgins death date as 26 Jan.1890.Wants-to close a mortg. on property.

ISSA.CO.PACKET GLEANINGS
PROBATE DRAWER-#101-121

#109:EST OF ISABELLA EDWARD CHAPMAN-minor heir(13 years old,Jan.20 1884)of decd.JOHN LOUIS CHAPMAN. Pet.of Guard.by Mrs.EMILIE CHAPMAN, mother. Bondsman, F.W.ANDERSON - July 1884-$250. Oct.4,1887, new bond & oath by Emilie Chapman-Security R.M.SMITH,C.S.JEFFORDS $2,100. 19 Aug.1893,State of Calif.San Bernadino Co. Issabella Chapman affidavit asking release from Guard.-now of age.

#110; Est.STEPHEN Smith-decd.2,July 1884 Issa.Co.,while traveling on a flat boat down Ms.River & left his prop. to D.F.PECK:Old delapidated flat boat, at Duncansby Ms. No heirs or relatives in state. Will submitted to probate by D.F.Peck-Aug.11,1884. Affidavit of J.L.ROOT who was on flat boat before Stephen Smith died and witnessed will-Spoken before him and other wit.J.H. STOWER, LEVI GORDAN,GEORGE WORTHINGTON-who reduced testament to writing. This was witnessed by A.J.WILKINSON & JAMES NICHOLS. **WILL:**"Giving to D.F.Peck his boat & contents." He had lived on boat in Issa.Co. for 30 days, nursed and boarded by D.F.Peck.

#110½ & #111;EST.OF DR.RICHARD C.WINSLOW'S MINOR HEIRS:ELIZABETH MAY-age 8on 8 Dec.1884-RICHARD PETTWAY WINSLOW,age 4-14 July 1884.Dr.Winslow decd.5 Dec.1884 intestate. **PET.FOR GUARD.**by mother SALLIE PETTWAY WINSLOW-Jan.1885. After Dr.Winslow's death Sallie P.Winslow moved to Hinds Co. temporarily for healths sake out ofthe "swamps", made 1887 A/C from Clinton and Pet.court to invest wards funds in order to pay mortg.on land R.C. bought from JAMES L.MAYFIELD-1883-Lots 6,7,8,Sec.2 T11,R8W;Lots 1,2,3,4,5,6,7,8,all of Sec.3, all Sec.4-920ac. **Nov.1890** SallieP. pet.court approval-remove wards to Clinton M. permanently to be close to College. Elizabeth May called Lizzie Mae & Maysie.

#112;EST OF JOHN C.CALHOUN-Intestate.-dec. his home near Arcadia Ms.Issa.Co. 8 Nov.1884-no widow-SON BRISTO only living heir. Let.Adm.BRISTO CALHOUN(x) 18 Nov. 1884-Bond Sec.A.D.HUGHES(X): S.B.HARWOOD $1,000 each.**APPR.** 28 Nov.1884-P.H.BAKER--A.D.Hughes, S.B.Harwood. **Final A/C-**July 1889.

#113;EST.OF LOVELL UTZ;Let.Adm.WALTER C.FLOWERS, a creditor-11 Dec.1884. Utz died at BEN LOMAND PLTN.Issa.Co. 4 Dec.1884 intest.;pers. Est. worth about $2,000. Sec.Bond JOHN L.ROOT, STEVEN B.DUNCAN. Unmarried- no heirs. **Appr.**EMANUL ROSE,HENRY ROSE,J.C.ERWIN(IRVING on cover).**LETTER** dated Jan.7,1886 from Nebraska, to court of Issa. requesting itemized acc. of Settlement and itemized vouchers from Vicksburg Bank. Signed W.H.UTZ.

#114;GUARDIANSHIP OF ROBERT & POLLY MINOR,being over 14 and pursuant of a law passed July 14,1862 are entitled to pensions and need a guard. appointed-ask for their Grandfather ROBERT MINOR-Filed 4 Aug.1877. Guard Bond sec. JACOB COOPER & E.STOCKNER 4 Aug.1877
WILL AND EST.OF ROBERT MINOR;written 4 Apr.1883-Wit. AARON FRENCH, LEWIS WILLIAMS. Probated 30 Apr.1885-Book C of Wills p.138-Issa.Co. House & Lot (his res.)in Mayersville,all goods & chattels to Granddaughter POLLY MINOR
Special devises;TOMMY MOLLISON-one bay pony. ANN MINOR(relationship unstated)1 bay horse "Bill, 1-sorrel mule "Kate". (cont.)

ISSA.CO.PACKET GLEANINGS
PROBATE DRAWER #101-121

#114(cont.)RICHARD GRIGG-executive.
PET.OF ADM.by Polly Minor(x)now WILLIAMS.(Grigg has deceased)-
no widow-no children-no mention of G'son Robt.Minor. Filed Apr.
29,1885. Sec. SALLIE FOWLER & E.N.SCUDDER.

#115;Est.JOHN IRVING;resided at "ELLWOOD PLTN"but died at "HOLLY
RIDGE PLTN". Remains taken by E.B.LAMON from Ben Lomond to V'burg
then by R.R. to Natzhez.Billed est.$64.70.
WILL:Dated 26 July 1883-Codicil dated May 11,1885-Recorded 8
June 1885.1.To faithfull servant LYLA GREEN,living on Holly Ridge
Pltn Issa.Co., all my household and Kitchen furnishings now on
Holly Ridge-plus $1,000.
2.To bro.WILLIAM-sisters REBECCA IRVING & ELIZABETH IRVING HODGSON
now residing near town of Lancaster Eng. all balance of pers.Est.
money etc.-equal shares of all real est.his Ellwood Pltn.,undivid-
ed ½ int.,right title & int. in certain Island in Ms.River called
the CORDELL ISLAND, undivided 1/3 int. house & lot on Union St.
in Natchez. Exec. Wm.S.FARRISH. Wit.W.A.HEARD,T.G.REDDY,S.C.ELLIOT
CODICIL;Wit.DR.R.D.FARISH,E.B.LAMON. To Lila Green $2,500. To
SOPHY PITTS-2 horses and buggies.
Sister Elizabeth signed receipt-Old Parkside Quemmore-near Lancaster Eng.,24 Aug.1886-E.Hogdson. Exec.Bond $1,000. Sec.E.N.
SCUDDER,H.P.SCOTT. 1,June 1885.**APPR.**B.N.MILLER,H.J.FINCH,J.C.
CAPERTON. W.W.McDOWELL-worked on Holly Ridge(Overseer?)vou.#11-
1st a/c.**BILL;**$162.90-Apr.19,1886-R.L.Rosebrough & Sons, St.Louis
Mo., W.T.MORGAN agent, for erecting tombstone & iron fence around
grave of Irving in Natchez. Italian Marble-"John Irving of Lan-
caster Eng. son of David & Jane Irving (scratched out)b.July
25,1822-d May 11,1885. As of Oct.1887 Irving heirs still in Eng.
No widow--no children.

#117;GUARD.HAGAN NASH-minor son(7 years) of TRAVIS NASH JR.-mother
living-not able to adm. O.R.BANKS,agent & atty. of decd.files
for Guardianship 15 Sept.1885.

#118:EST OF REBECCA BREHM:Pet.Let.Adm.JOHN BREHM,husband. She
decd.15 Apr.1884. Est.consist of 80 ac.land-description on Pet.
Children;ANNA, LIDDY, JOHN H. of age;SUSAN, WILLIAM, LIZZY,
MAGDALELENE, ETTA, minors.Filed 5 Oct.1885. Rebecca had requested
John to sell 80ac. & take ch. to Ohio-better opportunity for
education. John requested permission of court for sale.No disposition.

#119;EST OF W.B.SHIELDS;decd intes.Mar.1885 at res.Issa.Co. Let.
Adm.Wm.K.INGERSOLL,a creditor.No widow -no ch. Filed Oct.8,1885
Sec. ED.S.BUTTS,THOMAS R.FOSTER.$5,000. **APPR.**C.W.DIGGS,M.B.KEL-
LOGG,HENRY ROSE, J.J.DIGGS,----EASTERLING- Apr.7,1886. One of
the bills submitted for probate-DAVID HART Supt.& Gen.manager of
telegraph and P.O. on "PROMISED LAND PLTN".
W.K.INGERSOLL,ADM. had a store at Shipland-made no a/c for 1887-
88. Sheriff of WarrenCo. gave reason for non-delivery of writ-
W.K."lying at point of death" 17 Mar.1888.
May 28,1889 DR.CHAS.J.INGERSOLL exec.of W.K.Ingersoll's est.
made final a/c of W.B.Shields est.Not.in papers to these relatives
MRS.LENORA BRANDON,Nov.1891-Not in Adams.Co.(penciled notation)

ISSA.CO.PACKET GLEANINGS
PROBATE DRAWER #101-121

#119-cont.-by Sherf."She has left my Co. & now living near Como,
West.Felic.P.La. ---MRS.M.SHIELDS, MINELL E.SHIELDS & DR.BISLAND
SHIELDS- Jefferson Co.Ms.; MRS.M.L.SHIELDS, Tchula-Holmes Co.
MRS.F.B.VAUGHN-Birmingham,Ala: P.R.SHIELDS JR.AND W.B.SHIELDS-
Birmingham,Ala. Only one kinship identified-Miss M.L.Shields
a sister-cannot be located May 1892. Final a/c 4 Dec.1892

#120;WILL OF ZENAS PRESTON;dated 13 Oct.1875;Filed for Prob.
Oct.7,1885 Bk.Wills "C"p.142,Issa.Co.Ms."Oligraphic" will proved
in court by R.M.SMITH, W.E.COLLINS, F.W.ANDERSON-Oct.1886.
"All est. real & Personal to my Beloved wife MARY ELIZABETH PRES-
TON. Plantation and res. "WADE LAWN". Benefit of Life Ins. $10,000
She must pay MRS. ELIZABETH SCOTT of Natchez $1,350. There is
a house and lot and vacant lot in Waterproof, Tensa P.La. with
conditon old servant Issa.Higgins(colored)to continue to live
in house. Date of death 13.Sept.1885 .APPR.R.M.SMITH,E.N.SCUDDER
LIVINGSTON PEYTON.
DOC.INC.IN PKT.RENUNCIATION by MRS. Eliz.M.Scott & SARAH A.SCOTT
in favor of Zenas Preston. U.S.A.St.of La. New Orleans Pa.New
Orleans,La. Mrs. E.M.Scott is widow of Sam'l C.Scott,decd. of
Natchez,Ms. Miss Sarah A.Scott of same place. Zenas Preston of
Issa.Co.Ms. --all temporarily in this city. Heirs and relation
of SARAH BELLSINGER-MARTHA E.SCOTT & CHRISTIAN A BELLSINGER,decd.
   "For consideration of $1,000 to them paid by Preston-do relin-
quish & renounce in favor of Preston & his heirs all claims a-
gainst Preston- and any monies arising, obtained by Preston
about the year 1856 from above relatives,decd-and notes given
year of 1865 & other indebtedness of 1875."Signed; Eliz.M.Scott,
Sarah E.Scott,Zenas Preston. Wit. A.T.JANIC, A.J.ARMSTRONG. Recorded in Issa Co.Ms. 28 Oct.1889.

#121;EST.DANIEL A. ADAMS-int.,11 Apr.1885. Pet.Guard.13,Nov.1885
by CAROLINE ADAMS(X)-widow and mother-3 ch.MARY ELLA,½yr.4 Nov.
1885;MABLE(NOBLE?)3 yrs.Dec.1885;LILA,6 yrs.Sept.1885.   Bond
Sec.A.A.CHEEK, KIZZIAH PITTMAN,H.H.PITTMAN $300. Adams bought
160 ac.with Cheek and Pittman. Widow needs to sell for wards
1/3 int.

DRAWER 122-138
#122;EST.BENJ.BEARD;decd.8 Jan.1863-Leon Co.Tx. Person.Est.con-
sisted of one U.S.Bounty Land Certificate # 89327,dated 1838,
granted under act Mar.3,1855-"granting bounty lands to certain
officers & soldiers of U.S.-Certificate 120 acers. No kin.
H.C.COFFIELD was original Adm.of Est. and sold the Bounty land
Warrant to DAVID MAYER. Mayer tried to register warrant and was
turned down. 2 years search found Let.of Adm.& Bond of Coffield
that had never been recorded by Jeffords, Clerk of Court of
Issaq.Co.Ms. Hon.W.G.Phelps, Chancellor of 4th Dist.Judicial,
recommended Mayer getting his own Adm:papers and then sending
Warrant. Let.Adm.11Jan.1886 by David Mayer.

#123;EST.HENRY STERN;Decd."Clover Hill Pltn" 5 Nov.1885,intest.
LET.ADM. PAULINA STERN, wife, 13 jan.1886- Pers.est.-unpaid sal-
ary by R.STERN.Children HANNA,SIMON,ELLA STERN.**Bond sur.**L.HEIMAN
R.STERN,EMILMAYER $1,000.

ISSA.CO.PACKET GLEANINGS
PROBATE DRAWER #122-138

#124;EST.EBENEZER FOWLER;decd.Mayersville,Ms.30 Jan.1886 intest.
LET.ADM.SARAH FOWLER,widow. Son SANDERS FOWLER.Pers.Est.-small
stock of liquors & Bar fixtures $200.BOND sur.W.E.MOLLISON,H.H.
PITTMAN.APPR.SIMON HERZOG,H.P.SCOTT,R.D.GREEN.
By Sept.1887, Sarah is marr.again and now SARAH FOWLER YOUNG.

#125;EST.JAMES S.BELL:decd.Fitlers Landing.30Mar.1885-intest.
Was clerk at Gilbert and Ostroffisky Store on Fitlers Ldg. Only
heir:SISTER MRS. ALICE ORENDORF.LET.ADM.E.N.SCUDDER 4 Apr.1886,
BOND SUR.P.G.ALSTON,B.N.MILLER.

#126;EST.PHILIP GAINES ALSTON;decd.4 Oct. 1887 intest.Let.Adm.
by widow ARCOLA ALSTON. Issue;4,minors;PHILIP J.AND NAOMI ARCOLA,
PERCY GAINES, HALL ALSTON.20 Jan.1887. BOND SUR.DUNBAR HUNT,W.S.
FARRISH APPR.DUNBAR HUNT, LIVINGSTON PEYTON,T.Y.REDDY:9 Feb.1887
NAOMIE came of age 1891,boys last half of 1896.

#127-includes #120½,#128;two pkts.marked 127.EST.OF CHAS.T.SLATER:
decd."EAGLENEST PLTN"20 Jan 1887 intest. Est.consists of undivided
1/4th int.in Est. of Brother JOHN D.SLATER,decd. LET.ADM.BY JOEL
MYRES bro.-in-law-EMMA MYRES-Joel's wife is sister of Slater.
PRICILLA DAY-sister,ALICE DAVIS-sis. FINAL A/Cfiled 3 Oct. 1889.
APPR.ALTHA EVERHART,B.TONNAR,R.S.WOODBURY-10 Feb.1887.
ALSO CONTAINS EST.OF JOHN D.SLATER:decd.23 Oct.1885-Vicksburg,Ms.
intest.Was a res. of Issa. 640 acres called "EAGLENEST PLTN."
LET.ADM.by bro. Chas.T.Slater of Madison Par.La.Oct.27,1885.
No Widow or Children. 3 sisters.Pricilla Day,Emma Slater,Mrs.
Alice Davis.Charles died 1887 with out settling Johns est.and
on 4 Feb.1887, Emma and Joel Myers pet.for Let.Adm. for John.
FINAL A/C pub.23 Oct.1888

#129;EST.MICHAEL EVERHART:decd.11 Jan.1887-Issa.Co.intest.Let
Adm.ALTHA EVERHART-2 Feb.1887.Tract of land on Lake Lafayette,
Issa.Co. called "EAGLE EYE PLTN."his res.
WILL:Dated Jan.11,1887, Filed Feb.2,1887
Bro's.-GEORGE & ISAAC EVERHART- 1dollar each
Sist's-SOPHIA LANCASTER-ELLEN EVERHART-1dollar each
All prop. real & personal to my nephew ALTHA EVERHART and appoint
Altha Exec. wit. W.R.HARPER,attending phy.,J.P.TONNAR AT "Eagle
Eye Pltn."
HEIRS:GEORGE & ELLEN EVERHART-Oard Springs,Ind.:ISAAC EVERHART'S
heirs,Seymour,Ind.;SOPHIA COY-Westfield,Ill.:JOSEPH,JONATHAN,
ANNIE,WILLIE,LIZZIE EVERHART AND RICHARD REDMAN heir of JACOB
EVERHART decd.,Oard Springs,Ind.;LUCY EVERHART & minors IRA &
EDDIE-Oard Springs.Ind.;SOPHIA EVERT,Scottsburg,Ind.;ABIGAIL
VOORHIS,Kansas.

#130;EST.RICHARD WARBURTON:decd.5 Sept.1887 at Duncansby.Res.
"Woodland Pltn."Issa.Co.Ms. intest. NO WIFE-NO CH.in U.S.-LET
ADM.AD COLL. by W.F.WESTCOTT-9 Sept 1887.APPR.F.M.HALBERT:O.R.
DAUGHERTY:A.BUNN. ADM.BOND SUR.F.M.HALBERT:W.LACHS. One doc.
dated 5 Oct.1887,states R.Warburton "a foreigner,but owned prop.
in state and had contracted debts, no heirs-at-law in state"
Finala/c 1897.

ISSA.CO.PACKET GLEANINGS
PROBATE DRAWER #122-138

#132;EST.OF SCOTT THOMAS:decd.Oct.27,1885,St.Louis,Mo.where he had lived a number of years before death. Employee of Shickle Harrison & Howard Iron Co. Killed while tending iron castings pit. Platform fell into pit of red hot iron. Wife,KANSAS THOMAS- living in State of La. at time of his death,-later became KANSAS THOMAS JONES. Suit on behalf of minor heirs -LEANNAH THOMAS-6; SISTELLA THOMAS-7;suit compromised Jan.1888 in lengthy document with heirs netting $250 apiece. Kansas invested minors money in 40 acr.of land.PET.FOR GUARDIANSHIPby Kansas Thomas filed 22 Dec.1887-Suretty-W.M.SMITH & R.M.SMITH.Final a/c4 Nov.1891

#133;EST.OF JOHN A.CONNER:decd.at his res.in Issa.Co.Ms. 14 Oct. 1887-intestate. LET.OF ADMX. MATTIE M.CONNER,his wife. 2 minor children.Real & pers.est.½ int.in 160 acr.in Issa.co. 1 horse, 5 bales cotton-200 bu.corn-½ int.innotes$302-½ int.in a rent note $600 by H.C.PRESTON. Admx.bond filed 3 Jan.1888-bond surety F.W.ANDERSON,S.W.LACKS & CO. $1.000. APPRAISERS met at PIEDMONT Store(adjoins est. of Conner),16 Apr.1888-R.T.DINKINS:J.W.GRIFFIN: H.P.SCOTT. By April 1890 Mattie is MRS.MATTIE M. LEE.

#135;EST.OF ROBERT MOLLISON:decd. at MUSCADINE PLTN. Issa.Co.Ms. 28 Dec.1885-intest. NO WIDOW-NO CHILD. ½ int. in Muscadine Pltn. 1 horse-wearing apparell.LET.ADMX.IDA W.MOLLISON(joint tenant with Robert and wife of his partner in bus.-W.E.MOLLISON)17 Jan. 1889.W.E.MOLLISON,CLERK OF COURT,Issa.Co., bought out Roberts ½ int. from heirs-at-law,unnamed. BOND SURETY, W.E.Mollison, J.J.WILLIAMS-Jan.1889.

#135½:EST.OF WM.P.HICKS:late of Issaq.Co.,decd. 23 Oct.1889 at Sharon,Madison Co.Ms. intest. NO WIDOW, NO CHILD. Pers.Prop.- -1/4 int.in $3,000 life ins.Pol. LET.ADM.filed 25 Nov.1889 by W.G.ALLEN,a creditor. Bond surety-YEAMANS SMITH:JNO.W.HEATH $800, APPR.26 Dec.1889-W.O.BACON:E.A.WILSON:YEAMANS SMITH.

#136;EST.OF O.E.SMITHHART:decd.Mayersville,Ms. 1 Feb.1890 intest. Heirs;G.W. & WM.O.SMITHHART-brothers of Yazoo,Co.LET.ADM.by SAM DUNDAR SMITHHART(BRO.)3 Mar.1890.Pers.est.-1pair mules-cash in hands of MRS.S.S.NELSON,T.D.MILLS,PETER WYLEY about $500 total. APPR.3 June 1890 H.H.NUNISALLW(NUNNELLI_NUNNELLW)unreadable-JNO. TOWNSEND,H.WARREN. FILED IN THIS PACKET: a petition for adoption by THOMAS G.REDDY, OF MINORS OLIVE ENNIS SMITHHART,13;IDA SMITH- HART,8. Both parents(never named)dead and they have no guard. Children have been living with T.G.Reddy- He wished to adopt and change name to Reddy. States this is the expressed wish of the father(unnamed). 3 living Uncles-Sam'l Dunbar Smithhart- G.W.Smithhart & Wm.O.Smithhart-no other relatives to call upon. S.D.Smithhart agrees to adoption as does W.O.-no paper from G.W. NO COURT DECREE- On the Pet. for Adm. by S.D.Smithhart there is no mention of a widow or children for O.E.Smithhart---

#138;3 large pkts.Est.J.C.LYNCH & WIFE MATTIE F.LYNCH;1marked EST.R.LYNCH, 1marked Est.JAMES P.LYNCH.
1st PKT. JAMES C.LYNCH decd.at Duncansby Ms. 14 Jan.1891 and his wife MATTIE F. LYNCH followed him in death 3 days later 17 Jan. 1891, same place. 3 minor ch. RUBY, ROBT.RAY, (cont).

ISSA.CO.PACKET GLEANINGS
PROBATE DRAWER #122-138

#138;cont.JAMES PERCY LYNCH. LET.ADM.filed by WILL LACHS-17 FEb.
1891--Pers.Prop.-2 houses and a stock of liquors-groceries &
Tobacco in Duncansby,Ms. **VOUCHERS** receipts for $20 monthly for
children received by T.J.LYNCH,Cadeville,La. **APPR.**5 Nov.1891
by W.F.WESCOTT,J.H.COX,F.N.LESSER. $100 allowed Miss Wilson for
house service for children 1891.
PKTS.2 & 3 CONTAIN Vouchers for the childrens schooling and
maintenance, No Pet.for Guardianship here but R.M.Smith is their
guardian and signs all the vouchers.ROBT.RAY LYNCH was born Aug.
16,1882 and reached his majority ,1903. Had been schooled at
Baton Rouge University of La.and upon graduation resided at Ray-
ville La. JAMES PERCY LYNCH was a freshman at LSU in 1905-06
in Pre-med. Had attended school in Ruston,La.and Crystal Springs,Ms
Reached his Majority Jan.30,1906. In 1904, James P. had petitioned
the court to remove his disability of being a minor(hes 19) and
wants to enter into business with out reporting to court.Living
at the time in Crystal Springs,Ms. May have been denied for
he goes to LSU in 1905, or it could have passed and he made enough
to send himself to med school. Very little on RUBY LYNCH, 1903
she is in school at Cadeville,La. Living with T.J.Lynch.
WILL LACH is the postmaster at Grace,Ms.1891.
ONE OF THESE # 138 PKT.IS IN DRAWER #138 cont.to 160.

PROBATE DRAWER #138(cont.)-160

#138½;EST.JACK P.HAYS:decd.20 Jan.1892 at residence of mother
in Issaq.Co. intest. Undivided ½ int. in BRADFORD & ELLISTON
PLTN.800ac.cultivation,other wild lands. ½ int.in 50 head horses
& mules . WIDOW L.H.HAYS- no ch. **LET.ADM.H.H.DAVIS**,20 Feb.1892-
hes oldest brother of Mrs. Hayes,widow.MRS.E.E.HAYS,mother. THOMAS
W.HAYS,father,decd.**BOND SURETY:**JAMES CHILTON,W.S.WOOD,HENRY L.MAYER
Wm.PURNELL.26 Feb.1892, $7,000. **APPR.**Apr.21,1892 by W.M.HOLLY,JOE
MITCHELL,W.S.WOOD. **FINAL A/C filed** 8 Mar.1895.

#140;EST.OF ALBERT BRAZIL:WILL-written 10 July 1890-Filed-13
Aug.1890.Recorded p.148 Book C Wills-Issaq.Co.Ms. Albert decd.
13 July 1890.
1.All prop.to children-share & share alike. Not to be devised
until all chilren are of age.
2.Friend JAMES HIGHLAND to act as guardian of minor children.
PATSEY-17yrs.:JOSEPH-15 yrs.;MARY MAGDALENE-12 yrs.
Will written at "ONLEY PLTN"-Witnessed by S.H.HIGHLAND,ISHAM[X]
HARTFIELD.**APPR.**C.W.DIGGS,R.C.RICHARDSON,WARREN CADDOCK-24 Sept.1890

#141;EST.ALLEN NOBLE JR.(11yrs.)**GUARD.PET.& BOND**Joint Guard Pet.
of BURRELL HILL & GEORGIANA(NEE NOBLE)HILL. Georgiana is mother
of Allen Noble Jr. and Burrell Hill-stepfather. Bond $250-24
Oct..1890. Allen inherited ½ int. in 350 acres of land.

#142;EST.PRESTON HALL SMITH:decd.at res."ANNAVISTA" Issa.Co.Ms.
23 Sept.1892-intestate. **LET.ADMX.PET.**by the widow ANNA MARGARET
SMITH-13 Oct.1892. **BOND &SURETY-** R.M.SMITH J.P.HEATH-21 Oct.1892
$1500. **APPR.**by ALEX.BUNN,LIVINGSTON PEYTON,JUDGE P.MOBLEY-Dec.
1892. By 1900 the widow is MRS.ANNIE SMITH HART. **no children-
FINALa/c filed and allowed-**Dec.1,1902.

ISSAQ.CO.PACKET GLEANINGS
DRAWER #138(cont)-160

#144;EST.LAWRENCE H.GRANT:minor-H.R.CHILTON is Guard.in 1895.
R.M.SMITH Guard.in 1904. M.M.SPIARS Guard.in 1909(he's clerk
of court-Issaq.Co.).
Lawrence is son of JAMES GRANT,father(living)and LENORA GRANT-
decd.May 1888. In July 1895 Lawrence is in D'Evereux Hall Orphans
Aslym, Natchez,Ms. There until 1899.1909 he came to Mayersville
Ms. from Bliss, Okla to live with his brother.
**THIS PKT. IS VOUCHERS AND A/C by GUARDIANS. TWO MORE PKT. ONE
MARKED #144-145--THE OTHER MARKED #145 --CONCERN THE GRANT MINORS**

#144-145; more of LAWRENCE GRANTS VOUCHERS AND A/C by Guard.One
paper Dated 3 Jan. 1892 says James Grant,Father, takes Guard.
of MARY,THOMAS,LENORA, LAWRENCE GRANT. There is listed a description of land-undivided 4/5 int. in lot 6 Sec.26,T12,R8W; N part
of lot 3,Sec.37,T12,R8W-121 acres in all.
LENORA GRANT minor child of James and Lenora Grant(decd.) is
in ST.MARYS ASYLUM(orphan) Natchez,Ms. from 1895 to 1899, by
1903,Lenora is living in Jennings,La with her sister Mary Guth.
James Grant,father, living in Adam Co.Ms. in 1893
PURPORTED LAST WILL & TEST. OF MRS. ANNAS GRANT;written 30 Aug.
1890-rec.Bk."C"p.151 Issaq.Co.---She is living Rodney Ms."To
my sons,James Grant & JOHN GRANT,$2.00. To my daughter,MARY
MILLER AND HUSBAND ROMAN MILLER,live stock,money & notes remain-
ing. Roman Miller to be Adm. WIT.LYDIA M.SPIARS,J.McGRAW,W.H.
SCUDDER. **WILL & ADM.DISALLOWED BY COURT NOV.6,1890.**
INVENTORY of heirs of MRS.LENORA GRANT decd.Mary,Thomas,Lenora,
Lawrence---filed 30 Jan 1893 by Guard. James Grant.

#145;LENORA GRANT-minor- reaches 21 & asks discharge of M.M.SPIARS
her Guard. 2 Apr. 1912. **Vouchers & a/c by Spiars**
COPY OF PET.by James Grant for Guard. of his minor Children.
States-"Mrs.Lenora Grant decd.May 1888 leaving heirs Lawrence
H.-3yrs. Lenora-7 yrs. Thomas J.15 yrs. Mary-17 yrs. Filed 19
Nov.1892.

#147;GRAMLING HEIRS:PET.FOR GUARD.by R.O.GRAMLING,mother of 5
minor heirs and 1 adult male-unnamed- filed dec.1892. Father,
living,is A.D.GRAMLING-all live in Eustic,Lake Co.Fla.
MAGGIE R.,KATE EUDORA,CALLIE JONES GRAMLING-allover 14 choose
mother for Guard. in Pet.dated July 1892. Court appoints mother
Guard. of VIDA I.AND ADAM DANIEL JR. who are under 14.
These children have inherited the 1/6 undivided int. in N½ of
Sec.19,T12,R8W, 76 acres, from decd.sister EMMA GRAMLING. The
other 5/6 int. owned by LIVINGSTON PEYTON who buys their int.
for $600 in May 1893.

#148;LAST WILL & TEST.OF DAVID CURD:Dated 8 June 1889. Resident
of Issaq.Co.-"all real & personal prop. to wife ELIZABETH CURD
of Issq.Co.--Appoints her executrix." WIT:E.N.SCUDDER,M.B.KELLOGG
Proof of Will 28 Nov.1889,Filed for Probate 28 Nov.1889. Recorded
Dec.8,1892 Bk."C" wills p.153,154.
EST.OF ELIZABETH CURD:Exec.DAVID HART.Names legatees under Will
of Eliz.Curd(copy not included-see #150)minors-FRANCIS HILL,LIZZIE
McGEHEE & HARRIET CURD.Hart offers to court said minors are com-
petent to receive inheritance. Court orders Hart to pay (cont.)

ISSAQ.CO.PACKET GLEANINGS
DRAWER #138(cont.)#160

#148(cont.)--each legatee said amounts and at times named. Order filed Dec.7,1893.(See pkt.#150 for follow up)

#149;EST.OF JOHN MILLER:WILL-non-cupative-spoken 30 Aug.1890 at Chotard, Issaq.Co.Ms.-within 3 days of death. Wit.B.J.BAUSWELL, JAMES SCRUGGS,ALEX MOORE. "Bequeath to Step-daughters-MRS.EMMA HAMILTON & MRS.PATSY CHESTER all my real property of every description". Attested by witnesses-3 Sept.1890. Filed for Prob.25 Sept.1890.Rec.Bk"C" wills p.152. **LET.ADM.**JOHN M.CHILTON,a creditor 6 Mar.1893-states John Miller deceased 25 July 1890]¶note;dates for death are at odds with will date] NO WIDOW-NO CHILDREN-small tract of land E½ofE½ofW½of S10,T9,R8W-80 acres. **FIRST APPR.** May 1891 by H.R.CHILTON,B.J.BAUSWELL,WM.WOOD,J.MARSH. **SEC.APPR.** May 30,1893-J.P.HEATH,P.R.TRIM,BILL McGEHEE.**ADM.BOND**-surety $300 R.B.PHIPPS, MURRAY PEYTON Mar.6 1893. Court directs sale of land 6 Mar.1894.**PET.FOR SALE OF LAND** by Chilton 1 May1 1899. Sale and deed to HIRSH HEIMAN, 8 May 1901
¶NOTE: No further mention of will or legatees,-confusing packet-2 death dates-2 apprs.&Letters of Administration 3 years after death.

#150;EST.OF ELIZABETH CURD:Will dated 1 Feb.1893,Shipland,Ms. "Bequeath my good friend & benefactor,DAVID HART, all real & personal estate. That certain tract of land on which I reside-96 acr.S22,T11,R9W,Issaq.Co.
Bequests;2 grandaughters-Francis Hill & Lizzie McGehee(ch.of my decd.dau. ROMA ANN) & G.daughter HARRIET CURD(dau. of son DAVID CURD) sum of $350 each.·$100 per annum to each or $50 semi-annual 1st Jan-not to bear interest."
DAVID HART exec.--Wit.;SAM'L L.JONES:ALBERT R.NICOLS. Filed for Probate 11 Sept.1893. Recorded Sept.14,1893.**Appr.**A.R.NICOLS: S.L.JONES:N.H.BURTON 29 Sept.1893. **RECEIPT** of Legatees,1894,95, 96,97 signed-Mrs.FANNIE WILLIS(MRS.ED WILLIS):HARRIET CURD by Guardian PAULINE JACKSON: ELIZA McGEHEE- all from Shipland,Ms. Final a/c 4 Dec.1906. ¶NOTE; see Pkt.#148-related info.

#151;EST.OF JNO.L.GOODWIN:decd. intest. 26 Mar.1894 at HOMOCHITO PLTN. Issaq.Co.Ms. **LET.ADM.**LELIA LAFAYETTE GOODWIN (called FATIE) -widow: Minor children LEON,ETHEL,ERMA. No real est. **BOND SURETY**: L.HEIMAN, EMIL MAYER $665. **FINAL** a/c 20 Sept.1894.

#152;EST OF WALTER MAXEY:Decd. intest.-of Issaq.Co. Widow VINEY MAXEY files LET.ADM.May 6,1895 ¶NOTE:PAPERS ARE MARKED #155--WALTER S.MAXEY minor ch.is 16 on 11 Dec.1893. **Guard.Bond-from** Warren Co.Ms.by Viney- **BOND SURETY**;JAMES SCRUGGS:E.T.R.FOX. **PET. FOR GUARD.**dated 1 Oct.1895

#153;EST.OF LUCY PRICE:decd.intest, @8 Aug.1894, Greenville, Wash.Co.Ms. Res.in Issaq.Co. **PET.**of HENDERSON THOMAS claiming to be child and heir of Lucy price, asks that A.SMITH,Sherif.of Issaq.Co. be appointed Adm. 17 Oct.1891 (just as written). Names Wm.PRICE,husband;JANE CONWAY,JACOB JOHNSON & HARRIET WEEDIN her children-all full age. Smith appointed Adm.18---1894.
COMES Wm.Price to court to challenge Adm.Smith. Pet.states Henderson Thomas <u>alleges</u> to be son.--Lucy gave all her estate to (cont.)

ISSAQ.CO.PACKET GLEANINGS
DRAWER #138-160

#153(cont.)Harriet Weedin long ago. **COURT** orders Smiths adm.revoked, Nov.15,1894. There is mention of a filed NOn-Cupertive will of Lucy Price as Exhibit"A". Not included here.

#154;**EST.C.MOORE**:decd,Mayersville,Ms. 20 Feb.1896.**Pet.Let.Adm.**by widow ,MARGARET A. MOORE. Minor children CORINNE,4½ yrs;CHASTINE MOORE 2yrs.filed 2 May 1896. **BOND SUR.**MAX KILLIAN:H.P.SCOTT:7 May 1896. **VOUCHERS** to ch.in 1898 signed MRS.MARGARET KILLIAN-she married Max Killian,who decd Mar.1899. By Dec.1901 Margaret A.Moore Killian is Mrs. D.R.HARWELL, P.O.address Indianola,Ms. **GUARD.AD LITEM;R.M.SMITH.**

#155;**EST.JOHN Wm.FITZ**:of Issaq.Co.decd. at ST.Louis Mo. 21 July 1896--intest.--owned "COTTAGE HOME PLTN."**PET.LET.ADM.**by widow-EMMA F.FITZ-19 Aug.1896,names children ELISE COLUMBIA FITZ-22 yrs.;ROBT.Wm.FITZ-19yrs;OLIVER CORNELL FITZ 10yrs. **BOND SUR.** Fidelity & Deposit Co. of Maryland $500. The pltn.land description, Lots 1,2,3,4,6,7,8,S9,T13,R9W. Lots 1,4,& part of 5 S23,T13 R9W--Known as "Choctaw Land Dist." total acr. **498.**
July 26 1897,Emma files inventory from St.Louis Mo. By Dec.15, 1896 Elise is MRS. C.L.JACKSON,St.Louis Mo. By Aug.31,1898-the 2nd a/c Emma Fitz signs EMMA F.WALKER from St.Louis. **FINAL**;a/c Dec.4,1899.**LETTER** from Mrs. E.F.Walker to R.M.SMITH,Issaq.Co. from 929 Amsterdam Ave. New York, Dec.3,1901.

#155;**RIAL LIGHTS**; Pet.for Guardianship by JANE LIGHTS THOMAS, mother of 3 minor children of Rial Lights. MARTHA-19, 4 Feb.1876-ELIZ.,15, 27 Mar.1880-DORCAS,13, 17 Feb.1882.(the s on Lights is left off of the childrens name.)Pet.Filed 14 Oct.1895.**BOND SUR.** R.M.SMITH,LEON T.SMITH.

#158;**EST.OF O.R.BANKS**:departed life at Res. Issaq.Co. 2 Feb.1897, intest.**PET.LET.ADMX.** by widow CARRIE S.BANKS-4 Mar. 1897--sole heir-no ch.or g.ch. **BOND SUR.**W.M.HARRIS:L.C.DULANEY $300. **appr.** P.L.MANN:W.S.ANDERSON:FRANCIS GREEN-filed Mar.18,1898.Pltn. is not named as to where or value. **Final a/c 5 Dec. 1900.**

#159;**WILL OF MAX KILLIAN**:dated 23 Jan.1899."To my beloved wife MARGARET KILLIAN--everything".Names her Admx. Wit.W.H.SCUDDER, M.A.MOORE,MURRAY PEYTON. Filed for Probate-Mar.25,1899-Rec.BK "C"wills,p.161. Margaret Killian appointed Exectrix 27 Mar.1899. 14 U.S.BOnds transfered by title to Mrs. Marg.Killian Dec.6,1899 Marg.discharged from further accounts, May 8,1901.(See Pkt.154)

#160;**EST.OF MACKLIN STOKES**:decd.at res. Issaq.Co.Ms.1 June 1863. Pet.Let.Adm.by NANCY P.SCOTT of Warren Co.Ms. 2 April 1898-Granted and filed same day. **Bond sur.**H.P.SCOTT $100. No explanation for length of time between death and Let.Adm.

DRAWER #161-184

#161;**EST.OF HENRY GREEN**;decd.1June 1863.Pet.Let.Adm.by NANCY P.SCOTT- 2 Apr.1898.**Bond sur.** HENRY P.SCOTT,$100,same date.

ISSAQ.CO.PACKET GLEANINGS
DRAWER #161-184

#162;EST.OF ED ROBINSON alias MOULTRIE:Pet.Let.Guardianship by
EASTER R.FERGUSON -mother of minor heirs. 3 Oct.1894.
HARRY 13 yrs.on 9 Feb .1894   ALL ROBINSONS
KITTY 9 yrs. on 1 Dec.1894
ADOLPHUS 4 yearson 1 June 1894
BOND SUR.;HARRY ROBINSON & Wm.FERGUSON $100.

#164;EST.OF Wm.PURNELL:decd. 9 Mar.1899 intestate.Pet.Let.Adm.
20 Apr.1899 by widow O.PURNELL states small tract of land on
Ms.River-lower part of Issaq.Co.-there are 5 children over 21-
JOHN H.:Wm.R.:HENRY P:MILLARD R.:EDWARD T.PURNELL.
BOND SUR.R.M.SMITH:W.M.KAUFMAN $250. APPR.R.M.SMITH & W.E.COLLINS
May 1900 children petition court to release Mrs.Purnell from
bond and accounting. They want nothing from Estate. Final filed
Dec.5,1900

#165;EST.OF POMPEY WATSON:late resident of Issaq.co.Ms.decd.
8 Aug.1897. No widow. Pet.of son SAMUEL F.WATSON for Adm.18 Jan.
1898. Bond Sur. $100 I.LUCAS :JOHN W.HEATH

#166;EST.C.H.JOHNSON;decd.at a Levee camp in Issa.Co. Feb.1898
intest. ADM.AD COLEGENDUM-L.C.DULANEY Feb.23,1898. No relatives
or heirs after deligent search till Oct. 1909,

#167;EST.OF ROBERT L.MAITLAND-WILL. decd.Nov.1870-New York-a
merchant. Written 17 Apr.1868. Filed in Issaq.Co. Nov.10,1871-
Rec.in BK"C" p.193- 13 May 1910
BEQUESTS:Uncle-JAMES LENOX
         Aunts-JENNET LENOX,HENRIETTA A.LENOX,ALTHEA L.DONALDSON
         Sis.-ELIZABETH S.MAITLAND, JENNETT L.BELKNAP
         All to receive $200- also Miss CATHARINE T.WHITEHEAD.
MY SON ALEXANDER receive $25,000 at age 21
2other children to receive same at 21-one a daughter-neither named
in will.
BELOVED WIFE MARY CURRIE-all rest of personal& real prop.
Wife Mary Currie, son Alexander & friends JAMES DONALDSON,&
HENRY M.ALEXANDER to be executors & guardians.
WIT.-JAMES S.HUGGINS,New York;ASHBEL GREEN,New Jersey;EDWIN W.
EDWARDS, New York.
CODICIL;Jan.30,1869 concerned Presb.Church at Islip or Isliss
(old school) Proven in Surragate Court of New York, 31 Dec.1870.
Exemplified copys of Let.Adm. & Will sent from New York & filed
in Issaq.Co.Ms. Large amount of Real Est.in that Co.

#168;CHESTER A.BOLLING-minor;Pet. court to remove disability
of being a minor(hes 20) and in farming with older brothers ALBERT
L. & JAMES G. & CHARLES H.BOLLING. To obtain advances for crop
loans he needs to be able to mortgage his 1/4 int. in the land.
Granted for year of 1907 only. Land description incl.

#170;EST.OF HENRY P.SCOTT & WILL:written Aug.13,1899-Filed and
Prob. Oct.30 1899-BK"C" Wills p.162-Issa.Co.Ms. Decd. 19 Aug.1899
"To my wife NANCY SCOTT"--Everything real & pers. Real est. to
descend on her death to sons in equal parts--WILLIS H.SCOTT-
Grace Station,Ms. & FRANK C.SCOTT of Vicksburg,Ms. (cont.)

ISSAQ.CO.PACKET GLEANINGS
DRAWER #161-184

#170 (cont.)Sons & friend W.E.MOLLISON, share equal claim against Freedmens Savings & Trust Co. NANCY SCOTT Executrix; WIT; FRANCIS GREEN, MRS.MATTIE FOSTER- at Garcia or New Kansas, Issaq.Co.Ms. Final a/c May 1904--Land description.

¶NOTE-next pkt.out of sequence

#169; EST OF T.B.COWAN-WILL:dated 7 June 1899 at Esperanza Pltn. Issa.Co.Ms.Cowan decd. 16 July 1899-
"Give & bequeath to all my first cousins-$25 each-upon applying for same and proving identity."
"To my friend WmR.TAYLOR of Esperanza $20,000 in Capitol Stock of Greenville 1st National Bank. Also real estate I own in Greenville,Ms.-Livery stable, shops & etc.occupied by A.S.OLIN- & cottage house formerly belonging to J.C.HEAD"
"To my friend P.L.MANN who now lives with me on Esperanza Pltn.- all these certain 4 plantations in Issa.Co. "Lakeside"-"Hopedale" "Fair Field" and "Esperanza"-all pers.prop. on said Pltns.-- all money on hand,-all cotton unsold- $500 Capitol stock 1st National Bank Greenville,Ms. to be in full payment of any sum I owe him- all stocks,merchandise and accounts in stores on the pltn.--any other property not mentioned"
"Appoint P.L.MANNN Exec.& Adm."
WIT.:W.G.ALLEN:E.M.JORDAN:JAMES T.DUNBAR.Proven 24 July 1899 Rec.BK"C"p.164-165-Issa.Co.Ms. The following people challenge the Will Dec.1901-oneyear after final decree on Est.of Cowan; SAM'l R.COWAN-Lockhart,Tex.:A.F.COWAN Bertram,Tex.;MARY E.CABINESS Sea Willow,Tex.;MRS.M.C.SMART, Goliad,Tex.;MRS.M.T.HANDY Goliad,Tx W.C.& MARK H.COWAN of Leaky,Tx. DEFENDANTS-P.L.Mann,Wm.R.Taylor deny they are 1st cousins and state that only MRS.JOSIE DORSEY, Yazoo,Co.Ms.;MISS MATILDA COWAN,(nowdecd.);MRS.IRENE WHITEHEAD OF Thomaston,Ga. & MRS.HICKS, Warren Co. are 1st cousins and had been settled with- and will was lawfully proven in court with final Decree Dec.4,1900. W.R.Taylor in Rankin Co. by 1901.

#172; EST.MASON BARTLETT KELLOGG-WILL: Filed Mar.17 1900 Rec.BK "C" p.165-166.
Turo Infirmary, New Orleans,La. Nov.19,1899.
"To my nephew JOHN BLAKE KELLOGG of 19 W 42nd St. N.Y.City--all of my real & pers.est.-- Appoint JOSEPH HIRSH of Vicksburg,Ms. my Executor". Will mailed from N.O. to Hirsh same day as written-Kellogg was undergoing Surgery. He deceased 11 Feb.1900 still under care of Drs.in N.O.-Hirsh filed for Adm. 17 Mar.1900.
Appr.HARRY BAUGH,C.A.FITLER,LOUIS BOWERS.

#173; ADOPTION OF ISIDORE LUCAS STOUT; 11 years old-son of A.J. STOUT AND LULU SIRRONIA STOUT-married 9 Dec.1888-divorced 5 Dec. 1893 in Issaq.Co.Ms. Lulu took her maiden name-Sirronia. Dec.Term of court 1900 Isidore Lucas of Issq. Co. petitions for adoption and changing name of I.L.Stout to Isidore Lucas Jr. Agreed to by mother Lulu Sirronia-father can't be found,-agreed to by Grandmother ANNIE LUCAS. Decreed as so-4 Dec.1900.

#174; EST.OF JOHN HEATH:decd.intest. 2 Oct.1900. JAMES P. HEATH-son is Adm. Bond sur. JOHN W.HEATH,T.A.HEATH(sons of John)cont.

ISSAQ.CO.PACKET GLEANINGS
DRAWER #161-184

#174-cont.and R.E.FOSTER 23 Oct.1900. Johns daughter is N.E.FOS-
TER. **APPR**.26 Nov.1900 by G.D.ANDREWS:R.E.HOLBERG:THOS.W.STEWART.
FINAL a/c Dec.1901.

#175;**EST.DAVID STRACHAN**;decd.Jan.14,1901. ROBERT STRACHAN -Adm.
Documents included;-papers concerning sale of 6 acres of land
to I.A.CORTRIGHT-dated 1904.--One concerning Life Ins. settlement
due JANE STRACHAN,now deceased and willed to ELIZA SMITH-dated
1909.--A Bill of Complaint by MARGARET NASH et-all vs. D.& R.
STRACHAN dated 1900. Dismissed in 1901.

#176;**EST.OF FANNIE WALKER**:decd.25 Feb.1901-Shiloh,Issa.Co.Ms.
PET.LT.ADM.by JOSEPH NASH states that Fannie's husband C.D.WALKER
decd.8 Feb.1901. JOSEPH & CATHERINE NASH are her mother & father.
Brothers and heirs, GUS, JOE, CORNELIUS NASH ,& WINNIE WASHINGTON
Sisters-KATIE, EUGENIA, LEAH & NELLIE NASH. Filed 7 June 1901.
BOND SUR.T.A.HEATH & B.F.LACEY $600.

#177;**EST.FRANCIS GREEN**:decd 17 Oct.1901-**WILL** dated 4 Sept.1901.
Resided at Grace Station, Issa.Co. Ms.
Bequest"To my wife JULIA E.GREEN & our 7 children-ANNIE E.(now
McRAVEN):FRANCIS GREEN JR.,JULIA E.:WILLIAM:MATILDA:VIOLA & Mc-
KINLEY GREEN. All real & Personal Property. Julia E.Green to
be executrix & guardian--at her death Daughter Annie E.McRaven
to take over. Filed 25 Oct.1901.Rec.Will BK"C"p.168.
Annie E. becomes Extrix. 21 Jan. 1921--makes 1st & Final a/c
stating all heirs are of age & living. Viola-now Thames-Shelby
Co.Tenn;Matilda-now Scott, S.C.; Julia-now Butler-Vicksburg,Ms.
PET.for dismissal as Adm. 25 Feb.1924. William signs Dr.W.A.GREEN-
Shelby Co. Tenn.;McKinley Green-St.Louis Mo.;Francis Green Jr.-
Wash.Co.Ms.

#178;**EST.OF H.H.NUNALLEE**;late of Issa.Co.Ms. decd. 16 Sept.1901
at Monroe,La.**PET.LT.ADM**.by MAGGIE L.NUNALLEE-widow. Children-
BEAUREGARD W. 14 Yrs.:NASHTI R. 11 yrs.;MARGARET E.9yrs;HARDY
H. 6 yrs.;29 Oct.1901. **BOND SUR**.FLORA B. LEE, B.B.WARREN $2,000.
APPR.R.E.FOSTER,G.H.SIMRALL,G.W.CARTER.---Store house and stock
of goods at Arcadia,Issa.Co.Ms.--mules,horse,live stock and farm.
Tract of land -part of ARCADIA PLTN. bought from J.H.NELSON.
Maggie L. and children are in Monroe,La.-1901-02.
¶NOTE; NUNALLEE ALSO SPELLED NUNNALLEE]

#179;**EST.OF JNO.McYOUNG**:of Clover Hill,Issa.Co.Ms.-decd.29 Oct.
1901-intest. **PET.LT.ADM**.by HANNAH McYOUNG-widow (no ch.) 5Nov.
1901.Small army pension. **BOND SUR**. JOSEPH STERN $50.

#180;**EST.OF KITTY O'NEAL**:-**WILL**- dated Mayersville,Ms. 26 July
1895. "ALBERTA BROOKS & HUBERT O'NEAL inherit house & lot. Alberta & g.ch.KITTIE share black calf. Son JIMMIE gets household
furnishings,1 cow."Witnesses;MRS.E.BLAND,MISS M.B.JONES(alias-
MRS.M.B.FOSTER);MR.H.P.SCOTT.
MRS.LOUISA LAWSON asks Will to be probated 28 Oct.1902.Probated
and filed Nov.1902.

ISSA.CO.PACKET GLEANINGS
DRAWER #161-184

#181; EST.OF JOSEPH BAKER-WILL-dated 13 Nove.1901-Issa.Co.Ms. "all land on front of "PROMISE LAND PLTN" T11-doesn't say to whom--wife LUCY BAKER appointed executrix."Wit;EMILY DIGGS,JOHN FLORIDA,R.B.SHIELDS. **PROOF** of will offered 5 May 1902. **BOND SUR.** I.J.COLLINS $300.

#182; EST.OF JAMES H.COX:decd.--Dec.1902 at Duncansby Ms.-intest. **PET.LT.ADM.**of CHAS.L.COX,brother from Madison Co.Ms. states these Bro.& Sis. A.V.COX-Alexandria,La.;N.G.COX, Tishimingo Co.Ms.; LULU COX-Tishimingo Co.Ms.;JOSEPH B.COX- Fortsmith Va. Pet.dated Jan 5,1903. **DECREE** of insolvency filed by Chas.C.Cox 28 Apr.1904- after all debts are settled. **APPR.**JOHN GRIFFIN,W.H.BROWN,I.FREID- BORG-5 Jan.1903. Same men on Bond Surety,$1,000. Est.consists of drugs & goods in store at Duncansby,Ms.

#183; EST.ALEXANDER BUNN; late of Issa.Co. decd.at "VALEWOOD PLTN" Issa.Co. 29 Mar.1903-intest. **PET.LT.ADM.**SARAH A.BUNN,widow. 2 dau. FLORA B.BRYAN & GEORGIE BUNN-both over 21-1 May 1903. Admtrx.dismissed after final a/c 6 Dec.1904. 2 daus.sign waiver from Tenn. Husband had sold property before death to Worthington & he paid Est.$8,000. **BOND SUR.**EMIL MAYER,GEORGE ROBINSON $3600. **APPR.**E.MAYER:E.J.BRYAN:Wm.GRIFFIN.

#184; LAST WILL & TEST.OF SARAH FOWLER:dated 20 Sept.1900-Mayers- ville Ms. "This is the last Will & test.of me, Sarah Fowler-alias YOUNG-,revoking all other wills & codicils---Bequeath all property real & personal to son SANDERS FOWLER & dau.BETSY GINKERM-in equal portions. N½ of lot 1 in Block G in town of Mayersville,Ms. Exec.D.STRACHAN & JAKE COOPER." Wit.LUCY HINES,ISONE WATSON,D. STRACHAN. Filed for Prob.6 Feb.1901.Rec.WBK"C"p.167. Admitted to prob.May 4,1904.

#184; EST.OF NICHOLAS YOUNG:decd.sometime 1863. Sister IDA S.DIGGS pet.to Adm. & colect small pers.est.of wages & pay & bounty due him by U.S.Govt.for service in late War of Rebellion.$150. Pet. dated 28 Apr.1903. Bond sur. $250, C.W.DIGGS & L.H.HIGHLAND

¶NOTE: two packets of #184¶

DRAWER:#188-203

#188; EST.& GUARDIANSHIP OF HENRY & ARTHUR WILLIE & LOUELLA FOE: minor heirs of ISAAC FOE(alias EUTAW CHESTNUT). Guard.paper taken out by sister ADALINE FOE June 1905-so that the minors could collect a pension from U.S.GOVT.(a Pvt.Co.I,Reg.T.U.S.C.Vol.Infan- try) to be paid until children are 16, beginning Mar.2,1904-- which brings forth the conclusion that Isaac Foe decd. in that year..Original Cert.No.612638 USA,Bureau of Pensions-issued for soldier pensioned as "Isaac Foe".

#189; 2pkts.EST.OF JOSEPH STERN; of Issa.Co.Ms.decd.15 July 1905 intest.**LET.ADM.**by SOLOMON STERN-eldest son of JOSEPH & ROA STERN 26 July 1905.Children;SAM:HENRY JAKE:HANNAH & CECILE STERN.**BOND SUR.**R.M.SMITH,EMILMAYER,SAM STERN_$6,000.**APPR.**R.M.SMITH,LIVINGS- TON PEYTON,ISAAC HERZOG. Stock of goods in store,some live(cont.)

ISSA.CO.PACKET GLEANINGS
DRAWER #188-203

#189(cont.) stock & household effects-real estate in Memphis, Tenn. Sale of stock of goods made at Clover Hill store May 1906. HANNAH STERN IS HANNAH HYAM-wife of L.H.HYAM & living in McGehee, Ark. by 1906. Sam,Solomon & Hannah over legal age by Dec.1906.Jake & Cecile still minors-Cecile 8 yrs.in 1906. #2pkt.contains vouchers

#190;EDNA FORD-GUARD.MINOR HEIRS OF ROBERT McCANN:
Pet.states Edna Ford is mother of Eliza McCann-16 yrs.and Peter Williams,19 yrs. Also Mother of Robt.McCann-decd.18 June 1905. in Issa.Co.Ms.-unmarriad-no ch.-intest.-Member of KNIGHTS OF EPITHIAN SOCIETY -ins.of $400, Nov.3,1905. **BOND SUR.** U.S.Fidelity & Guaranty Co.---Eliza McCann signs receipt in Nov.1909 as Eliza Durman.

#190½;EST.OF E.B.DICKEN: Decd. 6 Apr.1906-in Issa.Co. W.W.CATCHINGS APPOINTED Adm.by court 7 May 1906. From items reported in sale of prop.-his business was a bar or saloon in town of Mayersville, Ms. **BOND SUR.** C.C.SANFORD,JOHN GRIFFIN $1,000. **APPR.** W.H.SMITH, V.A.KILLIAN,SAM STERN.

#191;L.T.WADE'S MINOR CHILDREN(GUARD); Pet. for Guard.by L.T.Wade father of W.R.WADE 14;LOUISE HOYT WADE 12;L.T.WADE JR.10;ALICE GRAY WADE 5;JANE WADE 2; devises of Last Will & Test. of W.W.RIFE late of Bolivar Co.decd.Apr.1905--Pet.dated May 23,1906.**BOND SUR.** J.K.HAZLIP,LOUIS KLEIMAN $4,500. **Certified** copy of Will of W.W.Rife of "Rifes Pltn"Bolivar Co.Ms. attached. Will dated 8 Jan.1903.Probated & Recorded 19 Apr.1905 Bolivar Co.Ms.
"I give--MARY LOUISA POWELL-1/4 of real & Per.Prop.
To heirs of GEORGE WADE   "   "   ""   ""
TO Children of Lawrence T.Wade   ""   ""   ""
Other 1/4 divided thus;CHARLES WADE 1/3; My nephew RIFE SIBLEY of Dardinelle Ark.1/3;MARY JANE BURR & her sister ANNIE,dau. of decd. bro. THOMAS C.RIFE-1/3.
Property to be sold for cash & distributed to heirs.HOLCOMB D. CHANEY & JOHN V. BURRUS to be Exec." Wit.;J.W.MASON;W.R.JONES.
LAND DESCRIPTION: L 6,7,8,Sec.4;L 1,2, Sec.5. N.diagnal parts of L 3,4,Sec.15;L 2 lying W of Straight Bayou in Sec.15;L 8 in Sec.15, all in T21,R8W. 514.81 acres.

#192;EST.OF MARY DORSEY: decd at "RESERVE PLTN",12 May 1906-intest **PET.LET.ADM.** by JAS.RICHARDSON(her son) states Mary decd. possessed of a pension warrant on US Treas. for sum of $24. Heirs 4 children-JAS.RICHARDSON,HESTER NASH,ABBY BROOKS,HENRIETTA RICHARDSON- filed 4 June 1906.**BOND SUR.** $50,R.B.PHIPPS,EMIL MAYER.

#193;EST.OF ELLEN WALKER: res.of Issa.Co.Ms. decd. 28 Apr. 1906-intest. 5 heirs,children-HENRIETTA WALKER(of age)JOSEPHINE WALKER ANTHONY WALKER,RUTH WALKER,ISAAC WALKER-minors.**PET.LET.ADM.** by J.A.McGRAW-28 Apr.1906. **BOND SUR.** W.H.SCUDDER,W.W.ELLIOTT -28 June 1906 $100. **Pet** by McGraw to cultivate or lease farm land 5 July 1906. **Probate** of claim by Dr.W.W.Scudder made out to JOHN & ELLEN WALKER-beginning of bill July 1900. **Taxes paid** on 40 ac. N½ Lot 2 Sec.28,T12,R9 in 1907 by JOSEPHINE now WILLIAMS. **FINAL** a/c 28 Mar.1914 all ch.in Tunica,Ms.living on R.I.A.ABBEYS place. All over 21-ANTHONY WALKER IS DEAD

ISSA.CO.PACKET GLEANINGS
DRAWER #188-203

#194;EST.OF LEE ALBERTUS SMITH:decd.2 July 1901-St.Mary Parish
La. Certified copy of succession from that parish states--MRS.
MARY IONE ROCHEL(Smiths widow) was appointed natural Tutrix of
minor & only child MARGARET INEZ SMITH. Signed IONE A SMITH.
Marg. inherited 1 undivided ½ of property-put in her possession
as legal usufructuary of other undivided ½. **GUARD.BOND** filed
in Issa.Co.Ms. July 19,1906. Bond sur. R.M.SMITH & J.P.HEATH.
PARTITION deed rec.p.519 DBK-S-Issa.Co.-Land description in
T12-R8W.**PET**.to sell wards land 6 July 1906-offer of $4,000.
¶NOTE:See Pkt.#62-Prob.Drawer 56-80 Issa.Co.Ms.-R.M.Smith- for
background of family. EMR. Vol.II pg.52.
Brief wrap up--Lee Albertus Smith was son of Robt.M.Smith & Margaret S.Smith- 14 years old when his father died 1877. He inherited 1/7 int. in "CLOVER HILL PLTN". Final a/c of that est.by
ROBT.SMITH JR. Jan 1906-states Lee A.Smith decd-sister Lou married
to J.P.Heath, LAWRENCE,PRESTON bros.also decd.]

#195;GUARD.OF OSCEOLA & JNO.MORRISON-minors;Pet.for Guardianship
to be given to JOHN MORRISON by Oceola who is over 14-9 Mar.1906.
GUARD BOND sur. D.W.GEARY,W.J.VOLLAR. John Morrison is "next
best friend"and has had custody & care of both minors since the
death of their mother GRACE M.GIBSON in 1904.
INCLUDED in pkt.is a doc.of suit brought by DENNIS M HENNESSEY
dated May term 1913. Hennessey,a life long res.of Issa.Co.Ms.
and 40 yrs old. States;"That the said minors Osceola & J.W.Morrison,are his nephews-sons of his sister Grace M. Gibson-who died
1904 intestate .--That said Grace also left 6 other minors,
ELIZABETH, GRACE, BEATRICE, CHRIS & ANNIE MORRISON & an infant
only a few hours old who died onlya few months old. Annie died
1908 age 14 yrs. Petitioner immediately upon the death of his
sister -took Beatrice & Chris,William C. & a few months later
took Eliz. & Grace & Annie to live with him & took care of them
etc.-Grace M.Gibson decd. was a colored woman, a negro, an octaroon and never legally married. The natural father of all her
children was a white man-caucasion-a Scotchman & subject of
Great Britian, whose name is JOHN MORRISON. Grace at her death
left some property-live stock and 160 acr.land.(descrp.included)
in Sharkey Co. on which there was a valuable lot of timber. That
Grace had also bought for her minor son Osceola 120 acr. of which
8 acr.has been in cultivation since 1903--40 acrs. in John W.'s
name-30 acrs. in cultivation since & including 1898----Doc. goes
on to accuse John Morrison of using land and selling timber-
never paying other children anything-and raising children to
hate white and black folks."
ANSWER;by John Morrison May 1914-"Admits Grace was Octaroon &
mother of all his children -that she died 14 Nov.1904-denies
Dennis Hennessey ever paid for their upkeek & education-states
that he was not naturalized & when he bought & paid for land
he put it in the name of Grace,Oceola & John W.-he had continued
the use of same since had worked & paid for it. States that
Hennessey had never been anything but an annoyance to him and
interfered with his labor & business. That the children had lived
with Graces mother for a time because the small ones needed a
mother, but all had returned to the home he had built on the
prop.and had been with him full time the last 2 yrs.(cont.)"

ISSA.CO.PACKET GLEANINGS
DRAWER #188-203

#195-cont. No disposition in this folder--penciled notation on folder "Remaned to File Nov.1921.Possibly more of this on file in Sharkey Co.Ms.

#196;GUARD.CECILE STERN-ward; SOLOMAN STERN petitions for Final Decree as Guard.of Cecile-ward becomes 21,8 Feb.1918. Approved May 9 1918. Cecile agrees to final a/c & signs in Greenwood,Ms. her residence-Apr.101918. **a/c & vouchers**

#197;GUARD.H.G.STERN: Final decree of Guardianship of Soloman Stern for H.JAKE STERN--14 Feb.1910-stating, Jake came of age 26 Jan.1910.**a/c & vouchers**-Final filed Feb.17,1910

#198;MRS.ALICE POINDEXTER CHILTON-WILL: Will not in folder. A note dated Raymond Ms. June 5,1907 by JOHN M.CHILTON requesting the will be mailed to him for use in a distant county. **PET.LT.ADM** 21 Nov.1908 by John M.Chilton states Alice P.Chilton decd.10 Nov.1906. Stated the will was witnessed by E.W.STILES & ALICE P.STILES and he was nominated in will as exec. Real est.in Issa. & Hinds Co. Ms. Insurance Policy $5,000. Will approved and admitted to record Issa.Co. 15 Dec.1906.

#199;EST.JOHN H.BREHM; decd. at Fitler,Ms. 3 Nov.1904-intest. Widow NANNIE T.BREHM pet.for Lt.Adm.3 Jan.1905. Children ALMA, WILBUR & BESSIE BREHM.

#200;EST.HENDERSON HILL; decd.Mar.1905 in Issa.Co.-Widow HATTIE HILL request court to appoint B.F.LACEY Adm. of small est. 19 Apr.1905. Bond sur. ALEX MASON,S.H.HIGHLAND.

#201;GUARD.HATTIE,LAURA,MARY BOOKER-minors; Children of FRANK BOOKER. Let.Guard. granted to B.F.LACEY 16 Nov. 1907. Mother ELVIRA BOOKER pet.court to appoint Lacey Guard. She used wards funds to purchase house and lot in Vicksburg,Ms.and took them there to live with courts permission. Deed & Plat in this folder .Lot bought of SARAH J.& JOHN W.HARRIS.Rec.Warr.Co.Bk#113,p.215

#202;EST.GRANT YOUNG: decd.at Valley Park,Ms. 19 May 1907.Left surviving him 1brother.Let.Adm. to F.Birdsong-Sheriff of Issa.Co. 3 Mar.1908. Est.consist of a judgment against Yazoo & Miss.Valley RailRoad for $300 for the killing of decd.minor Grant Young by one of their trains. 2 heirs;SIDNEY SIMMONS,12 yr.GEORGE HOUSTON 10yrs. now living in care of AUNT MOLLIE MILLER.

#203;EST.MARGARET HUGHES HOLMES: decd.at Grace,Ms. 5 Mar.1908- DAN HOLMES -her husband & only heir-Petitions for Adm.2May1908 Bond Sur.J.H.CAHOUN,JOHN DIGGS $300.

ISSAQUENA CO.MS.
SONS OF CONFEDERATE VETERANS APPLICATION PAPERS
ISSAQUENA CAMP NO.538,MISS.DIV. ORGANIZED 1906
   These records were found among the papers of Dr.W.H.Scudder
of Mayersville,Ms.He is deceased. They are now in the hands
of his grandaughter, Mrs.Jack Schults nee Gertrude Langford,
of Rolling Fork, Ms.
   The applications give the birthdate and place of Applicant-
parents, and service record of father.

STEWART FLOYD ALFORD-b.June 8,1873,Goshen Springs,Rankin Co.Ms.
   Father-Stewart Floyd Alford, Mother-Aurora Hoy.Service of
   Alford Sr.-Pvt.Co."Madison Rifles" 10thMs.Regt.Infty.Later
   entered Quartermasters Dept.under Maj.Hilliard until end
   of war. Application dated April 30,1907

HENRY WADE BENSON-b.Feb.18,1878,Fountain Hill,Ashley Co.Ark.
   Father-JOHN PORTER BENSON.Mother-MARY GEORGE WIGGINS. Service
   of J.P.Benson-Pvt.in Capt.Smith'sCo.,Wrights Regiment in
   Ark. He was still living in May 22,1909 and a member of United
   Conf.Veterans Camp no.216(Pat Cleburn) Ark.Div.,Fayetteville,
   Ark. Application dated May 27,1909.

WILLIAM WARREN CATCHINGS-b.Aug.15,1862,Madison Co.Ms.Father-
   William Warren Catchings. Mother- Georgianna Dulaney. W.W.
   Cathings entered Conf.Army 27 Apr.1862 as 1st.Lt.of the Vicksburg Volunteers--later served in Co.H 2nd Ms.Batt.&48th Ms.
   Regt. As attested by F.M.FOLKES,2nd Lt.same Regt. they fought
   in"nearly all (if notable)of the battles in Northern Va.,in-
   cluding Gettysburg & the 1864 campaign and seige of Petersburg

DR.VICTOR M.CROTHERS-b.Sept.24,1886,Washington,Adams Co.Ms.
   Father-PHILIP HOGGATT CROTHERS. Mother-ALICE HAZLIP. P.H.
   Crothers entered C.A.---1862 as Pvt.in Co.C,4th Ms.Cavl.Mabry's
   Brigade,Forest's Comd.Surrendered at Gainsville,Ala.with
   Reg.and honorably discharged. Appl.dated APR.21,1913.

GEORGE FREDERICK EICHELBERGER-b.Mar,29,1870,near Forest,SCOTT,Co.
   Ms. Father-WILLIE FRANKLIN EICHELBERGER. Mother-MINERVA_____.
   Joined CA Apr.8,1864, Pvt.Co.K,2nd Regt.Ms.Cavl.,C.S.A.Captur-
   ed May 4,1865.Paroled May 16,1865,Columbus,Ms. with Lt.Gen.
   Richard Taylor's Troops. Letter attached shows two other
   dates and places of enrollment,service,and discharge. Appl.
   dated May 19,1934

H.P.FARISH-b.Sept.15,1880,Mayersville,Ms.Issaquena Co. Father-
   ROBERT DAVIS FARISH. Mother-CAROLINE HARRISON POWER. R.D.
   Farish joined CA(no date)Pvt. Co.I 39 Reg.Ms.Inf.served until
   May 12,1865,paroled at Meridian Ms. Appl.dated Apr.30,1907
   Living Mar.15,1907,and a Vet.member of Gen.Nat.H.Harris,No.
   1607 Ms.Div. Camp. Mayersville,Ms.

J.D.FARISH-b.Aug.4,1887,Mayersville,Issaquena Co.Ms.Brother
   to above H.P.Farish. Same Info.

STEVEN POWER FARISH-b.May 31,1891,Mayersville,Issaquena Co.Ms.
   Father WILLIAM STAMPS FARISH.Mother KATHERINE MAUDE POWER.
   Appl.date,May 1,1907. No War record-but father a member of
   UCV Gen.Nat.Harris,Camp No.1607,Mayersville,Ms.Mar.15,1907

CONFEDERATE RECORDS OF ISSAQUENA CO.MS.

REV.ELMER C.GUNN-b.Oct.11,1883,Isney,Choctaw Co.Ms. Grandfather
JOHN GUNN, Grandmother-NANCY SHOEMAKER. John Gunn entered
C A Mar.1863, Pvt.Co.E 24 Cav.Bat.Paroled May 13,1865,Gainesville,Ala. Appl.dated Nov.1909.

JOHN KIRKLAND HAZLIP-b.July 8,1868,Cold Springs,Wilkinson,Co.Ms.
Father-SAMUEL W.HAZLIP.-Mother-MARTHA KIRKLAND. Samuel W.
Hazlip entered serv.Apr.1862,and joined as a Pvt.,Co.E,21st
Ms.Reg.Inf. in Va.with second list of recruits from Wilkinson
County Ms. Appl.dated May 1,1906

OLIVER H.KEEP-b.6 Jan.1868,Glen Anna Pltn.Issaquena,Co.,Ms.
Father HENRY V.KEEP. Mother-SALLIE B.COLLINS. Henry V.Keep
was a Capt. in Swamp Rangers,Vicksburg,Ms. Later Lt.Col.in
3rd Conf.Regiment. Appl.date-June 10,1922

E.B.LAMON-b.Jan.22,1855,Livingston,Madison Co.Ms. Father-
E.B.LAMON.Mother-SUSAN CONGO. Entered early part of 1863-
Pvt.Co A, 1st Ms.Reg.,Withers' Artillery. Paroled at Jackson
Ms.at end of war. Appl. Apr.30 1907

EARLY NESMITH-b.20 Dec.1869 near Martin, Caliborne Co.Ms. Father
CORNELIUS ROBINSON NESMITH. Mother-MARTHA ROZENA TREVILLION.
C.R.Nesmith entered service Spring of 1862-Sgt.in Claiborne
Guards, Co.K 12th Ms.Reg. Twice wounded. Surrendered with
Gen.Lee at Appomatox. Certificates attached dated 1922 say
C.R.Nesmith,deceased,was a member of The Camp of Conf. Vet.
of Claiborne Co. Appl.dated May 25,1922

DR.WALTER HOWARD SCUDDER Sr.-b.Sept.18,1861,Holly Retreat,Wilkinson,Co.Ms. Father-JAMES BLAIR SCUDDER. Mother-CELETE EMBREE.
J.B.Scudder entered serv. Spring 1862-3rd Lt. Co.D,38th Ms.
Regt.Inf.,"Wilkinson Guards". Died of Measles at Okolona Ms.
June 18,1862. Buried in Conf.Cemetery Okolona,Ms. Appl.dated
Mar.4,1907.

WALTER HOWARD SCUDDER Jr.-b.July 8,1892,Mayersville,Issaq.Co.Ms.
Father-DR.W.H.SCUDDER-Grandfather-JAMES BLAIR SCUDDER.
Mother-MARIE GERTRUDE PEYTON.Grandmother-CELETE EMBREE.
Same info. as above. Appl. Mar.4,1907.

WALTER HAZEL SMITH-b.May 21,1875,Mayersville,Issaquena Co.Ms.
Father-MARSHALL R.SMITH.Mother-JENNIE FOOTE ALSTON. M.R.Smith
was color bearer for Co. F,Schultz Battery,Kemper's Light
Artillery of S.C., C.S.A. Surrendered with Gen.Joseph E.
Johnston's army, at Greensboro, N.C. April 1865. He was
living Mar.15,1907(date of application)and Sec.for U.C.V
Camp #1607,Mayersville,Ms.

GILLIAM MERRIWETHER SMITH-b.Dec.25,1880,Mayersville,Issaquena
Co.,Ms. Brother to Walter Hazel Smith, above.Same Info.

FREDERICK A.SMITH-b.Aug.24,1873,Hazlehurst,Copiah Co.Ms.
Father-ISAAC L.SMITH. Mother-NANNIE E.FAIRCHILDS. Fredericks
home address is Smedes,Ms.and he is a Plantation Manager.
Father's service record-(Pvt.in pencil with ?)Co. F.,6th
Regt.Ms. Inf.,Col.Thornton.Joined Sept.9,1861.Dated 1907.

CONFEDERATE RECORDS OF ISSAQUENA CO.,MS.

MARSHALL M.SPIARS-b.Feb.28,1875,Mayersville,Issaq.Co.Ms. Chancery & Circuit Clerk of Issaq.Co. Father-JAMES SPIARS. Mother LYDIA MARTHA BROOKS. Record of father;Enlisted first-Apr.12, 1861 at Pensocola,Fla.in 10th Regt.Ms.Inf."Yazoo Rifles",Mose Phillips, Capt.After 1yr. reenlisted as Pvt.in Co.K,1st Ms. Regt.Cavl.,Capt.W.S.Yerger of Yazoo City. Appl.date-Apr.26,1907

HARRY LEE SUGG-b.Dec.13,1892,Mayersville,Issaq.Co.Ms.School boy. Father-LUCIUS DUNCAN SUGG. Mother-LEILA ALICE ABY. Father enlisted Oct.6,1861 as Pvt.inCo. K, 1st La.Cavl.,Col.John S.Scott.Paroled near Gainesville,Ala.May 13,1865. Grandfather-Wm.R.SUGG was a member of Capt.Geo.P.McLean's Co. in the 4th Ms.Regt.,Cavl.,was killed in small fight near Sharon,Ms. Feb.29,1864. Appl.date Apr.30,1907,father still living & member of Camp of U.C.V #1607,Mayersville,Ms.

ABY DUNCAN SUGG-b.Aug.3,1888,Mayersville,Issaq.Co.Ms. Clerk. Brother to above Harry Lee Sugg. Same Info.

SAMUEL H.SUGG-b.Oct.28,1873,near Port Gibson,Claib.Co.,Ms. Merchant. Half brother to above two Suggs by Lucius Duncan Sugg's first wife LAURA HUTCHINS. In this folder is a handwritten list of battles L.D.Sugg fought in and remark that upon mustering out in Ala. he rode horseback to his home in Claiborne Co.Ms. Other info. same.

LIVINGSTON PEYTON-b.Dec.6,1859,Raymond,Hinds Co.Ms.Landing Keeper.Father-MURRAY M.PEYTON. Mother-MALVINA ALSTON. Enlisted Aug.1861. 1st Lt.,Co.A.,3rd Ms.Regt.Inf."McWillie Blues". Father still living at application date Mar.4,1907. and a member Camp U.C.V.#1607,Mayersville,Ms.

STEPHEN FRANCIS POWER-b.Dec.20,1868,New Orleans,Orleans Parish, La. Father-MAJ.STEPHEN FRANCIS POWER. Mother ROSINA JOHNSTON HARRIS. The son is a Theological Student. Father enlisted Mar.23,1863-as a Capt.of Co.H, Miles Louisiana Legion.Pro.to Maj.at West Point,Ga. Mustered out Apr.15 1865. Appl.date Mar.23,1907

MARSHALL WHITE-b.Jan26,1890,Mayersville,Issaq.Co.,Ms. Student and Clerk. Father FREEMAN FRANCIS WHITE. Mother-KATE COMER McGRAW. Father enlisted Dec.1861 as 2nd Sgt.,Co. A, 3rd Mo. Cavl.,CSA. Surrendered & paroled near Shreveport,La. about Sept.1865. Still living and member of Camp of UCV in Mayersville at date of application-Mar.10 1907.

¶NOTE<The Camp of the United Confederate Veterans(UCV)as refered to in the above documents was the GEN.NAT.H.HARRIS,#1607, Miss.Division at Mayersville,Ms. These applications were made to UNITED SONS OF CONFEDERATE VETERANS, Headquarters Camp Issaquena, #538, Mayersville, Ms.>

METHODIST EPISCOPAL CHURCH,SOUTH,CLOVER HILL CIRCUIT WAS ESTABLISHED IN 1877 IN MAYERSVILLE, ISSAQUENA CO.,MS. THE CIRCUIT INCLUDED <u>MAYERSVILLE, HAYS LANDING(BEULAH) AND DUNCANSBY</u>.ALL OF THEIR RECORDS ARE IN THIS ONE BOOK. MRS.LUCILLE SHIPP OF MAYERSVILLE IS CUSTODIAN, HAVING RESCUED IT FROM AN OLD TRUNK GIVEN TO HER BY Dr.W.H.SCHUDDER,PRACTICING PHYSICIAN OF MAYERSVILLE,MS.,UNTIL HIS DEATH.

MARRIAGE RECORDS

John W.McCUE to LIZZIE COLLINS,Apr.2 1878 by Rev.H.J.HARRIS
Earl MILLER to Janie COLLINS n/d by Rev.H.J.Harris
Dr.J.C.ROBERT to Miss Fannie HARRIS-Jan.26 1879-Rev.Harris
J.E.HARRIS to Sue E.BUCKALOO-Feb.11,1879   "
Osker GRAMLING TO Ella TAYLOR-Jan.6 1880-Rev.J.H.SHELTON
RichardBANKSTON to Mattie DAVIS n/d by   "
C.M.WILSON to Ell GRAMLING n/d   "
Dr.W.H.SCUDDER to Marie Gertrude PEYTON-Vicksburg,Ms.Apr.15 1890
                by Rev.F.M.WILLIAMS P.C.
Livingston PEYTON to Idella G.SPIARS-Mayersville Church,Feb.10
                1886 by REV.M.H.MOORE P.C.
R.M.SMITH,Jr. to S.Eunice WOODRY-Mayersville,Jan.1 1890 by Rev.
                Rev.V.D.SKIPPER
James P.HEATH to Lurena SMITH-Clover Hill,Apr.9 1890-Rev.Skipper
J.L.PERKINS to Florence MAYFIELD-Vicksburg,Ms.Apr.14 1890
James W.ALEXANDER to Attie WILLIAMS-Tyrus,Ms.Oct.7 1891 by Rev.
                F.M.WILLIAMS
Warren CATCHINGS to Rosa Lee SMITH-Mayersville,Oct._1893-Rev.
                T.W.BROWN
Jas.PLEASANTS to Sidney SMITH-Mayersville Oct._1894-Rev.Brown
Dr.V.M.PERRY to Belle GAWLEY-Satartia,Ms.Nov._1893
John GRIFFIN to Dot ANDERSON-Duncansby,Ms.,Mar._1896-Rev.W.T.
                GRIFFIN
C.B.SMITH to Frank H.ANDERSON-Duncansby,Nov.25 1896-Rev.Griffin
Rochus VANDENING(?)to Annie Laurie WINTERS-May 25 1897-   "
E.M.JORDON to Mary SUGG-June 9 1897-Rev.Griffin
W.M.HOLLEY toMRS.S.H.JAYS-June 30 1897-Rev.Griffin
John VANDENANBORG(?)to Mary Malinda Jane WARD -Nov.18 1897-Rev.
                Griffin.

DEATH RECORDS

R.M.SMITH-1893
Mrs.N.L.KILKEY-May 28 1879
Mrs.Mary COLLINS-1881
Miss Lizzie COLLINS-Feb.6 1879
Mrs.E.C.HILL-July5 1877
Mrs.McGHERKIN-1882
Miss Lou ERVIN-died n/d
Miss Rena GARRETT-died n/d
H.W.TILLMAN-died n/d
Miss Emily ELLIOTT-Jan.17 1882
Walter J.SMITH-died n/d
Mrs.Rebecca BREHM-Apr.15 1884
James L.MAYFIELD-Aug.31 1885
Miss Emma GRAMLING-Oct.5 1885
Miss Lydia BREHM-Sept.13 1886

ADULT BAPTISMS

Miss Clara GRIFFIN-Mar.2 1879-Rev.H.J.HARRIS
Miss Lizzie HILL-Mar.2 1879   "
Mrs.Arcola ALSTON-June 3 1877- " F.M.FEATHERSTEN(?)
Miss Ula GRAVES-June 3 1877   "

CLOVER HILL CIRCUIT M.E.C.S.
ADULT BAPTISIMS (cont.)

Miss Anna E.BREHM-Aug.10 1884-Rev.M.H.MOORE
Miss Lydia BREHM   "   "   "   "   "
Mrs.Fannie C.SPURLOCK-Feb.2 1885-Rev.W.L.C.HUNNICUTT
Miss Susan E.WOODRY-Oct.18 1885-Rev.Moore
Miss Emma G.CARLILE-Dec.6 1886   "
Mrs.Mollie FUQUAY-Spet.18 1887-   "
Jas.W.ALEXANDER-July 22,1888-Rev.V.D.SKIPPER,PC
Miss Ima May SHORT-July 22 1888   "
Edward N.SCUDDER-Sept.30 1888-   "
John Drew BARNER-Mar._1889   "
Ada Louise GILKEY-Aug.21 1890-Rev.F.M.WILLIAMS P.C.
Nettie G---HENLEY-June 7 1891-Rev.John A.ELLIS P C
Ollie Virginia HENLEY "   "
Floyd Rufus HENLEY   "   "
Miss Sidney I.SMITH-Nov.7 1891   "
Clifton Ballon(u)SMITH-Sept.14 1892-R.S.ISBELL,La.Conference
Miss Belle GAWLEY-   "   "
Miss Frank Hill ANDERSON-Dec.21 1892-Rev.John W.CRISLER P C
Miss Allie May SMITH-Nov.25 1894-Rev.Thos.W.BROWN P C
James P.HEATH-Nov.25 1894-   "
Ella BONNAR-July 31 1898-Rev.W.T.GRIFFIN
Hattie BONNAR-   "   "
Mrs.Nellie MARSH SMITH-Apr.21 1901-Rev.M.M.BLACK

INFANT BAPTISIMS

Miss Naomie A.ALSTON-June 3 1877-Rev.F.M.FEATHERSTON
Philip ALSTON   "   "
Gertrude PEYTON   "   "
Eva HILL-Feb.24 1878-Rev.W.L.C.HUNNICUTT
Thos.Jefferson GRAMLING-June 1 1878-Rev.H.J.HARRIS
Vida Imboclew(?)GRAMLING-Oct.23 1878-   "
Katie Eudora GRAMLING-June_1876-REV.J.A.B.JONES
John Howard McCUE-Jan.30 1879-Rev.H.J.Harris
Alvernon Keep ANDERSON-Mar.26 1879-Rev.Hunnicutt
Percy Gains ALSTON-Mar.30 1879-Rev.Harris
Willie A.ALSTON   "   "
Willie COLLINS- n/d   Rev.HUNNICUTT
Eol Vandorn MILLER-Oct.20 1879-Rev.Harris
Ruby E.BENNETT-Nov.30 1879-   "
Nora E.FOLKS-Apr.19 1884-Rev.M.H.MOORE
Maggie L.BREHM-Apr.23 1884-   "
Etta BREHM   "   "
Gertrude BREHM   "   "
Howard P.KIRKLAND-Oct.19 1884-Rev.C.G.ANDREWS
Norman KIRKLAND-   "   "
Mamie Lee PHILIPPS-Oct.21 1884-   "
Robert S.COLLINS-Feb.1 1885-Rev.W.L.C.HUNNICUTT
Mamie W.COLLINS-   "   "
James W.SPURLOCK-Feb.2 1885-   "
Anna Choplain MILLER-Apr.11,1885-   "
Otho Singleton MILLER-   "   "
Byron Lera PITMAN-May 2 1885-   "
Thomas J.COLLINS-Oct.25 1885-   "
Mary E.GRAMLING-Nov.15 1885-Rev.M.H.MOORE
Mayfield H.FOLKES-Dec.5 1886-son/Wm.Folkes & wife-Rev.Moore
Wm.C.MILLER-Nov.6 1886-son/Earl MILLER & wife   "

CLOVER HILL CIRCUIT,M.E.C.S.
INFANT BAPTISIMS (cont.)

Cegis(?)M.SPURLOCK-Nov.24 1886-son/Jas.SPURLOCK & wife-Rev.Moore
Hays CARLILE-Dec.5 1886-Rev.M.H.MOORE
Florence CARLILE-   "   "
Susan G.CARLILE-   "   "
Mary E.CARLILE-   "   "   ,Parents of above 4 are
                                   JOHN CARLILE & wife
Justin W.McGRAW-Mar.25 1887- Rev.M.H.MOORE
Curtis R.McGRAW-   "   "
Joanna G.McGRAW-   "   "
Eunice E.J.McGRAW-   "   "   Parents of above 4 James
                                             McGRAW & wife
Pearl FUQUAY-Nov.27 1887-   "
Geneva FUQUAY   "   "   Par.Wm.& MollieFUQUAY
Stephen Myer RUSS-Dec.6 1887-   "
Adam Daniel GRAMLING-Dec.11 1887-Rev.Moore-Par.A.D.GRAMLING & wife
Celete(?)SCUDDER-Apr.28 1889-Rev.Skipper-Par.E.N.SCUDDER & wife
T.A.HEATH Jr.-Oct.22 1888-son/Dr.&Mrs.T.A.HEATH-Rev.Skipper
Lydia PEYTON-May26 1890-dau/L.PEYTON & wife-Rev.F.M.WILLIAMS
Shirley PEYTON-____1887-dau/   "   " "   " N.H.MOORE
Izora(?)BOWMAN-____1887-Dau/Robt.BOWMAN & WIFE-GrandMoth.Mrs.PITMAN
Robert Marshall SMITH-June7 1891-son/R.M.& S.EUNICE SMITH-Rev.Cris
Idella Gertrude PEYTON-June 7 1891-dau/Livingston & Della PEYTON
Walter NICHOLS-Oct.28 1891-son/Joseph & Jennie NICHOLS-Rev.Crisler
John Wesley CRISLER-May 7 1892-son/Rev.John W.& Annie I.CRISLER
Walter Howard SCUDDER,Jr.-July7 1892-son/Dr.&Mrs.W.H.SCUDDER-
                                              REV.D.A.LITTLE P C
Monita SCUDDER-Feb.26 1893-dau/E.N.& SEYMOURA SCUDDER-Rev.Brown
Katie RICE-___1893-dau/MRS.M.B.RICE   "
Fayssoux(?)SCUDDER-Nov.12 1893-par.E.N.& SEYMOURA SCUDDER- "
Mary HEATH-Nov.25 1893-dau/JNO.W.& ANNIE HEATH-   "
Mary Elizabeth SCUDDER-July 14 1895-dau/Dr.W.H.& G.SCUDDER-"
Livingston PEYTON Jr.-Dec.13 1895-son/LIVINGSTON& IDELLA PEYTON-
Dorothy Conpland(?)TAYLOR-Apr.18 1897-dau/C.C.TAYLOR & wife
Sarah SCUDDER-Oct.10 1897-dau./E.N.SCUDDER& wife-Rev.W.T.GRIFFIN
Calendar(?)Irving SCUDDER,same date/same parents-   "
William Anderson-July7 1898-son/John & Dot GRIFFIN   "
Clifton Bolm(?)SMITH-July 7 1898-son/C.B.& Mrs.Frank SMITH "
Susan Elizabeth-dau/L.& IDELLA PEYTON-July 24 1898   "
O.P.SMITH-Oct.8 1899-son/R.M.&EUNICE SMITH   "
Thomas Bedford GRIFFIN-Mar._1901-son/Wm.GRIFFIN & wife-Rev.Black
John Wesley GRIFFIN-Sept.23 1901-Rev.M.M.BLACK.

(?)after a name tells you the writing was hard to decipher and
I have written a good guess.
¶The book contains the <u>original</u> register of members in <u>Mayersville</u>-
a <u>revised Register brought up to date in the</u> 1890's,-and the
original <u>HAYS LANDING CHURCH(BEULAH)</u> Register. The Mayersville
Register has the earliest dates.
I HAVE NOT INCLUDED THESE LISTS. BUT I DO HAVE A COPY OF THEM.
ANY INQUIRIES WILL BE ANSWERED.

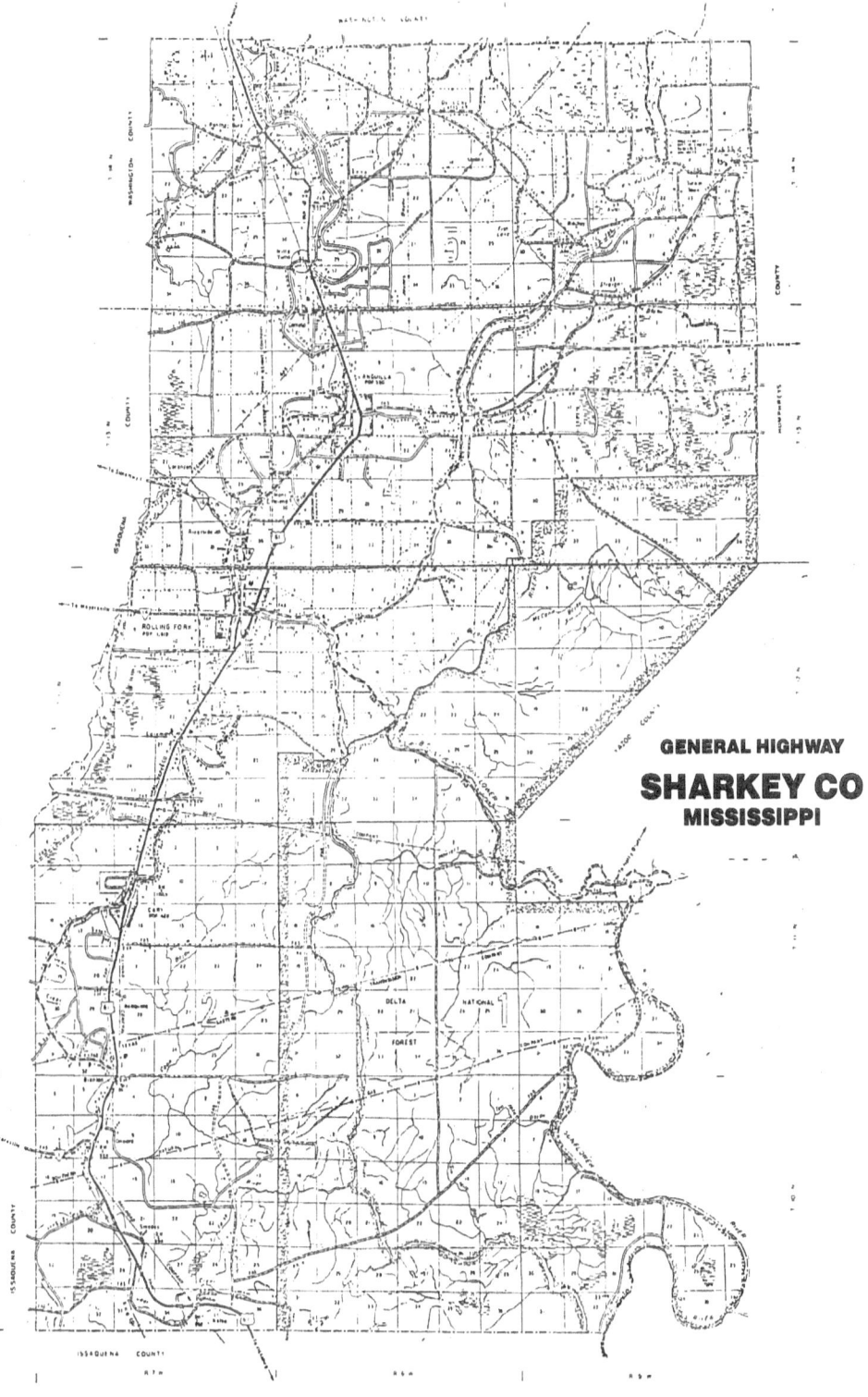

Sharkey County
Mississippi

Most Favorably Located Of All the Counties in the Rich Yazoo-Mississippi Delta. Undergoing a Period of Unprecedented Growth.

COURT HOUSE AT ROLLING FORK, MISSISSIPPI

SHARKEY COUNTY OFFERS BETTER INDUCEMENTS TO NEW COMERS THAN ANY OTHER PART OF THE SOUTH

Issue Issued by Sharkey County Progress League, Rolling Fork, Miss., July, 1919.

SHARKEY CO.MS. was made a county in 1876. Parent counties-Washington-Warren-Issaquena. Rolling Fork is the county seat. The Probate records and the Chancery Court records are all together, filed under Chancery Court (hereafter-CC). The Wills are recorded in books and the intestate Estate packets are on the CC Docket and filed in the CC boxes. Numerous divorce cases in the years-1876 to 1900. Many suits filed against Estates. The abstracts presented here were chosen for their genealogical facts.

SHARKEY CO. CC-1876-1900

#1;H.C.PINDELL,EXEC.VS.H.L.J.HARRIS et al.Bill of complaint;**Original Bill** filed 10 June 1876,states the Defendants on 15 Jan.1865 contracted a promisary note payable 6 mo.after the Civil War-$858.29 with interest at legal rate. Note was for certain supplies for plantation owned by Helen L.Johnstone Harris in Sharkey Co.Complaintants claim debt was made by Helen before her marriage to Rev.Geo.C.Harris Aug.21,1862.(femme sole)She possesses in her own right,lands and tenements in Sharkey and a part is known as her "Helen Place"-and a part is described towit;Sec.25 T13, R7W. The contract and Note was due Pindell as executive of H.G. VICKS est.as she had made this contract to H.G.Vick before he deceased in Dec.1859.
ANSWER by defendants;They admitted signing above contract in 1865,but want the court to know that Mrs.Harris made the debts before her marriage and was still an infant under 21 years of age,before 15 Jan.1859.They(Helen and Geo.Harris)argue that the Exb."A" is merely a bill-not a promissary note and that the statue of limitation had run out in 1865,and surely out by 1876. Further regarding "A" she,Helen, was then a marr. woman in 1865 and could not legally contract on her own. She also says the bill is not a valid or legal claim against them. They aver the contract was made in Confederate Treas.notes and not U.S.Dollars and not worth $858.
DEPOSITION;H.C.Pindell says he is from Louisville Ky. 54 or 55 years old(not certain which)in Aug.15,1878.States he is the executor of H.G.Vicks est.**[NOTE**:Vicks'will proven in Probate court-Wash.Co. 4 Feb.1860]Mrs. Pindell is aunt of Vicks.
DEPO.Geo.C.Harris Clergyman-41 years old-States his wife Helen was engaged to Vick who was killed in a duel in or near Mobile [some records say New Orleans] He made a will shortly before duel-devising Helen L.Johnstone the pltn."VICKLAND" in Wash. Co. (now Sharkey Co.)in 1860.
DEPO:MRS.MARGARET L.JOHNSTON,mother of Helen-resident of Madison Co.Ms. "ANNANDALE PLTN." age 69.STates she was appointed Guard. of Helen in 1849.
T.M.MILLER Attorney for defendants. W.G.PHELPS for complaintants W.C.PERCY,HON.opinion. Court ruled in favor of def.Helen & Geo. C.Harris 13 Sept.1879. Pindell Appealed to Supreme Court in 1879. Appeal denied 14 Apr.1882.

#3;**D.R.PETIT vs unknown heirs of CHRISTOPHER W.SMITH,decd.in** 1874.Filed Oct.1876.D.R.Petit citizen of Richland Pa.La. Smith late of Shar.Co.Ms.**ORIG.BILL** states J.T.MARSHALL gave Petit(in payment)a note(lien) of $100 that Smith owed him dated June 29,1870-due 11day June 1874. Smith died intest. & Petit wants to sell land belonging to Smiths est.for debt.No heirs found. (cont.)

SHARKEY CO.CC-1876-1900

#3-cont.**DOC**.included-copy of orig. indenture Deed of JAMES T. MARSHALL & wife ALVERMAN MARIA MARSHALL from Warren Co.to C.W.SMITH 29 June 1870. S½ofW½of S.W./4,Sec.19,T13,R6W.40acrs.more or less-tenements etc. Land in Issa.Co.now Shark.Co.Deed filed in Shark.and Issa.Co.

#4;**RICHARDSON & MAY vs.MARY S.FOOTE etal**;Mary S. Foote received notice of suit 6 Nov.1876 in Macon,Ms. She was the widow of W.H.FOOTE-son of JUDGE H.W.FOOTE of Macon,Ms.On the face of this notice paper,handwritten-"This suit dismissed by order of T.W.MILLER,complts.Atty. this 13th Sept.1884"
ORIG.bill of complaint;states the et als are R.A.ALLEN-partner of W.H.Foote and EUGENE CLARK & D.C.CASEY-all of Shar.Co. filed May 1873. Foote was decd.and Allen the surviving partner-owed $5,747.11 to Richardson & May-notes due 1873 were secured by D.T. to land and store Foote claimed to own.(in town of Rolling Fork). A.H.MAY-resident of New Orleans,La.D.G.PEPPER,agent and trustee of R.&M.Co.-partners with Richardson.
DEPO.of EDMUND RICHARDSON-Sept.6,1877 states hes 60 years old, res.of Jackson,Hinds Co.Ms.-merchant & Planter. States that DR.E.C.CLEMENTS & wife ANNIE FOOTE CLEMENTS-for $300-deed to Mary S.Foote a lot-house-store June 6 1873.(Dated 1yr.later-clerks error) Mary,in turn sells lot-house-store to D.C.CASEY & EUGENE CLARK-for $1,105 in 8 May 1875. Richardson disputes date of deed of Clements to Foote saying he had a lien and disputes sale to Casey & Clark.**DEPO**.of Mary S.Foote at Macon,Ms. ROBT.C.PATTY, clerk.States she had sold a parcel of land given to her by her grandmother PATTON-land in Huntsville,Madison Co.Ala. for $500 to her father-in-law Judge H.W.Foote. Her(Mary S.)husband W.H. Foote used the money to buy lot from E.C.Clements and built store.Mary did not know William Foote had given a D/T on property to R.& M. until it was done. This depositon dated 3 June 1882.

#5;**EMELINE REEVELY vs SAM'L REEVELY**(inside papers spell-REEVELIN-REVELIN);12 Dec.1876-Bill of Divorce. They married ---1868-issue 1--Alice living in care & custody of mother. Alice about 12 in Apr.1877. Emeline Reevely about 27 years old. Decree final Oct.8 1877-child remanded to custody of mother.Res.on NittaYuma Pltn. Grandmother of Alice-Nancy Tucker.

#6;**N.W.PARKER vs LEANNA PARKER**:Bill of divorce-19 Dec.1876. Nathaniel W.Parker-26 yrs.old farmer married Leanna 27 Feb.1873. Leanna Parkers father was PETER GALES res.of WEEPING WILLOW PLTN.4th Dist.Shark.Co.Ms. Final decree Oct.8,1877.

#7;**SPENCER WATKINS et-al vs ELIZ.HUDSON**et-al;Bill of complaint by Spencer Watkins & EDGAR P.WALKINS-executors of G.M.WALKINS deceased,of Montgomery Co. Maryland against-Eliz.Hudson(husband JOHN HUDSON,deceased);MELISSA J. ELLIS & W.H.ELLIS her husband both of Shar.Co.Ms.;EMMA J.LOVE & ROBT.H.LOVE,her husband both of Yazoo Co.Ms. Melissa and Emma are daughters of Eliz.&John Hudson. G.M.Watkins decd.17 Nov.1871,testate-will proven 4 Apr. 1871. **Partial Inv**.of Greenbery M.Watkins est.inMaryland, shows 9 promissary notes of John Hudson-total $5,000-payable $500 each-1873-74-75-76-78-79-80-81, 8%annual int.Lease of land(cont.

SHARKEY CO.MS. CC PACKETS-1876-1900

#7(cont.)for 99 years-from Jan.1872-Land description was in
WashCo.Ms.in 1872-now Sharkey Co.Ms. Sec.16,T14,R4W. Failure
to pay any note forfiets the deed.None have been pd.& executives
want Hudsons est. administered and courts to rent or sell lease
on land.**DEPO.**of Eliz.Hudson given in Yazoo Co.Ms.
BOND surety of G.M.Watkins est.administration in Maryland;JOHN
G.TRUNDLE, GEORGE PETERS,Wm.BREWER, Wm.HUDDLETON.
No dispensation in pkt.

#7½;EST.OF MISS ELLA C.ROBERTSON;decd.2 Apr.1877.**Will**-noncupative
dated Apr.3 1877. Spoken 1 Apr.1877 to W.D.BROWN-Wit.MRS.IDA
WRIGHT,MRS.ALICE V.BROWN,JAS(N.or W.)ROBERTSON, LULA C.ROBERTSON
& others."I want Lula(meaning her sister Lula)to have any land
& this house, and I want you(meaning the ascriber W.D.Brown)to
have my part of the mules & cattle(meaning-her undivided int.
in est. of L.ROBERTSON". She died in W.D.Browns home on NA.....
PLTN.(can't read the name)Shar.Co.Ms. A.D.& ALTA R.ALDRIDGE
of Wash.Co.Ms.consent to probate of will. Relationship not stated.

#8;J.OSTROFFSKY vs J.H.ROBERTSON(Sheriff of Shark.Co.)&Morris
& Co.: Injunction to prevent sale of Ostroffsky's property in
Rolling Fork,Ms. May 1877.

#9;CHARLES FISHER vs ROSE FISHER: Bill of Divorce.Filed Oct.16,
1877.Charles and Rose Fisher were Married Aug.1872.Final-8Apr.1878

#9½;STATE OF MS.vs H.M.CONNER(Habeas Corpus)20 June 1878. WASH
SMITH claims Conner did shoot to kill him on WATSON's place
11 May 1878.

#10;HENRY LEWIS vs EDITH LEWIS:B.of Divorce.Filed 26 Nov.1877.
They were married 8 Aug.1872.Final decree 8 Apr.1878.

#10½;EST.OF SARAH W.ANDERSON:decd. W.C.H.McKINNEY adm.petitions
court in Apr.1878 for saleof personal & Real property to satisfy
creditors-T.T.ORENDORF:J.W.DUKE:N.R.ANDERSON:F.W.ANDERSON.D.N.
ANDERSON:W.C.H.McKINNEY:J.W.WICK:J.W.BISSELL. One bill to Sarah
Anderson's Est. from N.R.Anderson shows a coffin bought Mar.17,
1878-Shroud & wagon hired for burial-deduction being Sarah decd.
at that time. **Prop.**sold July 1880-S.DOVER purchaser.**Final** a/c
13 Jan.1881.**VOUCHERS** show-Nov.1872-6 months board for self &
Husband $180 in a/c with D.N.Anderson. 1873 House rent for 18mo.
$216 to same person. July 1880 Cash collected from H.G.PARHAM
for house rent $22.00.

#10 3/4;SIMON BELL vs MARIA BELL ;B.of Divorce,filed 20 Aug.1878
Marr.10 Feb.1868.Simon 37 yr.old has lived in St.past 2 yrs.
Final 21 Jan.1878.

#11;(missing from files but listed in CC Docket).H.H.KAIN vs
JAMES McGINNIS et al(CHRISTOPHER,MARY JANE,ANNIE,ELIZ.McGINNIS)
Bill of complaint filed July 8,1878. Citation issued to W.F.
FITZGERALD June 28,1879. Pet.for Guardianship Ad Litem Mar.7,1879.
Depo.N.R.ANDERSON,T.G.PARKS,D.R.PETTIT,J.T.MARSHALL,T.M.FOLKS.
Oct. 1879.

SHARKEY CO.MS. CC PACKETS-1876-1900

#11½;EST.OF NELSON FULTON;decd.Nov.1878 in Shark.Co.Ms.**Pet.for** Adm.by W.H.BARNARD Dec.1878,states est.small crop of corn & cotton in field-no relatives in State. T.T.ORENDORF & J.A.C. SHRADER-bond surety. **Appr.**21 Dec.1878 by M.C.TAYLOR,M.C.PENDERGAST, D.N.ANDERSON. **Final&** discharge of Adm.25 Mar.1891.

#12 3/4:FANNIE OSTROFFSKY vs JOS.H.ROBERTSON et al(R.Cohn of Issaq Co.Ms.)Fannie ask court for Writ of Injunction to prevent seizure of mercantile prop. to settle debt, and for the return of Gold watch by Robertson, given as security for debt until case pending in court is heard. Injunction bond security;Fannie, C.J.PETERSON & JOHN S.JOOR $400.Jan.22,1879.

#13;WOLF AARON vs JOHN CHAFFEE & SONS(Wm.H.& CHRISTOPHER JR.). 2 big Pkts.marked Box 1.Chaffee & sons are citz.of New Orlean,La. AAron charges Chaffee & sons with not returning deed to a certain parcel of land situated in Rolling Fork,Ms. Thisdeed given as security for $1500 borrowed for mercantile business.Deed dated 10 Aug.1877. Fannie Aaron-wife of Wolf-ask deed to be canceled as all monies have been paid.**INJ.**bond signed by W.Aaron,H.H.BEIDENHORN,HENRY MAYER.,7 July 1879-Warren Co.Ms.**DEPO.by** WM.ROBERTS-30 yr.old Rolling Fork res.-carpenter. IRA A.CORTRIGHT in his ¶deposition of Oct.1880 speaks of a riot 1875 which had caused many people to leave the area and depress the economy,lowering the value of prop.and goods. Fannie states her age as 28 and a res.of Rolling Fork,Ms.**COURT**s decision in favor of Aaron & wife 26 Oct.1881. Chaffee & Son appeal 13 June 1882. Settled in 1884 with sale of Store lot--not residence.

¶**RIOT:** See next page for story on the riot of 1875,taken from the vertical files of the Rolling Fork-Shark.Co.Library on the History of Rolling Fork,compiled by the WPA.Written by Ruth Walker.

#14;MARY F.MARTIN vs G.W.BURTON et al.Title confirmation-July 1879.Mary's husband HENRY N.MARTIN a citz. of Warren Co. & JONES S.HAMILTON,citz.Hinds Co.Ms. joined in Bill of Complaint against G.W.Burton of Louisville Ky. & others who claim to have an interest in land that was sold for taxes May 1869. Seeking Title confirmation to land bought from Levee Commission Sept. 1877 for taxes by W.C.CAGE & HENRY W. MARTIN. Martin in May 1878 deeds his half to wife Mary F.--W.C.Cage,11Mar.1878,sells his to Jones S.Hamilton Wash.Co.Land descp.included-640 acres. Oct. 1879 WM.M.PRATT also interested in land and mentioned with Burton. His appearance later withdrawn. Last document dated 14 June 1880-DECREE PRO CONFESSO.

#14½;LIZZIE TURNER vs JACOB TURNER:Bill of Divorce-filed Sept.9, 1879. They were married Issaq.Co.Ms. 5 Jan.1871.Dep.by HENRY TURNER & BENJ.BALLARD for plaintiff. No final in pkt.

#15;WASH ARNOLD & MARY ARNOLD;B.of Divorce filed Sept.8,1879. Married 1 Feb.1878.No final.

#15½;EST.OF ENOCH TUCKER;(Ward of W.C.H.McKINNEY)**Guard.bond** dated July 14,1879 by McKinney and W.H.BARNARD $600. Enoch Tucker is son of ISAAC TUCKER decd.in 1870. Enoch over age 14,chooses McKinney as his guard. Est. consist of $50--1/3 int. in proceeds

LOCAL HISTORY OF ROLLING FORK,MS.COMPILED BY WPA. STORY WRITTEN BY RUTH WALKER. FOUND IN VERTICAL FILE 100 IN ROLLING FORK-SHARKEY COUNTY LIBRARY,300 EAST CHINA STREET,ROLLING FORK,MS.

Negro riot in 1875

¶In 1875, there were 25 white men living in the neighborhood of Rolling Fork while 400 negroes were drilling every night at ¶Cary and 400 more at the Cammeta place about 30 miles away.__.T. Casey(first initial too faint to read)was riding every night patrolling the roads while his wife & small son,age 8,stayed close at home,fearful at the sound of even a cracking twig because the negroes were threatening to burn the town, kill all the male children and men,take the young women for their wives and make the old women their cooks.

The Southerners were in a helpless state because their guns had been taken from them after the war. Gov.Adelbert Ames from Mass.,now Gov. of Ms.(later impeached)-was sending guns to the negroes at Rolling Fork, These were being shipped via Vicksburg and a clerk on the wharf boat there"caught on" and billed the goods to a white man at R.F. However, the white men, afraid to take possession of them, organized a deer hunt,and came in with four or five deer which they showed ostentatiously in the town. In the confusion and excitement,they put the ammunition and arms in the wagon with the deer on top and with that as an excuse for their gathering, they were able to cut up the deer and divide the Winchesters at the same time without the Negroes realizing what was happening.

In the meantime Colonel Ball, a Baptist preacher from Blue Mountain, gave up preaching until the riot might be settled.He was also a lawyer and he called a meeting of the best colored people and white people in an effort to make peace by talking things over.He spoke beautifully to the crowd assembled,and then called on Jake Black,a negro,to express his feelings.

Jake replied;"Well,I never made a speech before and I am not like the Colonel here who sits with his feet upon the table. What I know and what I got to say is the old bottom rail is on top and I say"stomp 'em ,stomp 'em,stomp 'em!"

That closed the meeting and Col Ball ordered the capture of the negroes who were the leaders. Mr.Casey captured "Colonel Noah Parker" who had been acting as squire and thus passing sentence onthe white men of the community. The affair was rather brief. Mr. Casey road up to the store where Parker was lounging.

"Parker,I want you."

"What does this mean? Does this mean an insurrection? Where's your writ?"

"Here it is",and pulled out his gun."Get on your mule."

The seven leaders caught were shot at the Charlie Williams place this side of Cary.

¶In the 1880 census of Sharkey Co.,D.C.Casey was the the only Casey listed. He had a brother living in Hollandale, J.T.Casey as reported in the 1899 Deer Creek Pilot. He could have been the one of this story, and living in R.F. at the time this episode took place.   AW

SHARKEY CO.MS. CC PACKETS 1876-1900

#15½(cont.)of land sold in Georgia(looks like Contra) received Jan.15,1883 of McKinney,by Enoch.

#16;ANNA B.HUNT et al vs GEO.M.KLINE et al.Orig. bill filed Sept.9,1879 by Anna on behalf of Herself and children Vida,David & George F.Hunt,------the children of David(decd.)and Anna B.Hunt. All minors. Defendants--GEO.M.KLINE,A.WARNER & DAN SEARLE(surviving partners of Geo.C.Kress & Co. of Warren Co.Ms.) & ABIJAH HUNT. David Hunt decd.Sept.1878 in Jefferson Co.Ms.while on a visit.His residence was in Sharkey Co.on"Georgiana Pltn'! where he and Anna B. had lived since their marr.in 1872.(land description here) Apr.1879 David gave a D/T to Wm.S.HARRISON(decd.by 1878) & ISAAC BONHAM on said lands as security for indebtedness. 1877 David was adjudged to be bankrupt and GEO.F.SWAN was appointed assignee of Hunt by Bankruptcy Court and ordered to sell land at public auction-24 Mar.1879. Geo.M.Klein purchased for $1,000 the bankrupt interest-then on 23 July 1879 sold his int. to Abijah Hunt for $14,533.70--warning Hunt, that Anna B.Hunt could exercise her right to homestead of 80 acrs.and dwelling house and outhouses not to exceed $2,000 value. The court alloted the same to Anna B. & children 13 June 1881. Commissioners to allot Homestead;EUGENE CLARK;W.W.MOORE & Wm.GIBBON.
Related info. David Hunts'will-Will bk "A" pg.6.also abstracted in this vol.

#16½;EST.OF SAMPSON L.WILLIAMS;decd.June 1879.Adm.Wm.GIBBON. Bond Surety,EVAN B.SHELBY & A.C.SHELBY-20 Nov.1879. Gibbons was a creditor and also a relation-bro.-in-law-Gibbons wife being sister to decd. APPR.Mar.4,1880 by JAS.H.MOORE,B.R.MOORE, J.M.McCALEB.**PET.**for sale of Pers. prop. Sept.10,1880.**Relatives**; MRS. ELLA FARR,Magnolia,Ark.:MRS.EMMA FRAZIER,Camden Ark.**Final** a/c and discharge of Adm. Mar.25,1891.

#17;N.W.PARKER vs MARTHA EVANS PARKER:married 29 June 1878; Bill of complaint by Mr.Parker states he had discovered Martha to be the lawful wife of WILLARD EVANS of Wash.Co.Ms. and wants his marriage declared null & void. Sept.10 1879.

#18;BEADY GALES vs TYLER GALES;B.of Divorce filed Sept.10,1879. Marr.24 Dec.1874.Residents of Sharkey Co.more than 20 years. IssueWESLEY GALE,3yrs.& living, ADELINE GALE who died at 6 mo. Mother asks custody of Wesley. Final filed Dec.13,1880.

#19;CHARLES WILLIAMS vs RACHAEL DOVER WILLIAMS.B.of Divorce to a Common-law marriage begun July 1866-terminated Aug.1878 [CLAUSE IN CONSTITUTION OF St.of Ms. adopted 1868-recognized com.law marriages of 10 year duration] Pltns mentioned in bill CAMERON PLTN. EGYPT PLTN.,TILLMAN PLACE. Filed 16 Sept.1879. CROSS bill filed by Rachael Dover Oct.16,1879. **ISSUE**-JOHN WILLIAMS,12 yrs.& ANGELINA 10 yrs..NO FINAL DATE.[Marriage records of Sharkey Co. show Charles Williams marr. Sylvia Kelly in 1877]

#20;JOHN TAYLOR vs PENNY ROBERTSON TAYLOR;.Bill of divorce filed 16 Sept 1879. Married 1 Mar.1878.Decree final 16 Oct.1879.

#21;W.D.BROWN vs.ANDREW WORTH of Wash.Co.Ms.&J.O.STEVENS,Shark.Co Bill of interpleader-filed 24 Sept.1879.

SHARKEY CO.MS. CC PACKETS 1876-1900

#22;JOHN D.WATTS vs MARY A.WILLIAMS et al;B.of Complaint filed
24 Sept.1879 by John Watts a citz.of Sunflower Co.Ms. Defendants
Mary(Margaret)A.Williams-lunatic now inmate Asylum,Jackson,Ms.
and W.C.H.McKINNEY her guard.Shark.Co.Ms. Watts holds notes
on est. of her decd.husband and wants payment. Mary's husband
SAMPSON WILLIAMS decd.June 1879 . Mary was adjudged of unsound
mind & committed 12 Jan.1877. She was the owner of Pltn.DANOVER
PLACE.(see #16½ and #23 for more of this.)

#23;EST.OF MRS. MARY A.WILLIAMS.ward(non composmentis). **Writ**
for committment to Insane Asylum filed Nov.1876.Petitions for
writ by JAMES J.WELLS,her cousin;JOHN F.CHANEY her ½ bro.:W.B.
BARNARD:J.C.HALL:FLOURNOY SHELBY all Shark.Co. and near relatives
and M.J.CHANEY,her ½bro. of E.Felica.Par.La. Drs.B.GOODMAN &
A.M.WADDILL testified to insanity at hearing.Jury of 12 men;Wm.
LAWSON:R.A.ALLEN:I.P.ALEXANDER:T.F.KEISER:HENRY FLOYD:S.A.HILL:
W.E.BAGGETT:L.A.MOORE:E.C.ESTMAN:.S.B.ALEXANDER:R.G.MAXWELL:T.C.
WATSON. **DATE** of Mary's death is never stated but order for Guard
McKinney to present all papers to ADM.MIKE J. CHANEY ½bro.of
La.,is filed 13 June 1881 and litigation on est.went on untill
1893. **PET.**by J.C.HALL-June 1883 states he had purchased all
heirs interest in est.and he alone will settle & takes exception
to McKinneys final a/c. By Oct.1893 McKinney is finally discharged when court approves his final a/c. M.C.MARTIN mentioned as
a creditor of est.

#24;PACKET MISSING;CC docket;P.M.KEHO vs EDGAR WOOD JR.et al;Orig.
Bill filed Oct.13,1879.Demurrer filed Oc.13,1879. Nov.13,1880
S.L.HUSSEY letter. June 13,1881 order of abatement-due to death
of complaintant.

#25;RUEBEN BYRD vs J.H.ROBERTSON,Sheriff;Oct.14,1879,Writ Habeas
Corpus.

#25½;EST.OF WILLIAM,ALICE MAUD,GEO.DUNCAN & LUCY MYERS:minors-
wards. Children of William(decd)& Mary C.Myers. Adult children
F.C.MYERS(son of William and decd.wife HENRIETTA F.WELLS MYERS
she decd.before 1850 when F.C was less than a yr.old. Henrietta
was the dau. of Sam'l W.Wells-his will & est. is abstracted in
Vol.II EMR.p.37)AND R.S.MYERS,son of Wm.& Mary Myers. **LET.**of
Guard.issued to Mary C.Myers 12 Jan.1880-N.R.ANDERSON surety
on bond. **Wm.Myers** decd.27 Dec.1876. The time lapse was explained
thusly-the life Ins. Co. holding the policy Wm.left to his child
ren had gone insolvent and now was paying 15% on claims. There
was no other est.left to Children. Oct.22,1894 Geo.D. now 22yrs
Guard.dismissed.Oct.28,1891 Maud over 21- R.S.,Alice,F.C. and
Wm. release Guard Mar.1890. F.C.MYERS name was FRANCIS C.

#26;WILLIAM MERIDITH vs HENRIETTA WILLIAMS:B.of Div.Dec.5,1879.
Decree granted June 14,1880

#27;FRANCES COLEMAN vs BENJ.COLEMAN;B.of Div. Jan.12,1880. Case
dismissed as stale on motion of clerk, Oct.28,1890

#27½;ADOLPH JOEL:esparte-lunatic. Mar.9,1880

SHARKEY CO.MS. CC PACKETS-1876-1900

#28;BILL STUBBLEFIELD vs JOHN W.STUBBLEFIELD:B.of Div. Apr.2 1880. Case dismiss as stale Oct.28,1890

#28½;EST.OF MOLLIE K.SHELBY:ward-minor. Father THOMAS J.SHELBY Pet.for letters of guardianship May 30,1880.Surety on bond A.C. SHELBY. Mollie K. owns 1/3 int in pltn.in Shark.Co.called CHI-COREA,E½ of NE1/4,Sec.15,T12,R7W, which Mollie inherited from Grandfather R.P.SHELBY.[ROBERT PRINCE SHELBY's est. is thoroughly covered in Vol.II,EMR, Issa.Co. records.] **Sale**;Mollie K. sold her 1/3 int.in CHICCREA to WM.GIBBONS-Jan.20,1881, and her mother EMILY M.SHELBY consents to sale.EVAN B. & A.C.SHELBY-bros.of Mollie Kate are co.-tenants in the land.

#29.W.M.BAKER vs EASTER BAKER:B.of Div.May 31,1880-Many depositions and case dismissed June13,1881

#30;Missing from files-CC Docket lists MARY E.GIBBONS et al vs J.C.HALL et al;Bill of complaint filed May 29,1880

#30½;EST.OF DAVID HUNT et al(wards DAVID,VIDA,GEORGE.:ANNA B. HUNT of Adams Co.Ms. Pet.Lt.Guard.9 Feb.1880. She is mother of David,Vida,George Hunt and Widow of David Hunt,decd.**Bond** sur.ABIJAH HUNT & B.GOODMAN. David Hunt,the father decd. Sept. 1878-Will is abstracted also in this vol. It is recorded in WBK"A"pg.6,Shark.Co.Ms. IN his will he states he never wants S½ of GEORGIANA PLTN. sold or encumbered in any way. **LT.Guard.** states that David Hunt left to his widow & ch. no est. real or pers.,except that portion which would by Law descend to them as a homstead. After his death his est.was declared insolvent and the providings and homestead are pending in court. **TWO** sets of Bonds-second set dated May 1890 and Surety was PROSPER DeMARCO of Natchez and says Anna and ch. are from Adams Co. Natchez.Ms. **INV.**of Est.made for 1881 thru 1890 totaled $7,031.25 and filed Oct.17 1891.David,Vida & George owned small tract in Sharkey inherited from Uncle James Hunt. **Court** orders sale of small homested(80 ac.). Bro-in-law to Anna,Abijah Hunt had cleared and managed this small inherited land.

#31;CC:D.McDONALD vs S.DOVER & JOHN S.JOOR,SHERIF.B.of Complaint Filed 22 May 1880. Dispute over promissary note.

#31½;EST.OF CHAS.CARROL PARSONS;ward & minor.Pet.Lt.Guard.filed June 19,1880 by step-mother M.L.B.PARSONS.**Vouchers**;1887-90 Room board and tuition in Memphis. 1893 Holly Springs-St.Thomas Hall tuition sent by Wm.BRITTON.1894-back in Memphis.**a/c filed** July 14, 1890 covered 10 years-gave amounts coming to Chas.C.Parsons as from T.WILBUR est. July 19 1880;C.T.LIPPITT est.Aug.1881; Willbur est.Nov.1881;Lippett est Oct.1882. Mrs. T.A.BRITTON handled the funds. Some connection with Mont Helena Mercantile Co.GEO.C.HARRIS, Wm.BRITTON,GEO.C.HARRIS JR.directors Oct.21,1893. No clue to fathers name or relationchip to Wilbur & Lippett ests.

#32;missing from files:A.V.BROWN et al vs H.E.SHANNON;Marshall-June 15,1880

#32½;EST.OF JAMES SMILEY;decd.28 Mar.1880.Pet.Lt.Adm.filed Oct. 20,1880 by Wm.J.CHANEY a creditor. Intestate-no known heirs(cont.)

SHARKEY CO.MS. CC PACKETS -1876-1900

#32½ cont.Adm.bond secur. G.Y.STEWART,CREATH SHELBY.

#33;Wm.LAWSON vs B.SINAI et al:et al being JULIUS SINAI & H.G. STEVENS, Justice of the Peace. B.of compl.and injunction filed 14 Aug.1880. Lawson & Sinai Bros. in co-partnership in saloon since Dec.1878-conducted in building on lot in Sinaiville.[town adjacent to McKinneyville(later called Anguilla)] John S.Joor, Sherif.of Shark.Co.Ms. appointed by court to be receiver of saloons assets until dispute resolved-May 1881. F.MYERS,JAMES H.CORTRIGHT,-----HOLLINGSWORTH are summoned witnesses and give depo.21 June 1881. **Court**finds against complainant. Lawson.

#34;two pkts.M.H.PEMBERTON vs JNO.T.MIZELL et al;B.of complt. filed 30 July 1880. LYLE CLARK soliciter for Pemberton. Defendants Jno.T.Mizell of Orange Co. Fla.;THOMAS B.WARD of Madison Co.Ms.; JAMES H.CORTRIGHT;ALLEN NICKERSON:CYRUS LAWYER:T.T.ORENDORFF:T.J.ORENDORFF:IRA A.CORTRIGHT,all of Shark.Co.Ms.**Orig**.bill states-Pemberton(called Major)was owner of 1/4 int.in a saw mill on Indian Bayou-formerly owned by E.G.CLARKE & CO. and also timber rights on Sec.33 & 34 T.13,R7W..Pemberton leased to Mizell for 3 years this prop. from Jan.1879 for $2,100 rent-½in good lumber,½ in money- not paid. Mizell was a res.of Shark. Co. at time of making lease with Pemberton-since has left for State of Fla.(Jan.1880). He sold all prop. he owned in Ms. and signed over his lease & prom.notes from J.H. & Ira Cortright & Nickerson to THOMAS B.Ward who in turn signed to the Orendorff brothers. Cyrus Lawyer was co-signer on prom.notes of Mizell to Pemberton. **INJUNTION** issued July 30,1880 to all defendants to cease all action on matter till heard in court.**LET**. from W.E.HAY complaining that the mare he bought from Mizells sale ran away before he got her home and he wants his money back! S.B.ALEXANDER & O.F.BARNES were wit.in case May 25,1881.**Depo**. 10 Dec.1881 by Mizell states hes 33 yrs.&resi.of Melrose,Fla. He had a sister living with him in Rolling Fork,named FANNIE. **other deop**.EUGENE CLARKE,31,resi.Shark.Co.Ms.JOSEPH KEITH,JOHN HARSH owner of Hotel Harsh.
Bill dismissed by agreement of all parties 14 Feb.1882-sharing court cost.

#35;WACHENHEIM & HERMAN vs H.E.SHANNON et al;B.of Complaint filed Nov.19,1880, mentions BETTIE C.SHANNON & W.W.SHANNON. Final Dec.13,1882

#35½;EST.JAMES HUNT:[related pkt.#30½-Bro.David Hunts,est.decd] Adm.ABIJAH HUNT-Bond security JAMES H.CORTRIGHT & IRA A.COURTRIGHT-both dated 4 Dec.1880. James Hunt decd.28 Nov.1880. Abijah only surviving bro.of James and his land adjacent to his. 5 Jan.1892 final a/c accepted by court. Pkt.mainly contains vouchers on est. **David**,Vita & George Hunt ch.of David Hunt,decd, are heirs to James Hunt est. As widow of David, Anna B.Hunt and sister Mattie H.Moore had conveyed their int.to Abijah in 1881.Land descr.and tax receipts made out to M.& J.HUNTet al. Bill of Dr.T.J.MURRAY,Onward Ms. dated from Apr.9 to Nov.8,1880 shows he doctored him in Vicksburg 3 days-then in May at CAPT. MOORES res.for 4 days. Legal fees of McLAURIN & McLAURIN.

SHARKEY CO.MS. CC PKTS.1876-1900

#36;NELSON POTTER vs HENRIETTA POTTER;B.of Divo.filed Feb.26, 1881. Dismissed Oct.28,1890.

#36½;EST.OF ABNER TRUCKS & ELLEN TRUCKS:minor children of JOSIAH TRUCKS decd.Nov.1879 intest. Mother of ch.died Jan.1878(before Josiah) She was the dau. of Wm.CLARK who Pet.for Let.Adm.on Josiah est,9 Dec.1880. **Guard**.pet.and bond same time.JOHN HARSH secu.on bond. **Est**.-small tract of land-198 ac. Sec.28,T10,R5-wooded,swampy land on lower Sunflower River. Pet.to sell land for maintanence of ch. GRAND MOTHER JANE CLARK--sister to Mrs. Trucks is CATHERINE CLARK. CATHERINE EMMERSON,Vicksburg,Ms.; MATILDA RINE,Yazoo Co.Ms.:ALIN CLARK Shar.Co. are nearest kin.

#37;ALLEN JAMES vs.ALICE JAMES;B.of Divo.filed Apr.9,1881.Granted Dec.15,1881

#38;EST.OF JOE CHRISTIAN;(inside spelled CHRISTIANSON)decd.20 Apr.1881-intest.-no relatives resi.of State.**Lt.of Adm**.by W.H. BARNARD,M.D. 22 Apr.1881-Bond sur.T.J.ORENDORFF.**Appr**.& Inv. 25 May 1881-paper blank.

#39;JACOB TURNER vs LIZZIE TURNER;May 20 1881-Bill of divo.Dismi. 1890

#40;BANKS SPRIGGS vs SYLVIA SPRIGGS:May 24 1881;Bill of divo. Dismissed 1890

#41;CAROLINE S. HATCHETT vs J.R.HILL:Bill of complaint-filed May 27,1881-Dismissed 1890

#42;MATTIE HARRELLL vs J.P.HARRELL:Bill of divo.July 15,1881-granted Dec.14,1881

#43;JOHN R.CAMERON vs STEPHEN GALES:B.of Complaint filed 13 May 1881-states Cameron,a resident of Madison Co.Ms.,owned and resided part time on WEEPING WILLOW PLTN.on Deer Creek. On 11 June 1875, Gales contracted to buy 560 acr. for $13,000, handwritten agreement-deed not executed until 1881.Mentions EGYPT PLACE. Land description. By 1881 Gales defaulted on yearly payments and Cameron seeking to cancel deed. **Gales** files cross bill Sept.1881. Settled Sept.1884 in favor of Cameron.

#44;JOHN W. CRENSHAW vs MARY CRENSHAW:B.of divor. June 16,1881. Granted June 13,1882

#45;AMY O.ALEXANDER vs WM.MULLER et al[S.B.ALEXANDER & JOHN S.JOOR]Bill filed June 28,1881

#46;J.D.STEWART et al vs W.H.McDOWELL et al;B.of compl. filed Sept.21 1881.Bills filed for non residents-no proof of publication. Bill dismissed Sept.21 1881

#47;JAS.D.STEWART,GEO.Y.STEWART vs MARY CARR et al;B.Compl.Sept. 27 1881 states-Stewarts from Hinds Co.Ms. Mary Carr from Logan Co.Ky.;JANE M.GLENN from Montgomery Co. Tenn.;MARY E WRIGHT(cont.)

SHARKEY CO.MS. CC PKTS.1876-1900

#47 cont.from Bibb Co. Ga. Affirmation of Tax Title. Land descp. included that was sold for taxes in 1868 to Levee Comm. In 1879 the commissioners S.GWIN & W.S.HEMINGWAY conveyed title to Jas. & Geo.Stewart. Title confirmed 13 June 1882.

#48;missing

#49;ANNIE PARRISH vs.JOHN PARRISH;B.of divor. Oct.17 1881.Grant. Dec.15,1881

#50; STEPHEN LANE vs MAHALA LANE; Oct.22 1881-B.of divor.Dismissed

¶Note;From # 50 to #364 I have picked only the Est.or occasional suit of interest.

#52;EST.OF DAN COSBY;decd.1Aug.1881-intest. LT.OF ADM.filed Oct.1.1881 by A.B.PITTS states court refused to appoint any relative due to incompetancy and he applies. B.Surety, W.H. BERNARD,E.DEUSTER:**Statement by John Cowan**; Cosby was tennant on Anguilla Pltn. of J.W.VICK in 1881-rents of which were due Cowan as surviving husband of MRS.L.V.COWAN-dau.of J.W.Vick. Pitt was general manager under J.W.Vick & kept all acc. Vick divided the proceed of Pltn.among his Ch. **DAN COSBY** had small per.assets & 271 acr.land. Pitt asks court to sell assets Dec.1882 to satisfy debts of est.and sustain Cosbys children.Affadavit by THOS.J.LOVE & Robt.(X)LOVE Dec.1881 Madison Co.Ms.states BRIMAGE PATTERSON,BETTIE WEBB,NICHOLAS GOODLOE,CALVIN GOODLOE & ROSA GOODLOE are legitimate ch.of Cosby.PET.by Brim.Patterson as next best friend of heirs ANNIE,MARTHA,DAN JR.,ELLA,&SAM COSBY filed June 1883 asking for cash settlement. **Final a/c** filed Mar.1885 and Exception to it filed by Patterson Feb.1886. ¶[see pkt.149 and 150 for related facts.]

#53;EST.OF J.P.WALKE:decd.2 Oct.1881-intest. Lt.of Adm.filed Dec.1881 by T.T.ORENDORFF a creditor. Adm.B. sureties JOHN HARSH T.J.ORENDORFF. Walke worked land belonging to J.M.McCALEB.Final a/c 1892

#54;EST.OF MRS. ELIZA LEIGH CLARK:decd.Dec.1880-intest.-no est. but had a small $2,000 Life ins.policy on son EUGENE CLARK who died 19 Dec.1881. No surviving husband-4 children EDW.D.CLARK, S.JACKSON CLARK,PEARL LEIGH CLARK & your pet. LEIGH CLARK. Edw. full age but S.J.& Pearl are minors. Lt.of Adm.by Leigh Clark filed Apr.8,1882.Ed.Clark & J.S.JOOR sureties on bond.

#67;EST.OF PATIENCE HARRIS:of Sharkey Co.Ms.decd.16 Aug.1882. WILL dated 12 May 1882.Wit.J.S.JOOR,N.T.BAGGETT;-"MOLLIE C. WADDILL to receive tract of land(lengthy descrp.)all in Sec.8 T12,R6W,Sharkey Co.,with all on it and also all of Patience's person. prop. Appoints Wm.B.McQUILLAN exec." Will filed Sept.23, 1882,Probated Dec.4,1882. No inventory or appraisal, some hint of possible litigation over settlement.

#69;EST.OF LYDIA HODGES^{col};decd.15 Mar.1882-intest. Lt.Pet.Adm. filed May 16,1882 by Dr.W.H.HIXEN(later spelled HICKSON)a creditor.Affi.by Hickson,May 1890 on Final a/c made from Warren Co.Ms. ¶IN the 1880 census he is **DR.W.H.HICKMAN,WIFE:LAURA S.HICKMAN**

SHARKEY CO.MS. CC PKTS. 1876-1900

#70;EST.OF JEFF COTTON;decd.24 Nov.1882,Shark.Co.Ms.-intest.Lt.
Adm.to son BEN COTTON dated Jan.3,1883 to collect a $163 judg-
ment to Jeff Cotton from G.W.HOLLINGSWORTH that was pending
in court. Ben was appointed a special adm.and later Dr.A.Miller
was appointed Adm.13 Mar.1883.Cotton left a widow and several
minor ch. Final a/c Mar.25,1891

#71;EST.OF W.V.DOOLEY;decd.Shark.Co.Ms.Aug.1882.JULIUS SINAI
a creditor files Pet.Lt.Adm.24 Jan.1883.Bond Secu.J.H.CORTRIGHT,
FRED GRAFT.

#72;EST.OF E.T.BRIDGERS:decd.1 Dec.1882-intest.Lt.Adm.to W.H.
BARNARD -a creditor-filed 5 Feb.1883.Bond sur.T.J.ORENDORFF,
J.S.JOOR. Est.consists of about 60acr.land. Pet.for sale of
land May 11,1883,brings a summons to ALBERT BRIDGERS,a minor
and sole heir, living with his g.father Wm.BRIDGERS near Raymond, Hinds Co.Ms. Land sold Oct.7,1884 to S.DOVER,W.C.H.McKINNEY
Final a/c to court states that upon sale of land they found
that Bridgers had conveyed deed to JAMES D.STEWART & G.G.STEWART
in Nov.1881.

#77;EXPARTE NICK GOODLOE,etal;See #52 Est.of Dan Cosby. Court
orders sale of land coming to heirs of DAN COSBY decd. on 24
Sept.1884, because property not dividable. E.DEUSTER in his
deposition described land as uncultivated wild land -unsuitable
for dividing 8 to 10 ways. Sold to M.H.PEMBERTON & W.H.SHELTON
for $271.00 15 Dec.1884.

#78;EST.OF JNO.A.McDOUGALL:decd.12 Oct.1882 in Vicksburg,Ms.
a citz.of Shark.Co.Ms.Lt.of Adm.granted to A.O.HARDENSTIEN,a
creditor of Warren Co.Ms. Est.consisted of small personal and
a tract of land. McDougall never marr.-no rela.in state-28 Aug
1883-Bond sur.J.F.BAUM.G.G.PEGRAM. Hardenstein states McDougall
may have had a sister in Canada or Nova Scotia.Land desc. wild
and unimproved sold 1886 to ERNEST HARDENSTEIN.

#79;EST.OF W.P.ELLISON:decd.11 Aug.1883-intestShark.Co.Ms. B.
GOODMAN files Lt.Adm.22 Sept.1883-a creditor. Bond J.S.JOOR &
A.G.FLOYD.Final a/c &plea for discharge by Goodman states that
the supposed assets of Ellison's est. were never placed in his
hands-all were claimed by A.FOX of V'burg,Ms. & there was nothing to Adm.

#83½;EST.OF WALTER STANDARD; ward.Pet.of Guard.filed 11 Dec.1883
by W.H.HICKSON*states; he, Hickson,,.on 4 Dec.1879 in Wash.Co.Ms
lawfully wedded Mrs.LAURA STANDARD, who had 2 minor ch. WALTER
& ALICE STANDARD. On 4 Nov.1883 Mrs.Laura Standard Hickson died
in Shar.Co.Ms. leaving said minors. On Nov.29,1883, Alice Standard died. Walter,6 years old needs a Guard. as his mother left
him a tract of land in Wash.Co.Ms. Bond Sur.W.J.CHANEY & FRED
GRAFT. FINAL a/c and asking discharge as Guard. Hickson states
that MARION BAREFIELD of Wash.Co.,an uncle of Walter Standard,
filed for Guard.in Wash.Co. & it was also granted & he surrendered all belonging to Walter and also the boy to Barefield. The
est.was an undivided int. in 40 acr.in Wash.Co. which Hickson
¶*In 1880 census he is Dr.H.W.HICKMAN

SHARKEY CO.MS. CC PKTS. 1876-1900

#83½ cont. and Walter held together-Hickson giving his part to the boy to be used for his benefit.

#87;EST.OF CHARLES FLEMING:decd.31 Mar.1884-resi.Shark.Co.Ms.-intest. Bro.James G.FLEMING files Lt.of Adm.June 1884.Personal prop.worth $1200.**Appr**.14 Apr.1884 by JAS.C.MOORE,THOMAS McEVINS, S.B.ALEXANDER. J.G.FLeming a Citz.of Clayton Co.Iowa. also appointed Guard.of only child GRACE FLEMING 5 May 1884,to act in her behalf in Ms. Mother, Harriet Fleming,natural guard.in Iowa. James Fleming,Adm. asks court to allow sale of part of prop.and the pers.prop. to pay debts of estate. One interesting voucher;by W.WILTSE,Hardin Co.Iowa-"to board and lodge wife and child of Chas.Fleming-Sept.1,1881-Oct.1,1882-55 weeks-$330.00. Administration takes exception to claim. Order for discharge after Final a/c Mar.24,1890. ¶**note-see #89 for related facts**⌋

#88;Est.F.M.BAGGETT:decd.26 May 1882. ISAAC P.BAGGETT ask court to appoint him Special Adm. to pursue 2 suits pending in court brought before F.M.Baggett deceased; Baggett vs IRA.A.COURTRIGHT & BAGGETT vs MRS.A.C.WADDILL. Petition dated 19 Apr.1884. Adm. bond sureties;JNO.HARSH,T.T.ORENDORFF. Only 2 doc.in pkt.

#89;EST.OF GRACE FLEMING:ward,minor.See Pkt.#87. Tax receipts give land descrp.200 acr.Grace inherited from her father Charles Fleming.**Guard**.bond appointing J.G.Fleming, Elkport,Iowa,May 5,1884-sureties J.H.CORTRIGHT,J.E.BUTLER,FRED GRAFT-$2500, inc. in this pkt. In this petition James G. states Charles Fleming decd.30 Mar.1884 and at the time of his death was unmarried but left 1 child Grace Fleming.(Since Harriet Fleming was still living, they were either divorced or never married).**PETITION** for Lt.of Guardian ship by F.M.WILLIAMS of Hardin Co.,Iowa - dated 8 June 1888, states"that Grace Fleming is the minor daughter of Charles & Harriett Fleming,decd."Upon the death of Graces mother-Williams has applied for Guard. in Iowa, But the uncle J.G.Fleming continues to function in Ms.until 1890. **DOC.A CC RECORD-** undated- WILLINGTON WILTSE & THOMAS McEVINS vs JAMES G.FLEMING, HARRIETT T.NEILAND & GRACE FLEMING-of Iowa Falls,Iowa,Harding Co. [Grace's mother Harriett has remarried?] J.G.Flemings address is Elkport,Iowa. **PAPER** marked Inventory of real estate give land descrip. Some duplication of paper in Pkt.87.

#90;EST.OF FRANK & ELLIS BAGGETT:wards,minors-See #88.**Lt.of Adm**. & Guard. filed Oct.28,1884 by ISAAC P.BAGGETT, husband of F.M.BAGGETT who decd.May 26,1883,intest. Frank and Ellis are their minor children. Guard.bond sur.JOHN HARSH,W.H.HICKSON $400.Est.consist of undivided 1/3 interest in 85 acr. in Shark. Co.Ms. worth about $50 an acr.20 head of cattle,1mare,2 colts. **INV** made Jan.13,1885- no other papers.

#93;EST.OF MOLLIE K.SHELBY; ward-see # 28½. This pkt.hold petition by Mollie K.stating she is over 14 and her guard.,father THOMAS J.SHELBY had died and she wants her bro. E.B.SHELBY appointed her Guard.-8 Jan.1885. Bond sur.JOHN S.JOOR:L.W.INGRAHAM. One citation 1890 to Guard.for Final report.

SHARKEY CO.MS. CC PKTS. 1876-1900

#98;EST.OF L.C.R.CASEY;ward-LAURA CORNELIA RUSSELL CASEY. Lt. Guard.dated 1 Dec.1885 by W.H.SHELTON with sureties D.C.CASEY, T.T.ORENDORFF. In Dec.1885 Shelton made a trip to Ark. to redeem land sold for taxes that Laura had inherited from her mother Mrs.Laura Russell. Also in 1885 Shelton tells the court he is moving to Tx.and wishes to be removed as Guard.-Pet.for Lt.of Guard.-3 Sept.1886,by D.C.CASEY,states he legally adopted Laura Cornelia Russell (no date-or papers). Guard.bond sur. H.L.FOOTE,T.T.ORENDORFF $1,000. COL.JOHNSON of Camden,Ark. took care of collecting $400 rent & paying Taxes on Laura's land in Ark. Last paper dated 1897.

#101;EST. OF A.L.:M.R.:ZARIFFA AARON:wards & minor ch.of WOLF AARON decd. Guard.Bond filed by Mother of ch.,FANNIE AARON Feb. 2,1891-sure. H.H.& L.J.STADEKER of Madison Co.Ms. $800.Bonds on each ch. In Fannies petition she states ch.are residing in Claiborne Co. July 1899 Court releases Fannie as Guard. & accepts final a/c. ALEXANDER LUCRECE AARON 21 Aug.13,1897. MAXIMILLIAN RUDOLF AARON,address Columbia,Tn.,age 18,now married as of 25 Apr.1899. ZARlFFA's address is Grand Boulevard Chicago,Ill. Alexander L.Aaron is now his mothers attorney.

#103;EST.S.F.SHELTON:decd.16 May 1885-unmarr.-no chi.-intestate. Nearest relatives-mother,Mrs.Mary E.Shelton, Brandon,Ms.& 4 brothers;E.A.SHELTON,Brandon,Ms.;T.P.SHELTON,Boston,Mass.:F.E. SHELTON,minor without guardian,residing in Rolling Fork,Ms.& the petitioner W.H.SHELTON,of Rolling Fork,Ms.who files for Let.of ADM. 21 May 1885. Bond sureties;A.MILLER,W.A.ORENDORFF, $3,000. Appr.sheet blank.O.F.DUDLEY,D.C.CASEY,T.T.ORENDORFF were the appraisers.

#112;EST.OF R.J.HAMILTON:decd.26 Oct.1885-Shark.Co.Ms. Let.Adm. by I.A.CORTRIGHT filed 29 Oct.1885,states no relatives in state. Final a/c 1892

#115;EST.OF B.F.ELLINGTON:decd.18 Aug.1885.Pet.for Let.Adm.by Mrs.L.D.ELLINGTON,widow of decd.,filed 18 Dec.1885. Adm.Bond sur.T.T.ORENDORFF & JAMES H.CORTRIGHT.Letter in pkt.to McLaurin & McLaurin,Attys.-written from Percy,Ms. by Mrs.Ellington-states that she and her son are trying to hold on to the land to make a living for she and the children-unnamed. Final a/c Mar.1891

#119;EST.of JAMES S.BELL:decd.---1885-resided and owned property in Issaq.Co.Ms.;T.J.ORENDORFF nearest relative(by marriage) seeks Adm.of est. 11 Jan.1886. B.sureties;T.T.ORENFORFF & H.L. FOOTE. 19 Mar.1890 Adm.Orendorff reports no goods etc. have come into his hands and is discharged.

#126;EST.JOSEPH RUSSELL:decd.July or Aug.1884 in Shark.Co.Ms. intest. Pet.Let.Adm.Mar.6 1886 by G.M.BAGGETT. Bond sur.B GOODMAN,E.BYERLY. INV.& APPR.4 May 1886 by W.J.ELLZEY,A.HUNT,ABNER DEMENT-1 bay horse,1 wagon(to widow)& 1 watch in possession of DAVID RUSSELL. Final a/c 29 Sept.1887

SHARKEY CO.MS. CC PACKETS-1876-1900

#127;EST.MARY L.WATTS(MRS.)decd.16 Mar.1885 Shark.Co.Ms.-intest.
H.E.SHANNON pet.for Let.Adm.Mar.1886.B.sur.J.G.PARHAM,SUSAN
SHANNON. Shannon states Mary Watts died possessed of considerable
real & personal property in which he has an interest.**INV.&
APPR.**by J.S.JOOR,G.M.CHAMPION,HENRY(X)WHITE-3 Apr.1886. **Apr.7,**
1886 RICHARD LEE,father of decd.Mary Watts,petitions court to
revoke Shannons Adm.& appoint him. States"Shortly before her,Mary,
death in Mar.1885, she married N.W.WATTS. She had previously
been the wife of AUGUSTUS ROSEN (marr.autumn 1878). Aug.Rosen
died Apr.4,1884 Shark.Co.-their issue-3-RICHARD,JOHN,MARY ROSEN,
who live with g.father Richard Lee and their g.mother his wife.
No other relatives. After Mary died Watts made a sale to H.E.
SHANNON(relationship by marriage-bro.in-law scratched out)of
his 1/4 int. in the est.They were marr.only 3 weeks. Small tract
land wild & uncultivated near Sunflower River,& 25 acrs.cultivated".
Pet.by Richard Lee to court to give him custody of children
& Adm.over the est. **10 Apr.1886** Hon.WARREN COWAN suspends Shannon's
Adm.until further order of CC of Shark.Co.Ms. **Depositions** by
W.H.RUSHING,JOHN MAXWELL & LUTHER CHILDRESS and Shannon's answer
to Lees suit. **ORDER:**undated-of C.C. revoking Adm. & saying not
necessay to Adm. on said estate.
¶IN THIS PKT.and marked #127-a deed Feb.1882,rec.DB"C"p.102-103
PATIENCE HARRIS-indenture to HARSH & ORENDORFF : S.F.SHELTON
& W.H.SHELTON ,Trustee. Harris est.in #67]

#134;GEORGE ANNA,AMALINE CLARK,Wm.HENRY HARRIS:wards-Pet.Guard.
by father Geo.(x)Clark Citz.of Shark.Co.Ms. filed 13 Aug.1886.
He is step-father of Wm.H.Harris. Their mother CHERRY CLARK
decd.&her est.was a benefit certificate in the Independant Order
of Son & Dau. of Jacob of America(Order of society for colored
people.) Bond.sur.by JAMES H.CORTRIGHT,JAMES LEE,who report
27 Oct.1890 that Geo.Clark could never collect the benefit certificate,and ask dismissal of the bond. Granted same day.

#154;EST.HENRY STEEL:decd.Aug.1886 Shark.Co.Ms.-intestate. Mar.
1887 A.L.NEAL(a creditor)applys for Let.Adm.Special to collect
a judgement against MONROE GLENN of $40 in favor of Steel,pend-
ing in court.Adm.B.sur.MRS.B.KENT,T.J.KENT. Case was settled
and Neal dismissed Oct.1890.

#155;EST.W.F.BARROW:decd.8 Nov.1886-intest.Shark.Co.Ms.-no liv-
ing relatives in state. J.E.BUTLER pet.for Adm.Ad Colg.15 Nov.
1886. Butler is a creditor -est.owes him $25 for burial expens-
es. JAMES CORTRIGHT & JOHN KELLY bond sureties.

#156;EST.E.P.CORTRIGHT:decd.15 Dec.1885 intest.-unmarried. His
bro. JAMES H.CORTRIGHT pet.Let.Adm. Sept.1887. Bond sur.H.J.Mc-
LAURIN,I.A.CORTRIGHT.

#157;EST.J.B.BAILEY:decd. 28 Nov.1887-intest.-Shark.Co.Ms.-no
relatives in state. 29 Nov.1887 I.A.CORTRIGHT(creditor)pet.Let.
Adm. Bond sur.H.E.SHANNON,WALTER McLAURIN.

SHARKEY CO.MS. CC PACKETS-1876-1900

#158; EST.ROBERT EMMET HARVEY:decd.28 Nov.1887-Shark.Co.Ms.intest
Pet.for Let.Admx.by mother MARTHA J.HARVEY,filed 7 Jan.1888.
She states hes her only son-2 daus.,MRS.HOPE H.CHAMPION, EVA
HARVEY,both over 21 sign with mother asking discharge after
final a/c Mar.1890. There is a 3rd dau.JULIA not mentioned in
this packet. Bill by Drs.ORENDORFF & HARPER-treating Robert
E.Harvey for Hematuria.
¶NOTE:Robert & his mother and several small children are buried
in pasture across Deer Creek east of Mounds Cemetery South of
Rolling Fork on Mounds Pltn. This piece of land on 1905 Map
of Sharkey Co. belongs to Mrs.Champion-inherited from her mother.
See related packet#253.]

#159;EST.LEE WONG:decd 19 Dec.1887 in Anguilla,Shark.Co.Ms.intest.
BRO.LEE JOU petitions for Let.Adm.9 Jan.1888.Small stock of
goods in store. SAM LEE & DIN GEY sureties on bond.

#167;EST. CARRIE IRENE & BURLEIGH SHANNON;wards.-H.E.SHANNON
father of dau's.Carrie & Burleigh , pet.for Let.Guard.9 Mar.
1888 for purpose of instituting a suit to recover minors prop.
in Shark.Co.Ms. G.Bond surety C.J.PETERSON. In pet.for final
discharge the suit was dropped without recovery and he request
court to release him Mar.1890. Granted Mar.1891. Shannon also
states the girls have interest with him in small realestate
and it takes every penny to school & keep them.

#168;EST.OF BYRON HENDRICKS:ward-minor heir of SAM'L D.HENDRICKS
Guard.bond by MRS.S.E.HENDRICKS- surety by JNO.W.HENDRICKS-30
July 1888. No Let.of Guard.included here. Final report & request
for discharge by Mrs.Hendricks filed Oct.1890 states Byron possessed a small est.left to him by an uncle who resided in Tenn.
Value $75-80.This money only prop.received by her. Does not
state if Sam'l Hendricks is the uncle-or if Mrs.S.E. is the
mother.

#168½;EST. H.G.STEVENS;decd.3 Oct.1888-Shark.Co.Ms.intest.
Pet.Let.Ad.Coll. by W.H.BARNARD-at the request of the widow
of decd.L.R.STEVENS-Oct.17,1888. Bond Surety-L.R.Stevens & W.B.
BARNARD-$1,000.**MAR.1889**-DOUGLAS STEVENS pet.court for Let.of
Adm. stating"H.G.STEVENS decd. owning 296 acr.land,some cash,
certain debts due est.,4 horses,1 mule,1cow. Douglas is the
son of JOHN STEVENS, A SON OF H.G.STEVENS by his 1st marriage.
There are 3 children by a 2nd marr. whose names & addresses
are unknown but Douglas thinks they are in Tx. Douglas is nearest
of kin in State & by law wants Adm. & for Barnard to turn over
all assets."**MAR.1890**-Barnard asks release from Ad.Coll.Adm.
showing vouchers paid to Douglas & L.R.Stevens. No Adm.Bond
included here for Doug.Stevens.

#171½;EST.SAMUEL McCOMB:decd.-E.B.McCOMB special Adm.to conduct
pending suit in Court of Claims in Wash.D.C. against US GOVT.
Bond sureties L.W.INGRAHAM & J.J.RESTER-Nov.3,1888. a/c for
1890-suit still pending. A/C for 1891 same. Court granted him
leave for no further reports until claim settled. Nothing more
in Pkt.

SHARKEY CO.MS. CC PACKETS- 1876-1900

#188;EST.OF C.J.PETERSON:decd.18 Nov.1889.NONCUPATIVE WILL made 1½ hours before death at Rolling Fork,Ms. at his residence. Witnesses;JOHN W.HENDRICKS:W.H.RUSHING:W.W.HALSELL:JOHN O.ROBERTS. "Iwant my partner to have half of all my property that I now own, and my 2 brothers the other half." J.L.ROOT was the partner. Brothers unnamed. PET.let.Adm. Jan.9,1890 by W.K.McLAURIN states he is a creditor of est. & no one has applied for Adm.& the real & Pers.Prop.& debts & claims of est. need Administrating. Bond surety H.B.ADEN:J.H.HURD- $2,000.

#193;EST CYRUS LAWYER;decd. May 1890-intest.-Shark.Co.Ms. M.H. PEMBERTON files for LET.ADM. 12 July,1890.Bond sur.G.M.BAGGETT: R.L.McLAURIN-$400.Oct.22,1890 Pemberton files a petition to court for recovery of certain funds from MINNA LAWYER-the widow of decd.Oct.27,1890,Minna Lawyer files motion to set aside clerks granting Let.of Adm.to Pemberton.Oct.28,1890 Minna answers Pembertons request for certain funds[rent on store & part of crop on small tract of land]stating the rent and land exempted to her by law as widow of decd. and needed for care of their 4 children-the oldest 8 the youngest 3. Pemberton claims a debt owed to him by est. INV.& APPR.returned & filed Oct.27,1890 by J.H.COOK,JOS.THOMAS,JIM HOLLINGSWORTH,NED(x)ROBINSON,CHAS. FISHER. OCT.29,1890 court dismisses Pembertons petition against Minna Lawyer. Annual A/C-1891-1892.

#201;EST.SPIVEY DOUGLAS:decd.Sept.30,1890-NON CUPATIVE WILL Egremont,Ms.Oct.3,1890(when set to paper) reads "On nite of Sat. Sept.27,1890 at his usual place of resi.and where he had resided for 4 years- Spivey Douglas, in his sickness & approaching death, in presence of H.L.FOOTE & DR.W.R.HARPER his attending phy.,made the following will---"."Realizing my dangerous condition, I desire H.L.FOOTE to take charge of all my prop. & money in Shark.Co.Ms.-pay debts($1 or$2 to S.McCOMB) and funeral expenses,doctors fees,& pay the rest to mother(she knows how much) and desire Foote & Harper to hear my statement-as to my other prop. they know what to do with it." Foregoing statement made at Douglas's residence on COUNCIL BEND PLTN.where he died on Sept.30,1890. PROOF of Will-Dec.30,1890.CONSENT of next of kin for will Probate sworn to in Noxubee Co.Ms. by GEORGE W.,JOHN T.,ABRAHAM DOUGLAS, only full brothers now living. Mothers name LUCY DOUGLAS. 15 Nov.1890. PET.Let.Adm.by H.L.Foote 30 Dec.1890 states he,Foote, owed Douglas $1100,which constituted all of the est. B.sureties;W.D.BROWN:W.R.HARPER-same date.

#202:EST OF LLYOD GUNDY:decd.30 Dec.1890-intest.-no widow. 120 acr.land Shark.Co.Ms. Pet.Let.Adm. by RILEY L.GUNDY,son of LLoyd Gundy. 6 other heirs-NAPOLEON,MANAH,AMANDA,PEARLY,STELLA,SARGENT GUNDY- 3 are minors.Pet.filed Jan.21,1891. Dr.B.GOODMAN & Wm. GIBBONS surety on bond. Later-1892 they ask court to release them from bond & N.GUNDY is new surety. INV.&APPR.June 29,1891 by A.A.DUANE:OMER HUNT,C.C.MILES-CLAIM against L.N.O.& T.R.R.CO. compromised-train killed 2 mules Final a/c Sept.1892. LETTER in pkt.from BREWER & BREWER Atty.of Clarksdale,Ms. to CLEMENTS & WRIGHT of R.F. dated June 28,1920 on behalf of client, a grand child of Gundy-WILLIE B.WILLIAMS RHODES, asks them to check owners of the 120 acrs.Claims interest in same.

SHARKEY CO.MS. CC PACKETS-1876-1900

#206;EST.OF J.J.UNDERHILL:decd.10 Oct.1890-intest.-Shark.Co.Ms.
Pet.Let.Adm. by widow GEORGIA L.UNDERHILL-20 Apr.1891. Adm.Bond
sur.G.M.BAGGETT,MRS.K.W.JOOR. **INV.& APPR.** stock shows Underhill
was a druggiest. FREDERICK GRAFT:C.W.ROGAN:IRA A.CORTRIGHT are
appraisers Sept.7,1891. Est.heavily in debt for stock in drugstore
and sale of stock ordered by court does not meet obligations.
Est.declared insolvent Oct.23,1894.//Other CC packets not totally
abstracted here,#250 orders sale of lot in Rolling Fork which
was conveyed to Underhill by H.L.FOOTE Dec.27,1889. This packet
mentions Jeff Underhill Jr. a minor child. Lot bought by R.S.MYERS
$150-Mar.1894.

#207;EST. DAVID KLAUS:decd.18 June 1891 in Natchez,Adams Co.Ms.
Place of resi.Cary Ms. Bro.EDWARD KLAUS,partner in business
of Klaus Bros.Cary,Ms. petitions for Let.Adm.27 June 1891 &
ask court to probate last Will & Testament of David Klaus, written in Natchez,22 May 1891,while there ill. "To my beloved mother
$500----Sister-in-law LENA S.KLAUS,wife of bro.Edward--proceeds
of Life Ins.policy $3,000---everything else to bro.Edward & appoints
him Exec." Wit.ISAAC SHLENKER of Natchez, JULIUS LEMLE.
Proof of Will-affadavit of Shlenker in Natchez.**Let.testa**mentary
issued 6 July 1891 to Edward Klaus.**Final** a/c & discharge 27
Mar.1894.Voucher by mother of David Klaus written in German
& her name signed in German---Mrs. Babetta Klaus, in English.

#214;EST ADLINE NICHOLS:decd.May 1891-intest.Pet.Let.Adm.by
E.D.DINKINS-Oct.27,1891-a creditor of est. Bond sureties R.L.
McLAURIN,G.M.BAGGETT. **APPR.**of personal est.done 2 Feb.1892 on
premises of decd.-live stock & $200 cash by W.A.CROCKETT,W.C.H.
McKINNEY,A.G.FLOYD. **TAX rec**eipt shows Adeline Nichols owned
½ int. in 38 acr.W/2of SW/4,Sec.15,Twp.13,R6. **EX**ception to 1st
a/c filed Oct.1893 by PRESTON WILLIAMS guardian of minor RENA
NICHOLS. Related pkts.#225-#241

#215;EST.ISAAC P.BAGGETT:decd.June1888-resi.of Shark.Co.Ms.own-
ing 1/3 undivided interest in small parcel land,85 acr.Shark.Co.
2 minor children CHARLES ELLIS & FRANK, own other 2/3 all of
which was inherited from the wife & Mother Mrs.F.M.BAGGETT,decd.
Brother G.M.BAGGETT,pet.Let.Adm.nunc Pro Tunc 7 Nov.1889. Bond
sureties,N.T.BAGGETT,B.GOODMAN. Vouchers from Dr.'s in Louisville
Ky.May1888. Land descrip. on tax receipt for 1889. **REV.**W.C.HEARN
guardian of Char.Ellis & Frank who now reside in Talladego,Ala.
Final a/c 21 Aug.1895.

#225;EST.RENA NICHOLS;Minor ward. Guard.Pct.by EMMA WILLIAMS
15 Feb.1892-states Adline Nichols decd. 7 June 1891 leaving
2 children-RENA & HARRY NICHOLS. Harry had also decd. now and
she,Emma,is Renas Aunt and Rena is in her care and age 12.G.Bond
sureties PRESTON WILLIAMS & MALCOLM CAMERON. Chancellor Pintard
revoked,annulled the appointment in Oct.1892. Pet.for sale of
cows & mules for support of ward---no dispensation on these papers.

#234;EST. SAINT JOHN WILLIS;decd.23 Oct.1892-intest.-Shark.Co.Ms
Pet.Let.Adm.by widow & sole heir META N.WILLIS 14 Nov.1892.
Adm.Bond surety,JOHN WILLIS & Wm.BRITTON-$35,000. Court authorizes
Meta to complete & gather crops on VICKLAND PLTN.(leased by decd.)

SHARKEY CO.MS. CC PACKETS-1876-1900

Cont.#234-16 Nov.1892 and sell all or any of personal prop.
Appraisment dispensed with by Court-Assets far outweigh debts

#235:EST JOHN C.DENMAN:decd. intest. Shark.Co.Ms.6 Aug.1892.
Pet.Let.Adm.by widow,LIZZIE DENMAN,only heir-no issue -filed
4 Nov.1892, states John owned valuable pltn.& some pers.prop.in
Shark.Co. Adm.B.Sur.J.F.TAYLOR,A.G.BOYKIN $2,000, Nov.1892.

#237;EST.JOEL ORMAND STEVENS;decd.-only doc.in pkt.is Inv.&
Appr. which is BLANK.

#241;EST.RENA NICHOLS:[see #225-@214]minor ward. In pkt.#225
EMMA WILLIAMS petitions for guardian of Rena & court disallowed
it. New pet.for Guard.by PRESTON W.WILLIAMS, states Harry decd.
Feb.1892. Preston is an uncle & Rena resides with him. Pet.filed
Feb.24,1895. Guard.Bond sur.;W.H.BARNARD,A.J.WILLIAMS $400-Mar.
1893.Inventory-Personal-live stock. A/c for 1893 shows small
tract of land was sold. A/c for 1897 -a voucher to Emma Williams
for $25 for burial of ADLINE NICHOLS, in Vicksburg. More papers
on Williams exception to A/C by Adm.Dinkins of Adline Nichols
estate. See pkt.#214.

#244;EST.JOHN OSCAR STEVENS:decd.6 Jan.1893-intest.-Shark.Co.Ms.
Pet.Let.Adm.by S.T.STEVENS,son of John O.Stevens, May 1893.
Adm.Bond Sur.A.G.PARHAM & J.G.PARHAM 20 May 1893 $14. Other
heirs;P.W.:J.A;F.O. & MAUD E.STEVENS & his widow EMALINE E.
STEVENS. Inv.dispensed with by court.

#253;EST.M.J.HARVEY:[see #159]decd.29 July 1893-intest.-resi.
Shark.Co.Ms. Pet.Let.Adm.by W.M.CHAMPION,son-in-law of Mrs.
Martha J.Harvey,decd.,states her small est.-real & pers.,about
90acr.(tax receipt shows 116 acr.)on Little Deer Creek, 1½mi.S
of Rolling Fork, a house and lot in R.F. 3 heirs-HOPE, wife
of W.M.Champion-Eva & Julia Harvey all of legal age. Filed 21
Oct.1893. Adm.Bond.surety-Eva Harvey & D.C.CASEY $1,000 same
date.[Casey in 1896 asks court to discharge him from bond obli-
gation--does not like the way Champion is administring estate.
No appr.by court order. W.M.MANN rented land in 1893 for $500.
¶MARTHA HARVEY was the mother of ROBERT E.HARVEY(#158)and widow
of EVAN J.HARVEY decd. Martha J. was the dau. of Sam'l WELLS
& MARTHA A CHANEY(later McQUILLAN)]

#255;EST.W.H.& SYBILMAY CLEMENTS:minor wards. Let.Guard.and
Guard.Bond 2 Mar.1894 by DR.E.C.CLEMENTS, father. Surety on
bond,MRS.A.F.CLEMENTS, mother-$1,695. Sybil age 14 asks for
father as Guard. W.H. is 20. Money for minors from a partition
sale(case #229) JAMES MURRAY vs E.C.CLEMENTS. 13 Dec.1893 a
Pet.by W.H. Clements asking for father as Guard.to take charge
of his 1/5 of share in partition sale.Filed 2,Feb.1894.Mailed
from Bell Buckle,Tenn.where he was in school.Vouchers for Sybil
May show her at Industrial Inst. Columbus,Miss '96-'97-'98.By
July '98,money exhausted & Guard.dismissed.

#266-2 Pkts.;EST Wm.BRITTON JR.;ward- GEO.C.HARRIS Guardian.
One pkt. included only A/C & vouchers for 1895-96- paid to
Rev.PETER SEARS of St.Thomas Hall,Holly Springs Ms.for(cont.)

SHARKEY COUNTY MS. CC PACKETS-1876-1900

(cont.)#266;Williams schooling(military).Guard.Harris's checks are from Madison Station,Ms.-some to William,-some to Helena Mercantile Co.Inc.1886-H.J.FIELDS,Pres. -Wm.Britton-Manager (scratched out)-G.C.Harris,Director.Vouchers for 1896-97-98 show Wm.sometimes in Vicksburg- Bellevue High School, Va.Bedford Co. W.R.ABBOT principal of school-report card shows high marks and a complimentary note by Abbot. Board check to MRS. M.H.CROCKETT Apr.12 1896-check to MRS.F.A.BRITTON for board for Wm.Aug.1898 in Vicksburg. Still at Bellevue Va.1899. **Pet.** July 1898 by JULIUS SINAI asking release as surety on Guard. Bond. H.J.FIELDS & G.C.HARRIS JR. new sureties.
2nd pkt. Pet.for Guard.Filed <u>Jan.2 1894</u> by Geo.C. Harris,states WILLIAM BRITTON SR.decd. <u>24 Dec.1894</u>]¶NOTE;date on guard.papers nearly a year before death--could be clerks error-maybe should be Jan.1895] Wm.Sr. was a resident of Sharkey Co.He decd.leaving a 15 yr.old son Wm.Jr. whose mother had previously decd. Wm.Sr. second wife was Laura N.Britton who is the Admtx. of his est. **1st.**Guard.Bon filed Jan.20,1895;Sureties J.SINAI,GEO.C.HARRIS JR. $2,000.**2nd** Guard.Bond filed July 12,1898;Sure. H.J.FILEDS GEO.C.HARRIS JR. $4,000. **letter** dated 7/8/1900 -Geo.C.Harris says he has placed Wm.Jr. in a cotton House(CARREN & WARRICK) in Memphis- he receives $25 per month.**1900** Harris buys 160 acr. for Wm.'s use, at a tax sale-Sec.35,T13,R6W-Land previously bought from railroad by Britton Sr.& HOLLINGSWORTH. Britton died before it was paid for after buying out Hollingsworth. **1902**-Guard.dismissied-William of Age.

#273;**NON CUPATIVE WILL of JUNIUS MHOON**;CHARLES N.BLUM of Nitta Yuma,Ms. & 39 yrs.old, & DR.A.MILLER of Panther Burn Ms. are witnesses to will and give depositions as proof of will. Mhoon was a resident of Nitta Yuma,Sharkey Co.Ms. He decd.<u>19 May 1895</u>. Made the spoken will <u>30 Apr.1895</u> after an accidental shotgun wound(by his own hand)"**I am** badly wounded and want to tell you what disposition to make of my property.....policy for $2,000 in KNIGHTS OF HONOR-payable to my mother...also policy for $2,000 with NEW YORK LIFE..enough to pay my debts...surplus money & all my prop.to go to my Mother. This property is my place in Madison Co.Ms. & my prop.I own near Memphis Tenn." Junius had resided in Nitta Yuma 9 yrs. Will subscribed to paper by witnesses-23 May 1895. HEIRS:MRS.MARIE A.MHOON-mother; JAS.A & ROBT.B.MHOON-brothers;ELLEN MHOON-sister;JAMES MHOON, FOSTER MHOON & STANLEY MHOON,minor ch.of W.J.MNOON,decd.of Madison Co.Ms.and MARY MHOON,minor also ch.of W.J.Mhoon of Richland Pa.La.;W.S.BAILEY,minor ch.of MRS.BETTIE BAILEY,decd.of Rich.Pa. La.. John M.Foster grand father of minors-Jas.Prestley Guard.of Minors. **PET.LET.ADM.**by Jas.A.Mhoon bro.of decd-July 13,1895. C.H.Blum in hisdepo. for proof of Will states he is Sec.& Gen.Mgr. of THE BLUM CO.ofNitta Yuma and Mhoon was bookkeeper & office Mgr.-1885 till decd.

#278;**CC-GEO.C.HARRIS vs LAURA BRITTON-ADMX.WM.BRITTON,EST.**: Orig.Bill filed Aug.26,1895-Harris,complainant:-states Admx. Laura Britton has not paid probated debt to Harris of Brittons before his death-$2,500 secured by 25 shares of stock in Helena Merc.Co. Britton decd. Dec.1894. **Cross bill** filed by Laura

SHARKEY CO.MS. CC PACKETS-1876-1900

(cont.#278)Britton,Nov.23,1895-Warren Co.Ms. Pet.by L.Britton
Admx-May 13,1896 asking compromise-states she owns 20 shares
in Helena Mercantile and is willing to release & convey to G.C.
Harris if he will credit Wm.Britton's est. $1,000. Also she
will release interest Wm.Britton,decd.,had in two frame rooms
he added at his expense tothe boarding house on Mt.Helena Pltn.
In return Harris & his son G.C.Jr. are to surrender all claims
to Wm.Brittons est. **Court** orders suit compromised May 16,1896
& all conditions accepted.[see # 266]

#290;Est.& Will of HENRY RICHARDSON;dated Rolling Fork,Shark.Co.
Ms.11 Sept.1895."..to grand son ALBERT CANADA all real & personal
property except that further devised..towit..$2 to my son HENRY
RICHARDSON JR.----LIZZIE COBBLER nee NICHOLSON-$25.....Julius
SINAE shall act as Exec.and Guard. for grand son Albert. If
Sinae refuses to act ..J.C.WATSON be appointed." Witnesses;
W.P.BROWN:W.H.RUSHING:W.D.BROWN.Richardson decd. 26 Sept.1895.
J.C.Watson files Let.Adm.Oct.9,1895. Exec.Bond Sur. Julius Sinae
$500. MARTHA RICHARDSON ,daughter and mother of Albert Canada
and wife of ALEXANDER RICHARDSON.

#308;EST.ELIZA WILLIS:decd.WILL-recorded WBK"A"SHARK.CO.MS.p.24
Filed Aug.17,1896. "I Eliza Willis,relic of DEMPSEY WILLIS....
To my dau. RITTIE MATTEN-$1 cash
To the children of dau.HENRIETTA(now decd) $1 each-towit-WESLEY
POTTER:ALICE POTTER;LEWIS POTTER:GEORGE POTTER,ANTHONY POTTER
all known as the 5 children of NELSON POTTER.
To my beloved son GEORGE MURDOCK- 10 acr.taken from S end on
boundary of my home place on Little Deer Creek ,Sec.14,T12,R7W
bounded by COUNCIL BEND & BACONIA.
To my Son DENNIS WILLIS -all the balance of my home place-47 acr.
To my beloved dau.ANNETTE MILLER-all 53-1/3 acr. she now is occu-
pying on CHOCTAW BAYOU in SE1/4 Sec.17,T12,R6W.
To my Beloved son DEMPSEY WILLIS all 33-1/3 acr. now occupied
by him on Choctaw Bayou-same description above.
To my beloved son BENSON WILLIS-all 53-1/3 acr.now occupied by
him on Choctaw Bayou---same description above.
..All personal prop. of what ever kind.equally divided between
my 4 beloved children-ANNETTE MILLER;BENSON, DEMPSEY,DENNIS(now
residing with me at home place)WILLIS.
Dau.Annette nominated Execx...no bond required."
Dated 17 June 1896   ELIZA(x)WILLIS
WIT.WM.I.CHANEY:L.M.POWELL
PET.for Prob.of Will, states Eliza decd.20 June 1896.**Inv.& Appr.**
Dec.14,1896 by G.M.BAGGETT:JAMES H.CORTRIGHT,DAVE FRAZIER.

#322;EST.Wm.GIBBONS;decd.in Jackson Ms. 10 Apr.1897-resi.Shark.
Co.Ms.MARY E.GIBBONS,widow, Pet.Let.Admx. 4 June 1897. Adm.Bond
sur.Wm.GIBBONS JR. & W.R.HARPER. Son Wm.Jr. over 21. Est.finaliz-
ed July 1898.**[earlier records had no s on Gibbon]**

#324;EST.WILLIS THOMPSON;decd.intest.30 July 1897-only heir
is son SMITH THOMPSON who Pet.for Let.Adm. Aug.28 1897. Bond
sur.Wm.COMMODORE,N.W.PARKER-$200.

SHARKEY Co.Ms. CC PACKETS-1876-1900

#329;EST.WALTER LEE JEFFRIES: minor-In Pet.for Guardianship of Walter Lee- T.F.DEDMAN(called Frank) filed Dec.31,1897,states estate consists of small personal/$75-$100, real/ 80 acr.-35 in cultivation-states child lives in his house in Shar.Co. Doc.dated Jan.13,1898-Pet.of MRS.LIZZIE GRAY & MRS.LAURA STOKES sisters of MOSES JEFFERIES who decd. Dec.1894 intest.,leaving his widow MARTHA ROWENA JEFFRIES , who in 1897 married DRAYTON JONES. Martha decd. 19 Dec.1897 leaving the said Jones & her 4 year old child Walter Lee Jeffries her only heirs. Dec.1897 T.F.Dedmon,brother of Martha Rowena Jeffries Jones, filed for Guard.of minor Walter Lee Jefferies & clerk of Court in Vacation granted same 31 Dec.1897. Aunts claim Dedman too young-without property-no business sense-unmarried-no home & unfit to care for child. They ask Court to suspend appointment. So done by court,18 Feb.1898 by Chancellor Pintard until further review by court. No document included here to show reinstatement but T.F.Dedman served as Guard.of Walter Lee Jefferies until he was 21 25 Jan.1915. **4 Guard.bonds** & sureties;1. 30 Dec.1897- E.L.CRIPPIN,O.THORNELL $250- suspended by court. 2. Jan.1902 S.HERN & FRANK KETTLEMAN $250-this was set aside by request of S.Hern Feb.19,1907 because Y.& M, R.R. was passing thru lands of mincr & bond not sufficient to cover new value of Est. Frank Kettleman has decd.-3.9 Aug.1907 J.C.HOLLINGSWORTH & T.S.MOORE $1,200. July 1908 T.S.Moore accuses Dedmon of handling $1,100 in minors funds recklessly & wants release from Bond. 4.Aug.11 1908 J.C.HOLLINGSWORTH & MRS.W.F.BERESFORD-$1200.
Packet is large & full of voucher & a/c. Walter Lee Jeffries acknowledging receipt of final a/c/ payment dated Lucre,Ms. May 15,1915.

#334;EST.OF EUDORA J.BARNARD- 3 loose papers. 1. Motion to compell Adm.W.H.BARNARD to file account- motion made by heirs-at-law---A.C.WADDILL, J.H.CREATH, Jan.15,1901.
2.Order of Court to Barnard,Adm.,to file a/c since it had been more than 1 yr.his Adm.started.
3.14 May 1903 Waddill & Creath consent to Barnards discharge as Adm.

#335;EST.& WILL WM.M.AIKEN:decd. Will/handwritten letter-unwitnessed-dated San Francisco,Calif. Feb.15,1895 to his brother GEORGE R.AIKEN, Hollandale Ms.-devising all pers. & real prop. to him except "the prop. in San Francisco to wit- his Cigar Store & cash on hand & watch & chain--all to be sold and proceeds to pay burial--residual cash to NANNIE B.AIKEN" .18 Mar.1898 George offers the letter as Exb."A" in Proof of Will hearing. Wm.Aiken died in S.Fran Mar.1895, He had small acr.in Shark.Co. Ms. **Affadavits** by JAMES E.AIKEN of Wash.Co. also a bro. of Wm.'s and by JOHN H.CROUCH of Wash.Co.Ms. both on 18 Apr.1898 Will admitted to probate 9 May 1898-Filed Apr.20,1898.

#342;EST.WILLIE ELIZA MARKETT;minor-4 yr.old child of CLAUDIA J.MARKETT,decd. Pet.Let.Guard.-EMILIUS G.BARNARD, uncle-brother of mother--states Willie Eliza is child of William Markett,decd. in Shar.Co.intest.1893,and his wife Claudia J.Markett who decd. 19 Mar.1898. Estate consists land.64 acrs.rented by D.B.BARNARD Bond sur. W.H.BARNARD,10 Sept.1898.**Willie** Eliza Markett(cont.)

SHARKEY CO.MS. CC PACKETS-1876-1900

(cont.#342)deceased 1902, Court orders 2 debts to be paid. 1.W.D BROWN,atty.fees. 2. JAMES LINDSEY for board of ward, residual to Grandmother Mrs. ORA MARKETT-Jan.13,1904.

#344;EST.JOHN CANOVAN:decd.Oct.4,1898-intest. Pet.Let.Adm by MRS.BRIDGET M. CANOVAN,widow & only heir-24 Nov.1898. Adm.Bond surety M.W.HUGHES of Vicksburg, who gave his P.O.A. to PATRICK CANOVAN to sign bond for him- same date.

#347;EST.LYDIA LUSK; 1 loose paper-dated 10 Jan.1899-Appr.& Inv. report by Adm.JAMES SMITH.

#356-357;EST.MARION B.& ALICE E.COKER:(All loose papers,but later found a larger packet in another drawer containing vouchers and a/c)Minors. Pet.Guard.by MAUDE M.COKER-mother. Guard.Bond sur. R.S.MYERS & Wm.MYERS-$1800-8 Mar.1899. Some vouchers in loose papers and 1 document detailing the loan of $2,000 with land security and subsequent foreclosure & buying of land for wards.July 1906.[Maude is sis.of R.S.& Wm.Myers]

#359;EST.J.D.KNAPPER:decd. May 1897-Shark.Co.Ms. at his residence. No children- widow LUCY ANN KNAPPER has since decd.,and Let.Adm.applied for by SIMON DOVER a creditor, 13 Apr.1899. Est. in debt to Dover for $2,000. Real estate in Issaq.Co.Ms. Adm.Bond sur. BEN PEARL & A.K.MARTAK-15 Apr.1899 $200.

#360:EST JAMES CHOCK:decd.-intest.-Shark.Co.Ms. 2 Apr.1899- Widow AMERICA CHOCK. Children-MARY COOPER: WILLIAM,JAMES,MILLIE, JOSEPH CHOCK: MATTIE WILLIAMS; SADIE CHOCK,Widow of JORDAN CHOCK decd. and their 4 ch., GRACY ANN,EUGENE, ALFERD & PERCY CHOCK. All over 21 except grandchildren. By July 1900 Millie Chock is Millie BANKS.**BEN PEARL** of Anguilla Ms. files Pet.Let.Adm. 3 May1899 at request of aged widow America Chock. Adm.Bond Sur SIMON DOVER,A.K.MARTAK- $750.

#361;EST. ESTELLE BOYKIN MARSHALL;minor-Pet.for Guard.by H.J. MARSHALL, States he is husband of minor Estelle B. and she is dau. of A.G.BOYKIN a resident of Shark.Co.Ms. who decd.-intest.- 28 Oct.1898 and left 7 children. Filed 5 May 1899. Estelle Boykin married H.J.Marshall 23 Nov.1898 Shark.Co.Ms. Estelle asks for Husband discharge as Guard.12 Jan.1901 when she becomes 18. C.H.WALTON is Adm.of A.G.Boykin's estate. Guard.Bond sur. A.E. MARSHALL, HENRY GRAM. $1,000.

#362;EST.OF LENA BOYKIN-minor child of A.G.BOYKIN decd.28 Oct. 1898. Pet.Guar.H.J.MARSHALL 4 May 1899.Bond Sur. U.S.FIDELITY & GUARANTY CO. Marshall states Lena is under 14, and lives with him & his wife, Lena's oldest sister Estelle. **Guard.** Marshall discharged Jan.1910 when Lena married W.E.HOLDER, 21 Nov.1906

#363;EST.OF MELVIN BOYKIN:minor child of A.G.BOYKIN,decd.28 Oct.1898.Pet.Guard.by FIELDING B.BOYKIN,20 May 1899. Bond sur. H.C.FARRAR,R.P.CRUMP $1,000. F.B.Boykin asks court permission to resign Guardianship 8 Jan.1904. Reason-Melvins behavior.

#364;EST.MITCHELL BOYKIN:minor son of A.G.BOYKIN decd.28 Oct. (cont.)

SHARKEY CO.MS. CC PACKETS-1876-1900

(cont.#364)1898. Guard.FIELDING B.BOYKIN- Bond surety A.M.BOYKIN
& A.K.MARTAK $1,000- both 20 May 1899. Fielding states in petition
that Mitchell & Melvin live with him, their Uncle. There are
7 Boykin children of decd. A.G.Boykin. Fielding is a full brother
to A.G..Finala/c & discharge 11 Jan.1904-Mitchell over 21. Mitchell signs vouchers J.M.BOYKIN. **Pkts.** of all the Boykin minors
have a/c & vouchers.

SHARKEY CO.MS. WILL BOOK "A"

P.1&2. DANIEL KNAPPER: "Beloved son JOHN-1bay horse,1sorrel mare, farm implements, corn & etc.on SPENCERS PLTN. Wash.Co.Ms. All accounts of every discription except those to my dau.'s GRACIE & LUCINDA PATTERSON. Gracie-2 horse wagon. Lucinda,my large bed & bed clothes. All other prop.of all kinds to John. I desire Lucinda to live with John & he to take care of her". John to be exec.Dated 30 Jan.1877-Nitta Yuma,Shark.Co.Ms. DAN(x)KNAPPER. Wit.CHAS.W.WILLIAMS,R.W.LINTON,HENRY STEVENS,W.A.LISBORG. Proven for Probate 13 Mar.1877.

P.3,4,5,COPY OF SUCCESSION OF JAMES JACKSON IRBY: sent from N.O. Second District Court for Parish of Orleans. Filed 7 Oct.1878. Will dated July 30,1878-New Orleans- Oligraphic. "..divided ½ to my wife VIRGINIA -½ to children JNO.ROBIN McDANIEL IRBY, SANDERS IRBY, Wm.RATCLIFFE IRBY & JAMES J.IRBY JR. -equal div. 3 Ins.policies-& the commercial firm of J.J.IRBY & SON. Wife Virginia R.Irby & son Sanders appointed Exec."Proofs filed with Pet. by W.R.Irby 16 Jan.1879 in Shark.Co.Ms.

P.6,7,;DAVID HUNT-written from Jefferson Co.Ms. "..beloved wife ANNA & my living children & any to be born thereafter....equal parts of all my estate, real & personal. Wifes portion to be held only during her widowhood. DUNBAR HUNT to be Exec. & if he decd. his brothers ABIJIAH & JAMES HUNT to act jointly....request that S.½ of GEORGIANA PLTN.in Shark.Co.Ms. neither be sold or encumbered."Dated 6 June 1878. Wit. CLAUDE PINTARD, JOHN S.VAUGHN, EDGAR W.BAKER. Their depositions for proof of will taken in Jefferson Co. 26 Apr.1879.

P.8,10;THADDEUS C.S.FERGUSON of State of Va.,city of Lynchburg. "...had given his 7 ch.(unnamed) their inheritance over the years...Dau. MRS.DUNNING...Son-in-law MR.LACY's debt to be forgiven....Wife ALEAN H.FERGUSON..Wife and son-in-law M.C.JAMISON co-Exec....To grandson,his namesake, and son of PARKER FERGUSON, a small silver box that was presented to him(the decd.)by Lynchburg Agri.& Mech.Society 13 Oct.1879.....To old friend JUDGE DAVID E SPENCE, gold eye glasses." Wit.DAVID E.SPENCE,W.H.OTEY, PETER J.OTEY. Filed for Probate in Va.Nov.5,1879 and in Shark.Co Ms. 9 Feb.1880.

P.12;EDWIN STEVENS -Shark.Co.Ms. "To my Beloved wife MARY E. STEVENS all land & appertinences there on...for her lifetime.. on her death to be divided between son JOHN H.STEVENS & the 2 children of son W.C.STEVENS...Wife Mary E.to be Exectx." Dated 9 Dec.1884. Wit. DANIEL BROWN,Issaq.Co.Ms.;M.HAMBERLIN, Shark.Co.;A.H.JOHNSTON ,Yazoo Co.Ms.

P.13;JAMES NICHOLS-Shark.Co.Ms. "...to brother ANTHONY WILLIAMS all real & Pers. prop., PRESTON WILLIAMS appointed exec."Dated Aug.10,1885. Wit. PRESTON WILLIAMS:N.W.PARKER: CYRUS(x)SAMUEL

P.16;MOLLIE BYERLEY-Cary Ms.Jan.12,1888."Land in Sec.17 & 8,T11, R7W-conveyed to me by my brother DR.B.GOODMAN by deed-shall descend to my living children, equal parts....Husband FRANK BYERLEY shall control annual rental income on interest in land until ch. are 21..." Brother & husband Joint Exec. Wit;N.T.BAGGETT, W.O.BLAND,EDWARD BYERLEY.

SHARKEY CO. WILL BOOK "A"

P.17,18,19;MARY ANN LEE Sharkey Co.Ms."...to JOAN LEE,my youngest child..my homested - to wit;SE 1/4 & S½ of SW 1/4 of SE 1/4 of Sec.34,T13,R6W,& 12 acr. in SW corner of SW 1/4 of Sw 1/4 of Sec.35,T13,R6W...husband RICHARD LEE(father of Joan Lee) to have control until his death & be her,Joan,Guard. If Joan dies without issue, the above mentioned homested to be divided equally to the rest of my children.ANNIE EARVINE & S.E.STEVENS and the AUGUST ROSEN children & their heirs. " Dated 5 Oct. 1892. Wit.C.WALTON,W.A.CROCKETT,W.A.CONNELL. Filed for Probate Mar.27 1893.

P.27;JOHN E.BUTLER: Shark.Co.Ms. "...to my dau. EVANAH BELLE KELLY all my prop. real & personal -not to be sold or disposed of until her youngest child, GEORGE KELLY, comes of age.... grandson JOHN BUTLER KELLY ..gold watch...to EDWARD B.PRIDMORE, $1.00. N.T.BAGGETT,friend, exec. Evanah Belle is wife of JOHN KELLY." Dated 22 June 1897. Wit. C.H.WALTON,J.E.MEEK,A.L.NEAL. Codicil added Nov.3,1898 names the children of Evanah Belle & John Kelly. JOHN BUTLER,KATE,CLAUDE,CLIFF,GEORGE,NANNIE & ROSA KELLY. Wit.to codicil; A.L.NEAL,W.H.CLEMENTS,E.D.ROBERTS.

P.30-35;MARY BULLUCK VICK PHELPS,Nitta Yuma,Shark.Co.Ms.7 July 1900."...to daus.NANNIE PHELPS GEORGE & MARY PHELPS PIOLA CASSELI, my house & lot on corner of 9th & Market St.Louisville,Ky. ...to dau. ELLEN BODLEY PHELPS,all real estate in Boliva Co.Ms. .....son HENRY V.PHELPS and daughters to share alike in estate in Shark.Co. to be Administered by Execs.in trust. Execs.sons-in-law-Mary P.husband RENATO PAOLIE CASSELI--PETER GEORGE husband of Nannie P. & son Henry Vick Phelps." Mary B.V.Phelps husband was DR.A.J.PHELPS. 12 pages of detailed division to all concerned and the task set forth by execs. Interesting will Names DR.R.C.CRUMP & JOHN DURST-friends, RINALIN PAOLI CASSELI, ALONZO PHELPS GEORGE-grandchildren. Wit.to will A.MILLER,W.D. LONG,J.HIRSH. Filed for Probate Feb.12,1901.

P.36;JOHN W.BROWN 24 Feb.1901 "...to my wife ETTER BROWN..all property real & personal in her lifetime. After her death..to J.T.L.&PERLIE BROWN, my legal heirs." Wit.H.J.WRIGHT & JNO.S. JOOR. Probated 27 June 1901

P.37;NANNIE PHELPS GEORGE 28 Feb.1901,"...to my husband PETER GEORGE, all prop.real & pers. & $5,000 to be paid out of my mothers,Mary B.V.Phelps estate as decreed in her will. Husband to be Exec. Son ALONZO J.PHELPS GEORGE to inherit all on death of Nannie & Peter George." Wit.J.F.RHODICALS,JNO.H.DURST. Probated 3 Oct.1901.

P.38:NATHANIEL RUTLEDGE ANDERSON,3 Apr.1894 Shark.Co.Ms."...to my brothers & sisters(unnamed)all real & pers.est. Nephew Wm.S. ANDERSON of Issaq.Co.Ms. Exec." Wit.A.L.NEAL,H.JAMES,T.J.KENT. Prob.14 Nov.1901.

P.40;WALTON SAUNDER City of San Francisco,Calif.21 July 1900 "...my wife MARY FRANCES SANDERS,our child MARY WALTON CATHERINE 6 yrs.old. ..Left all to wife & trust to her motherly love to care for Dau.Wife Execx.& Guard.of child."Wit.ALFRED J.(cont.)

SHARKEY CO.,Ms. WILL BOOK "A"

(cont.SAUNDERS)MORGANSTERN,San Francisco;K.D.McCANN,San Francisco, Filed in Calif .5 Feb.1902. Filed in Shark.Co. May 12,1902.

P.43;ELLA WIXON Shark.Co.Ms.8 Mar.1897 "...to my sister IDA WIXON,my interest in undivided land being bought by my father M.BOZEMAN." Wit. A.H.JOHNSON,W.J.ADDISON.Prob. 6 Jan.1904

P.43.MASONIC LODGE NO.25-certificate of Insurance 13 Nov.1899 Masonic Benefit Assn. "I,HENRY M.MICKEY of Cary,Ms. age 40 yrs. bequeath this cert. unto SUSAN MICKEY $5.00, MINA KEMP & HENRY MICKEY $5.00-remainder to CARRIE MICKEY ,who is now in possession of THOMAS & EMMA GIBBS.23 Dec.1903. Execs.friends A.H.FOREMAN, A.A.DUANE,IRA COSTLEY." Wit. L.W.FOREMAN,C.L.WATSON,WILL HOOD. Probated Mar.14,1904.

P.45;FRANK KETTLEMAN Shark.Co.Ms.(no date on Will-in proof of will it states on or about Sept.1,1902) "...to my son TONY, Lot 2,Sec.32,T11,R5W.Shark.Co.....to my son Will, Lot 1,Sec.32, T11,R5W...Wife LUCY shall live in the homestead with Tony & Will & have a support her natural life....Granddau. SELMA KETTLE- MAN, 40 acr.Lot 3,Sec.33,T11,R5W.on Little Fish Lake, where her father lived(unnamed). Daus.ANNIE,IDA,JESSIE KETTLEMAN...re- mainer of real estate...all to pay to sister LILLIE the sum of $200 each when she arrives at 21 yrs. or marry, in lieu of land. J.C.HOLLINGSWORTH ,Exec." Wit.H.W.McCORMICK,Yazoo Co. C.H.PERKINS. Prob.24 Oct.1904.

P.46;SILAS BALDWIN Mar.11,1905 -Member of St.Elmo Lodge No.114, order of K&P-"..my policy to wife SARAH." wit.JOHN HOPKINS, AARON GULLIE. Prob. Apr.1,1905.

P.47;JAMES HARRISON MOORE. Harrodsburg,Ky.Co. of Mercer.Sept. 21,1901."I appoint my beloved son DANIEL LAWSON MOORE,and my beloved grandson,JAMES HARRISON MOORE JR.,my Exec.....to my son Daniel L. the premises on which I reside,known as Hilldale, which I value at $8,000..I bequeath him this prop.at this low valuation because he sold it to me at a nominal price...to Grandson & namesake,JAMES HARRISON MOORE,my farmon Lexington pike-263 acr..value $15,000...to ANITA MOORE & MINNIE B.MOORE,children of son Daniel L,..each 10shares Mercer Nat.BankStock...to BELL PAYNE $100...to OLIVIA ROCHESTER $100...to MARY McCALEB $100..to ESTHER MORSE $100..to KATHERINE KEIGHEE $100..to BERTHA HEBB $100..to LILLIE McCALEB $100...to THOMAS MOORE of Honduras,son of LAWSON & BETTIE MOORE $100...to DANIEL L.MOORE JR.,my nephew, the distiller,$100...to my 2 nephew WILLIAMD.MOORE & DR.J.H. MOORE,each $100...to MARY BACON MOORE,VIRGINIA MOORE,DANIEL MOORE & JOHN B.MOORE,children of my son BACON MOORE, each $1... to Grandson BACON R.MOORE, $100,and direct if he will take an education,my grandson James Harrison Moore pay the expense out of est.I have bequeathed him...Medical books to my nephew DR.J.H MOORE...BookCase & other books to MACK MOORE & HARRY MOORE my grandsons...remainder contents of house divided between son Daniel L.&grandsonJamesHarrison Moore Jr....all pers.prop.on farm..direct Exec.to sell...proceeds divided equally between son Daniel L. & g.son J.H.Moore Jr...remainder of prop.-real- & pers...sell...and son Daniel L.'s share to be made equal with

SHARKEY CO.MS. WILL BOOK"A"

(cont.J.H.Moore)in amount received by g.son J.H.Moore Jr.and then the rest divided equally between them...TO MR.WALLACE BARTLETT & MR. BRAYER MOORE $100...g.son H.H.Moore Jr. gold watch...ggson VINCENT R.BARTLETT,my gold seal & chain. My $2,000 scholarship in the Central University..wish my Exec.to use...aiding 2 deserving young men. Should any legatees attempt to break this will,...hereby cut off from any lot or parcel of my estate." After J.H.Moores signature is this sentence--"The advances heretofore given BOWMAN MOORE is hereby confirmed, is Total..That is all he receives from my estate." Wit.E.H.GAITHER,LOTTA LANG. **CODICIL** Sept.22,1902...."I give to my Grand dau. MARY MERSINGLE WHILDEN my house & lot on Mooreland Ave.that I bought of MILLS, now occupied by CHELF family, free from any int.whatever of her husband." Same Witnesses. Will proven for Probate in Ky. Oct. 2,1905. Rec.in Shark.Co.Ms.Jan.4,1906.(also rec.Wash.Co.Ms.)

MARRIAGE BOOK I, SHARKEY CO.MS. Nov.19,1876-Dec.30,1880

KEY TO ABBREVIATIONS:* His mark; Li.-license;Bd.-bond;nt-no return
Page 1
*ANDERSON WALTON-ISABELLA BUCKNER-19 Nov.1876 by H.PICARD.Bd.
  *JAMES PENWRIGHT
Page 2
*JAMES PENWRIGHT-LUCY COOPER-19 Nov.1876-by W.T.BARNARD MBS.
  Bond.*ANDERSON WALTON
Page 3
*TONEY HAWKINS-NANCY VALENTINE-13 June 1876-by W.T.BARNARD MBS
  Bond *ANDERSON WALTON
*NED JOHNSON -NANCY MODLEY-13 June 1876-by ELDER BOWIE.Bond
  *LLOYD GUNDY
Page 4
*GOERGE POINDEXTER-EASTER FAIRFAX-8 June 1876 by ELIAS SPRIGG
  elder Bap.Ch. Bond *ALONZO WASHINGTON
*JAMES BYAS-EMMA WASHINGTON-24 June 1876-by EDWARD PARRY,pastor.
  Bd.*SIB GIBSON
Page 5
BENJAMINE SOMERS-MAGGIE DAVIS-5 July 1876-by L.H.WILSON,Min.
EDMUND MONTGOMERY-ADELINE BEDWELL-1 July 1876 by W.DAMRON
Page 6
WASHINGTON SMITH-RACHEL TELLIS-8 July 1876-by JAMES BYAS
JOHN DOLL-FANNIE SMALL 13 July 1876-by L.H.WILSON,Min.Bd. L.W.
  ROGAN
Page 7
GEORGE RIDLEY-SUSAN ANN WILKINS-23 Sept.1876 by P.H.JOHNSON,JP
GEORGE W.HOWARD-CELESTE FLORENCE SMITH-26 Oct.1876 by EUGENE
  CLARK,MBS also signed bond.
Page 8
*JOHN WESLEY CLARK-MARGARET SMEDLEY-13 Nov.1876 by Elder JOHN
  KNAPPER. Bd.*KYE HINDSMAN
JERRY WILLIAMS-LIZA MASON-26 Oct.1876 by EDMUND PERRY.Bd.J.S.JOOR
Page 9
*JAMES BOOTH-MARGARET WELSH-28 Dec.1876 by E.P.PERRY.Bd.JAMES
  CARRINGTON
JAMES CARRINGTON-NANCY WHEELER-Li.21 Dec.1876,nt Bd.*JAMES BOOTH
Page 10
WM.CLARK-RITCHIE RANDALL-Li. 8May1876-nt-Bd.DAVID HUNT
*JOHN CARSON-FANNIE BRADFORD-Li.27 May 1876-nt-Bd.*DAVID JACKSON
Page 11
*SIB GIBSON-MARY WHEELER-Li.15 July 1876-nt-
FRANK ANDERSON-FRANCIS JOHNSON-Li.7 Aug.1876-nt
Page 12
WALKER GRIFFIN-PARLEE BOYD-Li.18 Aug.1876-nt
HIRAM PARKER-AILSIE WILLIS-Li.23 Sept.1876-nt
Page 13
ISAAC BOOKER-VIRGINIA YOUNG-Li.30 Sept.1876-nt-Bd.J.S.JOOR
PATTERSON MORELAND-AMANDA HILL-Li.25 Oct.1876-nt.BD.DENIS MOODY
Page 14
*JOHN PIERCE-ADELE DeNAY-Li.7 Nov.1876-nt.Bd.*GABRIEL NORMAN
JAMES BANKS-ANN WASHINGTON-Li.2 Oct.1876-nt-Bd.DAVID HUNT
Page 15
JOHN SMITH-MARY WILKES-Li. 11 May 1876-nt.Bd.HARRISON SMITH
*WILLIAM RUSH-JULIA GREER-Li.28 Oct.1876-nt-Bd.*HENRY HILLIARD

MARRIAGE BK.I,SHARK.CO.MS. 1876-1880

Page 16
*JAMES RUSSIN-CATHERINE RUSSELL-Li.21 Mar.1876-nt.Bd.*COLLIN
   WILLIAMS
*SILAS BALDWIN-MARTHA HARRIS-31 May 1877-by EDWARD PERRY,Pastor
   *GEORGE DORSEY,BOND
Page 17
*FRANK ROBINSON-CLARA GREY-Li.7 Apr.1877-nt-Bd.*FRED DOVER
*LEVI THOMPSON-ADALINE WASHINGTON-Li.21 Apr.1877-nt.-Bd.*WARNER
   MILES
Page 18
*WARNER MILES-ELIZABETH WILLIAMS-28 Apr.1877 by Rev.JAMES BYAS
   Bd.*LEVI THOMPSON
B.F.COATS-REBECCA GRIFFIN-26 Apr.1877 by EUGENE CLARK-MBS.
   J.M.WEST bond.
Page 19
*THOMAS CRAWFORD-ELLEN WILLIS-Li.21 Apr.1877-nt-Bd.*SILAS GRANT
*ELLIOTT WILLIAMS-CORNELIA WILLIAMS-26 Apr.1877 by W.B.McQUILLAN,
   JP. Bond *HENRY WILLIAMS
Page 20
*PINK RIVERS-SUSAN BURKS-22 Apr.1877 by Rev.W.DAWSON.Bd.*RICH.ROAM
J.G.PARHAM-ALICE GERTRUDE STEVENS-29 Apr.1877 by Rev.H.R.CALDWELL,
   M.E.Church South. Bd.A.H.COOK
Page 21
*GEORGE JACKSON-LIZZIE CREFT-7 May 1877 by Rev.NELSON COLLINS.
   Bd.*ISAAC SIMILTON
*ALBERT McPHERSON-MARY ANN WHEAT-Li.5 May 1877-nt.Bd.*FRANK TAYLOR
Page 22
*RICHMOND PAYNE-CELIA HENRY-19 Nov.1876 byW.T.BERNARD,MBS.Bd.
   J.H.EPPS
*KYE HINDSMAN-JOSEPHINE HINDON-Li.26 Dec.1876-nt-Bd.*DENNIS MOODY
Page 23
*ANDERSON HUGHES-ADELINE JONES-Li.11 Nov.1876-nt-Bd.*HARRISON
   McPHERSON
*DAVID RIGHT-GRISELLY DAVIS-Li.13 Nov.1876-return not dated
   by JOHN KNAPPER. Bd. R.L.WRIGHT
Page 24
*WESTON BLAIR-RITA DANIELS-Li.13 Nov.1876-nt-Bd.JOHN NAPPER
*NATHAN SMITH-SARAH DAVIS-19 Nov.1876 by W.T.BARNARD,MBS. Bd
   IRA A CORTRIGHT
Page 25
*CHARLES MYERS-MELEINDA ELLIS-20 Nov.1876 by L.H.WILSON,Min.
   Bd.*STEVE HUMPHREYS
*JOSEPH CHAMBERS-COURTNEY COLEMAN-21 Dec.1876-by L.H.WILSON,Min.
   LINDSEY JOHNSON
Page 26
*STEWART HUSTON-CARRIE SEESTRONG-Li.18 Dec.1876-nt.Bd.L.JOHNSON
PETER MARTIN-MINERVA EVANS-23 Dec.1876 by CHRIS HAUSER,JP.
   Bd.*LEVI WILSON
Page 27
*AARON SMITH-KATIE GRAHAM-28 Dec.1876 by L.H.WILSON,Min. Bd.
   *GEO.GRIFFIN
*DENNIS MOODY-MARIA MORELAND-9 Jan.1877 by Elder JOHN NAPPER.
   Bd.*THOMAS CLARK
Page 28
JAMES H.WADE-JENNIE TUCKER-5 Jan.1877 by L.W.ROGAN,JP.Bd.G.M.
   BAGGETT

MARRIAGE BK.I SHARK.CO.MS. 1876-1880

JAMES SYLVESTER-SALLY TUCKER-5 Jan.1877 by L.W.ROGAN,JP. Bd.
   JAMES H.WADE
Page 29
*HIRAM REED-EVANA PIERCE-6 Jan.1877 by J.A.C.SHRADER,MBS,also Bd
H.M.HOGG-MARY HAWKINS-10 Jan.1877-by W.B.McQUILLAN,JP. Bd.W.D.
   BROWN.
Page 30
CHARLES CARROLL-MRS.EMALINE WOOLFOLK-11 Jan.1877 by L.W.ROGAN,JP
   J.J.WELLS, bond.
GEORGE HAUSER-ISSA HOGG-11 Jan.1877 by L.W.ROGAN,JP.Bd.*ALONZO HOGG
Page 31
JOHN PARISH-ANNIE WEEKS-21 Jan.1877 by R.L.WRIGHT,JP. Bd.WM.RIGSBY
*CHARLES MITCHELL-ISABELLA JONES-Li.20Jan.1877-nt-*ANANIAS ROGERS,Bd.
Page 32
*LONDON DANSLER-ELIZABETH BROOKS-25 Jan.1877 by Rev.Elder BOWIE.
   Bd.*FRIDAY CLAYTON
*GEORGE HILL-JOAN CALHOUN-1 Feb.1877by Elder JOHN NAPPER.Bd.*JOHN
   WOODRUFF
Page 33
*MINUS DIXON-ANNIE CLEMENTS-Li.8 Feb.1877-nt-Bd.*MOSE ANDERSON
*CHAS.CARSON-MATILDA GIBBS-Li.10 Feb.1877-nt-Bd.*HAMILTON SAUNDERS
Page 34
*HILLIARD WHITE-CELIA PETWAY-17 Feb.1877 by E.PERRY,Pastor.
   Bd.*CHARLES CARSON
*HAMILTON SAUNDERS-MARY STINSON-Li.10 Feb.1877-nt-Bd.*H.WHITE
Page 35
*PETER EMORY-JENNIE SPEARMAN-25 Feb.1877by GEO.JONES,MG- Bd.
   *DENNIS MOODY.
GEORGE EVANS-SUSAN DANDRIDGE-Bond dated 17 Feb.1877-surety
   *CHARLES MURRAY.No Li. or wedding date.
Page 36
*JUDGE SPEARMAN-LUCY ANN HINTON-25 Feb.1877 by GEO.JONES,MG
   Bd. *MOSE JENKINS
*MOSE JENKINS-MELIA OLIVER-25 Feb.1877 by GEO.JONES,MG-Bd.
   *JUDGE SPEARMAN
Page 37
*CHARLES WILLIAMS-SYLVIA KELLY-Li.22 Feb.1877-nt-Bd.*LEE BRONSON
*TOLBERT BROWN-TILDA GIBSON-3 Mar.1877 by EDW.PERRY,Pastor.
   Bd.*SILAS BALDWIN
Page 38
*RICHMOND HARRIS-MILLIE SMITH-15 Mar.1877 by E.PERRY,Pastor.
   Bd.J.H.SHRADER
*WASHINGTON GOODLOE-CLARISA ANN SMITH-Li.7 Mar.1877-nt-Bd.
   *PATRICK MAY
Page 39
*SILAS SIMILTON-AMANDA WYNN-Li.10 Mar.1877-nt-Bd.*ALBERT JACKSON
Page 40
*LARRY LAUGHLIN-MARY JONES-19 May 1877 by EDMUND PERRY,Pr.&
   D.M.MICKEY,Ir. Bd.DAVID HUNT
*THOMAS CASH-MILLY CANNY-Li. 16 May 1877-nt-Bd.*Wm.LANCASTER
Page 41
*ANDERSON FRAZER-MATTIE ROBINSON-29 Mar.1877 by ELIAS SPRIGGS
   Bd.*SIMON BELL
*ELI WARE-CATHERINE McINTYRE-20 Apr.1877 by W.M.McQUILLAN,JP
   *JEFFERSON MONROE

MARRIAGE BK.I,SHARK.CO.MS. 1876-1880

Page 42
W.B.BARNARD-HENRY(I)G.STEVENS-18 Apr.1877 by Rev.W.R.CALDWELL,
  MECS. Bd. HENRY FLOYD
*GREEN MITCHELL-FLORA LOVE-20 May 1877 by W.T.BARNARD,MBS-also
  bond
Page 43
*WEST JACKSON-SALLIE BOZE-Li.19 May 1877-nt-Bd.*EDMUND CARTER
*DAVE JOHNSON-ELIZABETH WILLIAMS-Li.25 May 1877-nt-Bd.BEN LEWIS
Page 44
*Wm.DUNCAN-CHARLOTTE WILLIS-9 June 1877 by GEO.JONES,Min. Bd.
  *SIMON BELL
*NATHAN HILL-EMILY JONES-Li.10 June 1877-nt-Bd.*ALEX YOUNG
Page 45
*JOHN WOODRUFF-EASTER ROSEN-Li.22 June 1877-nt-Bd.JERRY BALLARD
*JOHN JOHNSON-JUDY KELLY-7 July 1877 by Elder D.BOWEN.Bd.J.G.DAVIS
Page 46
*JOSEPH HOGG-MOLLIE ONEIL-11 July 1877-by EUGENE CLARK,MBS. Bd.
  GEORGE HAUSER
BENJAMIN F. EZELL-JOANNA BOYKIN-26 July 1877 by R.S.WRIGHT,JP
  Bd.*J.P.LIVINGSTON
Page 47
*GEORGE WILLIAMS-MARTHA HUGHES-28 July by JAS.BYAS,Elder.Bd.
  *SILAS BALDON
*HENRY RICHARDSON-ANNIE WILLIAMS-Li. 4 Aug.1877-nt-Bd.J.A.BRITTON
Page 48
*GEORGE JACKSON-MILLIE JONES-Li.11Aug.1877-nt-Bd.*WASH SMITH
JACK LINDSEY-AMANDA HAWKINS-11Aug.1877 by D.M.MICKEY,MG. Bd.
  *Wm.JOHNSON
Page 49
*JOSEPH HARPER-ANN MICKEY-12 Aug.1877 byD.M.MICKEY,MG. Bd.
  *ANTHONY CRUMP
*JAMES LACY-SALLIE PARKER-16 Aug.1877 by W.T.BARNARD,Pres.Board
  of Sup. Bd.*SIMON COOPER
Page 50
*BEVERLY PAYNE-CLARA GARDNER-Li.28 Aug.1877.Bd.*ISAAC CHAMLIN
*GEO.A.WILLIS-AMERICA SMITH-Li.1 Sept.1877.Bd.Wm.W.MOORE
Page 51
JOHN C.DENMAN-LIZZIE MANOR-4 Sept.1877 by JNO.W.JONES. Bd.
  W.A.ORENDORF
*DAMAN WALKER-MAHULDA ROWE-3 Sept.1877 by(no sig.)Bd.*LEWIS
  WIMS
Page 52
A.S.WHEELER-LOUISE CARLYLE-4 Sept.1877 by R.L.WRIGHT,JP. Bd.
  W.H.SHRADER
*R.W.PARKER-MRS.BIDDIE SWINNEY(SWEENEY)-8 Sept.1877by F.M.FEATHER-
  TON,MG. Bond C.A.STAUB
Page 53
*CALVIN WILLIAMS-REBECCA PARKER-20 Sept. by Rev.W.DAWSON.Bd.
  *FRIDAY CLAYTON
W.H.SHRADER-EMMA WHEELER-4 Oct.1877 by Rev.H.R.CALDWELL,MECS.
  Bd.A.S.WHEELER
Page 54
*INEE HENRY-MARY PHILLIPS-Li.1 Oct.1877-nt-Bd.*PETER EMERY
*PETER DIXON-FANNIE WATSON-7 Oct.1877-by *MANUEL KING. Bd.
  *ADAM MITCHELL

MARRIAGE BK.I,SHARK.CO.MS. 1876-1880

Page 55
*HENRY SCOTT-MATILDA CHAMPLI(A)N-Li.10 Oct.1877-nt-Bd*ISAAC
  CHAMLIN
ANDREW PATTERSON-DELEST WHITTERKER-Li.17 Oct.1877-nt-Bd.
  ISAAC CHAMLIN
Page 56
*ELIJAH HAMPTON-NANCY DUCKET-Li.18Oct.1877-nt-Bd.*SAM MORDECAI
JAMES B.WESLEY-ELLEN TOWNS-Li.30 Oct.1877-nt-Bd.*JIM BOOTH
Page 57
*Wm.JONES-AMERICA GIBSON-9 Nov.1877 by EUGENE CLARK,memb.of
  Board of Sup. Bd.*JAS.BUCKINGHAM
*GREEN MELVILLE-ANN GIBBS-3 Nov.1877-by D.M.MICKEY,MG. Bd.
  *JOE HARPER
Page 58
*JAMES SMITH-KITTY GREENWALL-8 Nov.1877 by Rev.JACKSON HILL.
  Bd.JACK HILL
*ALFRED HAYS-AMANDA MACK-17 Nov.1877-by Elder JOHN KNAPPER.
  Bd.*WASH WILLIAMS
Page59
*SAMUEL BANKS-MARY FURNCHESS-12 Nov.1877-by ELIAS SPRIGGS.
  Bd. *SIMON BELL
*OS SAM-DELIA ADAMS-9 Sept.1877-by R.L.WRIGHT,JP.Also bond
Page 60
J.A.OVERBY-ELLEN I.SHRADER-17 Dec.1877 by R.L.WRIGHT,JP. Bd.
  HENRY PICARD
*HENRY FORD-MARY KELLY-Li.13 Dec.1877-nt-Bd.*CHAS.HOWARD
Page 61
GUY McCOY-JOSEPHINE JEANS-15 Dec.1877 by W.B.McQUILLEN ,JP
  Bd.L.A.LLOYD
JOHN OTTO-MOLLIE BROWDER-21 Dec.1877-by W.B.McQUILLEN,JP
  Bd. THOS.G.PARKS
Page 62
EMMANUEL LILLY-FRANCIS WILLIAMS-Li.21 Dec.1877-Bd.*WILSON
  BRANDINGAX
BLANK
Page 63
*WILST CALAWAY-HANNAH GREENSHIP-26 Dec.1877 by *EMANUEL KING.
  Bd.*JAMES CAREY
*AMBROSE BOOKER-HARRIET SMITH-Li.26 Dec.1877-nt-Bd.*THOS.CRAWFORD
Page 64
*CHARLES FAIRCHILD-NETTIE ANNE WILLIS-1Jan.1878 by L.W.ROGAN,JP
  Bond VIRGIL PARKER
*SPENCER BATES-MATTIE KNUCKLES-27 Dec.1877 by L.W.ROGAN,JP.
  Bd. A.M.WADDILL
Page 65
*SAM ROBINSON-RINDA HIGHTOWER-Li.31Dec.1877-nt-Bd.*COL.ELLERBY
THOMAS DAY-LOU PERKINS-Li.3 Jan.1878-nt-Bd.AUGUSTINE CHEW
Page 66
*ERNEST MILES-HARRIET WILLIAMS-Li.3 Jan.1878-nt-Bd.J.H.ROBERTSON
*LINDSEY JOHNSON-VERTENA ROGERS-Li.15 Jan.1878-nt-Bd.WILLIAM
  FISHER
Page 67
*ROBERT WILLIAMS-SALLIE JACKSON-10Jan1878 by AARON CHASE. Bd.
  *NED HUDDLESTON
N.C. CRANE-FRANCES J.REYNOLDS-3 Feb.1878 by Rev.H.R.CALDWELL,MECS
  Bd.S.D.PARKS

MARRIAGE BK.I,SHARK.CO.MS. 1876-1880

Page 68
*JAMES DAVIS-CAROLINE MELTON-13 Feb.1878 by Rev.W.H.WILLIAMS
   Bd.*ARTHUR BATTLE
*BROWN RUTLEDGE-ANNIE GARRISON-7 Feb.1878 by JACK HILL,Min.
   Bd.*MOSES MAIRCIER

Page 69
*JESSIE SCOTT-ROSA WARREN-Li.8 Feb1878-nt-Bd.*JASON CUNNINGHAM
*GREEN MELTON-TINSEY CRENSHAW-Li.11 Feb.1878-nt-Bd.E.B.SHELBY

Page 70
*WASHINGTON ARNOLD-MARY SMITH-Li.11Feb.1878-nt-Bd.*CHAS.FIELD
*WILLIAM SMITH-MARY GIBBS-14Feb.1878-by JACK HILL.Bd.*AMBROSE
   BOOKER

Page 71
*HENRY WRIGHT-LUCY MARTLEY-Li.16Feb.1878-nt-Bd.J.K.BRUZELIUS[a]
*EAD THOMPSON-ANNIE MALONE-Li.21Feb.1878-nt-Bd.*MOSES MALONE

Page 72
J.A.KETCHERSIDE-ELLEN CHRISTESON-Li.28Feb.1878-nt-Bd.*G.W.BOYKIN
*ADAM BROWN-POLLY HOWARD-14 Mar.1878-by JACK HILL.Bd.*MOSES
   MARCIERS(MAIRCIER)

Page 73
*GEORGE CONLEY-EMILY COX-Li.5 Mar.1878-nt-Bd.JUDGE POWELL
*WILLIAM MITCHELL-CHARITY GAUNT-7Mar1878-by Rev.GEO.JONES. Bd
   *WASHINGTON HARRIS

Page 74
PATRICK MAY-EMILY STAPLE-Li.6Mar.1878-nt-Bd.*WASHINGTON HARRIS
JOSEPH SMITH-FANNIE BAKER-Li.7Mar.1878-nt-Bd.WILLIAM BAKER

Page 75
*ARCHIE GEE-JULIA McELROY-Li.7Mar.1878-nt-Bd.*WHITMAN HILL
*PETER FISHER-CAROLINE TOWNSEND-Li.8Mar.1878-nt-*ESAN TEA

Page 76
CHARLES McLEMORE-FLORENCE DICKINSON-Li.11Mar.1878-nt-Bd.
   G.M.BAGGETT
W.A.COALTER-LUCY O'NEAL-14 Mar.1878 by Rev.H.R.CALDWELL,MECS
   Bd. W.B.McQUILLEN

Page 77
*JAMES HILL-MARY WATKINS-Li.19Mar.1878-nt-Bd.*THOS.REEVLEY
*FRANK HICKMAN-LUCY PALMER-3Apr.1878-by L.W.ROGAN,JP. Bond
   R.Y.MAXWELL

Page 78
M.C.HELMICH-L.G.JONES-Li.3 Apr.1878-nt-Bd.J.G.PARHAM
*ROBERT SPELLER-LIZZIE RUSHING-Li.10 Apr.1878-nt-Bd.*HOLLIS
   GRAY

Page 79
*CHATMAN PHILIPS-ARY MILLER-Li.13 Apr.1878-nt-Bd.*BEN PRADER
*WASH PATTERSON-ROXANNA ROBINSON-Li.20 Apr.1878-nt-Bd. *CYRUS
   SHELDEN

Page 80
*SPENCER WRIGHT-EMMA MURRAY-Li.22Apr.1878-nt-Bd.*ISAAC CHAMLIN
*JOHN TAYLOR-PENNY ROBINSON-Li.22 Apr.1878-nt-Bd. T.J.ORENDORF

Page 81
*JOE ROBINSON-MARY ANN THOMASON-Li.25 Apr.1878-nt-Bd.*WALTER
   GRIFFIN
*DOC HARVEY-MARIA VIVENS-Li.2 May 1878-nt-Bd.*SAM'L FISHER

Page 82
*HENRY DUNN-SALLIE EDWARDS-Li.6 May 1878-nt-Bd.JERRY WASHINGTON
*THOS.WEBB-JOANNA JOHNSON-Li.9May 1878-nt-Bd.G.Y.STEWART

MARRIAGE BK.I SHARK.CO.MS.-1876-1880

Page 83
*SOLOMON COX-MARGARET DICKINSON-Li.10 May 1878-nt-Bd.JUGE POWELL
*HENRY BARKSDALE-JULIA EMERY-26 May 1878 by JACK HILL. Bd.J.B. WESLEY

Page 84
*DANIEL HENDERSON-ADINE DONALD-Li. 16 May 1878-nt-Bd.Wm.WALKER
*ADAM MICHAM-ELZY CALDWELL-Li.16 May 1878-nt-Bd.*DENNIS MOODY

Page 85
CALVIN WATSON-MILLY MARSHALL-Li.20 May 1878-nt-Bd. HAYWOOD FERBY
*Wm.JOHNSON-ELMIRA HICKS-Li.8 June 1878-nt-Bd. TONY HAWKINS

Page 86
BREDERICK BROOKS-ELIZA HARSH-19 June 1878 by Rev.H.R.CALDWELL,MECS. Bd.JAMES H.CORTRIGHT
JOHN S.JOOR-KATIE E.WADDILL-27 June1878 by C.J.WINGATE.Bd.GEORGE Y.STEWART

Page 87
N.W. PARKER-MARTHA EVANS-Li. 29 June1878-nt-Bd. CHAS.W.WILLIAMS
*ISAAC MURPHY-HENRIETTA SCOTT-Li.4 July 1878-ny-Bd.*LUMFORD HOPKINS

Page 88
CHARLES*LEE-FANNIE JONES-Li.6 July 1878-nt-Bd.GEO.W.BUTLER
SAMUEL H.SHRADER-FRANCES ADAMS-Li.21 Sept.1878-nt-Bd.JOHN W. WRIGHT

Page 89
*MURPHY RHODES-HESTER JOHNSON-Li.18 July 1878-nt-Bd.*WHITMAN HILL
*CAP WILLIAMS-JULIA ANN GARDNER-20July1878 by Rev.*EMANUEL LESTER, Bd.by LESTER

Page 90
*ANDERSON HARRIS-FLORA SPRIGGS-Li.26July1878-nt-Bd.*Wm.WALKER
*EDMUND CARTER-ELLEN SWINEY-Li.15Aug.1878-nt-Bd.*JOHN WILLIAMS

Page 91
*NOAH GEE-CLARISSA BYRD-5Sept.1878 by W.T.BARNARD,MBS. Bd. *WHITMAN HILL
*LOUIS GANT-MARGY PIERCE-Li.24Sept.1878-nt-Bd.P.C.PURVIS

Page 92
*JOSEPH SCHOALIN-CASSANDRA CAGE-Li.1Nov.1878-nt-Bd.*CHARLES HAMILTON
ELIJAH*WILSON-ALICE KEY-Li.1Nov.1878-nt-Bd.*THOMAS DUNCAN

Page 93
B.J.GORMAN-MARTHA(MATTIE)WESTON-Li.13Nov.1878-nt-Bd.B.J.BRANTLY
JOHN WELL-MRS.SARAH THOMPSON-Li.15Nov.1878-nt.-Bd.T.J.WARD

Page 94
*JAS.NICHOLS-AGNES HARRIS-Li15Nov.1878-nt-Bd.T.J.WARD(hes Dep.Clk.)
*CHARLEY JACKSON-EDITH WILLIAMS-Li.2Dec.1878-nt-Bd.*SANDY AGEE

Page 95
H.E.SHANNON-BETTIE C.MALLETT-Li.20Dec.1878-nt-Bd.T.J.WARD
GUST.ROSEN-MARY L.LEE-Li.21Dec.1878-nt-Bd.T.J.WARD

Page 96
*AUSTIN VALENTINE-ROXIE ARMSTEAD(ORNSTEAD)Li.23Dec.1878-nt- Bd.*ALEX ACHE(OCHE)
[writing on these pages -horrible]
*LEM TERMANT(TENANT)-LAURA EDWARDS-Li.26Dec.1878-nt-Bd.*KENNEDY BOYD

MARRIAGE BK.I SHARK.CO.MS. 1876-1880

Page 97
*ANDERSON JACKSON-LIZA JACKSON-Li.25Dec.1878-nt-Bd.BOB WILLIAMS
*HENRY CARTER-FLORA JACKSON-Application dated 25Dec.1878-Li.not issued-Bd. BOB WILLIAMS
¶THESE Li.dated Christmas day !Dedicated Clerk!]
Page 98
*ISAIAH ELLIS-CAROLINE CRAIG-Li.26Dec.1878-nt-Bd.EDWARD HUDSON
*Wm.CHILDS-MARY CARTER-Li.27Dec.1878-nt-Bd.*JOAB HARRIS
Page 99
*RICHARD LUCKETT-ELIZABETH JOHNSON-Li.31Dec.1878-nt-Bd.*HOWID (could be DAVID) NATHANIEL
J.R.WEEKS-CINDA BOYKIN-Li.2Jan1879-nt-Bd.B.L.BARNES
Page 100
¶Writing horrible again]
FRANK*WILLIAMS-FRANCIS SIMILTON-Li.3Jan.1879-nt-Bd.ALBERT*FARROW
JOHN*LEWIS-CHARLOTTE JONES-Li.8Jan.1879-nt-Bd.RUEBEN*WILLIAMS
Page 101
FRED*JOHNSON-MOLLIE IMONT or SMART ormaybe DURST-14Jan.1879 by H.PICARD. Bd.CHAS.*MATTHEWS
CHAS.*MATTHEWS-ANNIE BROWN or BURN-Application 14Jan.1879-no Li.issued-Bd.FRED*JOHNSON
Page 102
J.R.CALDWELL-ABBIE BRITTON-Li.16Jan.1879-nt-Bd.JOHN*GORDON
WILLIAM*BELL-SARAH BRITTON-Li.17Jan.1879-nt-Bd.JOHN*GORDON
Page103
ELBERT*WATSON-ALVINA REED-Li.18Jan.1879-nt-Bd.JACK MAKES ?
WILEY HARRIS-GEORGIANA STEPHENS-25Jan.1879 by GEO.*JONES. Bd. JESSE THOMAS
Page 104
R.PARKS-GEORGINA REYNOLDS-Li.21Jan.1879-nt-Bd. E.P.BRIDGERS
DAN*GRIFFIN-PATSY WASHINGTON-Li.23Jan.1879-nt-Bd.T.J.WARD
Page 105
W.G.PHELPS-VIRGINIA THOMPSON-30Jan.1879 by STEVENSON ARCHER. Bd.T.J.ORENDORF
T.J.WARD-MARY J.WEST-9Feb.1879 by J.G.DAVIS,MBS.Bd.JNO.GRIFFIN
Page 106
THOMAS*DUNCAN-NELLIE BURNS-4Feb.1879 by Rev.JOHN KNAPPER.Bd. ALFRED*WINN
J.W.STUBBLEFIELD-BELLE WIGGINS-9Feb.1879 by W.T.BARNARD,MBS. Bd.GEORGE POWELL
Page 107
JAMES*THOMAS-EDIE JOHNSON-Li.10Feb.1879-nt-Bd.GEORGE*GANT
EDMOND*YOUNG-CARRIE ARCHER-14Feb.1879 by Rev.Eld.GRANT
Page 108
JOSEPH*JOHNSON-EDIE GALES-Li.14Feb.1879-nt-Bd.TYLER*GALES
KYLE*WILLIS-DORA STOWLES-22Feb.1879 by Rev.JOHN KNAPPER. Bd. J.P.GRAY
Page 109
JOE*COLUMBUS-SARAH LUSTON-20Feb.1879 by EMANUEL LUSTON,Elder. Bd.ELY*CRAIG
LOUIS SOULES-MINNIE STOWLES-Li.25Feb.1879-nt-Bd.J.P.GRAY
Page 110
ANDREW*BALDWIN-TENNIE CURTIS-28Feb.1879 by D.M.MICKEY,Pastor. Bd.GEORGE*WILLIAMS
WILLIAM*LANCHESTER-ANGELINE DANIELS-Li.18Mar.1879-nt-Bd.S.F. SHELTON

MARRIAGE BK.I SHARK.CO.MS.-1876-1880

Page 111
JIM*DAVIS-VICTORIA BYRD-3 Apr.1879by MASHOEK LOCKMAN.Bd.ROBERT
  *WILLIAMS
CHARLIE*THOMAS-ANNIE ROBERTSON-Li.5Apr.1879-nt-Bd.MONROE*DISON
Page 112
THOMAS*WELLS-NANCY HUNT-13Apr.1879 by Rev.M.D.MICKEY.Bd.LOYD*GUNDY
JOS.L.BARNARD-ELLEN WATSON-16Apr.1879 by J.C.BRADFORD,MG.Bd.
  I.A.CORTRIGHT
Page 113
ISAAC*THOMAS-AMY WILLIAMS-Li.16Apr.1879-nt-Bd. LOUIS*HAWKINS
HARRY*ROBINSON-PRISCILLA BROWN-Li.22Apr.1879-nt-Bd.N.R.ANDERSON
Page 114
PERRY*SEALS-EMMA HILL-26Apr.1879 by EMANUEL KING,Pastor.Bd.
  A.G.FLOYD
Wm.*HARRIS-HESTER JACKSON-Li.28Apr.1879-nt-Bd.ALEX*EUSTIS
Page 115
EDMOND*BOLTON-RHODA JAMES-Li.8May1879-nt-Bd.GEO.*THORNTON
Wm.*GRAY-BASH WILSON-15May1879by Rev.W.H.WILLIAMS.Bd.ALEX*GRIFFIN
Page116
OWEN*RANKINS-LIZZIE PARKS-10May1879 by MANUEL KING,Pastor. Bd.
  ISAAC*CHAMBERLIN
MURTON*GLASS-EMMA JENKINS-1June1879 by Rev.E.RUSSELL.Bd.SAMUEL*
  FISHER
Page 117
ED*JONES-EMELINE DONALD-18May1879 by Jno.HARSH,JP.Bd.J.H.ROBERTSON
Wm.FORD-ROSA JAMES-Li.19May1879-nt-Bd. EMANUEL*SIDNEY
Page 118
CHAS.H.HAMPTON-MARY POWELL-Li.21May1879-nt-Bd.BOB*PAYNE
SEBON*CARR-SUSAN JOHNSON-26May1879-nt-Bd.BEN*LEWIS
Page 119
JOHN*SMALL-SUSAN PINKARD-Li.June1879-nt-Bd.ANDERSON*JACKSON
JOSEPH DUKE-ALICE WELLS-25June1879 by R.L.WRIGHT,JP.Bd.DAVID WELLS
Page 120
JOHN*ROBINSON-CHARITY LANKSTON-26June1879 by Rev.JOHN KNAPPER.
  Bd.NAT PARKER
JOHN*HENRY LEWIS-LIZZIE ANN WELLS-30June1879 by Rev.JOHN KNAPPER
  Bd.PARRET McDUFFEY
Page 121
ISIAH BROWN-DOLLY GRAHAM-10July1879 by JOHN HARSH,JP.Bd.LEWIS*
  HAWKINS
MORRIS*WILSON-ANNIE TAYLOR-Li.1July1879-nt-Bd.WILLIAM*HARRIS
Page122
ROBERT LINTON-ANNIE WILLIAMS-3July1879 by Rev.JOHN KNAPPER.
  Bd.C.H.HAMPTON
HYMAN*PATRIDGE-ADELINE JOHNSON-13July1879 by Rev.GEO.JONES.
  Bd.EUGENE CLARK
Page 123
ALICK*NATHAN-HANAH BATTLE(Battie)-19July1879 by M.LOCKMAN.
  Bd.S.R.DAWSON
JACK SANDERS-HULDA BROWN-13July1878 by Rev.GEO.JONES,&Rev.J.A.
  THOMPSON. Bd. EUGENE CLARK
Page 124
WILLIAM*PARHAM-ELVIRA JOHNSON-Li.15 July1879-nt-Bd.GREEN*MITCHELL
CALVIN DOVER-JENNIE MARSHALL-21July1879 by J.A.C.SHRADER,MBS.
  Bd.R.W.MITCHELL

MARRIAGE BK.I,SHARK.CO.MS. 1876-1880

Page 125
STEWART*TURNER-SUSAN ARMSTEAD-24July1879 by J.A.C.SHRADER. Bd.
    EDWARD*LONG
DAVE*FORD-FLORA SCOTT-24July1879 by H.G.STEVENS,JP.Bd.EDWARD*
    LONG
Page 126
HENRY*HARDING-MARY SMITH-31July1879 by Rev.GEO.JONES.Bd.ALBERT*
    STINSON
THOMAS*OWENS-SARAH WHITEHEAD-4Aug.1879 by DOCK BOWIE,Min. Bd.
    EUGENE CLARK
Page 127
FELIX*FRIEND-EMMA DILL-Li.1Aug.1879-nt-Bd.ALLAN*MASON
ANTHONY*LEWIS-CAROLINE DAVENPORT-3Aug.1879 by Rev.JAMES BYAS.
    BD.DANIEL*LAWSON
Page 128
M.T.SHRADER-LULA SHELTON-5Aug.1879 by R.L.WRIGHT,JP. Bd. HENRY
    SHRADER
ALLEN*WASHINGTON-FANNIE JOHNSON-18Aug.1879 by Rev.JAMES BYAS.
    Bd.RUBE*WILLIAMS
Page129
THOMAS*HILLIARD-ELISA HOSE-13Aug.1879 by Rev.W.H.WILLIAMS.Bd.
    J.R.CALDWELL
E.R.BANKS-HANAH FARRAR-Li.16Aug.1879-nt-Bd.R.W.MITCHELL
Page 130
WASHINGTON*ARNOLD-EASTER WHITE-18Aug.1879 by Rev.GEO.JONES.
    Bd.GILES*SWANSON
SIMON*BELL-NELLIE DAVIS-21Aug.1879 by Rev.W.H.WILLIAMS.Bd.
    JOHN*SMITH
Page131
ISAAC*WHITEHEAD-HATTIE SMITH-28Aug.1879 by MASHOEK LOCKMAN.
    Bd.EUGENE CLARK
ABRAM*DOSIER-NANCY FOSTER-4Oct.1879 by J.G.DAVIS,JP. Bd.
    JAMES H.CORTRIGHT
Page 132
FRANK VANVECOVEN-ALICE O.DAY-Li.18Sept.1879-nt-Bd. DANIEL BROUGHAL
CHARLES*MONTGOMERY-EMMA THOMPSON-Li.9Sept.1879-nt-Bd.GEO.*CLARK
Page133
DANIEL*ADAMS-IDA GIBBS-11Sept.1879,by GEO.JONES,Min./Bd.PAT.MAY
ANDREW*FERGUSON-MARIAH DAVIS-Li.11Sept.1879-nt-Bd.NATHAN SMITH
Page134
SAM*JOHNSON-MARIAH BELL-Li.11Sept.1879-nt-Bd.TONY*HAWKINS
WALTER CARTER-CELIA HARRIS-Li.11Sept.1879-nt-Bd.CHARLEY JACKSON
Page 135
ISAAC*WILDY-FANNIE WILDY-19Sept.1879 by Rev.JORDAN CHAVIS. Bd.
    HILLIARD*JONES
HILLIARD*JONES-KANSAS BLACK-19Sept.1879 by Rev.JORDAN CHAVIS.
    Bd.JOHN HARSH
Page 136
STEPHEN*LANE-MAHALA SMITH-Li.27Sept.1879-nt-Bd.TYLER*GALES
DANIEL*WEBSTER-SARAH LANE-Li.27Sept.1879-nt-Bd.ALEX*YATES

MARRIAGE BK.I,SHARK.CO.MS. 1876-1880

Page 137

CHARLES A.COLE-SUSAN NICHOLAS-5 Oct. 1879 by W.T.BARNARD,MBS.
  Bd. JOHN T.MIZELL
LEVI*WALLACE-JULY MOORMAN-8Oct.1879 by H.G.STEVENS,JP.
  Bond J.B.*MURRAY

Page 138
JOHN*LEE-HENRIETTA FRIARSON-19Oct.1879 by Rev.D.M.MICKEY. Bd.
  RICHARD*DAVIS
JOHN*BELL-MARGARET GIBBS-Li.13Oct.1879-nt-Bd.Wm.*CRUMP

Page 139

E.T.BRIDGERS-CARRIE E.MALLETTE-15Oct.1879 by T.C.BRADFORD,MG
  Bd.A.D.ALDRIDGE
ED*LEE-CATHERINE CARSON-22Oct.1879 by Rev.GEORGE JONES. Bd.
  JOHN L.WILLIAMS

Page 140

DAVE*YOUNG-SUSAN RIDLEY-Li.25 Oct.1879-nt-Bd.MERRIDY*SPRIGS
CHARLEY*BELL-ELIZA BOWIE-6 Nov.1879 by J.G.DAVIS,MBS. Bd.
  EUGENE CLARK

Page 141

RICHMOND FERGUSON-JENNIE EMLEN-30 Oct.1879 by Rev. W.H.WILLIAMS
  Bd. JUDGE *SPIERMAN
J.T.McALPINE-MALICIA SHADRACK-11 Nov.1879 by JOHN HARSH. Bd.
  W.B.WRIGHT.

¶ LAST PAGE IN THIS BOOK IS #204,AND WAS STUCK TOGETHER AND I MISSED IT.
THIS PAGE WAS NOT FULL SO AM ADDING IT HERE OUT OF SEQUENCE.
Page 204
DENNIS YOUNG-JULIANN COLEMAN- 31 Dec.1880-by Rev.JOHN KNAPPER.Bd.HANDY
      COMMODORE
*HANDY COMMODORE-EASTER LAWSON-Li. 30 Dec.1880. Bd.DENNIS*YOUNG

¶ WHEN A LICENSE IS NOT RETURNED DOES NOT MEAN THE MARRIAGE DID NOT TAKE
PLACE. USUALLY IT MEANS THAT THE MINISTER OR PRESIDING PERSON FAILED TO
GO TO THE COURTHOUSE AND RECORD THE MARRIAGE. THERE ARE INSTANCES WHERE
THE MARRIAGE NEVER TOOK PLACE BUT ARE NOT NOTED IN THIS BOOK. In 1887 A
TRIP TO THE COUNTY SEAT FROM SOME PARTS OF THE COUNTY,BY HORSEBACK OR BUGGY
MUST HAVE BEEN SOMETHING OF AN ORDEAL.

SHARKEY CO.MS.MARRIAGE BK I   1876-1880

Page 142
W.R.SAUNDERS-MRS.M.A.VINCENT-20 Nov.1879-byJOHN HARSH,JP-Bond
  *H.R.(or K)McKENSIE
JOHN TAYLOR-MINNIE REED-15 Nov.1879-by H.G.STEVENS,JP-bond*DENNIS
  WALKER
Page 143.
HENRY KERNAGHAN-CLARA WILSON-20 Nov.1879-by W.D.DORSON,Min.;Bond
  *SAMUEL FISHER
FELIX HUNT-MARY MILLER-7 March 1880-by REV.W.DAWSON:Bond JOS.
  L.BARNARD
Page 144
NAPOLEON MORRIS-ROSE MARTIN-Li.22 Nov.1879-no ret.Bond*SIMON
  BELL
*THOMAS JACKSON-EMMA LOUIS-23 Nov.1879-by DOCK BOWIE,Min.Bond
  *ANTHONY WALKER
Page 145;
*WILLIAM JACKSON-MARTHA WILLIAMS-Li.26 Nov.1879-no ret.Bond
  *G.Y.STEWART
J.J.SAUNDERS-E.C.BOYKIN-5 Dec.1879-by JOHN HARSH,JP:Bond W.R.
  SAUNDERS
Page 146
ROBERT E.EPPERSON-MOLLIE WRIGHT-7 Dec.1879-by JNO.W.JONES. Bond
  Wm.LAWSON
*MATT BASS-SALLIE WHEATLY-13 Dec.1879-by DOCK BOWIE,Min. Bond
  *WHITMAN HILL
Page 147
*OSEY ADAMS-HARRIET FORD-11 Dec.1879-by JOHN HARSH,JP. Bond
  *LEWIS HAWKINS
*WILLIAM BALLARD-ANNA CLEMENTS -26 Feb.1880-by REV.W.H.WILLIAMS
  Bond *DAVE FRAZIER
Page 148
*DAVE RUSSELL-LUCY GREEN-18 Dec.1879-by J.G.DAVIS,MBS:Bond
  *CALVIN WATSON
R.P.ISIAH-MATTIE CAYHILL- 7 Dec.1879-by REV.W.H.WILLIAMS. Bond
  *DAN HENDERSON
Page 149
J.F.CHANEY-ELIZA A.DUEWESE(or DUENISE OR DUEWISE)-21 Dec.1879
  by JOHN HARSH,JP: Bond JAMES H.CORTRIGHT
J.H.COKER-MILLIE SCOTT-23 Dec.1879-by JOHN HARSH,JP:Bond W.B.
  McQUILLAN
Page 150
*MONROE GLENN-LULA ROAN-23 Dec.1879-by ELDER SPRIGGS. Bond J.L.
  BARNARD
*DAVID GARRETT-MOLLIE LYNCH-by REV.W.H.WILLIAMS-25 Dec.1879
  bond *GLEN JONES
Page 151
MITCHELL KING-ELZIE VALENTINE-18 Jan.1880-by Rev.Elder JOHN
  KNAPPER. Bond *GREEN CLARK
*ISAIAH MURTON(MERTON)-MINDA GIBSON-1 Jan.1880-by J.G.DAVIS,
  MBS. Bond IRA A.CORTRIGHT
Page 152
*RICHARD HANSBERRY-SARAH SMITH-(min.signed Li.on wrong bond
  at bottom of page.)1 Jan.1880 by ELIAS SPRIGGS.Bond *ALEX-
  ANDER GIBSON.
*GEORGE KALFUS-EMMA ALLSIP(or ALLSIS)-Li.30 Dec.1879.Bond C.H.
  HAMILTON

MARRIAGE BK I SHARKEY CO.MS.1876-1880

Page 153
*ALFRED WINN-WINNIE WILLIAMS-9 Jan.1880=by JOHN WELLS JP.Bond
  *ALEX DANIELS
BENJAMIN POTITE-EMILY CONELY-15 Jan.1880-by REV.W.H.WILLIAMS
  Bond JNO.R.BAGGETT
Page154
JAKE OSTROFFSKY-ESTHER COHN-13 Jan.188 -by OMER HUNT,JP:Bond
  S.F.SHELTON
*ELIAS MAXWELL-CARRIE THOMPSON-__Jan.1880 by THOMAS GRANT.Bond
  RICHARD PARKS
Page 155
*MATT HUDSON-WINNIE DANIELS-16 Jan.1880-by JOHN WELLS,JP: Bond
  F.HARSH
MACON VALENTINE-MARY JONES-Li.21 Jan.1880-no ret.Bond *ALEX
  ROBINSON
Page 156
*FLENOY EATON-IDA AUSTIN-3 Jan.1880-by REV.W.H.WILLIAMS. Bond
  *JIM DAVIS
*D.L.SCOFIELD-MARY DOVER-Li.23 Jan.1880-no ret.Bond *MARTIN
  DAVIS
Page 157
REUBEN MASON-EMMA KAHILL- 29 Jan.1880-by REV.JAMES COLEMAN-
  Bond *PIERCE JOHNSON
J.L. WILLIAMS-FANNIE SMITH-26 Jan.1880-by GEORGE JONES,Min.
  Bond *JOHN PARKER
Page 158
*JOHN PARKER-LOU ROBERTSON-26 Jan.1880-by GEO.JONES,Min. Bond
  J.L.WILLIAMS
YORK EDMONSON(EDMONDSON)-DELIA EVERETT-Li.26 Jan.1880-no ret.
  Bond*FRANK ROBERTSON
Page159
* MARTIN PASCO-SOPHIA NAPOLEON-29 Jan.1880-by Rev.JAMES COLEMAN,
  MG. Bond *JIM FOX
*JORDAN BROWN-DENA HOUSTON-7 Feb.1880-by REV.JAMES COLEMAN,
  Bond M.C.MARTIN
Page 160
R.J.COLLIER-MATTY MATT-11 Mar.1880-by T.C.BRADFORD,MG: Bond
  G.W.MARSH
TOM PENDORVIS-MALA COVINGTON-Li.9 Feb.1880-Bond *GEORGE POWELL
Page 161
GEORGE MARTIN-ROSE FISHER-12 Feb.1880-by REV.W.H.WILLIAMS.Bond
  *Wm.BELL
A.L.WRIGHT-MINNIE ELLINGTON-18 Feb.1880-by T.BRADFORD,MG. Bond
  BROM BOYKIN(signs A.G.BOYKIN)
Page 162
*MOSES KEMP-CAROLINE MELTON-Li.14 Feb.1880-nt-Bond*HENRY WRIGHT
*JIM WILLIAMS-ALIS WILLIAMS-Li.14 Feb.1880-no ret.Bond *ROBT.
  MYERS
Page 163
Blank
*GEORGE ROSS-MARY ARCHER-Li.21 Feb.1880-nt-Bond *JOHN JACKSON
Page 164
*BILL WILLIAMS-EMMA BALLARD-Li.27 Feb.1880-nt-Bond*HENRY TURNER
*DAVE TOWNSEND-MARIAH BAKER-4 Mar.1880-by ELDER DICK BAKER.
  Bond *PETER FISHER

MARRIAGE BK 1-1876-1880

Page 165
RUFFIAN MORDICA-JANE TAYLOR-Li.1 Mar.1880-nt-Bond JOE WATSON
*NELSON MOSELEY-JULIA PRICE-4 Mar.1880-by REV.W.H.WILLIAMS,
  Bond THOMAS PRICE
Page 166
*TYLER GALES-ELLA JOHNSON-Li. 5 Mar.1880-nt-Bond JOHN ROBINSON
JOHN ROBINSON-MANERVA LEWIS-20 Mar.1880-by THOMAS GRANT-Bond
  *TYLER GALES
Page 167
N.B.HULL-MARTHA DENAS-5 Mar.1880-by L.W.ROGAN,JP:Bond W.R.WRIGHT
*ED STOKES-JANE BLACK-Li.10 Mar.1880-nt-Bond *GABRIEL OLIVER
Page 168
*GENERAL BLUE-DINAH JOHNSON-Li.11 Mar.1880-Bond *JAMES LEE
*MONROE DISON-GRACE ANN JOHNSON-Li.11 Mar.1880-nt-Bond *CHARLIE
  THOMAS
Page 169
*JEFF JONES-IBBIE BALDWIN-17 Mar.1880-by J.G.DAVIS,JP.Bond *JOHN
  JOHNSON
*ZEKE DAWSON-PENNY WILLIAMS-18 Mar.1880-by JOHN WELLS,JP:Bond
  FERD HARSH
Page 170
*SAM REEVELY-ELIZA ROBERTSON-Li.22 Mar.1880-nt-Bond A.J.PHELPS
*ENNIS COSBY-ANGELINE JOHNSON-22 Mar.1880-by JAMES H.CORTRIGHT
  member Board Supervisors,Shark.Co. Bond*ISAAC JOHNSON
Page 171
SAM BURTON-NANCY HICKS-28 Mar.1880-by J.G.DAVIS,JP.Bond*J.C.GIBSC
*JACK ROBERSON-SALLIE LEE- Li.3 Apr.1880-nt-Bond *SIMON BELLE
Page 172
*STEPHEN ARCHER-SARAH WHEAT-Li.10 Apr.1880-nt-Bond *W.H.HILL
BROWN(signs A.G)BOYKIN-ELLEN O'NEAL-14 Apr.1880-by T.C.BRADFORD,
  M.G. Bond JOHN C.DENMAN
Page 173
*JAMES HARRIS-VICEY JOHNSON-Li.17 Apr.1880-nt-Bond *SAM MORDICA
OLIVER WILLIAMS-JULIANN HILL-28 Apr.1880-by *MANUEL KING-Bond
  *J.L.HOLLINGSWORTH
Page 174
NATHAN B.DAVIS-JANE PATTERSON-22 Arp.1880-by H.G.STEVENS,JP.
  Bond*TONY HAWKINS
*COLONEL BROWN-HARRIET JENKINS-24 Apr.1880-[Return says HARRIET
  BROWN]by AARON CHASE. Bond *ANTHONY WALKER
Page 175
JAMES H.CORTRIGHT-CLEMANTINA ROBERTS-5 May 1880-by T.C.BRADFORD,
  MG of MEC South. Bond B.SINAI
*ELBERT HINES-AIRY PHILLIPS-Li.5 May 1880-nt-Bond *HILLIARD WHITE
Page 176
*PETER GALES-PEARLINE WINN-13 May 1880-by H.G.STEVENS,JP.Bond
  FRANK HARRIS
*TAYLOR LEWIS-ELVIRA DAIRY-20 May 1880-by AARON CHASE.Bond BILL
  WILLIAMS
Page 177
HERBERT THOMPSON-SALLIE WATSON-27 May 1880-by T.C.BRADFORD,MG
  Bond H.MOORMAN
AUSTIN PERKINS-MATILDA BELL-Li.28 May 1880-Bond*JOHN HOPKINS
Page 178
W.HENRY BARNARD-IDA CREATH-3 June 1889-by T.C.BRADFORD,MG.Bond
  W.C.H.McKINNEY

MARRIAGE BK.SHARKEY CO.MS.1876-1880

Page 178
R.C.HARRIS-MOLLIE D.HOOD-7 June 1881(Li.4 June 1880)by A.G.
   FLOYD,JP. Bond G.W.HOOD
Page 179
*ISOM COMMER-NANCY DANIELS-6 June 1880 by MANUEL KING.Bond
   LEIGH CLARK
*GABRIEL OLIVER-RACHEL JONES-Li. 7 June 1880.Bond*LEROY DOUGLASS
Page 180
*LEROY DOUGLASS-CHARITY BATTON-Li.7 June 1880.Bond*GABRIEL OLIVER
*D.JOHNSON-ANGELINE WILLIAMS-Li.12 June 1880.Bond *JOE DOUGLASS
Page 181
*JIM BELL-MOLLIE JONES-Li.2 July 1880.Bond*WILLIAM BELL
*DOCTOR ALEXANDER-FRANCIS KING-Li.2 July 1880.Bond PETER NORMAN
Page 182
*HENRY HARRIS-EDIE WILLIAMS-Li.2 July 1880.Bond.J.H.CORTRIGHT
JAMES LEE-ROSA McELROY-21 July 1880-by L.E.SIDNEY,Min.Bond
   GEORGE THORNTON
Page 183
*CHARLEY PHILLIPS-DILLA GRAY-Li.8 July 1880-Bond *DAN HENDERSON
ALFRED SMITH-DELIA WINN-Li.13 July 1880.Bond WILLIAM DRAYTON
Page 184
*THO'S REAVLY-AGNIS WYNN-Bond date 20 July 1880-no Lic.date
   no return-Bond *SAMUEL ERVIN.
*JONAS JONES-HULDY CURTISS-Bond date 22 July 1880-no ret.Bond
   *THOMAS JOHNSON
Page 185
JOHN WILLIAM GREEN-M.E.PENDARVIS-2 Feb.1881(Li.5 Aug.1880)by
   H.G.STEVENS,JP. Bond A.L.GREEN.
*BOTLEY JOHNSON-LUCY THOMPSON-2 Aug.1880 by *THOMAS GRANT.Bond
   *GUSTUS COBB
Page 186
*WILLIAM MERRIDITH-ELLEN JOHNSON-Li. 4 Aug.1880.Bond JERRY SMITH
   (signs JEYY WASHINGTON)
GEORGE WINKLEY-M.E.McCARTHEY-9 Aug.1880 by A.G.FLOYD,JP.Bond
   J.H.BAKER
Page 187
*LOUIS PRATT-LUCY SAMPLE-9 Aug.1880 by REV.J.H.PENNY.Bond
   *FRANK McDONALD
Bond only by WILLIAM BONDLESS &*MALCUM VALENTINE-14 Aug.1880
Page 188
LOUIS*DAVIS-CRECY SUTIN-Li.21 Aug.1880.Bond*JIM DAVIS
*CORNELIUS PRESTON-MALINDA GIBSON-28 Aug.1880,by REV.JAMES
   BYRAS. BOND,*GEORGE WILLIAMS
Page 189
*JOHN THORNTON-CATHERINE JONES-bond only 2 Sept.1880,CHARLEY
   LEE
FRANK L.STEVENS-BETTIE TEIFER-7 Sept.1880 by T.C.BRADFORD,MG
   Bond*GEORGE POWELL
Page 190
*WILLIAM WATKINS-ELIZA THOMPSON-Li. 15 Sept.1880.Bond*ALTIMORE
   WATKINS
*T.J.DUKE-BETHINIA GRICE-3 Oct.1880 by A.G.FLOYD,JP.Bond J.M.
   TURNER
Page 191
*CHARLES HILL-CHARLOTTE JEFFERSON-9 Oct.1880-by REV.W.H.WILLIAMS
   MG

MARRIAGE BK.I,SHARK.CO.MS.1876-1880

Page 191-cont.
*EDMOND CARTER-CARRIE SPEARMAN-Li.12 Oct.1880.Bond*NED HUDDLESON

Page 192
*JAMES LIGHTNER-MARY ELLEN HOLLIDAY-Li.13 Oct.1880 Bond with
 note attached by W.GIBBONS,states Mary Ellen his former slave
HENRY CARTER-FRADONIA EATON-21 Oct.1880by REV.W.H.WILLIAMS,MG
 Bond*ANDERSON JACKSON

Page 193
*ELIJAH RICHARDSON-PENNY TAYLOR-Li.22 Oct.1880.Bond*ZEKE DAWSON
*GEORGE COLEMAN-ELLA COLLINS-23 Oct.1880 by JNO.W.JONES. Bond
 FRANK L.STEVENS

Page 194
WARREN ABNER-RITTA BURNS-30 Oct.1880,Elder DANIEL VICTORY,Bond
 JNO.H.CLANCY
*LINDSEY ANDERSON-KATIE JOHNSON -Li. 3 Nov.1880.Bond *RICH.BAKER

Page 195
*JOHN JACKSON-LOTTA CLARK-7 Nov.1880-by Rev.VICTORY.Bond *GEORGE
 BELL
*ALBERT McFEARSON-AMY THOMPSON-12 Nov.1880 by REV.L.E.SIDNEY
 Bond *HENRY WILLIAMS

Page 196
S.R.DORSON(he signs DAWSON)-LUCINDA TURNER-24 Nov.1880by L.W.
 ROGAN JP .Bond *JOHN GORDON
*ADAM MEACHAM-JENNIE FERGUSON-5 Dec.1880 by REV.W.H.WILLIAMS
 Bond H.J.FIELDS

Page 197
L.W.INGRAHAM-SARAH WATSON-21 Nov.1880-by L.W.ROGAN JP.Bond
 B.H.WATSON
CHAS.H.FISHER-ELIZA P.CLEMENTS-1 Dec.1880 by------.Bond J.S.JOOR

Page 198
WALTER BROWNSON-ADELINE ROBINSON-14 Dec.1880 by REV.JOSEPH PENNE
 Bond *ALLEN ROBINSON
*FREDERICK MARSHALL-ISSABELA CARRINGTON-17 Dec.1880 by REV.JOSEP
 PENNEY. B(*SAM REED

Page 199
*RICHARD JENKINS-LENA SPURMAN-17 Dec.1880-by AARON CHASE. Bond
 *ISAAC GLAUTON
*Wm.CRUMP-MAY SANDERS-6 Jan.1881 by REV.D.M.MICKEY.Bond *WESLEY
 WILLIS

Page 200
*WESLEY WILLIS-ELLA WHITING-1 Jan.1881,by REV.JAMES BIAS.Bond
 *Wm.CRUMP
*RUEBEN MITCHELL-ADELINE REEVELEY-Li. 22 Dec.1880.Bond.*CALVIN
 DOVER

Page 201
JOE McBRIDE-MOLLIE SINGLETON-Li. 22 Dec.1880.Bd.*GEORGE WADDELL
*MACK McCULLUM-FLIXIE CONES-1 Jan.1881by REV.JAMES BIAS.Bd.
 *AUTREY LEWIS

Page 202
*BLANTON ISHMAEL-ANGELINE WINSTON-1 Jan.1881 by Rev.JAMES BIAS.
 Bond.*CEBON CARR
*MONROE DENNEY-ELLA SPEARMON-1 Feb.1881 by AARON CHASE. Bond
 *JIM DAVIS

Page 203
*MOSE ANDERSON-LOUISA REED- 30 Dec.1880 by J.A.C.SHRADER MBS
 Bond *EDMOND REED
*WARNER WILLIAMS- LIZZIE JOHNSON-31 Dec.1880 by Rev.JOHN KNAPPEF
 Bond WILLIAM JOHNSON

DEER CREEK PILOT..AUG.1,1891-DEC.31.1892--ROLLING FORK, MS.
EDITOR..SIDNEY W.LANGFORD --PUBLISHED ON SATURDAY

The excerpts presented here from the weekly newspaper were chosen for their geneological facts and to establish a persons whereabouts in the county of Sharkey. Society columns were headed; Rolling Fork, Percy, Cary, Anguilla, Auter, Fish Lake, Spanish Fort.

Aug.1,1891
GENERAL DIRECTORY

Judicial: J.D.GILLILAND- Circuit Judge 9th District.
T.M.GIBSON--District Attorney

COUNTY OFFICERS

N.T.BAGGETT-Circuit and Chancery Clerk

W.C.H.McKINNEY--Treasurer

A.J.WILLIAMS--Tax Assessor

S.W.LANGFORD--Supt.of Education

S.T.KAGLER--Supervisor   1st District

A.HUNT-Pres.   "   2nd   "

J.S.JOOR   "   3rd   "

H.J.FIELDS   "   4th   "

A.G.BOYKIN   "   5th   "

H.J.WRIGHT--Sheriff

SOCIETY NOTES BY PHOEBE (Rolling Fork)

MRS.HATTIE CAMERON is visiting relatives in Mayersville

W.P.BROWN is at home after a charming visit to Vicksburg.

MISS ELIZA CASEY went to Hinds Co. to recuperate from a recent illness

H.L.FOOTE journeyed to West Point to take place in a shoot.

LOUIS NICHOLSON returned from Canton and vicinity his former home.

NAT & ERNEST RATCLIFF from Gloster visited in Rolling Fork.

The home of MISSES LOLA DINKINS & MABEL CAMERON is again brightened by their return from Mayersville.

COL.BROWN returned from Ala.& Tenn. thoroughly recuperated from a recent illness

MRS.D.C.CASEY & little MISS CORNELIA left Wed. for summer vacation in Warren and Hinds Co.

DR.J.C.HALL & wife of Sharkey Co. are stopping at the Peabody in Memphis

DR.WALTER JONES & wife spent the week in Mayersville

PETITIONS FOR RETAIL LIQUOR LICENSE

J.M.HOLLINGSWORTH-Lorenzen Station,Ms. 4th Dist.

DEER CREEK PILOT EXCERPTS-1891-1892

Pet.for Liquor Li.Cont.

    M.Y.SHANNON- Rolling Fork.

Aug.8,1891

MISS EVA HARVEY recuperating from severe illness

DR. & MRS. CHAMPION paid a visit to R.F.

JNO.F.DINKINS was initiated into Mason.

Pioneer Lodge No.72, Knights of Pythias, held meeting in their Castle Hall,Anguilla,Ms. Lodge was instituted Mar.27,1891 with 19 charter members. Now number 39.

S.W.FERGUSON appointed Sec. & Treas. of Board of Ms.Levee Comm.

Aug.15,1891

CHRIS.LORENZEN applies for Liquor Li. for Lorenzen Station

GEORGE,from Columbus,& Robt.Foote of Macon, visit their uncle H.L.FOOTE in R.F.

MRS.WILL WAGGENER & children EMMA WAGGENER, ALICE BAGGETT, are guest of MESSERS G.M.&N.T.BAGGETT.

MRS.EMILY SHELBY visits in V'burg

Aug.22,1891

First bale of cotton brought in by WILL LANG,manager Helena Plt

MRS.R.K.CARR& children visit Centreville

LITTLE JEFFERSON UNDERHILL was first to have picture taken by visiting photographer Mr.Bell of G'ville.

MASTERS W.H.CLEMENTS & ARGYLE BROWN leave for Bell Buckle,Tenn. to attend school at Webb.

The new residence of HON.H.L.FOOTE on the Mound is nearly complete.

MISSES MARY HUBBELL,of Yazoo City,JENNIE BATTAILE of Anguilla visit R.F.

Aug.29,1891

PET.LIQ.LI. A.G.FLOYD-in Anguilla, 4th dist.

            W.F.WALKER- Egremont, 3rd "

            CHARLES A BREARD, town of R.F.

COTTON WORMS THREATEN CROPS

SCHEME TO SETTLE A COLONY OF GERMAN IMMIGRANTS IN THE SOUTH REALIZED.

PILOT WILL BE 8 YEARS OLD ON SEPT.8,1891

Sept.5,1891

D.H.MONTGOMERY has opened a school in old Union Church building

DEER CREEK PILOT

MISSES MATTIE BODIE & MINNIE HARREL left for Brownville,Tenn.to
to attend school.

LEE HAM rented the old drug store building and moved his stock
from the PEEK-A-BOO.

E.B.McCOMB,street supervisor,has a crew filling mud holes and
cleaning out ditches.

J.E.BUTLER is the established Undertaker

CIRCUIT COURT DECISIONS
    JERRY MYER-guilty of murder of GEO.HILL
    KIRBY BIRD guilty-shot R.R.conductor HOWARD at Egremont.
    ESSEX JOHNSON,WILLIS JOHNSON,JAS.PENWRIGHT,JOHN GREEN,guilty
      burning colored church Pleasant Green Baptist.
   JUDGE WASHINGTON, murder trial, cont.
    BANISTER WILLIS, assault--fined
    JOHN CHISHOLM-shooting on Hiway-fined
    J.A.C.SHRADER JR.-assault with intent to kill--cont.
    H.E.SHANNON-Pointing pistol,Assault & Battery---cont.
    ALFRED RUSHING-burglary-cont.
S.H.& W.P.SHRADER-carrying concealed weapon-plead guilty-fined
A number of citizens fined for retailing on Sunday and 1
couple for fornication.

Sept. 12,1891
MRS.JAS.D.BRAZIER of V'Burg visits her sister MRS.JNO.Q.ROBERTS
of R.F.

LITTLE MISS SARA BLUM of Nitta Yuma spent the week with MISS
ESTHER SINAI

FRED GRAFT appointed Alderman on resignation of DR.W.R.HARPER
Town of R.F.

Among arrivals on morning train, MISSES ANNIE & FANNIE CLEMENTS,
MRS.MARY H.BELL & JUDGE & MRS.H.W.FOOTE,Macon,Ms. & MRS.
PATTY & daughter of Atlanta,Ga.

JERRY MYER SENTENCED TO HANG FOR MURDER OF Geo.Hill.

Sept.19,1891
HON.WALTER McLAURIN visits R.F.

Hon.A.G.McLAURIN & son ANSOLOM JOE of Brandon visit R.F.

MRS.IDA ROBINSON is very ill at residence of CAPT.J.E.BUTLER.

THOS.McMAHON appointed agent for HillCity Oil Mills

Miss KATIE ELLIS returned to Bolton after 2mo.visit with relatives in Anguilla.

TALK OF CONSOLIDATING SHARKEY AND ISSAQUENA COUNTIES

REV.J.A.B.JONES pastor of Race Street Methodist Church.

DEER CREEK PILOT

REV.MR.ROBERTSON paster of Anguilla Methodist Church

Sept.26,1891
School proposal at meeting in Anguilla, organized by COL.W.T.BARNARD, to build a high school. Attending, Messers DINKINS, FLOYD,ROBERTSON,McKINNEY,WALTON, NEWITT VICK.

Oct.3,1891
MURDER of CHARLES S.DAVIS of Hollandale, bartender for W.W.MILLER. Mulatto girl,LOU STEVENS, lured him outside of bar & he was shot by black, GRANT WHITE. The colored man and woman were hung together from Cletonia Bridge.

Pet.Liq.Li.FRANK HIRSH-on mouth of Sunflower River,called L'Arge

WOLF AARON'S building being fitted for M.Y.SHANNONS saloon.

Oct.10,1891
MRS.WILLIAM BRITTON has returned from visit to her old home in Madison Co.[She was HELEN JOHNSTONE HARRIS'S SISTER]

Oct.24,1891
H.J.FIELDS lost his steam gin & quantity of cotton by fire.

J.G.PARHAM left for New Orleans to purchase stock for his new store. W.C.FARMER has accepted position with Parham.

R.A.MANN of Issaquena Co. has rented BAGGETT BRO'S.,ROBERTSONS place and the north store of Pilot building. Mann & family will be moving to R.F.

Oct.31,1891
DR.GEO.C.HARRIS is visiting Deer Creek, contemplating erecting handsome residence on mound at Helena Pltn.for his son,G.C.Jr

CORTRIGHT & ROBERTS gin nearly destroyed by fire.

ANGUILLA NOTES; MRS.MARION & MISS DOLLY BAGGETT of V'burg visit Mrs.McKINNEY

MISS SADIE THOMPSON of Percy,Ms. & friend MISS PIERCE of Memphis visit MRS. WILL BARNARD.

MISS GERTIE TAYLOR visits Bolton Fair.

MISS CORRINE MANN will preside over Steele Bayou School

MISS MAGGIE ANDERSON of Anguilla has charge of school near Holldale--she is the bright star of Womens Suffrage--W.C.T.U.

DEMOREST'S FAMILY MAGAZINE for Oct. published portraits and biographical sketches of a number of Southern Beauties. MISS MAMIE PHELPS(MARY PEARCE PHELPS) daughter of Dr.ALONZO J. PHELPS of Nitta Yuma. Mother is g.daughter of Maj.Burwell Vick. "She has rich & haughty beauty of a young duchess, a figure that is regally imposing. Wealth,attractive & prestig

DEER CREEK PILOT

have been an "Open Sesame" to the White House & uttermost parts of country. Her blonde beauty is universally extolled".

Nov.7,1891
Announced for Nov.12, Marriage between HON.J.H.McLAURIN & MISS WILLIE D.PAYNE of 527 Park.Ave. Hot Springs,Ark.

BOB Smith of Issa.Co. employed by H.L.FOOTE on "Council Bend"Plt. will move his family to Sharkey Co.

ANGUILLA NOTES:MR.FLOYD purchased Hardee Pltn. on Little Deer Creek but will remain in Anguilla.

COL.FIELD & DR.BARNARD contemplate building large gin and oil mill in Anguilla.

DAN ANDERSON visits son at Grace Station

MISS GERTIE TAYLOR & MR.DAVID FARR return from Bolton.

MR. H.J.McLAURIN WIll open a law office in G'ville

Pet.Liq.Li.S.H.HOGIN-Watsonia Station, 2nd Dist.

Nov.14,1891
THOS McMAHON hired CHAS.SCOTT of Crystal Springs as bartender

DAN L.MOORE & wife of Ky.will spend winter with family of H.L.FOOTE

Pet.Liq.Li.E.OSTROFFSKY-Cary-2nd dist. S.W.LEE -Georgiana Pltn.

Nov.21,1891
MRS.S.M.CORTRIGHT is home after summer in New York State.

E.B.McCOMB & family move to Lorenzen Station to work for C. LORENZEN & CO.

SHARKEY POP. CENSUS 1890-8,382- 1880, 6,306

Nov.28,1891
Pet.Liq.Li. BEN PEARL-Anguilla,Ms.,4th dist.

MISS MAGGIE ALLEN is visiting her twin sister MRS.Wm.ROBERTS.

MURDER:JNO.ADAMS killed GEO.HAMPTON at Lorenzen Station. They were arguing over 10¢ in a crap game.

Dec.12,1891
Pet.Liq.Li. H.W.PHILLIPS-on Sunflower River-1st dist.

B.GOODMAN,BYERLY CO.,& KLAUS BROS. have merged into CARY MERCANTILE CO.

MRS.ALICE JOHNSTON,daughter of MAJ.M.HAMBERLIN is the teacher for the R.F. school.

DEER CREEK PILOT

Jan.9,1892

Goodspeed Pub.Co. is enjoined from delivering their history of Ms. by Lowry & McCardle. They charge infringement of copy write law from their recent publication of Miss. history. Suit is for damages.

Pet.Liq.Li.-T.P.HOUSE-R.F. in present Thos.McMahon business opposite Court House square
    W.W.MANGUM- Smedes-1st dist.
    A.K.MARTAK-Anguilla-4th dist.

MR.JNO.R.BAGGETT has rented Dr.J.C.HALLS' Danover place near Egremont

MISS SADIE SAUNDERS of Ky. is visiting her uncle DR.A.MILLER at Panther Burn.

MRS.Geo.N.LANGFORD & MISS ANNIE LANGFORD,from Brandon, are visiting their son and brother S.W.LANGFORD[Ed.Pilot]

MR.J.C.BRUCE has rented the Parham Hotel. He is the former manager of Dr.Hall's MOUNT place at Grace Station.

MRS.GEORGIE UNDERHILL is building a neat cottage east of H.J. WRIGHT residence.

MR.GEO.HILLhas succeeded JNO.L.BRANSFORD as depot agent. Mr. Bransford returned to his home in Loanoke, Ark.

Installation of Masonic Lodge officers- Wm.PINFIELD,Worshipful Master; N.T.BAGGETT-Senior Warden: C.H.BLUM-Junior Warden: DR.W.M.CHAMPION-Sen.Deacon: Wm.MYERS, Jr.Deacon:D.C.CASEY, Sec.: MOSE SINAI,Treas.:J.A.DINKINS,Tyler.

PROF.JAS.H.RITTER,composer of the overture "Chicorea" had it played by the Emma Warren band. He intends publishing it for sale-it is dedicated to the Plantation formerly owned by his wife MOLLY KATE SHELBY RITTER-called Chicorea.

BUSINESS FAILURE OF TWO POPULAR FIRMS in 5th dist. J.A.C.SHRADER & J.T.MANOR. Short crops-low price cotton-poor collections forced them to the wall

The Pilot Opera House has presented entertainment to the people of the area, weekly.

The cornerstone of the new Jewish Temple in R.F was laid Mon. with appropiate ceremonies. The building when completed will cost $7,000.

Jan 23,1892

The Board of Supervisors will meet to pass on Liq.Li. of H.W. PHILLIPS of Campbellville.

MRS.GEO.C.HARRIS & MISS HELEN are guest at Mt.Helena.

DEER CREEK PILOT

Jan.30,1892
JAS.S.RICHARDSON was elected president by Stockholders of Miss.
  Mills, to fill vacancy of brother JOHN P.RICHARDSON,deceased.

COL.JOHN W. HEATHS gin at Shiloh,Issaq.Co. burned destroying
  70 bales cotton. It was the largest Gin House built since
  war in Issaq.Co.

Feb.6,1892
FRED GRAFT resident of Shark.Co.for a number of years, renounc-
  ed allegience to William the Second,Emperor of Germany, and
  declared allegience to U.S.-and was made a citzen of America
  at present term of Circuit Court. Fred has enjoyed this pri-
  viledge for many years--post master of R.F.--voted in elections-
  served on juries--his citzenship never had been questioned!

The site of the Episcopal Church has been decided upon & building will begin. Committee decided on lot offered by MRS.
  FANNIE BRITTON in East R.F.

Feb.13,1892
MASTER LOUIS BRITTON is visiting his Aunt MRS.ST.JOHN WILLIS
  at Panther Burn.[Mrs.Willis-nee META NICHOLSON-Louis Britton
  is son of LAURA NICHOLSON BRITTON & WILLIAM BRITTON,Jr.]

Feb.27,1892
Contract let for Episcopal Church to Hester Bros. Lumber now
  being place on lot East of rail road. Structure to be in
  shape of a Cross-will cost $1,500.

MRS.M.J.HARVEY is building a 2 room cottage on a lot East of
  rail road. J.A.DINKINS-contractor.

MRS.GEORGIA UNDERHILL'S cottage in East R.F. is completed.

MRS.JENNIE M.CAPERTON & MISS ANNIE CLEMENTS visit Editor Langford, Mrs.Caperton leaves for Forest,Ms. Sunday evening.

DR.JNO.LOWRY,Dentist, opens office in R.F.

Mar.9,1892
MRS.Wm.GIBBON visits her sister Mrs.CASEY.

COL.BROWN,on behalf of Ladies Aid Society of Episcopal Church,
  presented the Methodist Church with a silver service.

Pet.Liq.Li. J.E.GRIFFING & R.E.FLANAGAN-Cary-2nd dist.

Mar.26,1892
MRS.JOSIE PHELPS BRUCE,young pretty wife of P.P.BRUCE,proprie-
  tor of Parham Hotel[Jan.9,paper had him J.C.BRUCE] took Nitric
  Acid to kill herself. Mother called Drs.CHANEY & HARPER to
  save her. Mouth & Throat severely burned. Mrs.Bruce had previously tried to shoot herself.

DEER CREEK PILOT

Apr.2,1892
Born to MR.&MRS.SIDNEY W.LANGFORD Apr.2,1892, at 6:15, a son.

MRS.A.L.JOHNSTON visits father MAJ.HAMBERLIN at Onward.

Apr.23,1892
Story on "HELEN JOHNSTONES GUARDS"-only Company in the South during the recent war to be outfitted by a woman, as well as the bravest Co. in Confederate Army. Equipped with the best & at her own expense. Co.elected CAPT.E.C.POSTELL of Canton as its first Commander. Its first flag (from the Canton Courthouse)was presented by Helen. Later she visited her "Guards" at Co.E.,24th Ms.Reg.to which they were attached. Postell later wounded at Chickamauga.

PERCY POINTERS: MISS FANNIE WATSON arrived Mon.to visit her sister,MRS.HERBERT THOMPSON.

MR.THOS.McMAHON left for Jackson Sun.Night to make his future home.

Apr.30,1892
MR.Wm.MYERS & bride,nee ANNIE McLAURIN of Fayette,Ms. arrived & proceeded to their home on "Lexington Place"

MRS.W.E.COURTS & sister MAY MEEK, of Watsonia, visit their mother in BAY St.Louis.

May 14,1892
MRS.FANNIE BRITTON is with her son Wm.Britton at Mt.Helena

May 21,1892
Wm.BRITTON IS postmaster of new Post Office at Mt.Helena.

HON.L.C.DULANEY & JUDGE ROOT from Skipwith,Issq.Co.,report levees holding with average of 2½ ft.above water.

MR.J.T.MANOR visits daughter MRS.J.C.DENMAN at Fish Lake.

May 28 1892
MRS.HENRIE BARNARD, visited here from Anguilla,and upon her return home took MRS.J.G.PARHAM with her.

June 4 1892
W.H.CLEMENTS returned home from school at Bell Buckle,Tn.

W.L.LIPSCOMB is the manager of META PLTN.[Percy Pointers]

Messers CARNATHAN & LOWE of Nitta Yuma & Wm.LANG of Vickland, & Messers PARISH & MOSELEY of Panther Burn were in town Sun. The boys looked tough after withstanding the storm of Sat.night.

June 11 1892
RICE CROPS of 1892 exceed 1891 by 50%.Cotton offers so little margin of profit, many have taken up rice again.

LEROY PERCY,Esq. of G'ville & COL.STOVALL of Coahoma are delegates to Democratic Convention in Chicago.

DEER CREEK PILOT

RICHMOND DISPATCH;"Statement made by Mr.McCabe at dinner of
   alumni of University of Va....of 1200 students at Harvard
   50 volunteered for Union Army...of 650 students of U.of Va.
   515 entered Confederate Army. 200 died in the conflict."

THOS.McMAHON is back."Rather be in jail in R.F. than walk the
   streets of Jackson"

FISH LAKE: A.R.DENMAN visits brother J.C.DENMAN
   MR.& MRS.SANDERS of Vickland spent Sat.& Sun with Mrs.HALL
   their(?)mother.
   KATIE DUKE of Nitta Yuma visited her Uncle & Aunt the J.C.
   DENMANS & grandma MRS.R.L.DENMAN.
   MR.& MRS.A.ADAMS of Gum Ridge visited MR.& MRS.A.M.BOYKIN.
   J.T.MANOR of Vickland visited Fish Lake.

June 18 1892
MALCOLM CAMERON of Nitta Yuma brought in first cotton bloom

W.J.PEPPARD of Percy also brought blooms.

THE NEW EPISCOPAL CHURCH...long article with description of
   chruch. First services June 19. Conducted by Rev.Dr.G.C.
   Harris, assisted by Rev.McGuire.

MISS LENA NICHOLSON has returned from school in Salem, S.C.
   & is visiting sister MRS.Wm.(LAURA)BRITTON at Mt.Helena.

June 25,1892
L.M.NICHOLSON left for Livingston,Madison Co. to rest a month.

H.J.WRIGHT has purchased the cottage built by Mrs.Mollie Kate
   Shelby Ritter on Race street for $8oo.

MISS OLLIE ALEXANDER home from school at Clinton.

SEE NEXT PAGE FOR COMPLETE LIST OF REGISTERED VOTERS FOR '92

July 16 1892
MRS.I.A.CORTRIGHT left for Syracuse,N.Y.to visit her parents.

MISS LUCIA PARHAM recites at Anguilla school exercises.
JESSE FIELDS brought down the house as "Tom" in the school exercises as did LAURA FIELDS with her"Prompt Obedience"sketch.

MISS MAYMIE HARRIS,Hazelhurst is visiting family of Dr.E.C.CLEMENTS

MR.TOM McCAUL is temporarily replacing depot agent Hill.

July 30,1892
JOHN HARSH,excitizen of R.F. now resides in Memphis,Tn.

MRS.J.G.PARHAM and daughters are visiting in Amite City,La.

Aug.6 1892
DR.JAS.F.ARCHER,son of Rev.S.Archer of Greenville,a graduate
of the Uni.of Louisville,will locate in R.F. From Sunflower Co.

DEER CREEK PILOT.

PUBLISHED WEEKLY BY
S. W. LANGFORD.

Entered at the Postoffice at Rolling Fork, Miss., as Second-Class matter.

TERMS OF SUBSCRIPTION:

Single copy, one year.................$1.50
For six months........................ 1.00
For three months...................... .50

SATURDAY, JULY 9, 1892.

Advertising Rates:

Transient Advertisements, each inch, first insertion............................$1.50
Each subsequent insertion............. 1.00
Larger advertisements contracted for at the most liberal rates.
☞All advertisements due when inserted unless otherwise agreed upon.

REGISTERED VOTERS.

The following is a complete alphabetical list of the registered voters of Sharkey county as compiled by Registrar N. T. Baggett, and includes all who can vote, or try to vote, at the coming elections. Those marked (c) are colored.

SMEDES.

Anthony, R A (c)
Courts, W E
Dorsey, Augustus (c)
Eggleston, Geo W
Farrar, J T
Ford, E W ( )
Hamberlin, M
Houston, Stewart (c)
Houston, Squire (c)
Howard, A G (c)
Jackson, J W (c)
Jones, George (c)
Jones, Richard (c)
Jones, Benjamin (c)
Kagler, S T (c)
Mangum, W W
Matthews, Lenzy (c)
Mosley, Ed
McAlpin, R E
Ratliff, F L
Royal, C C (c)

SPANISH FORT.

Hirsch, Frank

PHILLIPS.

Bright, J M
Carroll, A W
Dudmon, R
Edmondson, J C
Gray, M T
Gray, J C
Hamberlin, S L
Jeffries, M L
Lucas, G W
Phillips, H W
Ross, John
Screws, J N
Sharbrough, J W
Sibley, C G
Watson, J J

CARY.

Addison, W J
Allen, Nathan (c)
Banks, Haywood (c)
Brooks, F P P (c)
Byerley, Frank
Clark, S N
Darden, G T
Davis, Geo W
Davis, J G
Deane, A A (c)
Flannagan, R E
Foreman, D J (c)
Freeman, T T
Gowin, W T
Golden, A J (c)
Goodman, H
Griffing, J E
Hawkins, G S (c)
Hunt, Omer
James, A E
Klaus, Ed
Mims, O C (c)
Mickey, D M (c)
McBanie, D W
Ostrofsky, J
Ostrofsky, S
Pickel, J W
Robinson, F R (c)
Saunders, N H
Saunders, J J
Standifer, W S
Williams, Andrew (c)
Williams, Culbert (c)

ROLLING FORK.

Baggett, J R
Baggett, N T
Baggett, G M
Batton, J A
Booth, H
Breard, C A
Brown, A E
Brown, W R
Brown, W D
Brown, D H (c)
Brown, Robt (c)
Bruce, R M
Bruce, P P
Brazil, L T (c)
Butler, J E
Byram, Brook (c)
Caldwell, J K (c)
Carr, B K
Casey, D C
Champion, G M
Chaney, Wm l
Clark, Wm (c)
Clements, E C
Cook, J H
Cortright, J H
Cortright, I A
Craig, Eli (c)
Dawson, W D (c)
Dinkins, J A
Dinkins, E
Farmer, W C
Foote, H L
Gibbons, Wm
Graft, Fred
Harper, W R
Harvey, T H (c)
Higgins, Westley (c)
Hilliard, Tom (c)
Houston, R W (c)
Inalee, E A
Isaiah, R P (c)
Junkins, Jerry (c)
Jolley, W A
Jones, Frank (c)
Jner, Jno S
Kelly, John
Langford, S W
Luckett, C N (c)
Martin, M C
Miller, Andy (c)
McLaurin, R L
McMahon, Thos
Neal, A L
Orendorff, T T
Parham, J G
Penny, Jos (c)
Powell, H J
Ratliff, D
Roberts, Benj
Roberts, Jno Q
Roberts, Wm
Rogan, C W
Rogan, L W
Rogers, P S
Rushing, W H
Shannon, M Y
Shannon, H E
Shelby, E B
Smith, C E
Sturgis, J B
Suggar, S S (c)
Swint, Pope (c)
Thornton, C (c)
Walker, Frank (c)
Walker, W F
Wiggins, R G (c)
Williams, S A (c)
Wright, H J

ANGUILLA.

Anderson, N R
Anderson, D N
Anderson, T J
Arnold, W A
Awtru, Hannibal (c)
Barnard, W T
Barnard, W B
Barnard, W H
Barnard, E G
Battaile, C M
Batton, J C
Britton, Wm
Brown, J T L
Butler, Eugene T (c)
Butler, Geo W (c)
Camero, M
Champion, W M
Chisholm, Jno R
Connell, W A
Crockett, W A
Crockett, C W
Dinkins, H L
Dinkins, Paul
Dover, S
Ellis, W T
Ervin, A L
Everidge, B J
Fields, H J
Fisher, C H (c)
Floyd, A G
Floyd, A J
Hall, J C
Hall, J R
Harris, Geo C Jr
Hendricks, J W
Henry, R M
Hickman, Geo B
Hollingsworth, J M
Ingraham, L W
Johnson, S A
Johnson, Bryant E (c)
Joshua, E W (c)
Lambertson, R T
Lane, G F
Lee, Richard
Lindsey, James
Lorenzen, C
Mahaffey, W B
Martack, A K
Martin, W T
Merrett, T J
Moore, F R
Murray, J B
Myers, F C
Myers, R S
McEnnery, Thos
McKinzey, W C H
McKinzer, H K
Orendorff, W A
Parham, H G
Patterson, Brimage (c)
Pearl, Ben
Pinfield, H
Price, Julius
Redmond, J M
Richardson, James (c)
Richardson, R E (c)
Sidney, L E (c)
Sinai, Julius
Sinai, M
Stevens, J Oscar
Stevens, Douglas
Stewart, W H
Taylor, J F
Walton, C H
Watson, J C
Webb, J E
White, C L
Wise, Frank (c)

VICKLAND.

Abbott, J D
Bennett, E T (c)
Bennett, Sandy (c)
Bennett, M G (c)
Blum, C H
Boykin, A G
Boykin, D P
Baykin, F B
Brabham, W C
Carnathan, O N
Cloud, M R
Cole, C U (c)
Coleman, Sutton (c)
Cooper, J E
Crump, R P
Downing, H R
Downing, O N
Duke, J W
Durst, John
Foster, Lewis (c)
Gayles, Johnson (c)
Gayles, Otis E (c)
Hogg, H M
Klein, B n
Long, J W
Long, Jas A
Manor, J T
Mhoon, Junius
Miller, A
Mooreland, Pat (c)
Moseley, R J
McCoy H B
Parish, K N
Parker, H J (c)
Phelps, A J
Phelps, H V
Price, T H
Rogers, J M
Rogers, Jno A
Saunders, A A
Savage, W E
Shrader, J A C
Shraler, W P
Shaader, S H
Slaughter, F R
Sylvester, W C
Sylvester, N B
Trim, T F
Weeks, J B
Williams, P
Williams, A J (c)
Wright, R L

STRAIGHT BAYOU.

Baker, Ed (c)
Chase, N C (c)
England, R O
Shrader, W H

Total number registered in county, 384. White, 210; colored, 74.

—Those who failed to register already have reason to regret it, as they cannot take part in the election which is sure to be called in a few days to vote for or against prohibition in this county.

DEER CREEK PILOT
Sept.10,1892
SHARKEY Co. votes dry Aug.9, by majority voters

WILLIE BRUMFIELD of Murphy Bayou, visited his Uncle R.L.WRIGHT on Vickland.

MR.W.H.SHRADER is erecting a new residence at Auter.

Sept.17 1892
Grace;J.P.TONNAR of Eagle Nest Store near Grace, contemplates a storehouse on east side of rail road opposite Mrs.Harvey's house.

Sept.24 1892
MRS.H.E.SHANNON & children visit her mother in Vicksburg.

MRS.PEARL HOGIN visited her brother S.J.CLARK at Cary on returning to N.Y. from ElPaso Tx.

Oct.1 1892
MISS VIRGIE BARNARD of Anguilla,visited MRS.J.G.PARHAM.

DR.ORENDORFF went to G'ville to help organize Miss.Delta Medical Association.

Oct.22 1892
There was a small fire in the fine gin of CAPT.CAMERONS on "Weeping Willow" near Nita Yuma.

Oct.29,1892
MRS.M.C.MARTIN was thrown from a spring wagon by runaway horses. Dr.Orendorff hopes her injured spine will not be permanent.

Saw mill & gin of CORTRIGHT & ROBERTS near the depot was destroyed by fire. Gin was in receivership due to suit filed & pending court action.

Nov.12 1892
GEO.C.HARRIS JR.is now conducting a wholesale brokerage business in New Orleans.

Nov.19 1892
CLEVELAND GOING TO WHITE HOUSE & MIDDLING COTTON TO 12¢

SAM FARMER OF Rocky Springs,Claib.Co.Ms.visiting brother W.C. FARMER

It is probable that CAPT.& MRS.JOHN WILLIS & MRS.ST.JOHN WILLIS will make Vicksburg their home in future.

Dec.3 1892
Work was commenced on the Public School building in R.F.Mr.Dinkins is the contractor

MRS.ALICE M.SCHMIDT proprietress of Delta Hotel.

Dec.24 1892
R.M.SMITH,manager for H.L.FOOTE,will move back to Issaq.Co.

DEER CREEK PILOT
PETER MATHYS OF Issaq. rented part of "Forked Deer"and moved
   here.
Dec.31st last issue in this binder.

MARRIAGES TAKEN FORM THE DEER CREEK PILOT-1891-1892

Sept.26 1891
Married at residence of JOHN TURNER,Straight Bayou,Sept.22,1891
   by Rev.IRA B.ROBERTSON----Rev.J.W.JONES to MRS.J.E.PORTER.

MR.CHRIS HAUSER to MRS.LUCINDA JOLLY Aug.9 1891 by C.H.WALTON,JP
   at residence of groom on Sunflower River.

Oct.3 1891
JAS.W.ALEXANDER,editor of Mayersville Spectator, to MISS ATTIE
   WILLIAMS, daughter of Rev.& MRS.F.M.WILLIAMS at Methodist
   church, Tyrns,Ms. Oct.7,1891

JOHN F.DINKINS to MISS DREW COWAN,daughter of CAPT.E.D.COWAN
   Oct.8,1891 at Canton Ms. Methodist Church by Rev.T.B.HOLLIMAN

JENNIE M.DeBERRY to E.M.CAPERTON at Cruger,Holmes Co.Ms.Oct.8,189

Oct.101891
FRANK BYERLY of Cary to JUANITA H.PURDY, at residence of J.P.
   HAYS Esq. on "Bradford Pltn" Issaq.Co. Oct.7,1891

MR.TILLMAN SORRELL(conductor on Riverside train)to ELLA CAMMACK
   at Tuscumbia, Ala. Sept.16,1891

Nov.7,1891
Announced for Nov.12-marriage between Hon.J.H.McLAURIN & MISS
   WILLIE D.PAYNE of 527 Park Ave.,Hot Springs Ark. The big
   write up is in Nove.21 paper.N.T.Baggett-best man.Wedding
   took place in Hot Springs,Ark.

Nov.14 1891
Announcement-NAT RATCLIFF to LAURA D. WEST-Nov.18 1891 at "Oak
   Grove" Ms.

Nov.28 1891
Wm.ROBERTS to MATTIE ALLEN at "Old Auburn" residence of brides
   father near Learned,Ms. Nov.24,1891 by Rev.N.J.ROBERTS,of Utic

Jan.23 1892
MAMIE PHELPS daughter of DR.A.J.PHELPS of Nitta Yuma to PETER
   GEORGE of Chicago,Ill. Jan.20,1892 at the brides home. Rev.
   Wm.CROSS of G'ville officiated. MARY PHELPS sister of bride
   was maid of honor. HENRY GEORGE,brother of groom,best man.
   Couple to make home in Chicago where Mr.George is a wealthy
   & prominent manufacturer.

Feb.27 1891
MRS.STEVENS,widow of late CAPT.JOEL STEVENS to Mr.LANE,Feb.21
   1892 by Rev.Keene

MARRIAGES-DEER CREEK PILOT
Mar.26,1892

The following article was so blatant and typical of the reporting of the time, I could not resist including it here.

ELOPEMENT

The old saying that"Love,that mischievious god, laughs at locksmiths" was again verified last Monday night, when MR.B.F. TISDALE & MISS LINNIE C.LUSK eluded the vigilance of stern parents and were united in the happy bonds of wedlock in the parlor of the Delta Hotel, Dr.P.S.ROGERS,of this place,officiating,with MR.J.N.CRAWLEY,the popular night operator of the L.N.O.&T.office and MISS BESSIE DAVIS,both of this place,as attendants.

Mr. Tisdale has for the past year been depot agent at Erwin's Station onRiverside Div.and Miss Lusk is one of the Beauties of Lake Washington.

They were assisted in the elopement by MISS KATIE DUNCAN, of Hampton, who came down to see the knot well tied. The happy couple left on the midnight train for a short visit to Baton Rouge, the former home of the groom, and Miss Duncan returned to her home Tuesday morning to break the news gently.

It only remains for the parents of the runaway bride to bless their children and join the guest in wishing them "many happy returns". [paper pub.onSat.so date of wed.Mar.21,1892]

Apr.9 1892
J.E.GRIFFING of Cary to OLLIE McCARTNEY of Roxie,Ms.Apr.6,1892

Apr.16,1892
JNO.W.WILLIAMS of Warren Co.Ms. to MRS.BELLE STEVENS,Apr.17
   at Hollands Ldg. on Sunflower River.

May 8 1892
DR.JNO.L.DODGE,formerly of Pantherburn,now of Bolivar Co. Married
   May 5,1892 FANNIE MAY RICHARDSON of Bolivar Ldg.

Runaway marriage at Kent Hotel, May 6, between JAMES COTTLE &
   MARY EDWARDS of Silver Creek,Sunflower Co., by Mayor Butler
   of RollingFork.

May 28 1892
MR.R.T.DINKINS of Mayersville to MRS.DUTY of Memphis-in Memphis
   May21,1892

Sept.24,1892
LOWRY LAMB,grandson of Gov.Lowry, eloped with MISS IRENE LYERLY
   of Jackson, Sept.23,1892

Oct.1,1892
MISS MARY DePERRIN daughter of MRS.E.O.PERRIN of Parkland,Ky.
   niece of Dr.T.T.& Mrs.W.A.ORENDORFF WILL be married next
   Wednesday to THOS.C.CLYCE of Louisville,Ky.

Cards are out for the marriage of MISS LOTTIE OHLEYER TO DR.
   B.GOODMAN for Oct.5,1892 at Brandon,St.Lukes Epis.Church
[WRITE UP OF THIS WEDDING IN Oct.15 paper.Rev.H.W.ROBINSON
   officiated- Best man A.C.HUNT of Cary.-LALLIE LAMB,music-
   Bride given away by brother E.H.OHLEYER. MARY MASSIE-atten-
   dant as was DR.D.T.DARDEN. Brides mother-MRS.JOHN OHLEYER]

MARRIAGES DEER CREEK PILOT-1891-1892

Dec.3,1892
Wm.K.McLAURIN to MISS WILLIE C.ADEN at brides brothers home,H.B. ADEN in Valley Park,Ms. Nov.29,1892,by Rev.IRA B.ROBERTSON.

Dec.24 1892

Hymeneal*

The central thought for weeks in our little city has been the approaching nuptials of MR.N.T.BAGGETT & MISS ANNIE CLEMENTS.Miss Annie is the daughter of our esteemed townsman, DR.E.C.CLEMENTS,and has as an inheritage, a rare charm of mind and person, possessing all those qualities that go to make up a true,noble,christian woman. Modest and retiring in her disposition, her real worth is only known and appreciated by those who see her in her daily walks of life. To know her is to love her and those who know her best love her most.

Mr. Baggett has for a number of years filled the office of Circuit and Chancery Clerk of Sharkey county, and is an honored citizen and withal a christian gentleman. He comes from an old and honored Alabama family.

At 7:30 o'clock on the evening of Dec.21st, at the Methodist Church in Rolling Fork, the fond dream of two loving hearts was realized,and the brilliant wedding will form a beautiful background for a perfect picture of domestic bliss. The church was beautifully decorated by loving hands for the occasion, and never did a Queen look more queenly than did the bride. So fair, somodest, blushing under a silken veil. The ceremony was performed by Rev.F.M.KEENE in his own beautiful graceful style.

After the ceremony the invited guests retired to the residence of the brides's parents where a reception was held. The supper was grand. If a King could have stepped in he would have thought Mrs.Clements an adept in the culinary art, so successful was she in suiting the tastes of the most fastidious. The popularity of the happy couple was evidenced by numerous and elegant gifts from friends at home and abroad. Of all their friends who bring offerings of good will and congratulations none can be more sincere than the writers. May all the blessings that their mutual love can give be theirs throughout a long life, in which their moments of happiness may be like the dew drops of Heaven or the sands of the seashore, without number,and may they have "just enough clouds intheir life to bring on a glorious sunset."

¶* Hymeneal sent me to the dictionary:hy'me.ne.al,adj.-of a wedding or marria also hy'me.ne'an.noun-a wedding song or poem.
The writer of this article was obviously a good friend and admirer of this couple, for I found no other writeup that came close to this one in the flowery language, praise and detail.....almost a love song, or poem.
I had to share it with you readers.   A.W.

DEATH NOTICES-DEER CREEK PILOT-A WEEKLY NEWSPAPER-Aug.1,1891-Dec.31,1892 -Pub.on Sat. S.W.LANGFORD-Editor.

Aug.22,1891
Adm.Notice-J.P.WALKE,deceased Dec.21,1881.T.T.Orendorff,Adm.

R.F.BECK,ex-mayor of Vicksburg decd.Aug.19,1891. Age 48 & from New York.

Sept.12,1891
FLOYD PIERCE,son of F.G.PIERCE of Smedes Station.

Sept.19,1891
W.H.PERRIN,bro-in-law of Dr.T.T. & W.A.ORENDORFF,decd. at Parkland ,Ky. in his home.

MRS.T.P.SHELTON died of child birth at El Paso,Tx. Sept.14,1891 Mr.Shelton,a former resident of Sharkey Co.Ms. took her body to her home in Va.for burial.

Oct.3,1891
MRS.S.V.SHELTON died Sept.21,1891 at residence of son-in-law J.R.KIRKLAND on Oakley Pltn.Issaquena,Co.Ms. She was 67-maiden name OIVES-born near LaGrange,Tn. She was the widow of the late REV.J.H.SHELTON,to whom she was married at her fathers home in Anguilla,Ms. in 1858. A member of MEC South. Burial in Mayersville,Ms.

MISS SALLIE MAXWELL,niece of Mrs.JENNIE STEVENS-19 Sept.1891 Shaw,Ms.

Oct.17,1891
Mrs.IDA W.ROBERTSON,died Oct.11,1891,interred in family burial ground.

Oct.31,1891
PRENTISS STEVENS-32 died Oct.30,1891 in hospital in Vicksburg.

THOMAS FOOTE,son of Judge H.W.FOOTE of Macon,Ms.killed by accidental discharge of gun at own hand. He had loaded the pistol for his wifes protection against another tramp,and while passing through the room with harness on the floor, he tangled his feet,fell,and pistol discharged a bullet to his brain-instant death. He was a brother to H.L.FOOTE & MRS.DR.CLEMENTS (ANN FOOTE) of Rolling Fork,Ms.

Nov.14,1891
S.W.WATTS died Nov.6,1891. Interred Redwood,Ms. Young widow returned to home of father in La.

Nov.28,1891
CAPT.JOEL O.STEVENS died Tues.Nov.24 at his home on Sunflower River. Burial at family residence, with Masonic honors. He leaves a wife and 7 children(unnamed)

Dec.12,1891
CAPT.JOHN E.HOGIN died at Hotel Piazza Dec.8,1891. 50 years old,native of Jackson Co.Tn. Leaves a wife,2 sons, 4 daughters. 1 bro. ALEX A.HOGIN, 1 Sister,THURLA HOGIN.Funeral at Bethany church, Redwood,Ms.

LAURA BELL BRYANT, INFANT dau.of J.A.BRYANT,Dec.10 at Vickland.

DEATH NOTICES-DEER CREEK PILOT

Jan.9,1892
C.W.,son of CHRIS LORENZEN. Burial in Vicksburg

Jan.23,1892
CAPT.J.P.HAYS,died at Hays Landing,his residence,Issaquena Co.
   Jan.22,1892. He was 35 years old. His wife, who is the sister
   of H.H.DAVIS of Brunswick, survives him. He was a son of
   Judge Hays, late of Issaq.Co.

Mar.5,1892
Wm.GOODMAN died a week ago, and was buried by his brother Jonas
   GOODMAN in Greenville.
Mar.19,1892
M.Y.SHANNONS twin baby boy died Mar.18 & the little girl is
   dangerously ill.
May 14,1892
DUNCAN FARISH,7 yr.old son of MR.& MRS.W.S.FARISH,died May 12
   Interred at Natchez
June 4,1892
Wife of REV.G.T.STORY died May 31,1892 in Greenville
July 9,1892
THOS.D.McCALEB died July 8,1892 at Byrne,Tx. He left Vicksburg
   for Texas several weeks ago for his health. He died of con-
   sumption. W.D.McCALEB is the only surviving son of J.M.McCALEB
   3 of the boys having died in the last 7 years. Funeral held
   in Presby.Church in Vicksburg.

Aug.13,1892
JNO.C.DENMAN-36 yrs.old died Aug.6,1892. Interred at Vickland
   Cemetery. His widow survives him. Suicide at his home on
   Fish Lake, Shark.Co.Ms.
Aug.20,1892
C.D.ELLINGTON died Aug.18,1892 age 27 of hematuria.[OBIT:in
   theSept.24,1892 issue says:He was born in Utica,Ill. He died
   at his mothers home in Shark.Co. where he had been a resident
   of 20 years. His father and sister had previously died of
   hematuria]
Sept.17,1892
COL.LOVE, Wash.Co.Ms. Uncle of R.L.McLAURIN of Rolling Fork,Ms.
   died Sept.15,1892
Oct.1,1892
MRS.ELIZA McDANIEL died at residence of Wm.BRITTON,Mon.night
   and was buried at Union Graveyard, Anguilla,Ms. Wed. She
   had been an invalid for several months.(Paper pub.on Sat.)
Oct.15,1892
MRS.MOLLIE LANE, widow of Capt.Joel O.Stevens, died at her home
   near Holland landing this week.
Oct.22,1892
GEORGIE ROBERTS,small dau. of MR.& MRS.JNO.Q.ROBERTS died Oct.16.
OCT.29,1892
OBIT.OF ST.JOHN WILLIS-grandson of Maj.Henry Vick,founder[*] of
   Vicksburg,and descendent of 4th generation of Col.Harry Wash-
   ington,Revolutionary Soldier, thru the WINTER & RICKS family.
Wife is META NICHOLSON, of Madison Co.Ms. Willis deceased at
   Panther Burn, his home Oct.23,1892. Buried in Memphis from
   Christ Church. Parents Mr.& Mrs.John Willis, living.
*¶Newitt Vick founded Vicksburg.

EXCERPTS FROM THE DEER CREEK PILOT, A WEEKLY NEWSPAPER, SOCIETY COLUMNS. Pub.IN ROLLING FORK, MS.SHARKEY CO.Jan.7,1899-Dec.21, 1900. THOS.W.CAMPBELL,EDITOR,.Pub.every Sat.until Mar.10,1899, then on Friday.

Jan.7,1899
MISS GERTRUDE PARHAM has returned to Grenada to school.

BEN STURGIS will manage Baconia Pltn. next year.

REV.H.M.VANHOOK will be the Metho.Minister another year.

A ferry will soon be established at Hollands Landing.

BOARD OF SUPERVISORS:W.H.BARNARD,Pres.;E.KLAUS,B.L.BARNES,A.L. NEAL,M.HAMBERLIN. Co.Supt.of Ed. JOHN S.JOOR

United Daughters of the Confederacy meets every Mond.at 4 PM at home of MRS.J.S.JOOR,Pres.

Jan.14,1899
MRS.L.R.STEVENS visits her daughter MRS.WILL BARNARD in Anguilla.

MISS ALICE BAGGETT of Vicksburg is visiting the family of N.T. BAGGETT in Rolling Fork.

MRS.DINKINS is visiting her g'daughter MRS. W.E.STEVENSON.

MRS.W.A.JOLLEY gave a dinner party, in honor of the Natal day of her sister,MRS.H.L.FOOTE. Guest;Mesdames FOOTE, WALKER, HARPER, GOODMAN, MOSELY, McLAURIN,& MISS DARBY.

OLIVER CATCHINGS,son of GEN.T.C.CATCHINGS, is now a member of law firm CATCHINGS, HUDSON & CATCHINGS in Vicksburg.

Jan.21,1899
BURRUS SHANNON has moved to the CLEMENTS place at Egremont,Ms.

MRS.H.H.BOOTH(e)gave a candy pulling party for her nephew A.B. SIMS,who left for Newport News,Va. his future home.

MR.H.BOOTH(e)is the manager of D.L.MOORE Land & Lumber Co.of Lorenzen.

Rev.H.M.VANHOOK & family returned home with Mrs.VanHook's brother M.ORMAND,with them. He will remain here reading law under Messers McLAURIN & CLEMENTS

Misses THEODORE & MINNIE WALTON have been visiting their Uncle C.H.WALTON

Jan.28,1899
W.G.SWAYZE has rented Dr.HAMBERLINS place.

MRS.HATTIE WANDELL of N.Y. is visiting Uncle I.A.CORTRIGHT.

M.RUSSELL bought the HALL place which was occupied by H.L.FOOTE.

DEER CREEK PILOTS SOCIETY NOTES-1899-1900

MRS.T.W.CAMPBELL & ELLEN & LOUDOUN visit relatives in Vicksburg.

FRANK BYERLY announces candidacy for Co.Treasurer

W.P.DAWSON announces candidacy for Sheriff

DR.S.T.HAMBERLIN leaves Rolling Fork, for Cuba. He has received a hospital appointment.

W.E.COURTS announces for Sheriff.

Feb.11,1899
While passing an open grate Thrus.Morn., the clothing of MISS CORINNE PARHAM took fire & before extinquished she was painfully but not dangerously burned. DR.HARPER dressed the wounds & the young lady is doing well at this writing.

Feb.18,1899
MISS MARY BACON MOORE of Ky. is visiting her brother D.E.MOORE

PROF.N.B.HINTON IS a candidate for Supt.Ed.
W.P.SHACKLEFORD "   "   "   "   Tax Assessor
W.A.CROCKETT   "   "   "   County Treas.
C.H.WALTON   "   "   "   County Clerk
GEO.WEST & THOMAS McMahon   "   Sheriff
DR.A.MILLER   "   Representative

Feb.25,1899
WILL GOODMAN of Cary visits Rolling Fork.

R.C.PATTY of Macon,Ms. is visiting his uncle Hon.H.L.FOOTE

MRS.ROCENA YANCY of Coldwater,Ms. is visiting her daughter MRS. J.E.MEEK

Friends of MISS CORINNE PARHAM willbe pleased to learn she has recouperated from effects of her late accident.

CAL JOHNSON has gone in the cotton business with out procuring a license. He was caught stealing lint cotton on the Pltn. of CAPT.JOHN WILLIS at Percy & is closely studying the market reports from jail.

Mar.4,1899
The State Auditors office is receiving many applications for redemption of land sold for taxes Mar.1. A body of 5,500 acres of Delta land in Sharkey Co. was redeemed by MRS.BELLE KUPPENHEIMER of Chicago.,Ill. Accrued Taxes & Cost--$1,732.85

The plantation residence of NAILOR ROACH at Valley,Ms., 8 mi.from Yazoo City, was destroyed by fire.

SARGEANT STEPHENSON,of the 3rd Ms., who has been visiting his brother W.E.STEPHENSON,returned to his regiment in Ga. soon to be mustered out.

DEER CREEK PILOTS SOCIETY NOTES 1899-1900

DR.J.T.TAYLOR,formerly of Sharkey Co., now a resident of LaGrange Ky. visited friends here this week.

H.E.SHANNON had a small fire in his residence.

CLUB NEWS:
QUI VIVE CLUB met with MISS BESSIE TAYLOR.Choice music by MISS CORINNE PARHAM, recital by MISS KATIE JOOR,songs by CARRIE SHANNON(this club for very young ladies)
THE OLD MAIDS CLUB(for young ladies)
THE FORTNIGHTLY CLUB for the young married ladies.

Mar.10,1899--Pilot now issued on Friday.
MRS.D.B.MOORE's sister MRS.BUSTER of Ky. is visiting.

MRS.DINKINS left to join her sons in Waverly,La. her future home.

M.D.LANDAU,trustee, sold the NANCY V.CHISHOLM property to J.SINAI & SON for $2,000.

MRS.A.HUNT entertained a number of friends at her home in Cary,Ms in honor of her husbands birthday.

Mar.17,1899
By-line Vicksburg- At the sale Wed. of the JAS.S.RICHARDSON estate in Bolivar Co.,the entire landed interest of the "Dahomey" and other pltn. were bid in by P.M.HARDING of this place for the Equity Sec.&Mortg.Co.of N.Y. Lands sold contain 20,000 acres in cultivation.

MRS.BARNEY MARION & MISS BAGGETT spent Sund.with their sister, MRS.W.H.C.MCKINNEY at Anguilla,Ms.

Farewell reception given MRS.H.L.FOOTE by MRS.H.J.McLAURIN with members of the Fortnightly Club assisting.

Mar.24,1899
MRS.BURRUS SHANNON was appointed postmistress at Egremont upon the resignation of H.L.FOOTE

JOHN BAGGETT & JESSE FIELDS of the 3rd Ms.reg. were mustered out of service last week.

HON.L.C.DULANEY of Issaq.Co.announces for the Senate.

Though HON.H.L.FOOTE & family have left R.F. it is gratifing to friends to know they will have gone but a short distance. Mr. Foote closed a deal Sat.by which he became owner of that magnificent residence & pltn. known as the Dudley Place (Mount Holly,built by Margaret Johnson Erwin Dudley in '58) on Lake Washington.

Mar.31,1899
MR.& MRS.W.H.MALLET will make their future home in Nitta Yuma.

JOHN BAGGETT Jr. has gone to Waverly where he will manager store for his uncle.

DEER CREEK PILOTS SOCIETY NOTES-1899-1900

MRS.D.B.MOORE & sister MISS THERESE BUSTER left for Harrodsburg, Ky. to visit their parents.

Apr.8,1899
MRS.GLOVER of Ala. is guest of daughter MRS.W.F.WALKER of Egremont

MISS LAURA FIELDS is visiting relatives in St.Louis.

May 5,1899
DR.CLEMENTS contemplates making extensive alteration to his residence on Race Street. Adding another story and other changes Family will live with his son-in-law H.J.WRIGHT during remodeling. R.T.LEDBETTER is the contractor.

May 12,1899
Charleston S.C.--"The burning of GEN.WADE HAMPTONS residence near Columbia,S.C.,has excited warm sympathy through out the state and a conference has already been had here to take immediate steps toward replacing the structure.

MISS MARGIE FIELDS has returned from school at Blue Mountain.

MRS.ALEXANDER has as her guest,her son J.R.ALEXANDER & wife

MRS.& MRS.CLIFTON R.HOOD of Wash.Co. passed thru Sun.on way home, Mrs.Hood is the former LALAH DINKINS of this Co.

MRS.H.J.McLAURIN left for a visit with her mother in Hot Springs Ark.

J.M.BRIDGES' mother from Bolton is visiting.

MRS.PRENTISS BROWN of New Orleans is visiting COL.& MRS.BROWN.

May 26,1899
Invitation from MISS CORNELIA CASEY to attend commencement exercises at Blue Mountain June 7 & 8

MRS.& MRS.CHARLES CROCKETT & children left for their home in Greenwood after visitings parents in Anguilla.

June3,1899
MISS DORA CROCKETT is visiting her brother W.A.CROCKETT

MRS.W.E.STEVENSON & daughter MRS.CAMERON & MISS RUBY MANN have returned from a visit to Hinds Co.

MRS.THOMAS McMAHON left for Grenada Mon. to attend commencement exercises of the school which her sister Gertrude Parham attends.

June 9,1899
MISSES CORNELIA CASEY,SARA ALEXANDER, LADY BARNARD who have been attending Blue Mountain school,return home.

DEER CREEK PILOT SOCIETY NOTES-1899-1900

MISS ORA MANN has as her guest her cousins MISS FLORA BELL SIMPSON of Flora,Ms. & MAE FERGUSON of Ft.Worth,Tx.

June 16,1899
MRS.HATTIE WANDELL,after a visit of several months with her uncle I.A.CORTRIGHT, has returned to her home in New York.

PROF.W.PRENTISS BROWN & wife of Tulane University, are spending his vacation with parents Col.& MRS.W.D.BROWN.

Contractor LEDBETTER is rushing the work on CLEMENTS residence, and expects to have it ready in a few weeks.

FOR RENT-a store & dwelling combined-N.J.VICK,Anguilla,Ms.

June 23,1899
Work on the Vicksburg Nat.Military Park began Friday.Mr.G.C.HAYDEN assigned to this work by MAJ.WILLARD, commenced laying it off Sat.-beginning at the Warrington road on lands obtained from MRS.SALLIE MOSBY.

June 30,1899
COL.J.R.HALL is visiting his daughter in Texas.

RAY & JOHN BREARD of Fla.are visiting parents the C.A.BREARDs.

MISS NOLA MONTGOMERY has been visiting relatives in Madison Co.

MRS.S.T.HAMBERLIN & children leave for Canton to spend summer with her sister MRS.JOHN R.CAMERON.

EGREMONT NOTES:B.H.SHANNON's sister MRS.MULLINS from Tallulah, La.is visiting him for several weeks.

MRS.J.B.STURGIS has as her guests,2 sisters from Grace,Ms.

July 14,1899
WILLIE & GREEN WAGGENER are visiting their uncle G.M.BAGGETT.

MRS.L.W.ROGAN & family returned to Vicksburg after spending several days here with her son IRBY ROGAN.

July 21,1899
MRS.MARY PARHAM & daughter MRS.LUCIA BAKER are visiting the family of J.G.PARHAM.

Mesdames HILL, STEVENSON, HARPER, McLAURIN, GOODMAN, McMAHON,& BAKER of Trimble,Tenn. & MISS ALICE BAGGETT left Thurs.morn. to attend the Dinning given by MRS.H.L.FOOTE of Dudley,Ms. to the members of the Fortnitely Club.

July 28,1899
C.LORENZEN is leaving the Co.his friends regret to hear. MAJ.H.M. PEMBERTON has bought all of the real estate owned by Lorenzen & Co. at Lorenzen, including the gin house,store etc.
Nov.3 paper says-Lorenzen family will move to R.F. & occupy cottage on Deer Creek above the Sinai residence.

ISRAEL BORODOFSKY, IKE BERNSTEIN,HENRY KLEIN were admitted to citizenship at this term of Circuit Court.

DEER CREEK PILOT SOCIETY NOTES-1899-1900

Aug.4,1899
Contractor LEDBETTER will build a new store for C.H.BLUM,on the GWIN place near Grace,Ms. & move the old store over the line into Wash.Co.

Aug.11,1899
Delta Hotel changes hands;MRS.A.M.SCHMIDT & sister EMMA REDMOND sold to MR.& MRS.A.L.DENMAN. Mrs.Schmidt moves to Louisville Ky. Miss Redmond to Hot Springs, Ark.

Aug.18,1899
COL.D.C.CASEY spent Sund.in Hollandale with brother HON.J.T.CASEY

MRS.H.J.FIELDS & family returned home Wed.from a stay at Cooper's Well.

DR.ALBERT McLAURIN of Brandon,visited his brother here,accompanied by Dr.BERRY of Jackson,son-in-law of Gov.MCLAURIN.

Aug.25 1899
BRYCE ALEXANDER of New Orleans,La.is visiting mother.

MRS.MOORE of V'burg is visiting her brother W.A.JOLLEY

We are pleased to learn M.C.MARTIN & daughter MISS MAUD are recovering from a recent illness.

Sept.1,1899
W.I.CHANEY of R.F. offers a store for lease at Lorenzen.

Sept.8,1899
MRS.JAMES R.CLARK & son of Oneonta, La.are visiting MRS. G.L.UNDERHILL

Sept.15,1899
MISS KATE VICK,sister of N.J.VICK continues very ill in V'burg

H.L.DINKINS & wife of Waverly,La. are visiting DR.J.C.HALL

W.P.DAWSON formerly with Blum Co. is now with DAWSON, WINTERS of Panther Burn.

MISS SUNSHINE CLEMENTS left for Cleveland,Tn.to attend school accompanied by brother W.H.CLEMENTS who will spend a few weeks at Look Out Mt.

MISSES GERTRUDE & CORINNE PARHAM who left Sun.eve.for school at Oxford did not get any further than V'burg. A case of yellow fever in Jacksonprevented trains from stopping there. (in the next issue they left on Thurs.for Oxford via Elizabeth Ms. accompanied by mother MRS.J.G.PARHAM.

Sept.22,1899
MRS.H.E.SHANNON has as a visitor, her mother Mrs.WILLIAMS of Warren Co.

MRS.CAMERON is with her sister MRS.ROBT.MANN of G'ville who is very ill.

Sept.29,1899
Deputy Sheriff DAVE FARR visits relatives in Hinds Co.

DEER CREEK PILOT SOCIETY NOTES-1899-1900

J.W.SHARBROUGH of Patmos,passed thru town on way to V'burg.

MISS MARY ORENDORF won a scholarship to Industrial Institute& left for Columbus Ms. Mon.Night.

MISS OLLIE ALEXANDER& MISSES IDA & LADY BARNARD are at Blue Mt.Coll.

The record in the case of A.C.WADDILL vs S.L.HALL,et al, just completed and sent to Jackson. Covers 218 typed pages, 63,609 words. Took the clerk a month to complete. The largest record ever sent to Supreme Court from Sharkey Co.

Oct.6,1899
Board of Supervisors Notice to contractors for bids to build a school house at Cary,Ms.

GEO.C.HARRIS Jr.& wife are located at Mt.Helena for the winter.

MRS.ROBT.FLANAGAN of Cary,after a protracted visit to relatives in Ark. has returned home.

Oct.20,1899
MRS.FRANCIS MARRIOT,formerly of this Co.now lives in Saffordville, Kan.

DR.S.T.HAMBERLIN is attending his ill father MAJ.H.HAMBERLIN at Onward,Ms.

MRS.H.J.McLAURIN's mother MRS.M.E.PAYNE of Hot Springs,Ark. will spend the winter with her.

Oct.27,1899
DR.SAMP GOODMAN & wife arrived in Cary,Ms. Fri. from Va.

C.E.HEARN, Manager of Telephone Co. in Pine Bluff Ark. is visiting the family of his uncle N.T.BAGGETT.

Nov.3,1899
MRS.DUNCAN of Yazoo City was a visitor to her uncle H.J.WRIGHT. she is enroute to Richmond Va. & the convention of Daughters of the Confederacy.

GOV.McLAURIN has granted a pardon to J.A.C.SHRADER Jr., on condition he never indulge in intoxicating liquors or carry pistol.

Nov.10,1899
CAPT.W.W.MOORE of Watsonia, visited R.F.

HON.A.Y.GLOVER of Ala.has been visiting daughter MRS.W.F.WALKER of Council Bend Pltn. Mr.Glover was at one time a resident of the Delta and law partner & brother-in-law of the late SEN.ALCORN.

Contract for schoolhouse in Cary was awarded to S.J.BOZEMAN:$1440.

DEER CREEK PILOT SOCIETY NOTES-1899-1900

Nov.17,1899
MISS CARRIE SHANNON departs for Iuka,Ms. to enter normal school.

COL.D.C.CASEY closed deal on Lorenzen property. 1,000 acres-400 cleared & in cultivation.

Nov.24,1899
M.C.MARTIN willbe located at Mt.Helena next year.

MRS.H.J.McLAURIN & mother MRS.PAYNE spent several days in Mayersville with MRS.L.C.DULANEY.

Dec.1,1899
Middling cotton now bringing 7 to 16¢ a lb. with a firm market & prices looking upward.

Dec.22,1899
MRS.G.C.HARRIS spent several days here with her son at Mt.Helena.

M.MOORE of Harrodsburg,Ky.,returned home Thur.after a few days visit with his cousin D.B.MOORE.

Dec.29,1899
H.P.GREER went to Coldwater to visit parents.

J.W.SHARBROUGH & family spent Sun.here with MR.& MRS.C.W.BREARD. Mrs.Sharbrough & Children left for Natchez to spend holidays with her mother.

Jan.5,1900
NOTICE: The Blum Co.,Nitta Yuma-MRS.R.BLUM,M.A.BLUM & C.H.BLUM have purchased all interest of the CAMERON Est. & MALCOLM CAMERONS interest in "The Blum Co." of Nitta Yuma.

Two State Farms in Shark.Co.--Sandy Bayou & Forked Deer.

REV.ROBT.SELBY new Methodist minister & wife & children have arrived at parsonage.Mrs.Selby is daughter of late JUDGE H.F.COOK of Vicksburg.

NOTES from the Fortnitely Club;"We learn with sorrow that we will lose one/our most charming members,MRS.D.B.MOORE,who will reside in Ky.in the future."

Jan.12,1900
W.M.MANN came over from La.to be present at daughter ORA LEIGH MANN's wedding.

MRS.ROBT.MANN of Wash.Co.attended the MANN-FARR wedding and was the guest of MRS.W.E.STEVENSON.

Jan.19,1900
FRED GRAFT & son BERNHARD were visitors to the Hill City this week.

GEO.C.CORTRIGHT has gone to N.O. to attend Tulane University.

MR.&MRS.Thos.McMAHON have moved to the Reveland Pltn above Anguilla.

DEER CREEK PILOT SOCIETY NOTES-1899-1900

Feb.2,1900
JNO.R.BAGGETT,bookkeeper for McLEOD Lumber Mill at Nitta Yuma spent Sun.in town with friends.

DR.J.C.BOMMER & wife of Auter,were in the Hill City Sat.

Store & contents of FRANK HIRSCH at L'Argent on Sunflower River was destroyed by fire--arson suspected.

Feb.9,1900
In Supervisors minutes:G.B.McCALL was granted permission to erect telephone poles along public roads from R.F.to Indian Bayou Bridge.

MRS.Wm.MYERS of S.C.has been visiting R.S.MYERS. Miss ALICE MYERS accompanied her on her return home.

A.E.BROWN has disposed of his interest in store at Watsonia to H.A.DARDEN

MISS IRENE DAVIS visiting her sister MRS.H.W.HILL

MISSES MANN & JOHNSTON of Jackson, have been visiting W.M.MANN.

MRS.W.F.WALKER returned home after visiting relative in east Ms. and Ala.

Little FRANCES BAGGETT met with a painful accident-ran needle thru knee.

L.E.MANN left for Ashley,La.to manage a mercantile house there. D.D.FARR will look after his interest in L.E.Mann & Co.here.

Feb.16,1900
NOTICE; Charter of Inc.;Rolling Fork Oil Co.-JULIUS SINAI,BERNARD SINAI,G.M.BAGGETT,M.SINAI,W.H.BARNARD. Production of cotton seed oil-ginning--compress.

MALCOLM CAMERON has let contract for store building on Weeping Willow.

MRS.J.M.REDMOND & MISS JOSIE MANN left for Ashley,La. to visit their father W.M.MANN. Mrs.Redmond went from there to Opelousae, La. her home.

THE DARDEN CO. has bought J.H.BRABSTON's place North of town.

Feb.23,1900
CENSUS BUREAU ESTIMATES POPULATION OF U.S.AROUND 78,000,000. VAST INCREASE OVER 1890

MRS.HUGHES OF Issaq.Co.visits sister MRS.J.W.JOHNSON.

MRS.SARAH OWENS of Brookston,Ind. visiting dau.MRS.A.R.DENMAN.

DEER CREEK PILOT SOCIETY NOTES-1899-1900

Mar.23,1900
    W.E.STEVENSON,now in business in Morehead,Ms.,visited his family here and made arrangments with BOB LEDBETTER to build him a residence in Morehead.

COL.H.J.FIELDS,one of our most progressing planters, purchased the handsome residence of W.E.STEVENSON, on the north bank of Rolling Fork Creek, to take possession May 1.Our city extends a welcome to Mr.Fields & family

Mar.30 1900
MISS DOLLY BAGGETT of Greenville visits sister MRS.W.C.H.McKINNEY In Anguilla.

C.LORENZEN has rented a house in Greenville & will move family immediately.He has purchased large tract of timber land east of Leland upon which he will erect a saw mill.

Rolling Fork has lost one of her enterprising firms by the removal of L.E.MANN & CO. to Ashley,La. where they are extensively engaged in farming.L.E.MANN & MISS JOSIE,MR.& MRS.D.D.FARR will leave soon for their new home.

H.L.DINKINS,former resident of Shark.Co.,now of Waverly,La.visiting.

Episcopal Church services will be held at Nitta Yuma on 2nd Sun. of each month by REV.DR.G.C.HARRIS. In absence of regularly appointed house of worship, MRS.PHELPS has kindly offered her residence.It is hoped that a church will soon be erected at Nitta Yuma as plans are being considered.

Apr.6,1900
MISS ANNIE NUGENT of Jackson & little MISS MARSHALL of V'burg are guest of MRS.G.C.HARRIS Jr.at Mt.Helena

MRS.E.S.WEST,mother of Sheriff West, arrived Wed.eve.to reside here in house formery occupied by W.E.MANN.

Our young friend TOM BAGGETT has been pulling the bellcord on the Deer Creek Accomadation train this week and friends are pleased he will remain permanently.

D.B.MOORE,who for past 2 yrs.has been manager on"The Mounds" place,has returned to his old home in Ky.where he will reside in the future. R.E.STRATTON of Hollandale succeeds him as manager.

The new school house in Cary is just completed,turned over to the trustees--handsomest building of its kind in the Co.

COL.D.L.MOORE,who has been here for 2 mth.looking after his Pltn. interests, left for his home at Harrodsburg,Ky.

Apr.12,1900
MISS ANNIE NUGENT sister & guest of MRS.G.C.HARRIS Jr.has returned to V'burg.

DEER CREEK PILOT SOCIETY NOTES-1899-1900
MR.&MRS.J.E.MEEK left for Memphis Sun.Mr.Meek will go to Coldwater to visit his parents.Mrs.Meek will remain in Memphis several weeks.

Apr.20,1900
MRS.S.D.ROBERTS of V'burg visiting Brother N.J.VICK,Anguilla.

JNO.S.JOOR Jr. is now employed at D.L.MOORE's new store at Baconia.

MISS COOK OF V'burg a guest of her sister MRS.ROBT.SELBY.

SMALL POX IN THE CO.
Apr.27,1900
GEORGE CORTRIGHT ,who has been attending a commercial school in New Orleans, is home again.

GEO.C.HARRISJr. was in V'burg Wed.to attend WILKERSON-WILLIS wedding.

May 4,1900
We acknowledge receipt of invitation to attend a musicale given by MISSES PARHAM & PARKER, members of graduating class in Music at Woman's College, Oxford,Ms.

May 25,1900
MISS PATTIE GLISSON has gone to north western part of Texas to reside with an aunt.

June 1,1900
MRS.MAUD COKER & children left for Clio,S.C. to spend the heated season with her brother WILLIAM MYERS.

MRS.A.R.DENMAN of the Delta Hotel left for Louisville Sun.night. On return she will be accompanied by MISS LOVIE who has been attending school in Ind. H.E.HILL in charge of hotel.

COL.H.J.FIELDS & daughters MISSES LAURA & MARGIE & S.DOVER & daughters MISSES SELMA & MIRIAM,& MR.& MRS.W.C.H.McKINNEY & son WILLIE, all from Anguilla departed Sun.for Louisville Ky.to be present at the Confederate Vet.reunion. The gentlemen are delegates from PAT CLEBURNE CAMP & the young ladies are maids of honor to the Sponsor for the Miss.Division.

June 8,1900
Inviation from MRS.WALKER BROOKE to marriage of granddaughter LALLA BROOKE JONES, TO GEORGE W.EGGLESTON at Presby.Ch. Vicksburg, June 20,.900

June 15,1900
MRS.W.F.WALKER has gone to Demopolis,Ala.to attend marriage of her brother.

MISSES IDA & LADY BARNARD returned home from Blue Mt.school.

MR.& MRS.J.H.McLAURIN were host & hostess of an elegant "at home" Tues.eve.in honor of the "Misses PARHAMs". The young people from far & near assembled at the McLaurins beautiful Home. MISS PARHAM & MR.CAGE entertained the guest with some(cont.)

DEER CREEK PILOT SOCIETY NOTES 1899-1900
(cont.)beautiful music. Games were played..MISS IDA BARNARD won
the ladies prize & MESSERS ALEXANDER,CAMPBELL & CLEMENTS
cut for the gentlmens.

June 22,1900
MISS NOLA MONTGOMERY has returned from Greenwood where she spent
the winter with her uncle MR. BASKET.

June 29,1900
MRS.J.W.JOHNSTON spent a few days with nephew EDGAR JOHNSTON
at Carolina Landing.

GEO.C.HARRIS Jr. left for Jackson & the wedding of sis-in-law
Miss ANNIE NUGENT.

COL.D.C.CASEY has sold his place near Grace Station to HON.L.C.
DULANEY in Issaq.Co.

JOHN KELLY, successor of late J.E.BUTLER will continue business
at the old stand(undertaker)

July 6,1900
The Bell tower of the Epis.Church has been completed and the bell
placed in position. Bell is gift of CAPT.JOHN WILLIS in memory of son ST.JOHN WILLIS.

COL.H.J.FIELDS & family are now occupying handsome residence
on north bank of R.F.Creek after extensive renovations.

July 13,1900
Chancery Court Session;MATTIE R.CAMERON granted divorce from
MALCOLM CAMERON.
JACKSTUBBS granted divorce from AMANDA STUBBS

July 20,1900
MISS GLEN HOLLINSWORTH of Hollandale guest of Misses FIELDS

I.A.CORTRIGHT has gone north for the hot summer.

TOM FIELDS has returned home after absence of 1week in V'burg.

COUNT & COUNTESS CASSELLI are at Nitta Yuma visiting MRS.PHELPS
who is the mother of the Countess.

MISS REA POWELL of Dudley visits sister MRS.T.E.SIMS.

MISS CHRISTINE GRAFT left Tues.for Pentecost, where she will
be the guest of MRS.ALMA STEGALL.Brother BERNARD went with her.

July 27,1900
MISS IRENE DAVIS visits sis MRS.H.E.HILL

MRS.BARNEY MARION of Greenville is guest of sis MRS.W.C.H.McKINNEY
in Anguilla.

MISS GERTRUDE PARHAM, one of 6 contestants for State Musical
medal left for Crystal Springs,Ms.site of Contest.

DEER CREEK PILOT SOCIETY NOTES-1899-1900

MRS.JOHN OTTO of St.Louis,Mo.,who is engaged in mission work there is guest of her aunt MRS.H.J.FIELDS

Aug.3,1900
W.H.CLEMENTS is back from visiting relatives in Columbus & Macon,Ms.

Aug.10,1900
A.P.CAMERON of Madison Co. visiting brother Malcolm at Weeping Willow.

Aug.17,1900
Last night Rolling Fork was connected with V'burg and intervening points, by phone. A call box was placed in Meeks Drugstore. A first class exchange will be installed in near future.

T.J.KENT offers the well known Kent House Hotel for rent.

CAPT.W.W.MOORE,who has been enjoying the coolweather at Mont Eagle,Tn.passed down to Watsonia Sat.Eve. He expects to return to Tn.in a week or 10 day to finish the season there.

W.J.HIBLER of Lorenzen was circulating among friends here Tues.
Aug.24,1900
B.H.WOLFE of Copiah,Co. is visiting bro-in-law Sheriff WEST.

Cumberland Tele.Co. have installed poles and lines over town to subscribers. Exchange connected in about 2 weeks at Kent House Hotel.

Aug.31,1900
MRS.L.R.STEVENS returned to Hot Springs this week.

MRS.W.L.BARTLETT & son NELSON left for Ky.to visit her parents.

GEO.McCAUL don't care whether the trains get here on time or not as he has other matters demanding his attention...its a daughter! ¶[Mildred McCaul Baggett b Aug.26,1900]

MRS.SARAH THOMPSON & her daus.ELLEN & MITA,who have been visiting relatives MR.& MISSES WATSON the past summer,returned to her home in Canton Ms. Tues.

MR.&MRS.HUGHES & children accompanied by MR.J.W.JOHNSTON,returned to Friars Points after short visit to the Johnstons.Miss LITA HUGHES will stay and attend R.F.School.

Sept.7,1900
J.R.CLARK,a former resident of this place now from Golden,La. spent a pleasant day visiting his friends here.

¶[It seems that the new social thing was to "storm" a friends house unexpectedly & with a crowd. A number of such parties are written up,and sounds as tho the young people were quite adept at making their own fun]

DEER CREEK PILOT SOCIETY NOTE-1899-1900

MISS MYERS was "stormed" in the most approved manner Wed.eve.and to say the crowd enjoyed themselves is putting it mildly.

Quite a crowd came down from Anguilla Wed.Eve on a Hayride and "stormed" MISS LAURA FIELDS. She returned with the merry crowd.

MISS MATTIE FIELDS celebrated her 10th birthday Sept.4,by inviting her friends to spend the afternoon.

Sept.14,1900
MISS DORA CROCKETT of Greenwood guest of brother W.A.CROCKETT

MISS GERTRUDE PARHAM & MISS BESSIE TAYLOR left Tues night for Oxford. MissParham has accepted a teacher of music position at Malone Institute & Miss Taylor is a student. MISS CORINNE PARHAM will join them as soon as she is able to travel.

Sept.21,1900
GROVER FIELDS & ALLEN WRIGHT of Vicksburg will attend Bellvue High SChool in Va. this term.

MISS AUGUSTA WILLIAMS who has been a guest of uncle J.W.JOHNSTON the past summer left for her home in Edwards,Ms.

DR.J.T.TAYLOR of LaGrange,Ky. has been here looking after his planting interest.

MR.& MRS.Robt.PATTY left for Macon,Ms. their future home.

BEN ROBERTS will attend A&M College in Starkville,Ms.this term.

Sept.28,1900
C.W.CROCKETT & wife of Greenwood are guest of MRS.W.B.BARNARD

DR.JOHN FLAKE of Waverly,La.was guest of brother here.

MRS.DAY,mother of MRS.H.L.FLAKE is slowly convalescing from severe attack of fever.

SAM JOHNSTON spent several days with parents the J.W.JOHNSTONs.

J.W.JOHNSTONs smiling face will be missed as he takes charge of MAJ.M.H.PEMBERTON's pltn. Oct.1.

MRS.BEN STURGIS left Tues.for Grace to be present at the marriage of sister MISS JULIA LUM, Thurs.morn.

MRS.FRED GRAFT was called to Pentecost for illness of MRS.STEGALL nee Miss ALMA DUESE.

A.J.ADAMS of 5th dist. has leased Kent Hotel which is being overhauled & fitted with new furniture.

MRS.GEORGIA UNDERHILL has leased the well-known Parham Hotel. Under her managment it will retain its popularity with travelers.

DEER CREEK PILOT SOCIETY NOTES-1899-1900

Oct.5,1900
MRS.BERTA WADDILL & granddaughter are visiting MRS.J.S.JOOR.

Oct.12,1900
R.C.PLATT of V'burg spent Sun.with sister MRS.T.W.CAMPBELL.

CHAS.MONTGOMERY of Smedes,is the guest of his uncle D.H.MONTGOMERY.

W.C.H.McKINNEY of Anguilla,is building a handsome residence.

M.SAUNDERS formerly of Anguilla, now living in Tenn. reportedly quite ill with pneumonia & infant dau.very ill.

M.H.PEMBERTON purchased GEN.A.L.NEAL's lot on W.bank of Little Deer Creek near the parsonage. He will build on this lot and move his family in from Lorenzen.

CAPT.BILL SMITH will raise the wreck of the "Joe Sivley", near Cypress Bend on the Sunflower River & take it to V'burg for overhaul.

MAX DOVER,a citizen of Germany,granted American Citizenship in Circuit Court term.

Oct.19,1900
MR.& MRS.PRENTISS BROWN,were made happy by arrival of a little girl.Grandparents-Col.&MRS.W.D.BROWN.

MRS.& MRS.THOS.McMAHON(nee Hulda Parham)spent Sun. with her parents MR.& MRS.J.G.PARHAM

Oct.26,1900
L.W.ROGAN & sons WILL & HENRY,spent Sun.in town.

JNO.S.JOOR Jr. is now with Darden Co. at Watsonia

MISSES SUNSHINE CLEMENTS & KATIE JOOR are visiting MRS.H.L.FOOTE at Dudley.

MRS.GOODMAN & MISSES JOHNSTON & BYERLY of Cary guest of MRS.W.A.JOLLEY.

MRS.GEORGIA UNDERHILL has retired as manager of Parham Hotel

Nov.2,1900
Ameeting of Dau.of Confederacy at MRS.E.C.CLEMENTS to divise mean of raising funds to remove remains of Miss.Conf.Soldiers buried in Washington, back to this State.

MRS.SEARLES & sons guest of brother GEO.W.WEST.

MRS.COKER of Newport News,Va.visiting sister MRS.H.BOOTH(e)

DR.H.L.FLAKE comtemplates adding another story on his building near Deer Creek Bridge.

DEER CREEK SOCIETY NOTE-1899-1900

MRS.H.L.FOOTE of Dudley &MISS FOOTE of Louisville,Ky were guest of MRS.E.C.CLEMENTS(nee-Ann Foote)

MISS ALICE MYERS spent spring & summer with bro.WILLIAM in S.C.

Nov.9,1900
MRS.D.GALCERAN of Starkville,guest of sister MRS.R.E.STRATTON.

Nov.16,1900
BOARD OF SUPERVISORS:Resoultion by GEN.A.L.NEAL to build new courthouse here.

Nov.23,1900
Mr.HANEY of Amite,La. guest of stepson J.G.PARHAM.

MRS.HESTER of Meridian,guest of sister MRS.A.O.ALEXANDER.

On Mon. GEN.A.E.NEWTON of La.,guardian of ALMA & EMMETT NEWTON, sold to E.KLAUS at public auction, 900 acres in Sec.19,20, T.11. for $8,000.

The remains of DR.COX,who was killed by accidental discharge of his pistol,near Campbellsville,was taken to Learned,Ms. where he resided.

Nove.30,1900
Lovely home of MRS.B.GOODMAN of Cary was scene of birthday party of 7 year old daughter ROBBIE. MISSES PRESTON & EDITH CURPHEY of V'burg were guest.

Dec.7,1900
M.RUSSELL & family have moved into their new residence in town.

E.L.PASSMORE,of Canton & son-in-law of M.RUSSELL,expects to make Shar.Co. his home.

Dec.14,1900
COL.W.B.BARNARD is visiting daughter MRS.C.W.CROCKETT in Greenwood

MRS.S.R.STEVENS (L) will spend the winter with daughter MRS.W.B.BARNARD.

MRS.W.F.WALKER has as guest-parents MR.&MRS.GLOVER,Demopolis,Ala.

CHAS.H.FISHER one of the most respected colored citizen of the Co. died at home near Lorenzen of Small Pox,contracted while nursing a patient.

Forked Deer Pltn.leased several years by State as a State Prison Farm & G.M.BAGGETT is Sgt.in charge.

Dec.21,1900
MRS.OTTO of St.Louis guest of family of H.J.FIELDS.

MRS.W.R.HARPER of Bradford,Ind.guest of son DR.HARPER.

DEER CREEK PILOT SOCIETY NOTES-1899-1900

REV.ROBT.SELBY assigned to Brandon, REV.J.G.CAMMACK new Metho.Min.

COL.D.C.CASEY made a deal with J.J.SANDERS for him to run SHILOH Pltn.

We understand H.J.FIELDS has bought the old Barnard homestead at Anguilla. We trust this does not mean their removal from Rolling Fork.

Store at Egremont occupied by LOUIS BORODOFSKY was destroyed by fire. Building was owned by H.L.FOOTE.

LAST ISSUE OF THIS BOOK

MARRIAGES TAKEN FROM THE DEER CREEK PILOT-1899-1900
[Published on Sat.,until Mar.10,1899, then pub.on Friday]

Jan.14,1899
JULIAN THOMPSON to ELIZABETH DUKE,daughter of County Assessor,
    J.W.DUKE.By GEN.A.L.NEAL,Member of board of Supervisors.

June 30,1899
A quiet wedding ceremony was performed at the home of A.R.DENMAN
    onthe 21st by Justice BUTLER,the contracting partners being
    DOUGLAS STEVENS & MISS ANNIE COOK.

Sept.1,1899
T.E.SIMS TO MISS CORINE POWELL at home of bride in Rolling Fork,
    Aug.30,1899, by Rev.VAN HOOK,MES.She is the daughter of
    H.J.POWELL. Hes the son of the late CAPT.THOMAS SIMS of Va.

Sept.15,1899
C.L.DAVIS,station agent at Cary to MISS JULIA SIMMS,by REV.VAN
    HOOK at the Methodist parsonage,Thur.Sept.21,1899.

Dec.15,1899
The news of the marriage of MISS MITTIE BODE & J.W.LYLES,several
    days ago, took friends of both by suprise,but they all at
    once united in extending their hearty congratulations to
    the happy couple.

Dec.29,1899
MISS BURLEIGH SHANNON & CLYDE BOYKIN, of the 5th district,visit-
    ed Vicksburg Christmas day and on their return the young
    gentleman introduced his father to another daughter. In other
    words they were married while in Vicksburg. We extend con-
    gratulation to the happy couple.

Dec.29,1899
MISS MARY ELLA DARBY & HON.AUGUSTUS LOOMIS NEAL were united in
    marriage Dec.27,1899 inthe Coldwater,Ms.Baptist Church by
    Rev.MR.ELLIS of Senatobia,Ms. She is daughter of MRS.S.L.
    DARBY of Coldwater. Miss Darby has long been a music teacher
    in Rolling Fork, and the happy couple will be at home in
    the Parham Hotel, at RollingFork.

Jan.5,1900
ANNOUNCEMENT-MR.W.M.MANN invites you to be present at the marr-
    of his daughter ORA LEIGH MANN to DAVID DIXON FARR, Wed.eve.
    Jan.10,1900 at half past 8 O'clock at the Chapel of the Cross
    Rolling Fork,Ms. At home after Jan.19,1900.
WRITE UP of wedding in Jan.12 paper:MRS.A.L.NEAL(nee MISS DARBY)
    provided the music...bride entered leaning on arm of sister
    JOSIE MANN..groom attended by brother of bride,LEON MANN.
    Other attendants:GERTIE TAYLOR,GEO.C.CORTRIGHT, ELIZA ATKIN-
    SON, CLAUDE GOODLOE, JULIE GOODLOE, GEO.W.WEST, NINA MANN,
    Wm.H.CLEMENTS. Reception held at City Hall.

Jan.12,1900
MR.M.SAUNDERS of Anguilla to MISS DAISY BELL DORSEY,only dau.
    of MR.GEO.H.DORSEY of Vicksburg.Marriage celebrated at home
    of DR.GEO.B.DORSEY[From V'burg Herald-&only date says"happy event
    yesterday"—no date or paper publishing date]

MARRIAGES FROM DEER CREEK PILOT-1899-1900

Jan.19,1900
ALMA L.DUESE & G.E.STEGALL at residence of FRED GRAFT,Wed.Eve.
   Jan.16 by REV.ROBERT SELBY.

April 20,1900
JOSEPH SINAI,a rising young attorney of New Orleans,son of JULIUS
   SINAI of Rolling Fork, to be married Apr.25 in Natchez,Ms.
   In Apr.27 paper, the brides name is MISS ADER,and the wedding
   took place as announced.MR.& MRS.J.SINAI and the grooms bro-
   ther MOSES, attended the wedding.

May 11,1900
The country home of MR.& MRS.W.L.BARTLETT was the scene of the
   wedding between ANNIE VIRGINIA BRYAN,a native of Natchez,Ms.,
   to EDWARD GLASS, by REV.MR.ARCHER pastor of Presbyterian
   Church in Greenville,Ms.,May 6,1900.Future home Grenada,Ms.

July 20,1900
At residence of COL.W.B.BARNARD last week, REV.MR.McGOWN of
   Anguilla,united MISS SADIE THOMPSON & FRANK TAYLOR in marr-
   iage.(no date)

Aug.10,1900
MISS REA POWELL & ROBERT PATTY of Dudley,Ms., married in Greenville,Ms., Aug.8,1900

Aug.24,1900
The friends of "BUNNIE"SIMS were surprised to learn Thurs.Morn-
   ing of his marriage in Vicksburg to MISS LILLY M.ELSESSER,of
   Vicksburg. They will make their home at Boothe Station.

Nov.9,1900
MISS ANNIE HENRY to REV.M.McKEOWN,pastor of Anguilla Methodist
   Church at the residence of the bride near Anguilla, by the
   REV.ROBERT SELBY, Wed.Nov.7,1900

Dec.7,1900
Nov.20,1900, in Memphis,Tn.,J.H.REYNOLDS was wed to MISS ANNIE
   CHISHOLM of Ark. Jonesborough,Ark.,will be their future home.

DEATH NOTICES DEER CREEK PILOT-JAN.1899-DEC.1900
Pub.on Sat.until Mar.1899,then on Friday, weekly.THOS.W.CAMPBELL Editor.

Jan.14,1899
LIZZIE BUCKINGHAM,wife of James Buckingham,dropped dead at Grace Station.

Jan.28,1899
HON.WALTER McLAURIN brother of Hon.H.J.McLAURIN & GOV.A.J.McLAURIN died at the executive mansion in Jackson (no date-but between Jan 21 & 28) of meningitis . All brothers at funeral except Dist.Atty.SYLVESTER McLAURIN & HON.WALLACE McLAURIN. Burial in Brandon,Ms.

JUDGE H.W.FOOTE father of Hon.H.L.FOOTE & MRS.E.C.CLEMENTS(nee Ann Foote),one of the oldest & best citzens of Noxubee Co., died at his home in Macon, Sund.morn at 10. He was buried Mon. 2PM. Prominent in Macon 65 yrs., served as Circuit Clerk and in both branches of Ms.Legislature and as Circuit Judge. He was 80 yrs.old, prominent Officer in Confederate Army, and always had been a conservative, Christian gentleman.

MR.E.V.SAUNDERS of Anguilla-Jan.21,of pneumonia.

Mar.17,1899
Wm.PURNELL,County Treas.of Issaq.Co.died at Vicksburg last Thurs.

Mar.24,1899
The remains of MRS.ELLEN WATSON BARNARD ,who died Tues.eve. were carried to Anguilla Thurs.morn,followed by a large con course of sorrowing friends, and interred in the family burying grounds there.[Obit on same page]

May 26,1899
MRS.SIMS -mother of T.E.SIMS died at NewPort News,Va. May 22 1899.Ex resident of Shark.Co., leaves several children and a sister MRS. H.BOOTHE

June 30,1899
ATWOOD WILSON,a former resident of Vicksburg, drowned in Sunflower River near Holland Landing last Sunday.

THE 17 year old daughter of JUSTICE C.H.FISHER(c)of Lorenzen, who had just returned home from V'burg where she was attending St.Mary's Epis.College, was taken sick suddenly Wed.morn & died before medical assistance could reach her. Death caused by congestion.

July 28,1899
OBIT.-JOHN R.CAMERON(Colonel) deceased Madison Co. July 24,1899 He had extensive land interests in Sharkey Co.

Aug.11,1899
Tues morn.MASTER GUS MARTIN,son of MR.& MRS.M.C.MARTIN was taken with congestive chill. DR.HARPER was called but in spite of all that science & faithful nursing, the young man never rallied from the attack and his death occured early Thur.Aug.10

DEATH NOTICES DEER CREEK PILOT-1899-1900

Aug.25,1900
E.C.BLAKE,an old resident of Shar.Co.,died at home of FRANK MYERS Tues.morn.,after an illness of several months. A native of Vermont & of same town Adm.Dewey was born

Sept.8,1899
MISS SALLIE SANDERS,13 yr.old daughter of J.J.SANDERS of Cary, last week.

Sept.22,1899
Mother of H.E.HILL, illness of several months terminated fatally Friday. Remains to be interred at Holly Springs,Ms.

Nov.3,1899
OBIT:DR.A.M.WADDILL died in Tioga,Tex.Oct.13,1899 age 73. Veteran of Mexican and Civil War. Owned a large property in Shark.Co. Ms. & Madison Parish,La. Sold it all in 1890 due to ill health and moved to the Panhandle of Tex.and reinvested...poor crops & low prices..lost his investment...went to live with son ANDY WADDILL, who soon died. Dr.leaves a wife, a dau.-in-law & 2 g.children in Tioga,Tex. 3 Daughters,MARY WADDILL, MRS. UNDERHILL, MRS.J.S.JOOR & 3 g.children in Rolling Fork,Ms. & a brother MAJ.GEO.C.WADDILL of Chicago.

Dec.15,1899
Little MARION,the lovely little dau. of MR.& MRS.W.C.H.McKINNEY died at Anguilla Tues. Dec.12, a victim of that dread desease Scarlet Fever.

Jan.12,1900
MRS.J.E.POWELL-last Fri.afternoon. Buried Sat.from Methodist church.Leaves husband & 3 dau.,& a brother.

Jan.19,1900
J.H.COOK-Jan.16. Interred Union Cemetery Anguilla.

CURIOUS ITEM:"REV.H.F.SPROULA,the eloquent Vicksburg divine, will preach the funeral service of the late EDWARD VIRDEN SAUNDERS at 11o'clock this morn.at Anguilla, it being the anniversary of his death."

Apr.6,1900
After a lingering illness of several months MRS.KATE RITTER (nee MOLLY KATE SHELBY)died at the home of her mother yesterday morn. Apr.5,1900.Interred in Shelby family burial ground.

Accident at Booths Mill resulted in death of W.O.DUNBAR of Port Gibson. While felling trees for mill, one fell on him. Interrment in Port Gibson

Apr.20,1900
Last Thur. about noon, MARSHALL REAVELY was shot & instantly killed by IRBY L.ROGAN,a well known planter below town. Reavely was advancing on Rogan threatning to beat out his brains with a fence post in his hands. Failing to heed warning to halt he continued his hostile march,then Rogan fired,with above results.The courts preliminary examination resulted in dis-

DEER CREEK PILOT-1899-1900

(Cont.)charge of Rogan, evidence showing it of self defense.

May 4,1900
OBIT.MRS.T.J.KENT(nee BETTIE MILES)dau.of DENT H.MILES of Sartartia. She was born.Nov.25,1843--died Apr.30,1900.Sisters-MRS.M.J.HOGAN of V'burg,& late MRS.McLEOD of Yazoo Co. She married T.J.KENT in 1879,-moved to this Co.1881--Catholic. Remains laid to rest May 2.FATHER WISE of V'burg conducted the funeral rites.

MRS.T.W.CAMPBELL(wife of Pilot Editor)left for V'burg Wed.eve in response to a telegram of the sudden death of her sister MISS NANNIE E.PLATT.

May 25,1900
OBIT: Friends of H.K.McKENZIE sympathize in his loss sustained by death of his wife last Tue.eve.7 o'clock. She had long been an invalid. Leaves husband,and a dau.Funeral took place from her late residence Wed.Afternoon.

June 8,1900
OBIT.: MRS.H.S.GOODMAN,gentle,attractive wife of Dr.H.S.GOODMAN of Cary,died at V'burg where he took her for medical help. Married last Oct. the young bride from Va.,dau. of COL.S.B. POWERS of Cumberland Co. Va., had many friends who will miss her. Clad in her bridal robes the afflicted husband & father carried the body to her old Va. home for burial.

June 22,1900
OBIT: CAPT.J.E.BUTLER died June 20,1900,born in S.C...came to Delta 1847..76 years old..twice married..died a widower. Leaves 1dau. the wife of JOHN KELLY..she is the last of 3 children.Funeral conducted by Deer Creek Masonic Lodge.. burial in family cemetery.**[Kelly Cem.in Rolling Fork]**

Sept.28,1900
The remains of BLANTON MOORE Of Watsonia, who died of Hematuria at Leland Mon.night,were taken to V'burg Tues.morn. enroute to Port Gibson for burial Wed. morning.

Sharkey Co. is mourning the loss of another citizen..JAMES A. BATTON, who died at his home near Hollands Ldg.last week.

Nov.2,1900
J.MARSHALL WOOLFOLK accidently shot & killed himself on his plantation near Percy last week. Remains taken to V'burg.

Dec.7,1900
LAMAR MAXWELL,oldest son of MR.& Mrs.TOBE MAXWELL died of Hematuria. Interred here Tues. Dec.11,1900

Dec.21,1900
OBIT.: ORA MANN FARR(Mrs. D.D.Farr) died Dec.17 in La.only 11 months after coming here as a bride. Funeral was held in Episcopal Church in Rolling Fork, where she had been Christened,Confirmed & married.Leaves her young husband and tiny babe, father,bro.,2sisters.Buried in Union Cemetery by side of her mother.

Early records of Union Church, established 1868 near Anguilla, Sharkey Co.,Ms. Later moved to Rolling Fork,Ms.and called the Chapel of the Cross.

MARRIAGES---SOME NOT DATED BY PRIEST.
JOE CULLEN HALL,M.D. AGE 31 res.of Anguilla,to SARAH LOUISA BER-
  NARD,dau.of Wm.T.Barnard, in his residence in Anguilla,Ms.
Wm.R.HARPER M.D.of Rolling Fork,Ms.to ESTELLE BROWN,dau.of W.D.
  & ANNA R.BROWN in their home in Rolling Fork by Rev.G.C.Harris
1888-WALTER A.JOLLEY to MARY BUTTS SHELBY,dau.of EVAN & MARY C.
  SHELBY IN RES.OF H.L.FOOTE in Rolling Fork,by Rev.G.C.Harris.
1894-JAS.R.REDMOND to CORINNE MANN dau of Wm.M.& ANNA MANN,of
  Rolling Fork. The first marriage in the new Chapel of the
  Cross,Rolling Fork,Ms.,by Rev.Geo.C.Harris
1892-CHAS.D.BASS to S.G.GREENWALL by Rev.W.C.MAGUIRE at Ditchley,
  Washington Co. on July 28.
1899-JOHN S.MAYS-res.near Lyon,Ms. to MARY AGNES FONTAINE dau.
  of LAMAR FONTAINE & wife of Lyon,Ms.,by Rev.G.C.Harris in
  the Lyon Methodist Church before a full congregation.
BURIAL RECORDS---ONE NOT DATED
n/d THOMAS C.WATSON Jr.age 20-res.Rolling Fork,pneumonia.Buried
  Union Cemetery,Anguilla,Ms.by Rev.G.C.Harris
1880 MARY CLARK--by Rev.Jas.Foster
1880-Feb.5-JOHN COKER-61,res.Rolling Fork landing.Buried near home
  "   NANCY ANN COKER-17   "   "   "   "   "   "   " "
1881-JAMES BARNES-10mo.,Union Cem.Anguilla,by Rev.Jas.Foster
Jan.10-EARL BARNES-2½yr. "   "   "   "   "   "   "
Mar.18-W.E.HARRIS-in Union Cem.Anguilla,Ms. "   "   "   "
Mar.19-MRS.E.M.MOORE-20 buried at Cammack Landing.Rev.Foster
      MRS.SPENCER-Buried Lake Washington by Rev.G.C.Harris
      SAML.A.McKENZIE-in Union Cem.Anguilla,by Rev.Harris
      Mrs.MARY E.SHELBY-Pneumonia-in Rolling Fork,by Howell
                Logan
1887-THOS C.WATSON-buried in Union Cem.Anguilla by C.J.WINGATE
1895-Dec.2-EVAN SHELBY McCOMB-in Shelby family Cem.by Rev.Harris
1897-Jan.20-MARY WATSON-d.Jan.19-pneumonia,buried in Church yard
  Rolling Fork by Rev.G.C.Harris
1897-Aug.16-FREDK W.HAMBERLIN-10dys.in garden of family res.by
  Rev.G.C.Harris
1899-Mar. ELLEN WATSON BARNARD-Menengitis.Home cemetery at Dr.
  Barnards resi.by Rev.G.C.Harris

BAPTISMS 1868-1899-All do not have dates.
1868,Nov.28 MARGARET ELIZABETH GIBSON-b.May 18,1868,dau./ALBERT
  C.& HATTIE L.GIBSON
  CALLIE LOU GIBSON-b.Sept.4,1867,Dau/Wm.W.& R.E.GIBSON.
  Both the above in the family resi.Mayersville,Ms.(later named)
n/d-WILLIAM BERNARD BERNARD-by Bishop Green in W.D.BROWNS resi.
 "   JOEL CULLEN HALL-age 32 by Rev.Harris
 "   SARAH LOUISA(BARNARD)HALL-age 28 Parent W.T.BARNARD.These
      two bapt.in Union Church,Deer Creek,Anguilla,Ms.
 "   MARGARET ANTOINETTE WILLIAMS-age 35 by Rev.Harris,Union Ch.
 "   MARY LOUISA HICKMAN-age 29 by Rev.Harris,Union Church
1869-Jan.31-LIZZIE WEST BERNARD-age 20 by Rev.Harris
 "   Feb.7-WILLIAM BAILEY BERNARD-age23 son/W.T.BERNARD &MRS.BER-
      NARD(deceased)
 "   Feb.7-SALLIE WEST age 18
 "   " 9-GEORGE BROOKS HICKMAN-age 6

UNION CHURCH & CHAPEL OF THE CROSS, BAPTISIMS 1868-1899
1869,Feb.9,ROWENA WEST HICKMAN-b.Nov.13,1866 by Rev.Harris
n/d JOEL BERNARD HALL-b.Jan.13,1869,son/Dr.J.C.& SARAH L.HALL.
    The above 6 names all baptised in Union Church Deer Creek
near what is now Anguilla.
n/d WILLIAM GIBBONS age 1yr.,son/Wm.&--GIBBONS,in family home.
" JOHN HALL -age 6 mo. in Union Chap.by Rev.G.C.Harris
" THOMAS WATSON Jr.age 20yr.IN EXTREMIS by Rev.G.C.Harris
" MARY KATE SHELBY by Rev.G.C.Harris
" MARY WATSON " " "
" FANNIE WATSON " " "
" ___SCOTT " " "
" ___SCOTT " " "
1890-July 20,MARY WADDELL(WADDILL)dau/Dr.& Mrs.Waddell
" " KATE WADDELL JOOR
" " GEORGIA WADDELL UNDERHILL-all three are dau of Dr.&
   Mrs.Waddell and baptised in Rolling Fork,by Rev.W.C.McGuire.
1890-CHARLES WOOLFORK--IN EXTREMIS-by Rev.Harris
1880 MARY CLARK,adult, in Rolling Fork by Rev.James Foster
Mar.19,IRENE WINIFRED MALLET-adult
   J   ROBERT M.MALLET,age 21yr.
   J   GEORGE MALLET age 3 yrs
   J   JAMES B.MALLET age 5 yrs.
   J   WINNIFRED MALLET age 8 yrs
   J   JOSEPH GEORGE MALLET AGE 10yrs.

All children of ___ & IRENE W.MALLET.
By Rev.Jas.Foster

J Mar.20 CARRIE(MALLET)BRIDGES dau/___&Irene W.Mallet
Mar.21 WILLIAM LEECH PHILIPS-adult
" " JNO.FRANK BROOKS b.Mar.29 1879 son/FRED & ELIZA BROOKS
Mar.23 CHARLES COKER b.July 18 1872
" JESSU COKER b.Jan.11 1877
" WILLIAM COKER b.Aug.10 1879
" JAMES DECELL b.Nov.13 1865
" LULA DECELL b.July 16 1867
" JOHN DECELL b.Nov.13 1870
" GEORGE DECELL b.Oct.21 1871
" BEATRICE DECELL b.Nov.28 1873
" THOMAS SIMMS b.Oct.7 1874
" MINNIE SIMMS b.Aug.15 1878
" ARTHUR B.SIMMS b.Aug.22 1876
Apr.15 WILLIAM BAILEY ROGAN b.June 19 1875-son/L.W.& M.A.ROGAN
" IRBY ROGAN b.Dec.29 1873 " " " "
July 1 LINCOLN WILLIAMS-@17yrs.In jail,condemned to be hung July
                2-Bapt.witnesses N.T.BAGGETT,LAWRENCE HARRIS
July 18,ESTHER J.DUKE b.Nov.7 1879 on Vickland
" LIZZIE RAY DUKE b.May 3 1877
" KATIE DUKE b.Feb.11 1875
" CORA ELLINGTON b.Dec.29 1864
ALL BAPTISED BY REV.JAS.FOSTER UNLESS OTHERWISE STATED
1880
Aug.2 JNO.D.ELLINGTON b.Oct.4 1876   by Rev.Jas.Foster
" CLARE D.ELLINGTON b.Aug.4 1865   "
" LULU ROBERTSON b.Oct.1872   "
Oct.15 GEO.WASHINGTON CHRISTMAS b.Dec.25-at Skipwith,Colored,
      Sponsered by Mr.&Mrs.TURNBULL,by Rev.Foster at Skipwith
Oct.18 PURNILL SCOTT-SponMiss P.Scott by Rv.Foster,Lake Washingto
" WILLIAM BRITTON by Rev.Harris
Oct.20 EVA ELIZABETH McKENZIE b.Jan.12 1879 dau/H.K.McKENZIE
               & wife by Rev.Foster
J NOTE:Listed 1880cen.pg 127 as MATTELLE

UNION CHURCH & CHAPEL OF THE CROSS, BAPTISIMS 1868-1899

1880
Oct.20 SAM ALEXANDER McKENZIE b.July 24 1872 son/Mr.&Mrs.H.K.
McKENZIE
" LOUIS K.McKENZIE b.Jan.23 1870   "   "   "
n/d CORNELIA(RUSSELL)CASEY-Spon.Mrs.SHELBY,by Rev.G.C.Harris

1888
Apr.2 JESSEE(BANKS)HARMON-in Methodist Ch.RollingFork.Rev.Harris

1890
July 20 GARNET RIVERS HARPER dau./DR.W.R.& ESTELLE BROWN HARPER
 "   MARGUERITE JOLLEY dau/W.A.& M.BUTTS JOLLEY at Jolley resi.
                by Rev.W.C.MAGUIRE

1892
Mar.20 ELSINORE SHELTON-Spon.the mother,M.C.MYERS,MESSERS HARPER
                & W.D.BROWN
June 30 CORINNE(REDMAN)MANN dau/W.M.& ANNA MANN.Maguire,Rolling F.
 "   THOMAS McMAHON by REV.W.C.MAGUIRE at Rolling Fork
 "   WALTER H.LANGFORD   "   "   "   "   "   "

1893
Oct.16 MARGARET ANDERSON dau/DAN & --ANDERSON.
 "ORA MANN dau/W.M.& ANNA MANN
Oct.15 MARY LILIA HUGHES 5 yrs.dau/ARCHIE & MARY HUGHES
 "   JOSEPH JOHNSTON HUGHES son/ "   "   "   "
Nov.19 MADELAIN BREARD 10yrs dau/C.A.& --BREARD
 "   JOSEPHINE BREARD BREARD-no information
THE ABOVE BAPT.AT CHAPEL OF THE CROSS,ROLLING FORK,BY REV.HARRIS

1897
Jan.20 WILLIAM FITZGERALD WALKER b.Egremont,Ms.4mo.old-son/W.F.&
       WILLIE A.B.WALKER at Egremont Pltn.by Rev.Harris

1896
May 18 AGNES GRAY 7 mo.dau/DR.JAS.W.& MARY R.GRAY,at Clarksdale,M.
                By Rev.Harris

1897
July 24 THOMAS HARRISON FARRISH 6mo.son/W.D.FARRISH & KATE M.F.
        FARRISH At Mayersville,Ms.by Rev.Harris
June 20 NANNEBELLE ROWLAND b.Mar.12 1895 dau/DRW.& SARAH R.ROW-
                LAND
 "   JAMES MARION FAIRFAX DEWEES b.1896 son/T.B.&MARG.DEWEES
        At Robinson Springs by Rev.Harris
 "   EUGENE FERGUSON HINTON 3yr.son/CHAS.L.& DAISY HINTON at
        Robinson Springs by Rev.Harris
 "HOWARD LAFAYETTE MONTGOMERY b.May 6 1889 son/A.J.& S.A.
        MONTGOMERY by Rev.Harris at Madison Stn.
 "ARTHUR JENNINGS MONTGOMERY b.Apr.4 1891 (same as above)
 "   SHELTON b.Clarksdale. by Rev.Harris at Madison Station
 "DR.Wm.O.PORTER by Rev.Harris at Grace Station
 "MRS.PORTER   "   "   "   "   "   "
 "INFANT PORTER   "   "   "   "   "   "

1898
Apr.3 REXEL GOODMAN son/DR.& MRS.B.GOODMAN.Chapel of the Cross,R.F.
July 3 EGBERT MIDDLETON BETTS son/___&VIRGINIA BATTAILE BETTS
         by Rev.Harris at Chapelof the Cross,Rolling Fork,Ms.
Dec.27 ___HAMBERLIN son/DR.&MRS.S.T.HAMBERLIN at residence

1899
July 2 MARTIN COBB MARTIN &
 "   MINNIE,his wife,heretofore a Roman Cath.made vows at same
        time & was received into the congregation of Christs
        Flock by sign of the cross.Rev.Harris,Chap.o.t.Cross,R.F.

CENSUS 1880 SHARKEY CO. MS.
Random listings.
Enumerator J.A.THOMAS #113, started each page with household #1.
Supervisors Dist. #3-Beat #2 to Page 16,line 17.

Pg.1.
1-1;Watson,Louis(Wid.)	38		Farmer	Ms.	S.C.	Ms.
" ,B.E.	9	son		"		
" ,Z.C.	6	son		"		
Duncan,O.D.(f.)	50	Aunt	Housekpr.	Tn	--	--
Thompson,J.A.(m)	34	Boarder-Sch.Teach.		Ky.	--	--
2-2:Breeken,John	40		Ruler maker	Ire.	Ire.	Ire.
Keller,John(Wid.)	65		Ruler Maker	N.Y.	Switz.	Switz
22-22;Scott,T.F.	38		Farmer	Ala.	N.C.	N.C.
" ,L.A.	38	wife		Ms.	--	--
" ,M.H.(f)	12	dau.		Ms.		
" ,L.J.	11	dau.		"		
" ,C.H.	9	son		"		
" ,K.A.	7	dau.		"		
" ,Y.G.	4	son		"		
" ,J.C.	1	son		"		
Kane,T.B.(m)	22	Boarder-Farmer		Ire.	Ire.	Ire.
Sanderson,W.A.(M)	18	"	"	Ms.	Ala.	Ala.
24-24;Carter,B.F.(m)	24		"	"	Ms.	Ms.
" ,Rebecca	18	wife		"	"	"
" ,John W.	1	son		"	"	"

Pg.4
12-12;MELOMORE,Charlie	21		Farm Lab.	"	"	"
" ,Laura	21	wife		"	--	--
Arnette,Andrea	22	Boarder(wid/div)		"	--	--
14-14;West,John	21	single		"	Tn.	Ms.
Knight,Dan	30	married		"	Ms.	"
" ,Zutie	26	wife		"	--	--
" ,Mary	12	dau.		"	--	--
" ,Peggy	8	dau.		"	--	--

Pg.5
1-1;HICKS,A.J.	56		Farmer	Ga.	Ga.	Ga.
" ,Sarah	46	wife		Ala.	--	--
" ,N.C.	19	dau.		Ms.	--	--
" ,Sam	16	son	Farmer	"		
" ,Clementine	13	dau.		"		
" ,S.D.	11	son		"		
" ,J.P.	6	dau.		"		
" ,John	3	son		"		
BURTEN,Sam	20	Married		"		

Pg.6.
1-1;HUNT,Omer	35			Ger.	Ger.	Ger.
" ,Mary	28	wife		Ind.	--	--
" ,Minnie	6	dau		"		
" ,Carrie	4	dau.		"		
9-9;OSTROFFSKY,Jake	34	(w/d)	grocer	Pol.	Pol.	Pol.
" ,Sam	8	son		Ill.		
" ,Mannie	5	Son		"		
COHN,Esther	23	sis-in-law(single)		Ohio		
McLAREN,H.J.(m)	25	boarder		Ms.		
COHN,Myers	17	"	Clerk	La.		

CENSUS 1880-Sharkey Co.Ms. Random Listing

Pg.7

				Ms.	Ms.	Ms.
3-3;	----(Ink on Surname)	40				
"	,Mattie	30	wife	"	"	"
"	,Geary	14	son	"	"	"
"	,Mary	8	dau.	"	"	"
"	,Joseph	5	son	"	"	"
"	,Ada	3	dau.	"	"	"
"	,James	1/12	son	"	"	"

Pg.9

2-2;	CLARKE,Eugene	29	single	"	"	"
	ELISON,Pervis	25	boarder-Machinist	"	"	"
3-3;	POTTER,Nelson	52		Ms.	Ms.	Ms.
"	,Henrietta	30	wife	"	"	"
"	,Henry	15	son	"	"	"
"	,Wess	12	son	"	"	"
"	,Allice	6	dau.	"	"	"
"	,Gaines	3	son	"	"	"
4-4;	FURL, Tom	33	Far.Lab.	Ms.	Ms.	Ms.
"	,Adline	25	wife	"	"	"
"	,Mary	14	dau.	"	"	"
"	,Sarah	3	daul.	"	"	"
"	,Jake	9/12	son	"	"	"
5-5;	PURCELL,Caleb	31	" "	"	Va.	Va.
"	,Viola	28	wife	"		
"	Ben	8	son	"		
	QUIELLEN,Harris	27	" "	Ga.		
	MOTIN,Caroline	15		Ms.		
6-6;	SANDERS,Jack	28	Far.Lab.	Ms.	Ms.	Ms.
"	,Huldie	21	wife	"	"	"
"	,Winnie	7/12(April)		"	"	"
7-7;	BROWN,Newrie	56	Far.Lab.	S.C.	S.C.	S.C.
"	,Eiley	46	wife	Ms.		
"	,Alford	18	son	"		
"	,Bragg	16	son	"		
"	,Eula	14	dau.	"		
"	,Arthur	14	Son	"		
"	,Sallie	9	dau.	"		
"	,Charlie	5	son	"		
"	,Davis	11/12(July)son		"		
8-8;	GORDON,Diem(w/d)	60	Far.Lab.	Va		
	GRIFFIN,Ellen(w/d)	41	---	Md.	Md.	Md.
"	,Chatman	19		Ms.		
"	,Wm.	15	son	"		
"	,Christopher	10	son	"		
	BELLE,Nancy	24	Neice	"		
9-9;	CHASE,Emma(w/d)	56	Farm.Lab.	Md.	Md.	Md.
"	,Rachel	18	dau	Ms.		
	MURRIE,Wm.	35	boarder(married)	VA.		
"	,Maria	27	" "	Ms.		
10-10;	OWENS,Tom	41	Farm.Lab.	S.C.	S.C.	S.C.
"	,Sarah	22	wife	Ms.		
	CARTER,James	49	-- " "	"	Ala.	Ala.

Pg.10

4-4;	BOLTON,Miller	33	" "	"	Ms.	Ms.
"	,Lizzie	27	wife	"	"	"
"	,Cou--	5	son	"	"	"
"	,Nancy	5/12(June)		"	"	"
	WASHINGTON,Geo.	32	" "	"	"	"
	JONES,Wm.	23	" "	"	"	"

CENSUS 1880-SHARKEY CO.MS. Random listing
Pg.10.(Cont.)

5-5;DICKERSON,Willis	61		Farm.Lab.	N.C.	S.C.	N.C.
" ,Lizzie	47	wife		Ala.		
" ,Allice	18	dau.		Ms.		
" ,Rena	16	"		"		
" ,Mary	10	"		"		
EZELL,Sallie	8	Gr.dau.		"		
7-7;BUSH,Ramen	39		Farm.Lab.	Switz.	Switz.	Switz
GEE,James	2-					

Pg.11

3-3;CARSON,Henry(mu)	23		Farm.Lab.	Ms.	Ms.	Ms.
Fannie(B)				Ga.		
WHITEN,Jane(B)	43	Mother		"		
HUNT,Abijah(W)	28			Ms.	Ms.	Ms.
LONG,Hue(W)	50		Engineer	Ky.		

Pg.14

6-7;MOORE,Wm.(w/d/)	38		Farmer	Ms.	N.C.	S.C.
" ,Anne	14	dau.		"		
" ,Blanton	7	son		"		
" ,Tiny	4	dau.		"		
" Jonsie	--	son		"		
HEMPHILL,Fred	32		Agent	"		
WRIGHT,J.B.	27		"	"		
MOORE,Homer(B)	20		Servant	"		

Pg.18-Beat #1

11-12;BROWN,M.E.	33		Overseer	"	Ky.	Ms.

Pg.25

71-72;PARISH,Hopey(f)	60		Cook	N.C.	N.C.	N.C.
PARLEE,W.S.	20	Clerk for Farmer		Ms.	"	Ms.

Pg.26

107-108;CARPENTER,John	37		Farm agent	La.	La.	La.
108-109;WOODWARD,James	45	(Cripp.)Farmer		Ga.	N.C.	N.C.
" ,Caroline	44	wife		".	Tn.	Tn.
113-114;STEVENS,E.	70		Farmer	N.C.	N.C.	N.C.
" ,Mary	45	wife		"	"	"
" ,John H.	25	son	"	Ms.	"	"
" ,W.C.	23	son		"	"	"
HOLLAND,R.C.	35	bro-in-law	"	"	"	"
114-115;McALPIN,Alex(w/d)	55		Carpenter	Ga	N.C.	Ga.
" ,John	21	son,Married,Farmer	Ala.	Ga.	Ga.	

Pg.27

124-125;MURRAY,T.J.	25	Physcian single		Tn.	Tn.	Tn.
WATSON,J.B.	38		Farmer	Ala.	Ala.	Ala.
" ,Fanny B.	28	wife		Ala.	Va.	Ala.
" ,Julia M.	14	dau		"	"	"
" ,James K.	12	son		"	"	"
MONTGOMERY,B.B.(single)	25	Boarder,Teach.		Ala.	Ala.	Ala.
WOODCOCK,T.S.	" 39	"	Farmer	"	Va.	"
WATSON,Adaline	4	dau.		Ala.	Va.	Ala.
125-126;GREENWALD,G.	43		Farmer	Europe	Eur.	Eur.
" ,D.	42	wife		"	"	"
" ,Sophia	16	dau		N.Y	"	"
" ,Saml.	14	son		Ohio	"	"
" ,Phillip	7	son		Ms.	"	"
" ,Anna	6	dau		"	"	"
HAWKINS,Manuel(B)	6	orphan		"	Ms.	Ms.

CENSUS 1880-SHARKEY CO.MS. Random listing
The numbers do not follow any pattern, so it is very difficult to separate households. SUPERVISORS DIST.#3. ENUMERATOR DIST.#114, ENUMERATOR G.Y.STEWART - BEAT # 3

Pg.1
1-1-EARLEY, J.W.	23	farm.Lab.	Ms.	Ms.	Ms.	
11-13; HOLDERAFT, A.W.	33	" "	"	Va.	"	
" , Matilda	33	wife	Ala.	Ala.	Ala.	
" , Mary E.	14	dau.	Ms.	"	"	
" , Martha J.	8	dau.	"	"	"	
" , Va.A.	6	dau	"	"	"	
" , Henry D.	4/12	son	"	"	"	
McCLENDON, Frank		step-son				

Pg.3
28-29; MILLER, C.O.	32	Farmer	Mich.	Mich.	Mich.	
" , M.	22	wife				
" , Wm.	4	son				
" , Teresa	3	dau.				
" , Claude	1	son				
McEVOY, J.H.(single)	27	Farmer	Ga.	Ire.	Ga.	
29-30; GIBBONS, Wm.	63	Farmer	Eng.	Eng.	Eng.	
" , Mary E.	47	wife	Ms.	Tn.	Ms.	
" , Wm.Jr.	13	son	"	Eng.	Ms.	
HAWKINS, Martha(B)	30	cook	"	"	"	
BANKS, Flora(B)	13	servant	"	"	"	
HAWKINS, Phil	40	"	"	"	"	

Pg.4
41-42; FERRIS, W.D., Sr.	57	Farmer	Ky.	Va.	Ms.	
" , Amanda C.	49	wife	Ms.	La.	Ms.	
" , T.L.	28	son	"	"	"	"
" , W.D., Jr.	18	son	"	"	"	"
" , Louisa K.	16	dau.	"	"	"	
" , Va.A.	14	dau	"	"	"	
" , Margaret C.	10	dau.	"	"	"	
" , Geo.G.	8		"	"	"	

Pg.6
60-71; GOODMAN, B.	39	M.D.	Va.	Va.	Va.	
" , Annie L.	25	wife	Ms.	Va.	Ms.	
" , Sampson	5	son	"	"	"	
" , Willie	3	son	"	"	"	
POWELL, Laura	28	boarder	La.	Md.	La.	
71-72; HARRISON, Hal(B)	22	servant	Ms.	Ms.	Ms.	
SHELBY, Thos.J.	63	Farmer	Tn.	Va.	Va.	
" , Emily M.	50	wife	La.	La.	La.	
" , Creath	31	son	"	Ms.	Tn.	La.
" , Mollie K.	15	dau	"	"	"	
VALLEAN, Wm.G.	21	boarder "	La.	N.Y.	La.	
72-73; SHELBY, Evan B.	33	Farmer	Ms.	Tn.	La.	
" , Emma	31	wife	"	Ms.	Ms.	
" , Lela	5	dau	"	"	"	
POWELL, Judge	29	(Married)	"	"	"	
" , Ella	25	boarder	"	"	"	
" , Corinne	3	neice	"	"	"	
74-75; MILLER, Jno.	31	single Farm.Lab.	"	"	"	
BREWER, A.T.	35	" " "	"	Ala.	Ala.	

Pg.8
49-50; LEECH, W.E.	31		" "	"	"	
" , A.J.	31	wife		"	N.C.	N.C.
" , Freddie	8	son		"	Ms.	Ms.
" , Moseley	2	son		"	"	"
POWERS, John	55	boarder, farm.lab.	Ire.	Ire	Ire.	

CENSUS 1880-SHARKEY CO.MS. Random listing.Sup.Dist.#3,Enu.#114

Pg.9

100-101;GIBSON,James	26		Farmer	Ga.	Ga.	Ga.
" ,Lou	25	wife		Ms.	Ms.	Ms.
" ,Gen.Jackson	6	son		Ms.	Ga.	Ms.
" ,Wm.C.	4	son		"	"	"
" ,Sallie	2	dau.		"	"	"
JENKINS,John	18	single	Laborer	"	Ms.	"
BUTTS,Thomas	30	"		"	"	"
106-107;MARTIN,M.P.(C?)	29		Farmer	La.	La.	La.
" ,Mary L.	27	wife		"	"	"
" ,Lizzie	7	dar.		"	"	"
" ,Willie	5	son		"	"	"
" ,Maude	2	dau.		Ms.	"	"
CHANEY,M.J.(m)	50	boarder		La.	La.	La.
" ,Olive R.	24	"		"	"	"
" ,Sterling	15	"		"	"	"
ELZEY,W.J.(m)	28	"		Ms.	Ms.	Ms.
" ,R.N.(m)	22	"		"	"	"
GILMAN,Filmore	22			Ill.	Ill.	Ill.
107-108;BURNEY,Robb	23			Ms.	Ms.	Ms.
" ,Mary	22	wife		"	"	"
GRIFFITH,Dony	9	boarder		"	"	"
108-109;SHADDRICK,Mal	20	single		Ala.	Ala.	Ala.
GRIFFITH,Thomas	6	brother?		Ms.	"	"

Pg.10

122-123;WOODWARD,John S.	32		Ms.	Ms.	Ms.
" ,Meena	30	wife	"	"	"
" ,Florence	9	dau	"	"	"
" ,Frank	8	son	"	"	"
" ,Willie	6	son	"	"	"
" ,Earl	4	son	"	"	"
" ,----	2/12	son	"	"	"

Pg.12

83-84;STEVENS,H.P.	36		Farmer	Ga.	Ga.	Ga.
" ,Harriet	32	wife		N.C.	N.C.	N.C.
FOOTE,H.L.	24	boarder,Genrl.store,	Ms.	S.C.	Va.
BARNARD,Ellen W.	23	"		N.C.	N.C.	N.C.
EMMITH,Ann(B)	46		Cook	Ms.	Ms.	Ms.
SPRIGGS,Julia(B)	8		servant	"	"	"

Pg.14

140-141;WOMACK,Frank	44			Ms.	Ga.	N.C.
" ,Fannie	40	wife		Ala.	N.C.	N.C.
" ,Lucy	11	dau		Ms.	Ms.	Ms.
" ,Ella	10	dau		"	"	"
" John	8	son		"	"	"
" Sallie	7	dau		"	"	"
" Allen	5	son		"	"	"
" Frank	3			"	"	"
" Annie	80	mother		N.C	N.C.	N.C.
"Aurela	30	sister		Ms.	Ga.	N.C.
141-142;ROGAN,L.W.	33		Farmer	Ms.	Md.	Md.
" ,Mattie A.	24	wife		Ms.	La.	Ms.
" ,Irby	6	son		"	Ms.	"
JAMES,Wilson(B)	40		servant	La.	La.	La.

CENSUS 1880-SHARKEY CO.,MS. Random Listing S.Dist.#3,Enu.#114
Pg.14
```
142-143:McCALEB,J.M.     43            Farmer         MS.        Ms.        Ky.
         "    ,C.H.      44 wife                      "          "          "
         "    ,John      19 son                       "          "          "
         "    ,W.S.      13 son                       "          "          "
         "    ,Lily      10 dau                       "          "          "
         "    ,Thos.      8 son                       "          "          "
         "    Matthew     6 son                       "          "          "
      WILLIAMS,WASH(B)   36            Servant(w/d)S.C.         S.C.       S.C
         "    ,Nancy(B)   8                "         Ms.         "         Ms.
143-144;RICHARDSON,SAM   21(B)         Farm. Lab.     "         Ms.         "
      WOODMAN,Dick(B)    65             "    "       Va.         "          "
      HICKMAN,W.H.       23            Physcian     Ala.        S.C.       S.C.
         "    ,Laura     27 wife                     MO.        Mo.        Mo.
      STANDARD,Alice      7 dau(step)                Ms.
         "    ,Walton     2 son          "           Ms.
```
Pg.15
```
151-151;CHANDLER,T.C.    46                          Ga.        Ga.        Ga.
         "      ,L.M.    21 wife                    Ala.       Ala.       Ala.
         "      ,T.A.     1                          Ms.        Ga.       Ala.
151-152;HARRISON,R.B.    49            Farmer        Tn.        Va.        Va.
         "      ,V.E.    44 wife                    Ala.        Va.        Tn.
         "      ,Charles 15 son                     Ala.        Tn.       Ala.
         "      ,Lucy     9                          Ms.        Tn.       Ala.
```
Pg.16
```
161-162;WATSON,Jacob     22            Farm.Labr.    "          "          Tn.
163-164;WALKER,J.P.      46            Farmer       Va.         Va.        Va.
         "    ,Hallie E. 35 wife                    Ala.        Tn.       Ala.
      ADAMS,Thos.F.      20 boarder                  "          "          "
      DUNCAN,Roxy         6   "                     Ms.        Ms.        Ms.
```
Pg.17
```
186-187;STURGIS,H.F.     24            Farmer       Ms.        S.C.       S.C.
         "    ,Addie A.  20 wife                     "
         "    ,Oscar D. 3/12 son                    Ms.        Ms.        Ms.
191-192;BRIDGES,E.T.     28            Farm          "          "          "
         "    ,Carrie    18 wife                     "          "          "
      KELLY,Robt.         3 ---                      "          Tn.        "
         "    ,Hillery    1 ---                      "          "          "
192-193;CRENSHAW,Mary E. 24                          "         S.C.        La.
      PRIDMORE,Edward     9                          "         Ms.        Ms.
```
¶NOTE:The following 2 households have been enumerated twice,but
are again copied-information slightly different.See Census pg.6
Household #71-72 &#72-73
```
195-196;SHELBY,E.B.      33            Farmer       Ms.        Tn.        La.
*        "    ,Emma S.   30 wife                     "
         "    ,Lela       6                          "
196-197;SHELBY,Thos.J.   59            Farmer       Ms.
         "    ,Emily     45 wife                    La.
         "    ,A.C.      31 son                     Ms.
         "    ,Mollie K. 15 dau.                     "
197-198;DEWES(sp?)Eugene 23                          "         Ms.        Ms.
         "    ,L.A.      27 wife                     "          "          "
         "    ,Liniel A.  1 dau.                     "          "          "
198-199;FIELDER,M.A.     20 (single)Farmer           "          "          "
         "    ,Mary      55 mother                   "          "          "
         "    ,Sarah R.  18 daul                     "          "          "
```
*Emma S.Shelby's tombstone reads;b.1849-d.1883.So 31 in 1880.

CENSUS 1880-SHARKEY CO.,Ms.Random Listing.
VILLAGE OF ROLLING FORK
Pg.18

```
168-169;SIMS,Thos.M.      39         Farmer         Va.    Va.    Va.
    "   ,Harriet M.22 wife                          Ohio   Ohio   Penn.
    "   ,Thos,E.      5 son                         Ms.    Va.    Ohio
    "   ,Arthur B.    4 son                          "      "      "
    "   ,Mary E.      2 dau                          "      "      "
169-170;CASEY,D.C.        38         Farmer         VA.    N.C.   N.C.
    "        ,C.E.    35 wife                       Ms.    Ms.    Ms.
170-171;ALDRIDGE,A.D.     40         Grocer          "     Ky.     "
    "           ,A.R. 31 wife                        "     Ms.    Tn.
    "           ,W.O. 10 son                         "      "     Ms.
    "           ,Dudley 13 dau.                      "      "      "
    "           ,A.D.Jr. 3 son                       "      "      "
        POWELL,A.H.       55         Clerk          Md.    Md.    Md.
171-172;SHANNON,H.E.      28         Town Marsh.    Ms.    Ms.    Ms.
    "          ,B.E.  17 wife                        "      "      "
    "          ,Luna  3/12 dau                       "      "      "
        Harrell,Sallie 10 neice                      "      "      "
        BLACK,Lizzie(B) 40           servant         "      "      "
172-173;CORTRIGHT,Chester-38         Grocer         N.Y.   N.Y.   N.Y.
    "           ,E.   32 wife                        "      "      "
    "           ,Ida   8 dau.                        "      "      "
    "           ,Earl E. 4 son                       "      "      "
    "           ,Louise 19 sister                    "      "      "
    "            I.A. 28 (single)                    "      "      "
173-174;ROBERTS,Wm.       33         carpenter       "      "      "
    "          ,Maggie 32 wife                      Ala.   Ala.   Ala.
    "          ,H.J.   3 dau                        Ms.    N.Y.   Ala.
    "           ---   3/12 son                       "      "      "
174-175;HARSH,John        47     Dry goods Merch.Ohio    Va.    Penn.
    "        ,Henrietta 42 wife                      "      "      "
    "        ,Frank   12 son                         "     Ohio   Penn.
    "        ,Maud    10 dau                         "      "      "
        SHELTON,W.H.      21     Dry goods clerkMs.        Va.    Va.
    "           ,S.F. 23         County clerk        "      "      "
        McLAURIN,W.K.     23         Lawyer          "     S.C.   Ms.
175-176;CLARK,Eliza       55 (w/d)                  Tn.    Tn.    Tn.
    "        ,Eugene 29 son     Farmer              Ms.     "      "
    "        ,Leigh  25 son     Lawyer               "      "      "
    "        ,S.J.   18 son                          "      "      "
    "        ,Pearl  14 dau                          "      "      "
        LEIGH,T.          50 sister                 Tn.     "      "
176-177;AARON,Wolf        36         Grocer         Prus.  Prus.  Prus.
    "        ,Fannie 26 wife                        N.Y.   N.Y.   N.Y.
    "        ,Alex.S. 2 son                         Ms.    Prus.  N.Y.
    "        ,Max R.  1 son                          "      "      "
        CORSON,T.A.       24     Telegraph Op.      Ms.    N.Y.   Md.
        GOLDMAN,E.        15     Dry goods clerkLa.        Austr. Bavar
```

Pg.19
```
177-178;BLUM,Charles H.24            Grocer         France Fr.    Fr.
    "       ,Rebecca  23 wife                       Calif. Poland Poland
    "       ,Moyer A.  2
        YARATZKY,Meyer(sing)20 bro/in/law,clerkEng.        Eng.   Eng.
        GOLDEN,Saml.     " 32        butcher         "      "      "
        HERMAN,Saml.     " 21    dry goods clerk Europe    Eur.   Eur.
```

CENSUS 1880-SHARKEY CO.,MS.Random listing.
VILLAGE OF R.F.,cont.

Pg.19

178-179;BAGGETT,L.(f)	58	(w/d)		N.C.	N.C.	N.C.
" ,N.T.	23	son-Deputy Sherif.	Ala.	"	"	
" ,G.M.	27	son Farmer		"	"	"
" ,S.M.	25	son "		"	"	"
" ,B.B.	19	son		"	"	"
" ,A.G.	15	dau		"	"	"
179-180;BAGGETT,J.R.	31	"		"	"	"
" ,M.E	25	wife		Tn.	Tn.	Tn.
" ,Alice	6	dau		Ms.	Ala.	Tn.
" ,Ella	4	dau		"	"	"
" ,J.W.	2	son		"	"	"
" ,J?B?	3/12			"	"	"
180-181;JOOR,John S.	30	Sheriff		Ms.	S.C.	Tn.
" ,Kate M.	24	wife		"	Tn.	"
" ,Fairy S.	1	dau.		"	Ms.	Ms.
LAIRD,W.C.	22	Telegraph Op.		"	"	"
181-182;SHELBY,M.E.(f)	39	Boarding House		N.C.	N.C.	N.C.
" ,R.K.	16	son		TX.	Ms.	N.C.
" ,F.B.	21	son		La.	"	Ms.?
" ,K.A.	15	dau		TX.	"	N.C.
" ,Mary B.	12	dau		Ms.	"	"
" ,Evan B.	10			"	"	"
182-183;BELL,Mary H.	42	(w/d)		Ms.		
" ,Alice E.	20	dau		"		
" ,James	18	son		"		
183-184;CORTRIGHT,J.H.	32			Ms.		
" ,C.R.	20	wife		Ms.		
184-185;PURVIS,Eveline	49	(w/d)Housekeeper		Ms.	La.	La.
" ,P.G.	32	son Sch.Teach.		Ms.	N.C.	Ms.
" ,Sallie F.	27	dau.		"	"	"
" ,Lula	25	dau		"	"	"
" ,Rebecca	22	dau.		"	"	"
185-186;BUTLER,J.E	56	mechanic		S.C.	Va.	S.C.
" ,C.J.	42	wife		La.	Ire.	Tn.
KELLY,John	31			Tn.	Ire.	Ire.
" ,E.B.	22	wife		Ms.	S.C.	La.
" ,Wm.	5	son		"	Tn.	Ms.

The end of Rolling Fork

Pg.21

2u3-204;McQUILLAN,W.B.	55	(w/d) Farmer		La.	La.	La.
SIMMONS,Bettie	11	gr.dau.		Ms.	Ms.	Ms.
" ,Nancy	8	" "		"	"	"
" ,Anna	6	" "		"	"	"
204-205;BROWN,W.D.	47	Lawyer		Tn.	Tn.	Tn.
" ,Alice V.	38			Ms.	"	Ms.
" ,W.R.	20	son single		Ms.	"	"
" ,Estelle	18	dau.		"	"	"
" ,Mena	15	dau.		"	"	"
" ,Prentis	12	son		"	"	"
" ,Garnett	8	dau		"	"	"
" ,Argyle	4	son		"	"	"
STEWART,G.Y.	28	lawyer		"	Ms.	Tn.
ORENDORF(F),T.J.	26	"		KY.	Ky.	Ky.

DENSUS 1880-SHARKEY CO.,MS.-Random Listing.
Pg.22

221-222;	DUDLEY,O.F.(m)	22 single		Ala.	N.C.	N.C.
	McCARY,E.M.	45 mother		N.C.	N.C.	N.C.
"	J.F.	15 brother		Ala.	"	"
	DUDLEY,E.A.	24 sister		"	"	"
	BAGGETT,---	67 single Farm Lab.		Tn.	Tn.	Tn.

Pg.23

228-229;	HOGG,J.M.	49	Farmer	Ala.	Ala.	Ala.
"	,Mary	26 wife		GA.	Ga.	Ga.
"	,Jos.	22 son		Ms.	Ala.	Ala.
"	,Issaquena	20 dau		"	"	"
"	,Francis H.	17 son Farmer		"	"	"
"	,Mollie	18 dau-in-law		"	"	"
"	,Mary	6 dau		"	"	"?
229-230;	MAXWELL,R.Y.	47	Farmer	Tn.	S.C.	S.C.
"	,Mary	47 wife		Ind.	Ind.	Ind.
"	,R.E.Lee	18 son		Ms.	Tn.	Ind.
"	,John G.	-- son		"	"	"
"	,Jeff Davis	--son		"	"	"
"	,Mary R.	--dau.		"	"	"
"	,Jno.Gilbert	--son		"	"	"
	RUSHING,Wm.H.	--step-son				
320-231;	BRITTON,F.A.(f)	52	Housekpr.	N.C.	N.C.	N.C.
	PARSONS,MARGARET	35 dau.		Ms.	N.C.	N.C.
"	,Charles	5 gr.son		N.J.	Ohio	Ms.
"	,Fannie	2 gr.dau.		Tn.	Ohio	Ms.
	BRITTON,Wm.	27 son Farmer		Ms.	N.C.	N.C.
"	,Mamie	22 Step²Dau.(in-law?)		Ms.	Va.	Ms.
"	,Wm.Jr.	5/12 gr.son		"	Ms.	"

NO NUMBERS FOR THE NEXT 4 SURNAMES
Pg.24

---	WADDILL,A.M.	52	M.D.	Mo.	Mo.	MO.
"	,A.C.	48 wife		Ms.	La.	La.
"	,Mollie	24 dau		Ms.	Mo.	"
"	,Georgia	14 dau		"	"	"
"	,Berta	3		"	"	"
"	,Anderson	11 son		"	"	"
---	ROBERTSON,J.H.	33		"	Tn.	Ms.
"	,Ida W.	--		"	Ms.	"
---	WRIGHT,Rebecca	54		"	"	"
"	,W.B.	22		"	"	"
"	,H.J.	20		"	"	"
---	ROBERTSON,Lulalo	24		"	Tn.	"

NEW ENUMERATOR:W.W.GIBSON-DIST.#115-BEAT #4

For many pages of Mr.Gibsons survey there is one big mess. He apparently didnot understand the system of recording persons birth,Fathers birth,& Mothers birth places. So have only copied persons birth place. He also was told to reverse names and he did!!!!such as J.G.PARHAM--became PARHAM,G.J. As you read it remember the initials and first name are reversed. Some households were not numbered--I have marked them **n/#**.   KB

Pg.3

29-29;	CHAMPION,M.W.	23	Agent on PLT.	Ms.		
	DOWELL,H.Wm.	29 boarder,Drug.Clerk		Ky.		
38-38;	HAUSER,Charles	23 single Grocer		Ohio		
"	,Geo.(marr.)	28 bro.Clerk in Store		"		
"	,Issaquena	19 wife		Ms.		
"	,Eliza	11/12		Ms.		
	PEARL,Bird(m)	24 Sing. peddler		Russia.		

*CENSUS 1880-SHARKEY CO.,MS.Random Listing.Dist.#115-Beat #4
```
n/#  ;MATTELL,Charles    24        Farmer          Ms.
     "      ,Josephine   23 wife                   Ms.
```
Pg.7
```
n/#; ORENDORF(F),W.W.    31 single,Farmer          Ky.
```
Pg.8
```
76-76;CRAIG,Joseph       47 Time South Review      Va.
     "     ,Elizabeth    39 wife                   La.
     "     ,K.Laura      16 dau                    La.
     "     ,Lola Lee      9 dau                    Tn.
     "     ,R.Lorena      7                        Ark.
     "     ,J.Irving      4 son                    Ark.
```
Pg.9
```
n/#; BROWN,T.L.J.        36 Agent on Pltn.         Ala.
     "    ,C.Mattie      28 wife                   Ms.
     "    ,Bertie        7/12                      Ms.
n/#; HELMETT,C.M.        30       Farmer           Germany
       "   ,G.Laura      24 wife                   Ms.
       "   ,M.Frances    1-4/12 daul               Ms.
n/#; GREEN,G.Henry       26       Labor            VA.
```
Pg.12
```
71-71;HALL,C.J.          42       Doctor           Ala.
     "   ,L.Sarah        36 wife                   Ms.
     "   ,B.John         11 son                    Ms.
     "   ,W.Jimmy        10 son                    Ms.
```
Pg.13
```
N/#; HARRIS,L.R.         23    Agent on Pltn.      La.
```
Pg.14
```
111-111;CRANE,C.W.       33     Brick mason        Pa.
       "    ,Fanny       22 wife                   Ms.
       "    ,M.Alice      6 dau                    Ark.
       "    ,H.James      3 son                    "
n/#; SAUNDERS,R.Wm.      20        Farmer          Ala.
       "     ,Miranda    25 wife                   Ms.
     LINGANT,Wm.          6 son                    Ms.
       "     ,A.R.       11 son                    Ms.
```
Pg.15
```
72-72:HULL,W.R.          23        Farmer          Ms.
     "   ,Henrietta      32 wife                   Ms.
     HIGGINS,Katie       14 dau.                   Ms.
73-73;BRANCH,J.Martha    40        Farmer          Ms.
     "     ,E.Wms.       16 son                    "
     "     ,Annie        12 dau                    "
n/#; McELOWN,Whinney     24     Raftsman           Mo.
78-78;SHELTON,D.G.       37        Farmer          Ala.
      "     ,R.A.        35 wife                   Ms.
      "     ,Irene        4                        Ms.
79-79;BOYAKIN,Eli        21        Farmer          "
      "     ,Lucinda     25 sis                    "
      "     ,Sallie      45 mother                 "
80-80;MURRAY,B.Jones     32    raftsman            Ill.
      "    ,Judith       32 wife                   Ind.
82-82;PARKS,D.S.         27        Farmer          Ms.
      "   ,Georgiana     21 wife                   "
83-83;RENALDS,Mary       50(w/d)   Farmer          Ms.
      "     ,Caroline    19 dau                    "
      "     ,Raney       17 son                    "
      "     ,H.James     16 son                    La.
```
*GIVEN NAMES ARE REVERSED

*CENSUS 1880-SHARKEY,CO.,MS. Random listing-Enu.#115,Beat #4

Pg.16

92-92;COWARD,D.W.	24		Labr.	Ms.
",RENALD,Lingo	23		"	"
92-92;PARKS,G.Holmes	45		Planter	Ms.
",A.Emily	35	wife		"
93-93;DAVENPORT,Louise	58		cook	"
",Henry	7	son		"

Pg.17

124-124;ANDERSON,R.N.	52	sing.	Farmer	Va.
127-127;MYERS,C.FRANK	31		Farmer	Ms.
131-131;PIGGS,F.J.(w/d)	35	male	Farmer	Ire.
132-132;LAWSON,Wm.	32		Grocer	Eng.

Pg.19

",Emily	38			Ala.
149-149;NIXON,B.John	34		Merchant	N.Y.
",R.J.	40	wife		"
",Exine	10	dau		Mich.

Pg.20

155-155;McKINSEY,R.H.	40		Farmer	N.C.
",A.Dora	33	wife		Ala.
",Lewis	11	son		"
",Saml.	8	son		"
",Eva	6/12	dau		"
McMAHON,Maggie	18	neice		S.C.
NICHOLSON,D.	25	boarder		Ala.
RANDOLPH,Wm.	25	"		Ms.
MYERS,Robt.	26	"	Farmer	"
157-157;CONNELL,A.W.	33		Farmer	Ala.
",E.S.	29	wife		La.
",Ernest	7	son		"
",Infant	6/12			Ms.
158-158;SINAI,Julius	34		Merchant	Poland
",Sarah	34	wife		"
",Moses	13	son sells dry gds.		N.Y.
",Bettie	7	dau		La.
",Joseph	5	son		"
",Hutee	2	dau		Ms.
",Barnard	25	bro.single		Pol.
159-159;MYERS,S.Robert	25	single	Farmer	Ms.
STRINGEY,Ben	25	boarder		"

Pg.21

172-172;SAUNDERS,J.J.	21		Farmer	Ms.
",W.Jesse	15	bro. laborer		"

Pg.22

175-175:HARRIS,J.A.(m)	21	single		"
MAHAFFEY,B.W.	18	boarder		"
BROWN,Thos.	24	"	Painter	"
176-176;BARNARD,H.W.	31		Physcian	"
",H.Ida	20	wife		"
-------BARNARD,T.W.	59		Farmer	"
",J.Eudora	48	wife		"
184-184; ",Willie	7	gr.son		"
-------BROOKS,B.(f)	80	w/d		"
HICKMAN,R----	14	gr.dau		"
SHRADER,T.M.	27		Carpenter	Ala.
186-186; ",C.Lula	17	wife		Ms.

Pg.23

198-198;OTTO,John	33		Carpenter	Mo.
",Mary	18	wife		Ms.

*GIVEN NAMES ARE REVERSED IN #115 LISTINGS

```
*CENSUS 1880-SHARKEY CO.,MS.-Random listing.Enu.#115-Beat #4
Pg.24
203-203;GRIFFITH,Henry   45        Farmer      Va.
        "    ,Sarah      35 wife               Tn.
        "    ,Henry      17 son    Lab.        "
        "    ,Bila       11 dau ⎤              "
        "    ,Mary       11 dau ⎦ twins        "
        "    ,Joseph      9 son                "
        "     Albert      7 son                "
Believe the next group belongs in Griffith household above.
204-204;McAMERAN,Thos.   31 boarder  single    Va.
        ROWELL,David     50    "     w/d       Ms.
n/#;BARNARD,Eliza(m)     46 w/d    Farmer      La.
    "    ,Blackburn      22 son                Ms.
    "    ,W.Thos.        17 son                "
    "    ,G.Hamilkins    15 son ⎤              "
    "    ,Brasher        15 son ⎦ twins        "
    "    ,Clauand        11 dau                "
206-206;LEANETT,George   28        Farmer      Ohio
        "    ,Florida    20 wife               Ms.
        "    ,C.Hines    4/12                  "
207-207;JOLLY,C.George   35        Farmer      Ohio
        "    ,Lucinda    35 wife               Ms.
        "    ,Effa        7 dau                "
208-208;LACY,James       22        Farmer      Va.
        "    ,Sallie     18 wife               Ms.
        "    ,Rosa       2/12 dau ⎤            Ms.
        "    ,Re         2/11 dau ⎦ twins      "
211-211;BRADFORD,C.L.    38        Minister    La.
        "    ,E.Mary     31 wife               La.
        "    ,Hary       12 son                "
        "    ,Hissie      9 son                "
        "    ,Sallie      7 dau                "
        "    ,Julia      21 dau.               Ms.
212-212;GORMAN,T.B.      33        Carpenter   "
        "    ,Mattie L   18 wife               "
Pg.25
213-213:LEE,Richard      48        Farmer      "
        "   ,Mary        44 wife               "
        "   ,O.Anna      14 dau                "
        "   ,E.Sophia     8 dau.               "
214-214;ROSEN,August     34        Farmer      Sweden
        "    ,E.Mary     22 wife               Ms.
215-215;  "  ,Alfred     9/12 (Sept.)son       "
        PUTNELL,George   87 Boarder  Labr.     Ala.
216-216;WALKER,Wm.       36        Farmer      Ms.
        "    ,Elizabeth  37 wife               "
        "    ,James      15 son                "
        "    ,Mollie      9 dau                "
        "    ,Matthew     7 son                "
        "    ,Sallie      4 dau                "
        HENRY,Patrick    15 boarder            "

217-217;CHILDERS,C.THOS. 50                    Ala.
        "    ,Sarah      39 wife               "
        "    ,Kitty Jane 23 dau                Ms.
        "    ,Lou        17 "                  "
        "    ,Luther     16 son                "
continued on next page-------------------------
*GIVEN NAMES REVERSED BY *115ENUMERATOR
```

*CENSUS 1880-SHARKEY CO.,MS.-Random listing.Enu.#115,Beat #4
Cont.CHILDERS,C.Thos.
" ,Sallie   14 dau   Ms.
" ,Henry   12 son   "
" ,James   9 son   "
" ,Richard   8 son   "
" ,Thomas   6 son   "
" ,Matthew   2 son   "
" ,Emily   4/12(Feb.)dau.   "
218-218;SANDERS,R.James 38   Farmer   Ky.
   " ,E.A.Martha 37 wife   Ms.
   " ,Edward   10 son   "
   " ,Lee Wm.   8 son   "
   " ,Thos.   5 son   "
   " ,Infant   3/12(Feb)   "
219-219;TAYLOR,C.M.   54   Farmer   Ky.
   "   ,Sallie 52 wife   "
    SMITH,Ben   55 boarder single   Ms.
220-220;STEVENS,O.Joel 50 Steamboat man   "
   " ,F.Mary   26 wife   "
   " ,W.George 22 son   Pilot(boat)   "
   " ,L.Frank   21 son   Farmer   "
   " ,B.John   20 son   Pilot   "
   " ,E.Ed.   17 son   Labr.   "
   " ,Y.Joel   15 son   "   "
   " ,S.Levi   12 son   "   "
   " ,B.Eli   4 son   "
   " ,Maud   4/12(Feb.)dau.   "
221-221;McKINZU,A.Peter 28   Farmer   Scotland
   "   ,D.E.   20 wife   Ms.
   "   ,D.J.   1 son   "

Pg.26
224-224;TIFFORD,Lenard 50   Farmer   Tn.
   "   ,Betty   17 dau   "
   "   ,George 15 son   Labr.   Ms.
   "   ,Wm.   15 son   "   "
225-225;STUBBLEFIELD,Ben,38 boarder w/d   "
    BARNEY,Taylor 25 boarder single   "
226-226;BYSON,Peter   27   "   (Marr.)Farm. "
   "   ,Ellen   20 wife
    LANIER,Patience 5 (B)orphan   "
    *McDOUGALL,M.John 40 single Farmer   Nova Scotia
*Cannot tell whether McDougall belongs in the Byson Household
227-227;JONES,W.J.   62 w/d Agt.Steambt.Ldg. N.C.
   "   ,Martha 25 dau.single   Ms.
   "   ,Mary   22 dau   "   "
   "   ,M.Fanny 16 dau   "
   "   ,C.Wm.   15 son   "
   "   ,Benj.   21 son sing.Farm.   "
228-228;PENDEROIS,Jackson 26   Farmer   "
   "   ,Mary   24 wife   "
   "   ,Frank   2 son   "
   "   ,Caroline 5/12   "
229-229;HOOD,H.James   46   Farmer   Ky.
   "   ,Amanda 30 wife   Ms.
   "   ,Jenny   10 dau   "
   "   ,James   4 son   "
                                           "

*GIVEN NAMES REVERSED BY #115 ENU.

*CENSUS 1880-SHARKEY CO.,MS.-Random listing.Enu.#115-Beat #4

```
230-230;ODOM,M.James     50         Farmer      S.C.
        " ,J.Mary        45 wife                Ms.
        " ,F.Mary W.     14 dau                  "
        " ,John           8 son                  "
        " ,Mattie         5 dau                  "
231-231;MITCHELL,C.John 19 boarder sing.Labr.Ark.
        DODY,V.W.        40    "     "    "  Ga.
```
Pg.27
```
232-232;LINGY,James      57         Farmer      Md.
        " ,E.Mary        44 wife                Ms.
234-234;DIOMINE,Patrick  35         Farmer      Conn.
        " ,Catharine     28 wife                Ms.
        " ,Anna           5 dau                  "
        " ,Bernard       31 boarder sing.Raftman Conn.
        " ,Lucy          58 sister single        Conn.
235-235;BRICKELL,Daniel  47 sing. Farmer        Ireland
        NELSON,Earnest   28 boarder Labr.       Sweden
236-236;PENDEROIS,H.Tho. 20                     Ms.
        "       ,Mollie  22 wife                Ms.
237-237:COVINGTON,Taylor 30         Farmer       "
        "    ,Anna       26 wife                 "
        "    ,John        4 son                  "
        HARRIS,Hillman   45 w/d board.Labr.      "
238-238;WALKER,Wm.       26         Farmer       "
        "    ,Parmelia   26 wife                 "
        "    ,George      6 son                  "
        "    ,Mary Jane   5 dau                  "
        "    ,J.Andrew   5/12                    "
239-239;BROWN,L.Thos.    56         Farmer      Tn.
        "    ,Caroline   50 wife                Ala.
        POWELL,George    23 son    Labr.        Ms.
240-240:ONEAL,C.M.       24         Farmer      Ala.
        "    ,C.Jane     31 wife     "
        "    ,E.Jane     11 dau                 La.
        "    ,W.John      6 son                 Ms.
        "    ,E.Mary      4 dau                  "
241-241;MARCH.W.G.       32                     GA.
        "    ,J.Anna     24 wife                Ala.
        MOTT,Moranda     50 mother w/d          La.
242-242;KADIKIN,John     22         Farmer      Ireland
        "       ,Sallie  23 wife                Ms.
        "       ,Bell     8 dau                  "
     *  RANOR,Caroline    7 dau                  "
        "    ,Frank     10/12 son                "
243-243:  " ,Robert      38                      "
        "    ,Amanda     30 wife                 "
        "    ,Laura      14 dau.                 "
        "    ,Henry       9 son                  "
        "    ,Thomas      7 son                  "
        "    ,Leona       6 dau                  "
        "    ,Lulla       4 dau.                 "
```
*have copied sequence of names as recorded
244-244;TAYLOR,Richard 19 son ?   "
Taylor could possibly belong to Ranor household,hard to tell.
*GIVEN NAMES REVERSED BY #115 ENU.

```
*CENSUS 1880-SHARKEY Co.,Ms.Random listing.Enu.#115,Beat #4
Pg.28
253-253;MAYHAW,---        28      Farmer         Tn.
       " ,Mary           20 wife                 Ms.
       " ,Wm.             3 son                  "
       " ,Minie           1 dau                  "
         CHILDERS,Patrick 15 boarder   Labr.     "
Pg.30
267-267;PARHAM,G.J.       28      Planter&Agent  La.
       " ,G.Alice        23 wife                 Ms.
       " ,J.Henry         3 son                  "
Pg.31
n/n;BELL,F.M.             61 w/d    Blk.smith    Ms.
Pg.32
284-284;WALTON,H.C.       39      Farmer         "
       " ,G.Louise       38 wife                 S.C.
         FARR,Danl.       6 nephew               Ms.
       " ,Medora         28 sister single        "
285-285;ANDERSON,N.D      69      Farmer         Va.
       " ,H.Minerva      50 wife                 "
       " ,H.Margaret     21 dau.Music Teach.     "
286-286;Williams,Saml.    29      Labr           Ala.
       " ,Fanny          23 wife                 "
       " ,W.Rubin         8 son                  "
289-289;WILLSON,Wm.       27      Farmer         Ms.
       " ,Sallie         25 wife                 "
       " ,Marion          7 son                  "
       " ,Joseph          6 son                  "
       " ,Charles         3 son                  "
       " ,Minnie          3/12 (March)dau.       "
Pg.33
294-294:McKINNEY,H.C.W.   36 single Merchant     "
       "        ,H.C.,Jr.22  "    Clerk          "
         GRANGER,W.B.M.   23 board.sing.Teach.   Md.
*295-295:OWENS,B.L.       26  "    "   Clerk     Ms.
         MILLER,C.W.      23  "    "    "        Ky.
         TAYLOR,F.J.      31  "    "   Doctor    Ky.
*Believe Owens,Miller,Taylor should be in McKinney household.
297-297;PARHAM,G.Henry    31 Dry Gds.Clerk       La.
       " ,J.Mary         31 wife                 La.
       " ,H.Charles       2 son                  Ms.
298-298;DEUTSER,E.(m)     29 single Merchant     Russia
299-299;HICKMAN,B.G.      19 boarder Clerk       Ms.
300-300:DOVER,S.          33      Merchant       Prussia
       " ,H.Caroline     27 wife                 Hanover
       " ,B.Joseph        4 son                  Ms.
       " ,Selina          2 dau                  "
302-302;STEARN,G.H.       60 Magistrate& Clerk   Ms.
       " ,Elizabeth      40 wife                 "
303-303;HAUSER,Gust       30 single Grocer       Ill.
304-304;  " ,Christopher  32 w/d Merc.& Farm.    Ill.
       " ,M.A.            4 son                  Ms.
305-305:RICKARD,Henry     34 single,Merchant     N.Y.
         HOOKER,Frank     21  "    Clerk,        Ms.
309-309;MILLER,A.         25  "   Physcian       Ky.
310-310;BENTLY,S.J.       40      Farmer         Ms.
       " ,Issabella      36 wife                 "
       " ,T.Wm.          13 son                  "
       " ,Eulaner        11 dau.                 "
       " ,Oliver          5 dau.                 "
       " ,E.Mary          1 dau.                 "
```

*CENSUS 1880-SHARKEY CO.,MS.Random listing.Enu.#115-Beat #4
```
311-311;McMILLEN,Joseph  64 w/d   Farmer          Ala.
         " ,J.Eliza      50 wife                   Ms.
         " ,E.Mary       26 dau. single            "
         " ,Maggie       16 dau.    "              "
         " ,J.Bula       15 dau.                   "
         " ,Jenella      12 dau.                   "
312-312;BOHAM,Joana      30 w/d   House Kpr.       "
```
Pg.34
```
316-316;LIVERSINGER,John 55       Blk.Smith       Eng.
         " ,Elizabeth    36 wife                   "
         " ,Saml.        11 son                    "
         " ,A.Henry      11 son                    "
         " ,W.John       10/12(Dec.)son            Ms.
         " ,Henry Jr.    14 nephew,Blk.Smith       "
320-320;WIGGINS,Bell(f)  30 w/d/  Farming          "
         " ,John         13 son                    "
         " ,Eliza        12 dau                    "
         " ,Eddie        11 son                    "
         " ,Ella          8 dau                    "
         " ,Lilly         6 dau                    "
321-321;BOUSHILL,Thos.   30 sing. Farmer          Ala.
        DIXON,E.Mary     35 sis. w/d               "
         " ,Thos         17 son                    "
322-322; " ,Wm.          11 son                    "
        BOUSHILL,Peter   26 bro.sing.Farmer       Ala.
```
Pg.35
```
326-326;BALLINGTON,Frank 28 sing.  Labr.          Ga.
        BAILEY,W.J.      47 Marr.Steambt.man      Ind.
328-328;BROWNLEY,Danl.   32 w/d Labr.             Ms.
        COHN,Saml.       26 single  Merchant      Poland
        COLE,Chas.       31   "     Farmer        Ms.
331-331:DARNELL,T.Y.     34 w/d    Farmer         Ill.
```
Pg.36
```
340-340:HOGG,M.W.        28        Farmer         Ms.
         " ,Pricilla     30 wife                   "
         " ,Anny         11 dau.                   "
         " ,Wm.           9 dau.?                  "
         " ,Rebecca       7  "                     "
         " ,Eliza         5  "                     "
         " ,Edward        4 son                    "
         " ,Julius        2  "                     "
341-341:HELMICH,C.M.     41        Farmer          "
         " ,Sophia       36 wife                   "
         " ,Rosa         16 dau.                   "
         " ,Pollyann     13 dau                    "
         " ,John         11 son                    "
         " ,Robert        9 son                    "
         " ,Rachel        7 dau                    "
         " ,Corinne       5  "                     "
         " ,Hampton       1 son                    "
```
Pg.37
```
347-347:PENDEROIS,R.P.   51 (Billious)Farmer      S.C.
         " ,Mary         50 wife," Sick           N.C.
         " ,V.Mary       18 dau.     "            Ms.
         " ,Anna         16  "                     "
         " ,Tobias       14 son                    "
```
*GIVEN NAMES REVERSED BY *115 ENU.

```
CENSUS 1880-SHARKEY CO.,MS.Random Listing.Enu.#115-Beat #4
348-348:BARNES,T.S.      29      Farmer        Ky.
    "      ,Cathern  23 wife                   Ms.
    "      ,Ida       4                         "
    "      ,Edward   10/12(Aug.)son            Ms.
349-349:JONES,H.JOHN      32 single Farmer     Ms.
    "      ,A.Jane   26 sister single          Ms.
    "      ,Selina   19  "         "            "
    "      ,Thomas   21 bro.single, labr.       "
    "      ,C.M.     17  "         "            "     "
    "      ,N.Eliza  36 sis. single             "
```

REMEMBER WHEN READING GIVEN NAME & INITIALS ARE REVERSED

```
350-350:SHUMPORT,C.D.     29 single-Commercial Agt.  S.C.
Pg.38
n/no.  :ANDERSON,Wm.      28 single Farmer     Ms.
        ALEXANDER,O.S.    32 Boarder,Singl.Lab.Ala
    "      ,Moses    31   "     ,Marr. Farm.Ga.
    "      ,Hannah   35 wife Lab.               "
*359-359"  ,Sophia   14 dau                    --
    "      ,Gracey   11 dau                    --
    "      ,Thomas    9 son                    --
n/no   :BAY,F.RANSOM     39 w/d    Farmer      Ms.
360-360:BUCK,W.J         61        Planter     Ky.
    "      ,Emily    53 wife                   Ms.
    "      ,Charles  26 son    Farmer          Ms.
    "      ,Sophia   19 wife Seanstress         "
361-361:BLUM,Jacob       42        Farmer      Prussia
    "      ,Caroline 40 wife                    "
    "      ,Patsey   16 dau.                   Ms.
    "      ,Robt.    13 son                     "
Pg.39
362-362:BARNARD,B.W.     33        Farm.       Ms.
    "      ,G.Henri  21 wife                   La.
    "      ,West     10 son                    Ms.
    "      ,Virginia  8 dau.                    "
    "      ,Wm.Jr.    7 son                     "
375-375:BROWN,M.John     55 w/d    Farmer      Va.
        PHELPS,M.Charley18 boarder,singl.Lab.Ms.
Pg.40
n/no   :BLAKE,C.E.       46 single Mechanic    Va.
Pg.41
386-386:DONAVAN,Thomas 31           Farmer     Penn.
    "         ,Mary   26 wife                  N.Y.
    "         ,Wm.    11 son                   Mo.
    "         ,Una     8 dau.                   "
    "         ,Nancy   6 dau                    "
        CURTIN,James     19 Boarder,single,Lab. Tn.
387-387:ROBERTS,Ben      53        Mechanic    N.Y.
    "      ,M.Sarah  52 wife                    "
    "      ,C.Jacob  21 son single              "
    "      ,Q.John   19  "      "               "
393-393:BODAY,C.Fanny    45        w/d         N.C.
        BOLTON,C.J.      24 son,single,Farmer   "
        BODAY,L.Phillip  15 son    Lab.        Ms.
    "      ,Sallie   13 dau.                   Ms.
    "      ,Lula     11  "                      "
    "      ,Mitta     8 dau.                    "
```

CENSUS 1880-SHARKEY CO.,Ms.random listing.Enu.#115-Beat#4
Pg.42 GIVEN NAMES ARE REVERSED
```
397-397:BALLINGER,Leonidie 28    Mechanic      Ohio
         HOUSER,Martha     58 mother w/d         "
n/no   :GREEN,John        20 single Lab.        Ms.
         "     ,Layfayette 24        Farmer     "
400-400: "     ,Fanny      24 wife              "
         "     ,Orainy     4 dau                "
         "     ,Wm.        3 son                "
         "     ,Re Della   5/11(Jan.)dau.       "
         "     ,James     14 brother, Lab.     "
401-401:BROWN,Edmund       42 single  Painter   Ire.
```
P.44
```
416-416:BAILEY,P.O.        48        Lawyer     Ms.
         "     ,Augusta    27 wife              "
         "     ,Pinckney   19 son  Lab.         "
         "     ,Samuel     12 son               Ms
        --"--,Jones--------2-son-(Written in)"died Jan.1st 1880"
        --"--,Infant-------son-(   "     "  ) :  "    "    "
```
Pg.45
```
424-424:WATSON,E.Joseph 30         single Farmer  N.C.
         "     ,Annie     28 sister-single       "
         "      Mary      24    "       "        "
         "     ,Fannie    19    "       "        "
         "     ,C.Thomas 18 brother     "        "
426-426:ALEXANDER,B.S.    47                     Ms.
         "     ,O.A.      37 wife                "
         "     ,R.James    4 son                 "
         "     ,O.Mary     5 dau.                "
         "     ,Brice      3 son                 "
```
P.46
```
432-432:CHAMPION,M.G.(m)25 w/d   Farmer     Ga.
         "     ,G.Robt    10 son                 Ms.
436-436:CHAISING,F.J.     30       Farmer        "
         "     ,A.Eliza   19                     "
437-437:MATTELLE,M.J.(f)36 w/d Teacher           "
    ¶    "     ,Robert    21 son-single-Farmer  "
    ¶    "     ,Joseph    11 son-sick with chills- Ms.
    ¶    "     ,Minnie     9 dau                Ms.
    ¶    "     ,James      6 son                 "
    ¶    "     ,George     3 son                 "
    ¶ BRIDGES,E.C.         17 dau w/d            La.
438-438:CHISOLM,V.Nancy(f) 52   Farming          Ms.
         "     ,J.Thos.    20 son                "
         "     ,R.John     11 son                "
439-439:THOMPSON,T.Wm.     41                    Ohio
         "     ,Violet     37 wife               Ms.
         "     ,Andrew     15 son                "
```
P.48
```
n/n    :RITCHIE,W.J.       32 single  Farmer    "
        COLLINS,L.J.       22 single  Farmer    "
```
SUPERVISORS DIST.#3,ENUMERATOR DIST.#116,BEAT #5 BY W.B.BARNARD
P.1 GIVEN NAMES ARE REVERSED ALSO BY #116
```
1-1:HAMMERS,R.Thomas      58       Farmer    Tn.   Tn.   Tn.
     "     ,Jane          52 wife            Ms.   Ms.   Ms.
     "     ,L.John        27 son-single-Labr. "    "     "
     "     ,Elizabeth     22 dau. afflicted   "    "     "
     "     ,Anna          13 dau              "    "     "
(cont.next page)
```
¶NOTE:Listed in church records pg.108 as MALLET(T)

CENSUS 1880-SHARKEY CO.,MS.Dist.#3,Enu.#116,Beat #5,W.B.BARNARD
(Cont.1-1 HAMMERS)*Barnard also is reversing first names.

```
      HAMMERS,A.Susan      11 dau                    Ms.
        "    ,William       7 son                     "
      JOHNSON,Allen        20 boarder-singl.Lab."
2-2;TERRILL,Sarah          65 w/d                     "
        "    ,Morgan       20 son                    La.
        "    ,Leona        15 dau                     "
      YOUNG,Thos.           7 nephew                  "
      CARLISLE,John        18 boarder-single         Ala.
6-6:CLARY,John             47      Farmer           Ireland
        "   ,Elizabeth     53 wife                   Fa.
      PARISH,Anna          20 dau.-divorced          Ms.
        "   ,John           3 son                     "
      GAMBILL,Fanny        22 dau. marr.              "
        "    ,E.William     3 son                     "
        "    ,E.James     10/12 Aug. son              "
      WEAKS,Juline         13 dau                     "
7-7:SMITH,Charles          38      Farmer          Germany
        "   ,Mary          26 wife                    "
        "   ,A.Theodore     4 son                    Ms.
        "   ,G.Ida          2 dau.                    "
8-8:HENRY,H.CHARLEY        45      Farmer            Tn.
        "   ,E.Mary        25 wife                   Ms.
        "   ,E.Calvin(?)    6 son                     "
        "   ,N.Gidion       4 son                     "
        "   ,V.Eliza        1 dau                     "
9-9:GRICE,E.R.             30 w/d  Farmer           Ala.
        "   ,A.Nancy       60 mother w/d             Ga.
        "   ,F.Betty       19 dau   single           Ms.
10-10:CONNERS,James        24 single-Farmer         Ala.
P.2
n/n:PEMBURTON,H.M.         39 single Farmer          Ky.
P.7
62-62:STRINGFELLOW,Lewis 27        Labr.            Ala.
        "   ,Eliza         20 wife                    "
        "   ,Eddy           3                         "
      BULLIKEN,Betty       16 nice                    "
63-63:PAGE,Wyatt           27      Farmer           Ms.
        ",Janey            24 wife                  Ala.
      SASSAMAN,Barnard     10 bro.  Labr.             "
        "      ,Eugene      8   "                     "
        "      ,Blunt      19   "      "              "
```

#ENUMERATOR BARNARD REPEATS A FEW PAGES,THEN CONTINUES:
P.13
```
120-120:PERKINS,P.S.       47      Farmer           Ms.
        "   ,A.Margaret    30 wife                    "
        "   ,E.Mary        13 dau                     "
        "   ,H.Bob         11 son crippled            "
        "   ,A.Susan        7 dau                     "
        "   ,S.S.Samuel     3 son                     "
        "   ,A.Elizabeth    2 dau                     "
        "   ,R.James        1 son                     "
```
P.16
```
150-150:WILLIAMS,John      25      Farmer           La.
        "       ,Jane      20 wife                   Ga.
        "       ,James      2 son                    Ms.
        "       Infant    6/12     son                "
      WATSON,J.E           25      Teacher            "
```

CENSUS 1880-SHARKEY Co.Ms.Dist.#3,Enu.#116,Beat #5
P.16 cont.
```
151-151:BRANTLEY,John    40         Farmer       Ms.
        "      ,Delia    40 wife                 "
        "      ,Abe      12 son                  "
        "      ,Sallie   10 dau.                 "
        "      ,Mary      8 dau.                 "
153-153:BAYAFOURS,Thomas 34         Farmer       "
        "      ,Margaret 32 wife                 "
        "      ,Nada     13 dau                  "
        "      ,Lela     11 dau                  "
        "      ,Clifton   8 son                  "
        "      ,Ona       3 dau.                 "
        RANSOM,Bailey    17 son                  "
        THOMAS,Thomas    19 boarder              Ala
156-156:MARSTON,John     38         Labr.        Ms.
        WARE,Ann         28 boarder marr.        Ga.
        MARSTON,Mary     58 mother w/d           Ms.
P.17
161-161:VANVACOVAN,Willie 40        Farmer       La.    La.   La.
        "      ,Sallie   36 wife                 Ms.    Ms.   Ms.
        "      ,Henrietta 5 dau                  "      La.   "
        "      ,Henry     3 son                  La.
162-162:VANVACOVAN,Frank 22         Farmer       La.
        "      ,Alice    19 wife                 "
        "      ,Mary     60 mother w/d           La.
163-163:LATIMER,Dock*    23         Labr.        Ala.
        "      ,Hester*  25 wife    "            Va.
164-164:SIMMONS,Emeral*  21                      Ala.
        "      ,Louisa*  30 wife                 Va.
        "      ,Rosa      2 dau                  Ms.
165-165:WILLIAMS,John*   17         Labr.        Ms.
        "      ,Abraham   7 ---                  Ms.
        "      ,James     4 ---                  Ms.
        MARR,Thomas*     25 boarder-singl.-Lab.  Ala.
        CAMBESS,Isom*    50  "      w/d          "      "
166-166:WARREN,Frances*  23 w/d     Labr.        Va.
        "      ,William  12 son                  Ms.    Va.   Va.
        "      ,Ella      6 dau                  La.
167-167:BELL,William*    70         Labr.        Ala.
        "      ,Jane*    35 wife                 La.
168-168:CLOYD(?),Mc.(m)  37 boarder-singl.Farm.  Ky.
        RUTHERFORD,Jos.  16  "          "  Labr. "
```
¶Believe the next 4 households are really 1 household
```
170=170:ELLIS,H.William  40
        "      ,J.M.     28 wife
        "      ,Elizabeth 12 dau
171-171:ANDERSON,Eliz.   69 mother               S.C.
        TERRILL,David    24 boarder-single       Ms.
172-172:STACY,Hinds      24  "         "         "
        GILMORE,T.G.     40  "      w/d          "
        COLEMAN,Charles  35  "         Single    "
173-173:NOVELL,Thos.     45  "         "         "
        GRANT,Wm.        22  "         "         "
        DIXON,Ellick(B)* 23  "      w/d          Ala
```
*CANNOT READ OR WRITE

```
CENSUS 1880 SHARKEY CO.MS.Dist.#3,Enu.#116,Beat #5
P.18 INITIALS AND GIVEN NAMES ARE REVERSED
181-181:WILLIAMS,M.T     42 w/d      Farmer        Ms.
     "      ,Earnest     17 son      Labr.         Ms.
     "      ,Elizabeth   19 dau.                    "
     "      ,Ella        14 dau                     "
     "      ,Ida         13 dau                     "
     "      ,Ada          3 dau                     "
        GRAMLAIN,Daniel  19 boarder single          "
n/n:    TUNSELL,George   18 single   Labr.         Ms.
          ", Nicholas    21 bro.single,Labr         "
183-183:SAVAGE,Ann       70 Mother w/d              "
P.19
189-189:DIAMOND,L.R.(f)  59 w/d                    Ohio
     "        ,R.A.      24 son sing.dry gds.clerk       Ill.
190-190:HALEY,Mikeil     35          Farmer        Ireland
     "     ,Eliza        28 wife                   Ms.
     "     ,Fannie        3 dau                    Ms.
191-191:DIAMOND,C.John   24          Farm.         Ill.
     "       ,Elizabeth  19 wife                   Ms.
        COLETT,---       12 ---                     "
        ROBINSON,Lee      8 orphan                  "
192-192:CARROLL,Charles  34          Farmer        Ala.
     "       ,Emeline    36 wife                   Tn.
     "       ,Jeanette   9/12 Sept.dau.            Ms.
193-193:LOPER,Buck       33                        Tex.
     "     ,Susannah     21 wife                   Ms.
     "     ,Wm.           4 son                     "
     "     ,Leona         2 dau.                    "
        RILEY,Lee        28 boarder single          "
     "     ,George       24 bro."         "         "
195-195:ONEAL,Robert     28                         "
     "     ,Josephine    22 wife                    "
     "     ,Lenard       9/12 Sept. son             "
196-196:  " ,Earline     48 mother                 Tn.
     "     ,Harold       22 son single Farmer      Ms.
     "     ,Thos.        21  "       "      Lab.    "
197-197:  " ,Levy        18  "                      "
     "     ,John         16  "                      "
     "     ,Della        12 dau                     "
198-198:GILL,Nelson      31          Farmer         "
     "    ,Betty         25 wife                    "
     "    ,Clifton        6 son                     "
     "    ,Cran          10/12 son                  "
199-199:BOYAKIN,W.G.     55          Farmer         "
     "       ,Armelia    56 wife                    "
     "       ,Sanders    14 son      Lab.           "
     "       ,Coleton    10 dau                     "
     "       ,Eudora      4 dau                     "
     "       ,infant     9/11 son sick              "
        ADAMS,J.A.       20 boarder,singl.Farmer   Ms.

P.20
203-203:STEVENS,John     28          Farmer        Ms.
     "       ,Amelia     18 wife                    "
     "       ,Alma       3/12 March dau             "
        RAGEN,John       24 boarder single          "
```

CENSUS 1880-SHARKEY CO.,MS.Dist.3,Enu.116,Beat 5
P.20-cont.

204-204:BRIDGES,A.Mary	33 w/d	Farmer		Ms.	
LEWIS,E.Thos.	12	son		"	
" ,Benjamin	11	son		"	
" ,Elizabeth	9	dau		"	
" ,Cornelius	7	son		"	
BRIDGES,Pemberton	5	son		"	
ROGERS,John	26			"	
205-205:COLE,Charles	38			N.Y.	
" ,Emeline	20	wife		"	
n/n;WIGGINS,P.L.(m)	28			Ala	
" ,Leodecia	25	wife		"	
" ,Franklin	4	son		"	
" ,Jaba	3	dau		"	
" ,Gertrude	2	dau		"	
" ,Infant	6/12 Dec.	dau		Ms.	
" ,E.Mary	60	mother		Ala	
ELLIOTTE,Mattie	12	gr.dau		"	
" ,Addie	10	" "		"	
206-206:ELLINGTON,F.B.	47			Ky.	
" ,Elizabeth	37	wife		Ill.	Ill.
" ,Claird	15	son		"	
" ,Cora	10	dau		La.	
" ,John	4	son		Ms.	
207-207:ELLINGTON,Gilford	45			Ohio	
" ,Agnes	14	dau		Ill.	
" ,Hattie	12	dau		"	
" ,Ben	9	son		"	
" ,Lizzie	5	dau		"	
208-208:DUKE,William	35		Farmer	Ohio	
",Henrietta	28	wife		Ill.	
",Katie	6	dau		Ms.	
",Lizzie	5	dau		"	
",Esta	8/12	dau		"	

P.21

209-209:COULTER,Joseph	25	boarder	single	Ms.	
STAFFER,Abram	26	"	"	"	
210-210:FARRIS,Daniel	36		Farmer	Tex.	¶If Daniel is a
" ,Ann	30	wife		"	bro.to C.R. in
" ,Tillman	8			Ms.	the next house-
" ,Lobelia	6	dau		"	hold, I do not
" ,Eldora	4	dau		"	know whether they
211-211:HARRIS,C.R.	23	brother	Farmer	Tex.	are HARRIS or
" ,Mary	18	wife		Ms.	FARRIS
212-212:FLOYD,G.A.	30		Farmer	Tn.	
" ,Jane Mary	28	wife		Ms.	
" ,James	12	son		"	
" ,Cora	10	son(?)		"	
" ,Walter	6	son		"	
" ,Ida	3	dau		"	
213-213;WHEELER,William	30		Farmer	"	
" ,Elizabeth	16	wife		Ala.	
214-214:WHEELER,Augustus	32		Farmer	Ms.	
" ,Louisa	20	wife		"	
" ,Nevena	2	dau		"	

GIVEN NAMES & INITIALS ARE REVERSED.SPELLING OF SOME OF THE NAMES VERY SUSPECT!

CENSUS 1880-SHARKEY CO.,MS.Dist.3,Enu#116,Beat #5 [REVERSED GIVEN
P.21-cont.   NAMES & INITIALS]

215-215:	McCRAW,Thomas	40		Ms.		
"	,Martha	37 wife		"		
"	,Robt.	13 son		"		
"	,Elizabeth	10 dau		"		
"	,Eudora	7 dau		"		
"	,Henry	4 son		"		
"	,Thomas	3 son		"		
	CARLISLE,John	18 step-son		"		
216-216:	WILLIS,John	40	Farmer	Va.	Va.	Va.
"	,Sarah	29 wife		Ala.	Ala.	Ala.
"	,A.Elizabeth	15 dau		W.Va.	Va.	"
"	,D.John	12 son		Ohio	"	"
"	,Emma	9 dau		Ms.	"	"
"	,M.Frances	6 dau		"	"	"
"	,Martha	4 dau		"	"	"
"	,Unice	10/12 Aug.dau		"	"	"
	THOMPSON,Fanny	9 dau		"	Ms.	"
"	,Charles	6 son		"	"	"
217-217:	SHELTON,Vincent*76		Farmer	Ms.	"	Ms.
"	,Sallie *	25 wife		"	"	"
"	,Vince Jr.	1 son		"	"	"
	STRINGFELLOW,John	23 boarder-single		"	"	"
"	,Richard	22 bro.board.singl.		"	"	"

P.22

219-219:	SHRADER,A.James	47		Ala.	Ala.	Ala.
"	,E.Mary	48 wife		"	"	"
"	,William	12 son		Ms.	Ms.	Ms.
"	,B.Mary	18 dau		"	"	"
"	,Jas.Jr.	10 son		"	"	"
220-220: "	,W.H.	25 marr.	Farmer	Ala.	Ala.	Ala.
"	,O.Emma	24 wife		Ms.	Ms.	Ms.
"	,Hattie	3 dau		"	"	"
"	,H.Lament	21 son marr.	Farmer	"	"	"
221-221: "	,Fanny	18 wife		"	"	"
224-224:	REED,Hiram	20	Farmer	Ala.	Ala.	Ala.
"	,Vanecia	20 wife		"	"	"
"	,Viney	1 dau		Ms.	Ms.	Ms.
225-225:	MOORE,Nero	38	Farmer	Ala.		
"	,Emma	30 wife		Ala.		
"	,John	2 son		Ms.		
"	,Angelina	8 dau		"		
"	,Susan	6 dau		"		
"	,Ellen	4 dau		"		
226-226:	COOK,Charles*	50	Farmer	Ms.		
"	,Mary*	40 wife		"		
	FRY,L.*	23 boarder single		Tn.		
227-227:	PIOIMAN,(?)Willis*	30		Ms.		
"	,Juliann*	29 wife		"		
"	,W.John	12 son		Ms.		
"	,L.Charles	6 dau(?)		"		
"	,F.Mary	4 dau		"		
"	,O.Bage--	9/12 Jan.son		"		
228-228:	SUM,D.Marcus	36	Farmer	Ms.		
"	,Margaret	28 wife		"		
"	,W.Love	11 son		"		
"	,G.Julia	8 dau		"		
"	,Elizabeth	5 dau		"		

*Cannot read/write

```
CENSUS 1880-SHARKEY CO.,MS.Dist.3,Enu.#116,Beat# 5] #116 Enu.rev-
229-229:LONG.John        43         Farmer      Ms.  erses initials
         " ,Nancy        26 wife                "    and given names.
         " ,John,Jr.     11 son                  "
         " ,James         8 son                  "
         " ,Edward        6 son                  "
         " ,Ada           4 dau                  "
P.26
266-266:BOYAKIN,Solemon 50          Farmer      Ms.
         " ,Hester       45 wife                "
         " ,Eliza        15 dau                 "
         " ,Duncan       13 son                 "
         " ,Phaland      10 son                 "
        GREAR,P.George   21 boarder single      "
267-267:BOYAKIN,M.T.     40         Farmer      "
         " ,Elenora      35 wife                La.
         " ,John         17 son                 Ms.
         " ,Lucinda      14 dau                 "
         " ,Barney       16 son                 "
         " ,Edward        6 dau ?               "
         " ,Allen         2 son                 "
        DUKE,Thomas      23 boarder single      Ohio
        COLTER,John      20   "        "        Ms.
269-269:BANUM,George     28 single              Ill.
270-270:MOORE,C.         31 single              Ireland
         " ,R.F.         25 cousin              "
n/n   :EZELL,F.B.        25         Farmer      Ms.
         " ,Jolly        20 wife                "
271-271:" ,Theodore       2 son                 "
         " ,Mary Jane   3/12 dau                "
        FLANERS,W.C.     24 boarder single      "
         " ,D.T.         19   "        "        "
272-272:BOYAKIN,J.A.     22         Farmer      "
         " ,Ellen        22 wife                "
273-273:MANOR,T.J.       49                     Tn.
         " ,H.E.         39 wife                Ms.
         " ,L.W.         14 son                 "
         " ,John          6 son                 "
         " ,L.E.ROBT.  6/12 son                 "
n/n; HOOD,D.Wm.          35 single   Lab.       Tn.
     " ,George*          30   "        "        Ms.
       ,John              8 bro.                Tn.
274-274:SMITH,Lizzie*    24 sister              "
         " ,Molly         3 dau                 "
        DRUMNIGHT,Wm.*   25 boarder single      "
        BRYANT,Rubin     20   "        "        "
275-275:HILL,D.J.        30(or 50)  Farmer      Ms.
         " ,Martha       20 wife                "
         " ,Lucy       1-2/12 dau               "
¶NOTE:Enu.116 now goes backwards and picks up Pg.23-24
P.23
230-230:LINK,Hiram       39         Farmer      Ms.
         " ,J.Lelia      34 wife                "
         " ,L.Henry      19 son                 "
         " ,Leon          7 son                 "
         " ,N.Howard      5 son                 "
         " ,Albert        2 son                 "
*cannot read/write
```

CENSUS 1880-SHARKEY CO.,MS. Dist.3, Enu.116, Beat 5
Pg.23 cont. **REVERSED GIVEN NAME & INITIALS**

231-231:WRIGHT,L.R.	50	Farmer		Ms.
" ,S.S.	46	wife		"
" ,L.Richard	15	son		Ill.
" ,E.Florence	12	dau		Ms.
" ,O.Maggie	7	dau		"
" ,W.J.	27	son w/d	Farmer	"
232-232:MULLEN,Hardy	45		Farmer	"
" ,Mary	35	wife		"
ROBINSON,Jackson	50	single		"
HARBER,Daner	19	boarder single		"
233-233:HORD,Wm.	30		"	
" ,Martha	26	wife		"
" ,Rubin	2	son		"
" ,Wm.	9/12			"
" ,Robt	40	brother w/d		Tn.
234-234:McLARRAN,John(B)	30	boarder,singl.	Lab.	Ga.
ANTHONY,Wm.	22	"	"	" "
COOPER,Wm.	19	"	"	" "
236-236:GASSETT,Wm.*	24	single		----
n/n : TURNER,Joseph	25	single		N.C.
239-239:EVANS,Benj.	30		Lab.	Ms.
" ,California	26	wife		"
" ,Joseph	4	son		"
" ,Wm.	1-6/12	son		"
" ,James	4/12	son		"

P.24

244-244:WIGGINS,Robt.	21		Farmer	Ms.
" ,Fanny	20	wife		"
" ,Mary	60	mother		"
245-245:SYLVESTER,Nathan	55		Farmer	"
" ,Margaret	40	wife		"
" ,William	21	son		Ala.
" ,Eugenia	14	son ?		Ms.
" ,Estelle	12	dau		"
" ,End W.	9	dau		"
" ,Walter	7	son		"
" ,Robb	4	son		"
" ,Harriett	1-4/12	dau.		"
246-246:BARNES,Benj.	35		Farmer	"
" ,Sallie	28	wife		"
" ,Wallace	6	son		"
247-247:SYLVESTER,James	27			"
" ,Sallie	20	wife		"
" ,Lansen	9/12	son		"
247-247:CHAMPION,M.A.	65		Farmer	Ga.
" ,Emily	60	wife		"
" ,B.Walter	22	son single		"
248-248:CHAMPION,John	33		Farmer	GA.
" ,Fanny	26	wife		"
" ,John	2	son		Ms.
250=250;ROGAN,Jackson	35		Farmer	Ms.
" ,Lucinda	30	wife		"
" ,Jeff	18	son		"
" ,Amelia	13	dau		"
" ,John	10	son		"
" ,Edney	7	son		"

*cannot read/write

```
CENSUS 1880,SHARKEY CO.,MS. Dist.3,Enu.#116, Beat#5
P.24 cont.     REVERSED GIVEN NAMES & INITIALS
251-251:LEVINGSTON,John  25 boarder,single,Lab. Ms.
        PLATT,Joseph     25      "         "      "    S.C.
252-252:COTTEN,George    25      "         "      "     "
        "     ,Joseph    16                              "
```

P.27(out of sequence,and no pg.25)

```
277-277:KYLE,L.W          34      Farmer            Tn.
     "  ,Y.M.             26 wife                   Ala.
     "  ,Franny           16 dau                    Ms.
        NELSON,D.J.       40 single Farmer           "
        McGRANGER,Marshall(B)64 w/d servant          "
278-278:ROSS,H.J.         27      Farmer             "
     "  ,E.A.             26 wife                    "
     "  ,C.James           8 son                     "
     "  ,Charles           6 son                     "
     "  ,infant          4/12 dau                    "
n/n: FULGER,W.A.*         43 single Farmer          Tn.
```

Pg.28

¶NOTE<Enuemerator #116,Barnard,has two households #290-290 listed,one under **WELLES**, the other **WILLIS**. Information is identical. I will list it only once and take your pick of the surname!>

```
            WILLIS or
290-290;WELLES,John       60      Planter           Ms.
     "  ,R.Anna           46 wife                   Ms.
     "  ,W.Fanny          24 dau                     "
     "  ,John W.          22 son                     "
292-292:JONES,W.J.        35 single, Engineer       Ms.  Ohio  Ohio
293-293:WRIGHT,Adam       24      Farmer            Ms.  Ms.   Ms.
     "  ,Marian           18 wife                    "   Ill.  Ill.
        ELLINGTON,Lizzie   5 sister                 Ill. Ill.  Ill.
        COOPER,Wm.        21 single                 Ms.  Ms.   Ms.
294-294:STARLING,A.S.     27      Farmer            Ms.  Ala.  Ala.
     "  ,A.Ellen          19 wife                    "    "     "
295-295:LOGAN,James       52                         "    "     "
     "  ,A.Nancy          46 wife                    "    "     "
```

P.29

```
297-297:EPPERSON,Robt.    25      Farmer           Ala.
     "  ,Mollie           19 wife                  Ms.
```

P.31

```
323-323:COLNELL,L.S.      29      Farmer           Ga.
     "  ,Ella             21 wife                   "
     "  ,Maud              3 dau                   Ms.
        WEEKS/WEAKS,Joseph 23 boarder,singl.Far.   Ga.
324-324;  "  ,James       26 w/d
     "  ,Lucinda---18-wife(scratched through)"died Dec.26"b.
     "  ,Lizzie            4 dau                   Ms.
325-325:WILLIAMS,Charles  30 w/d Farmer            Ms.
     "  ,John             13 son                    "
     "   Angeline         11 dau                    "
n/n/ ;  DANS,Anthony*     33 single Farmer         Ga.
326-326:ALLEN,George*     28      Labr.            Ala.
     "  ,Lucy             22 wife                  Ga.
        WILLIAMS,Henry*   37 w/d Farmer            Tn.
     "   Rebecca*         28 w/d                   Ala.
     "  ,Anna*            20 dau w/d               Ga.
```

*CANNOT READ/WRITE   Cont.next page

CENSUS 1880 SHARKEY CO.,MS. Dist.3,Enu.116, Beat 5
Cont.household326-326; **REVERSED INITIALS & GIVEN NAME**

```
      WILLIAMS,Mamie        3 dau                    Ms.
         "   ,Rosa          5 dau                    Ala.
      COMMODORE,James*     57 w/d  cook              Ms.
327-327:HARSH,Ferdinand    29     Farmer             Ohio
         "  ,Elizabeth     27 wife                    "
         "  ,Claudius       3 son                     "
         "  ,Bell Mary    1-9/12 dau                  "
      KETCHERSIDE,Ellen    22 sister w/d              "
         "       ,L.Mary    5 dau                     "
      LAKE,Moses           28 boarder single          "
Pg.32
328-328:ORR,Alford         45 single Farmer           "
      BUTLER,Malinda       45 boarder singl.housekeeper Ms.
n/n: NICHOLS,M.J.          35 single                 Ms.
         "      ,R.H.      32 Marr.                   "
         "      ,Margret   25 wife                    "
331-331; "      ,Mary      30 sister single           "
         "      ,Alsey     28 single                  "
332-332:PHELPS,J.A.        45     Planter            Ohio
         "     ,V.M.       37 wife                   Ms.
         "     ,W.N.       14 dau                    Ky.
         "     ,V.Henry    12 son,Clk.dry gds.store  Ms.
         "     ,P.Mary     10 dau.                   Ms.
         "     ,B.N.        7 dau                    Ky.
      MILTON,J.C.          23 boarder,singl.bookkpr. Ky.
      GIBSON,L.L.          24    "       "  Teacher  Va.
333-333:BELLAR,John        28     Farmer            Ohio
         "     ,Sarah      25 wife                   W.Va.
         "     ,A.Mary      8 dau                    Ohio
         "     ,R.Dalbert   7 son                     "
         "     ,John        3 son                    Ms.
      COTTER,Edmond        19 boarder Labr.           "
334-334:TODD,Charles       27   "    single          Ky.
335-335;DONERT,John        30   "       "  Agt.on Pltn. Ireland
Pg.33
n/n ;FINGER,W.A.           45 single labr.           Tn.
342-342:HOWE,Robert        61     Farmer            Ohio
         "   ,Lucinda      48 wife                   Ind.
         "   ,Elanora      17 dau single              "
         "   ,Edward       13 son                     "
         "   ,Thomas       11 son                     "
         "   ,Robt.,Jr.     6 son                    Ms.
P.34
344-344:ISAAC,Jacob        36     Merchant          Prussia
         "    ,Martha      27 wife                    "
         "    ,Sarah       11 dau                    N.Y.
         "    ,George       7 son                     "
         "    ,Henry        3 son                    Ms.
         "    ,John         2 son                     "
         "    ,Lula       9/12 Aug. dau.              "
348-348:LAWSON,Johnson     26     Farmer            Ohio
         "    ,Emeline     25 wife                    "
         "    ,Albert      11 son                     "
         "    ,Mary         9 dau                     "
         "    ,Susana       6 dau                     "
         "    ,Lula         3 dau                     "
```

*Cannot read/write

HEATH-SMITH CEMETERY ISSAQUENA CO.,MS.

Located 1 mile S.of Mayersville,Ms.adjacent to the levee-about 100yds.east.Group of 3 mounds.An elderly resident of this area stated that he had always heard that MR.EDWARD C.TOY was buried in an unmarked grave on top of the largest mound,which is overgrown,impossible to investigate.The second largest mound is the site of the HEATH-SMITH private Cem.Enclosed by a wrought iron fence,well kept,the tombstones are especially beautiful.Location-Sec.4,Twp.12N,R8W:Copied by Alice Wade,Katherine Branton.Apr.1984

NORTH-EAST SIDE:

SMITH | ROBERT McCULLA SMITH JR. June 9 1848-May 27 1913-FATHER
UNICE W.SMITH Jan.28 1863-July 31 1913 MOTHER
HAMPTON PHARR son/R.M.& E.W.SMITH Dec.17 1896-Dec.22 1896
WALTER WOODRY son/R.M.& E.W.SMITH Aug.27 1893-Nov.9 1895
LINDA SIBLEY wife/ROBERT M.SMITH Jr.Nov.5 1854-July 26 1874
PRESTON HALL SMITH 25 Mar.1861-23 Sept.1892-WOW
LEE ALBERTUS SMITH Mar.22 1863-July 2 1901-WOW
LAURANCE WADE son/ROBT.M.& MARGARET S.SMITH Oct.6 1866-Aug.14,1890
WALTER J.son/MARGARET S.& R.M.SMITH Aug.8 1850-June 3 1883
MARGARET S. wife/ROBERT M.SMITH,Sr. Mar.9 1831-Sept.14 1907
ROBERT M.SMITH Apr.14 1812-July 5 1877
HAMPTON P.son/ MARG.S.& ROBT.M.SMITH Jan.24 1859-Jan.9 1876
WILLIE C.SMITH Aug.8 1850-June 3 1883¶SAME DATES AS Walter J. Smith above!

MARY ELIZABETH SMITH COLLINS May 19 1857-Jan.6 1934
LUCILE S.beloved dau/MAMIE P.& I.J.COLLINS,Sept.12 1900-Apr.6,1921
WILLIAM E.COLLINS Co.A 18 La. Inf.CSA no dates
ROBERT S. son/W.E.& M.E.COLLINS Dec.3 1882-Sept.3 1897
MAMIE PHARR COLLINS Dec.14 1879-May 24 1956
ISAAC JARRAD COLLINS May 30 1862-Aug.19 1938
IKE JARRED COLLINS,Jr. 1903-1946

FRONT ROW,NE CORNER
JAMES M.McQUAID Sept.9 1833-Nov.15 1865
FANNIE M. dau/M.R.& J.E.SMITH Oct.14 1872-July 15 1875
ROBERT WILLIAM son/DR.R.D.& CALLIE FARISH May 25 1883-Mar.12 1884

SW CORNER
THOMAS JEFFERSON COLLINS 1885-1952
TOM M.STUART Sr. Sept.3 1932-Mar.15 1979
BENNIE COLUMBA STUART June 28 1978-Apr.3 1983 son/Frank&Jane STUART

STUART | SHARKEY VIVIAN Sr. May 23 1897-Sept.12 1952-on ft/st Sharkey V.Stuart-F2 US Navy WWII
MARY ELIZABETH HEATH(Mayme)Sept.7 1905-Mar.14 1977
BENNIE HEATH STUART May 19 1930-Oct.5 1943
FAYE ODETTE STUART July 15 1927-Jan.15 192_
Infant child of JAS.P.& LOURENA HEATH d.July 5 1891

HEATH | JAS.P. 1858-1925
LOURENA S. 1869-1930

HEATH | JAMES PRESTON Mar.18 1897-May 17 1962
GRACE KESTENBAUM Sept.1 1898-Oct.10 1973
JAMES PRESTON HEATH Jr. Apr.18 1934-Oct.5 1943
LUCY HEATH BRYANT June 5 1923-Jan.31 1979
JAMES FLOYD BRYANT Ms.SM Sgt.Tech Sch.Sq.AAF WWII May26 1919-May 22 1969
MILDRED CATHERINE dau/BEN F.& ALTEE H.WHITE Dec.18 1928-Oct.5 1943

HEATH-SMITH CEM.(cont.)

WHITE | BEN F. Feb.3 1888-Apr.1 1945
      | ALTEE H. Feb.20 1895(still living Apr.1984)

WHITE | BEN F. 1921-1983
      | BONNIE E. 1912 _____

GRACE, ISSAQUENA CO., MS.
In the "Alley"north of Grace,Ms. on old Hiway 1.Fenced in side
   yard of house,1 grave-tall headstone
JULIA A.LUHM Feb.10 1880-July 29 1909 wife/BERNARD TONNAR

FITLER, ISSAQUENA CO., MS.
Grave markers located on Derr Pltn.Inc.Mr.Hershel W.Toombs,manager of Pltn.supplied the information and told me the original cemetery had been bulldozed by a former owner and the stones buried in a pile. They had dug up these three whole stones-many broken pieces-and reerected them with a fence around them. This was probably the original owner of this lands family by whom the community of FITLER was named.
C.A.FITLER 9/24/1849-9/14/1901 Woodman of the World"
"Eleane" dau./ JOHN & ELLA BREHM 10/16/1896-9/10/1898
THEO.W.FITLER 3/15/1879-7/21/1896

FITLER GENEALOGY:also supplied by Mr.H.W.Toombs.The dates given do not match the dates(birth)on the stones of C.A.& Theo.W.Fitler but the death dates are the same.
THEODORE FITLER,b.Oct.18,1815;d.1882;marr.1846,SARAH L.BRACEY
   of Jackson,Ms.,b.1824;d.1863.Theodore Fitler went South where
   he purchased a large plantation on the Ms.River near Vicksburg
   call FITLER'S LANDING.About the close of the Civil war,his
   wife being deceased,he,with his children, returned to Philadelphia,Pa. where,on Dec.24,1867,the following children were
   baptized by the pastor of St.John'sLutheran Church;Charles
   Alfred,19;Eugene Bracey,17;Mary Josephine,15:George Weaver,
   13.Dr.JosephPfeiffer Fitler(uncle of ch.)stood as godfather.
   There were 2 other ch.,Theodore,Jr.& William.
I include here only the family of son Charles Alfred Fitler,
   eldest son of Theodore and SarahBracey Fitler;b.1848(?)
   d.1901;marr.1873,SALLIE Z.HAYS,of Miss.;Issue;
      Theodore W.,b.1875;d.1896[tombstone says 1879]
      Elise E.,b 1877[its possible she marr.John Brehm,I have
                       no proof,but she is of the right age
                       to be mother of "Eleane" in the above
                       grave.]
      Ida May,b.1879;Marr.a Mr.Bowers
      George W.,b.1881
      Charlie Alma,b.1886
      Robert H ,b.1889
      Ellis A.,b.1893
      Hugh Bracey,b.1900
Theodore Fitler had visions of a town at Fitler,and had laid out lots, a water system, electricity, a bakery...but the mighty Miss.River decided to change course and left the town with out access to shipping.

VICKLAND CEMETERY-SHARKEY CO.MS.

Located on Highway 434,1 mile west of Delta City,Ms. In the center of the cemetery are 2 large Magnolia trees,under which we found some of the oldest graves. It had obviously been fenced in at one time. This is where we began,trying to work in family plots. Compiled by KATHERINE BRANTON & ALICE WADE,August 1985.

Beverly J.CLINKSCALES-Apr.7 1935-Apr.29 1974
Wm.F.CLINKSCALES-12 Feb.1910-4 Feb.1970
Son-Julian CLINKSCALES-Mar.15 1914-June 1 1964
Father-A.B.CLINKSCALES-Aug.22 1877-Oct.4 1954
Mother-Hattie S.CLINKSCALES-Sept.17 1878-Sept.25 1966

Robbie-Daughter of W.H.& E.SHRADER-June 24 1886-Sept.27 1902
Mother Emma O.SHRADER-dec.16 1855-Jan.26 1935
W.H. son of J.A.C.& M.E.SHRADER-Aug.11 1853-Sept.6 1898
Our darling- Rosa E.CLARKE-Dau.of J.A.C.& M.E.SHRADER-Wife of
   W.A.CLARKE- June 29 1864-Aug.29 1900.Age 36 yrs. 2 mos.
Willie A. son of W.H.& R.E.CLARK -Sept.1 1887-Aug.1 1904
(toppled headsone)Herbert-son of W.H.&R.E.CLARKE-Aug.30 1882-
   Oct.31 1890
Mollie-dau.of W.H.& R.E.CLARKE- Aug.30 1884-Aug.29 1884
John C.Burriss-son of Charles & Mollie LEWIS-Aug.2 1883-Oct.15,1883
Mollie SHRADER LEWIS-July 5 1859-Aug.24 1883-Age 24 yr.1mo.19days
Charles LEWIS-born in the Co.of Meath,Ireland June 29 1850-d.Feb
   26 1895
Harry-Son of F.V.& S.H.SHRADER-Jan9 1886-Sept.7 1899
John Sullivan DURST-Cpl.US Army WWI,Nov.18 1890-Aug.19 1979
Edith SHRADER DURST-May 31 1898-Apr.4 1966
Ladye SHRADER HARPER-Nov.28 1903-May20 1944
SHRADER {Wm.Pinkney-Nov.22 1867-Oct.11 1911
{Maude Slater-Nov.14 1879-May 30 1961
Alpha R. wife of W.P.SHRADER-Jan 14 1870-Apr.19 1896
"My dear Sister" R.SUMMERS-Nov.30 1830-May 7 1885,Age 51yrs.5mo.7da.
Mary Etta wife of J.A.C.SHRADER-Feb.18 1832-Dec.6 1904
J.A.C.SHRADER-Aug.8 1833-Feb.9 1909
Lincoln P.SHRADER-Jan.1 1902-July 28 1923
J.A.C.SHRADER,Jr. 1873-1906
Myra dau.of Mattie &J.A.C.SHRADER,Jr. Nov.16 1895-Aug.14 1898
   This is a beautiful stone-A sleeping baby on lower tier with
   lamb at rest on top. "Fold her,O'Father, in Thine Arms,and
   let her henceforth be messenger of love between our human
   heart and Thee."
SHRADER {Wm.P.,Sr. Feb.12 1901-Dec.12 1966
{Rebecca Ferguson-Aug.10 1898-no/date-but a fresh grave.

Margaret ROAN-Sept.10 1918- Feb.27 1966
James A.OVERBAY-Nov.5 1888-Oct.19 1918-Woodsman of The World
J.A.OVERBEY-Oct.15 1855- Jan.24 1890
W.J.FERGUSON-1870-1953-F/S
Our darling pet-Cora E.-Dec.29 1869-Dec.2 1883-13yrs.11mo.27days
   Only dau.of B.F.& L.D.ELLINGTON

ON NORTH EAST EDGE OF CEMETERY
W.R.WILSON-MSGT,US Army-Mar.30 1929-Jan.30 1972
James W.WILSON- Dec.31 1889-Mar.23 1 66

M.R.CLOUD- Dec.13 1829-Feb.27 1910

VICKLAND CEMETERY SHARK.CO.MS.
Ples Oscar SHEPPARD-Aug.9 1888-Sept.4 1954

W.E.VERNELL-1919-1928
A.C.VERNELL-1906-1922

VERNELL ⎡Will E.-1878-1950
⎣Donna B.-1884-1924

Ida LOPEZ- Nov.20 1889-Mar.25 1919
Charles N.LOPEZ- Aug.26 1876-Sept.26 1900
My husband-B.LOPEZ Feb.26,1849-Nov.20 1897
Lena LOPEZ-Apr.8 1885-Aug.26 1886
Walter M.LOPEZ-July 5 1895-Mar.19 1914
"Our diamond"Mary Leora LOPEZ-broken stone-no/date
broken foot stone-b.@1870-died Oct.6 1883-no name
A.Corbett LOPEZ-Dec.28 1892-June 1 1950
Mother-Savannah W.LOPEZ-Jan.11 1859-Apr.9 1940
Ira Eugene LOPEZ-Aug.6 1882-Mar.31 1934

J.G.BATES-Apr.16 1859-Apr.28 1920

George Franklin EZELLE-Jan29 1882-Oct.27 1931

A.J.FULTON-July 15 1858-Apr.21 1920
Lula Moody FULTON -Mar.30 1859-Oct.20 1921

WHITE ⎡Lillie Belle Cox-July 11 1885-Aug.3 1960--Mother
⎢J.H.WHITE-May 13 1887- DEc.20 1925
⎣Cora Lee dau.of J.H.& L.B.WHITE-Feb.3 1922-June 13 1922

Wm.H.FURR-MS.PVT.I CL.7Inf. 3Div.-Dec.17,1895-May4 1942

HICKS ⎡Haley David HICKS-Sept.28 1905-Mar.27 1953
⎣Jessie Isabell HICKS-July 14 1901-no/date

EAST EDGE
Elbert TACKETT-Pvt.1Cl.7Inf.32Div.-Oct.15 1921

Eugene,son of J.W.& M.STEVENS-Aug.18 1885-Nov.27 1904

Lottie Grace dau.of T.J.& Lottie C.HILL-Feb.23 1890,age 2 mo.
Lottie C. wife of T.J.HILL-d.Jan.29 1890.23 yrs.1mo.26 days
Clarence,son of T.J.& Lottie C.HILL-d.july 18 1886
Second row west of east edge
Clara Stephens BROWN-Jan.25 1886-July14 1953
Andrew Byron BROWN-Feb.24 1886-Mar.17 1959

CARR ⎡Ellen E.-1902-1949
⎣Harold J. 1898-19__

Father-W.W.RAINEY-no/dates
Annie A.RAINEY-Aug.13 1881-Nov.61887
Rether RAINEY-no/dates   These headstones are identical,Lamb on top
Elmo RAINEY   no/dates
Flat slab-Milton F.RAINEY Ms.PFC 555 Base Unit AAF WWII-Mar.14
    1922-July 13 1967
MARKER BLANK

VICKLAND CEMETERY SHARKEY CO.,MS.

S.E.EDGE
Birdie Olivia wife of P.G.HAMMETT-Sept.20,1893-Oct.9,1918

Wm.A.EVANS-Apr.22,1832-Jan.28,1889
Sallie Etta,Dau.of C.A.& W.A.EVANS-Jan23,1888-Sept.11,1888

Nettie,wife of S.N.JONES-d.Dec.29,1888-age (broken off)

BENJAMIN BROOKS-b.Jan.24,1876-Murdered by Bud Logue,Dec.12,1894

MIRIAM LUSK-Nov.17,1841-May 15,1891

ALICIA LEE CAGE-Ms.Nurse Ar.Nur.Corp.-Feb.29,1920

THOMAS HUGHES LANG Sr.-May 16,1877-July 26,1959
MARY CAGE LANG-Sept.20 1890-Oct.21 1970
Wm.DENNIS LANG-Ms.Tec.5-446 AAA-AW-BN-CAC-W.W.II.Jan.20,1920-
Feb.27,1964

MELVIN CHARLIE HALL-Pvt.USA,W.W.II. Feb.23,1908-May 21,1983
RUTH B.HALL-June 21 1907- Oct. 6 1977
L.H.HALL-May 19 1877-July 31 1905

SOUTH SIDE
Ethel Tucker,wife of RICHARD W.POSTON-Mar.8 1887-Mar.28 1919
TUCKER
ELIZ.ANN TUCKER(Mother)   ENOCH BRYANT TUCKER(Father)
Jan.16,1866-May22,1941   May 8,1862-Feb.13,1919
HORACE JOHN TUCKER-Oct.13 1889-Sept.16 1916
EDGAR EMERY TUCKER-Nov.23 1892-June 28 1905
FRANK R.TUCKER-Ms.PFC Btry. C-12-Field Arty.WWI.Jan.8 1894-
Feb.27,1961
NEWTON M.TUCKER-Sept.17 1905-Mar.30 1983

MIDDLE SECTION
LOUIS HARROLD WORCESTER-June 18 1863-Jan.18 1912
"Darling Son" RAY L.WORCESTER-June18 1894-Mar.14 1934

RICHARDSON | Robt.P.-Feb.17,1901-Jan.28,1971
           | Beulah S.-Jan.15 1900-Jan.31 1983

Wm.D.RICHARDSON-Capt.USAirforce.Oct.28,1930-Dec.19 1963

RICHARDSON | Wm.Deloach-Sept.27 1868-May 6 1939
           | Edna Turner-Mar.18 1871-July 8 1936
JOHN D.RICHARDSON-Ms.Pvt.Co.V. 110 Eng.WWI.Sept.22 1893-Sept.19,1969
Broken Marker

Wm.J.EPPERSON-Nov.15 1855-Nov.19 1900
ANNIE CARR EPPERSON BOYKIN-Feb.28 1872-Oct.10 1962
EDD BOYKIN-no dates
Son of W.N.& E.ROUSSEAU-Apr.26 1880-Nov.17 1891
Flat stone Mrs.Eliza F.TURNER-Mar.11 1831-June 10 1903

PRINTES BOYKIN-Aug.29 1894-June 11 1895
J.W.HERRON-Aug.10 1861-Dec.13 1969

BOYKIN | IDA B.-1866-1929-mother
       | FELON B.-1870-1932-father

VICKLAND CEMETERY SHARKEY COUNTY MISS.

NEFF | Matthews Park,Sr.-May 16,1893-Aug.10 1963
| Lara Lee R.- Feb.26,1894-June 29,1976

Mother-Bettie V.JONES-wife of B.L.Jones-Nov.23,1882-Aug.27,1918
Muriel R.NEFF-Oct.18,1918-Aug.22 1920

NEFF | David- 1852-1935
| Margaret V.-1859-1926

Slab broken off and laid flat-couln't turn it over

S EDGE OF Original Cemetery-walking South

John S.MANOR-son of J.T.& Ellen Manor-d.Oct.16,1888-5yrs.1mo.15da.
J.C.DENMAN-husband of S.E.Denman-Dec.16,1854-Aug.6,1892(Backside
    of stone-son of JOHN & RACHAEL DENMAN)

MANOR | J.T.Manor-June 13,1831-Feb.5,1924
| Ellen H.Manor-Apr.16,1843-Mar.27,1924

Harriet E.TRIM-July 13,1868-Aug.19,1951
Funeral marker- Mrs.Johnnie Bell TRIM-Dec.14,1907-June 16,1984
Harry F.TRIM-May 27 1894-Jan.8,1962

Randal-son of Doris & Lawrence NEAL-Apr.11,1952-(no other date)
A.Lawrence NEAL-Cpl.U.S.Marine Corp-WWII-Sept.101915-Sept.22,1981

Mollie WHEELER-Mar.14,1891-Mar.29,1959

CHANEY | Wm.Issiac-Feb.2,1882-Jan.8,1962
| Sarah Frances Whitson-Apr.4,1891-May 7,1960

Lucille Chaney CAYGLE-July 24,1919-Mar.22,1961
John Franklin CHANEY-Sept.6,1914-Aug.21,1962
Alma Cockrill CHANEY-Apr.30,1918-Sept.10,1972

Infant-F/S-no date
Infant-Dau.of J.E.& Katie COOPER-no date

COLSEN | Melvin Patton-July 26,1898-Oct.4,1973
| Susie Adams- July 6,1902-_____

Katie Dodd dau.of James & Katie HAMPSEY-Nov.6,1894-Jan.7,1901
James HAMPSEY husband of Katie Hampsey-July 29,1860-July 15,1896

Henry Freeman JOHNSON-July 9,1887-Feb.24,1919
Thomas JOHNSON-d.Aug.1,1889-age 33

Lois Evelyn BOYKIN-Jan.16,1912-July 12,1913
Infant son of W.E.& Maggie BOYKIN-June 25,1920
Wm.Edgar BOYKIN-1892-1925-Woodman of the World

BOYKIN | Margaret-1861-1928-Mother
| Albert M. 1867-1937

John Harry BOYKIN-Apr.9,1903-Feb.4,1909
Large patch of grass-couldnt see any stones in it

Tony STRINGFELLOW-1893-1913
Lela Stringfellow WATSON-1869-1949
J.R.STRINGFELLOW-Oct.6,1860-May 23,1906

VICKLAND CEMETERY SHARKEY COUNTY Miss.

Leona Belle STRINGFELLOW-Apr.19,1904-June 1,1905
Robert Mastin-son of J.R.& L.A.STRINGFELLOW-Aug.27,1885- June 25,1894
Infant son of J.R.& L.A.STRINGFELLOW-June 1888
Lum T.STRINGFELLOW-Oct.13,1890-Aug.17,1891
Docia STRINGFELLOW DYE-1890-1919

Wead F.BOYKIN-Oct.29,1883-Sept.19,1937
Zenobia Y.BOYKIN-Oct.29,1882-Aug.13,1963
Thomas BOYKIN-Pvt.Ms.Inf.CAS Dec.10,1894

WATSON | Jim W.-Sept.22,1890-June 6,1956
| Julie E.-July 1,1908-July 22,1973

Jesse A.WEEKS-Ms.Pvt.321 SNL TN 87 Div. Apr.5,1933
Claude Oliver WEEKS- May 26,1889-Jan.12,1926
Charlie WEEKS-Ms.Fireman-130D.U.S.N.-R-R-Jan 20 1922
Lucinda WEEKS-Mar.23,1863-Oct.32,1949

_anais Melton,son of _R.& M.S.BOYKIN___1885

Cpl.Jones SMITH-Co.H-24 Ala.Inf.CSA

Belle-wife of C.E.WIGGINS-May3,1849-Mar.20,1899

SYLVESTER | Elizabeth W.Jan.27,1868-Dec.13,1916
| Wm.C. Sept.5,1859-Jan.28,1935

Mattie May COLBERT-June 5,1877-Oct.23,1887

Lenora Carnathan dau.of T.M.& M.H.BOYKIN-Nov.7,1867-Aug.13,1885
Willie(Miller)Leon son of Geo.W.& Anjaline BOYKIN-Sept.4,1879
       Oct.7,1886
Eudore BOYKIN-dau.of G.W.&Angeline BOYKIN-wife of Thad.C.WHITSON
       Aug.28,1876-Oct.29,1896

LOOSE MARKER-Geo.B.-son of A.K.& C.MARTAK-Jan.24,1900-July 24,1903

Abner J.ADAMS-1892-1976
Mabel W.ADAMS-1892-1975
Susie A.Hampsey-wife of A.J.ADAMS-1869-Apr.13,1901
Willie J.-son of Abner J.& Susie A.ADAMS-Dec.3,1894-Sept.30,1898

William Wallace BOYKIN-June 12,1872-Mar.24,1877
BURIED HEAD STONE
Minnie,wife of A.L.WRIGHT-4 Mar.1862-Aug.12,1890

FAR N EDGE UNDER TREE MIDWAY
Jewel E.CURNUTT-June 27,1902-Nov.10,1978

¶FEB.18,1986,we continue cataloguing this cem. Someone had made an effort to clean,and a number of broken stones have shown up. Some we could match up, some not and we recorded what wording we could decipher from them.   K/B & A/W

VICKLAND CEMETERY-SHARKEY CO.MS. FEB.1986
Starting south end of middle road,on east side,broken pieces
Bottom of piece--d.Aug.21,1884
Buried-Lamb on top-name can't read-----son of A.D.& ---RUSSELL
    b.1884
GUESSING-Harry Haynes,son of L.E.COLBERT b.Aug.11,1871-d-----

Richard BROWN,Nov.15,1852-Oct.10,1927.(Mason)
Aley A.S.-wife of R.BROWN, Mar.10, 1865-Jan.16,1895
Flat stones only initialed-W.A.E.--I.B.--I.B.
              | Irwin d. Nov.2,1884-aged 2?
Children of |
R.& A.BROWN | infant b & d June 28 1889

Frank W.BROWN, June 25,1891-May 3 1904
Alexander BROWN, July 4,1885- Dec.7,1932

Lizzie, wife of G.H.HOPSON, Sept.8,1874-Sept.27,1891

Luther J.WHEELER,Oct.6,1880-June 6,1950   Twins?
Lura H.WHEELER Oct.6,1880-Mar.1,1948
Lura H.b 10-6-1880, d.3-1-1948 WHEELER[same as above on another]
Augustus S.WHEELER,Co.C 24 Ms. Cav. CSA (no dates)
Clara Wheeler CARNATHAN, 1890-1911
Mattie, dau.of A.S.& LOU WHEELER,d.Jan.14,1888,age 3y,11mo.10days
------(broken off)wife of AUGUSTUS WHEELER,b.Jan.18,1861-July 18,
                      1896
Henry C.FARRAR- no dates
Gertrude S.FARRAR, 1892-1961

Thos.W.SCOTT, Nov.19,1872-Sept.20,1943
Alma Mary Wilson SCOTT,Mar.23,1876-June 25,1957

Interesting rolled stone like a bolster sitting off by itself on
the south east side of the middle road:
Mrs.Mary A.JONES,wife of R.B.JONES, 1852-d.July 3,1923

THESE ARE ALL TOGETHER IN AN OUTLINED PLOT:
W.T.McGRAW,b Dec.1,1840-d.Sept.201891
Robert E., son of W.T.& M.E.McGRAW,d.Oct.24,1884 age 17y,3m.12d
BROKEN HALVES FITTED TOGETHER:
Eldora,wife of Wm.G(or C)OWART,b.Feb.6,1873-Oct.8 1889
Wm.R. son of W.T.& M.E.McGRAW, Oct.9,1884-9y,7m,14d

Lucinda WOMACK,wife of J.M.ROGERS,July 18,1831-Aug.10,1910
Jefferson Lee, son of J.E.& A.G.ROGERS,b.Sept.4,1886,age 5m,14d
Addie B.Elliott,wife of J.D.ROGERS,Nov.2,1868-Aug.22,1899

Mattie Lucille SMITH,Aug.18,1914-Jan.26,1918

Dora Bertha WALTERS,Oct.21,1897-May28,1906
Burlie WALTERS,Feb.9,1889-June 20,1901

A.J.RUSSELL(I think)b.Dec.1860-d.Oct.1860(broken ½s that fit)
Infant-son of --& E.-RUSSELL,b.1885-d 1888

Thom.Harry,son of T.H.& E.-PRICE,b Jan.1890-d 189_
SMALL STONE UNREADABLE

VICKLAND CEMETERY-SHARKEY CO.MS. FEB.1986
Starting under a large cedar tree midway of cem.east of middle road-working north.
Lawrence C.SYLVESTER,1880-1932
SYLVESTER | Sarah M. b Nov.17,1858-d.Jan.19,1930
         | James M. Oct.30,1853-May 31,1935
Virginia Ruth SYLVESTER, b.Feb.2,1895-Oct.31,1979
Effe D.SYLVESTER, Mar.4 1872-Aug.8,1885
James Dewey SYLVESTER,July25,1898-Mar.12,1952
Enoch Hampton SYLVESTER b.Jan.1882-d Dec.1884
Roly L.SYLVESTER 1889-1941
SYLVESTER | Willard H.,b Sept.6,1886-Aug.6,1956
          | Virginia G. Dec.13,1885-Feb.21,1951
THIS SYLVESTER HAS TWO STONES:
Louis Earl SYLVESTER-Oct.27,1894-Aug.14,1929-Father
"   "   "   Ms.Pvt ICL 3 Amm.Train,3 Div.-Aug.14,1929
James O.SYLVESTER, Ms.Pvt. ICL 581 Inf.83 Div.Sept.27,1889-Jan.15,1936
Annie L.,dau.of E.M.& M.A.SYLVESTER,b.Aug.24,1892-Dec.3,1901
SYLVESTER | E.M.,b.Oct.21,1865-June 17,1937
          | Annie Davenport, his wife, b.June 19,1867,-----------
Margaritte S.ANDERSON, Nov.25,1909-June 14,1958

C.L.GILL,July 16 1880-Jan.2 1919
J.Orin GILL, Aug.17,1879-Jan.25,1904
Edward O.GILL,son of Geo.L.& Minnie GILL,Oct.17,1912-Mar.18 1940
Minnie McMurchy GILL, 1886-1976-Mother
Woodberry C.GILL Jr.PFC US ARMY WW11 Oct.29,1918-Oct.26,1979
Ella Wheeler GILL Mar.15,1893-July 17,1981
Woodberry Clifton GILL Dec.21,1873-Oct.3 1961
Naomi Wheeler GILL Oct.31 1878-Dec.24 1915
Eva Dorris-Dau.of R.N.& A.B.GILL,Mar.10 1918-Oct.7 1920
GILL | Annie Bell Feb.18 1881-Sept.7,1960-Mother
     | Robert N. Sept.2 1878-Jan.9 1935-Father
Clinton GILL Nov.16,1908-Oct.31 1931

Luther Polk LOCHRIDGE, Tn.Capt.Inf.(dates buried)
Hazel Lochridge HEMPHILL June22,1894-Nov.191942
Lucius S.HEMPHILL June 6,1859-May 6 1945
James Polk LOCHRIDGE Oct.10 1916-Aug.29 1964

Infant son of Mr.&Mrs.S.E.BOYKIN Sept.4 1925
S.J.BOYKIN Mar20 1832-Dec.25 1890
Alma Bibb Boykin WILLIAMS May 19 1894-Dec.31 1969
S.E.BOYKIN Nov.15 1890-Jan.4 1927
Ellen,Dau.of J.& E.O'NEAL, wife of A.G.BOYKIN Dec.27 1852-Feb.22 1887
A.G.BOYKIN Feb.17,1858-Oct.28 1898
Elizabeth O'Neal BOYKIN Dec.5 1854-Jan.4 1948 Mother
Clifton L.BOYKIN Ms. Tec 5 US Army WWII Mar.28 1913-Sept.3 1969
Blanch N.BOYKIN Dec.8 1908-Jan.31 1960
Marvin H.BOYKIN Sr. Apr.17 1903-Oct.17 1972
Carrie E.,wife of D.P.BOYKIN Jan26 1891-July 24 1922
Duncan Pierce BOYKIN Feb.24 1867-Oct.2 1919
WE ELECTED TO STOP CATALOGUING HERE. THE WEST SIDE OF MIDDLE ROAD IS THE NEWEST SECTION.

STRAIGHT BAYOU, SHARKEY CO., MS.

On the hiway quadrant map in Sec.13, across a damed slough from the Straight Bayou Baptist Church. Mound on west end is the starting point. All the early graves are recorded, and some with early birthdates. Later burials we only recorded the family names.
Mar.8,1986 by A.Wade & K.Branton

Aubrey HOLLOWAY 1929-1931
Lula A.BOYD 1869-1943
Wm.M.BOYD 1869-1945
Eunice BOYD 1900-1909
Wm.M.BOYD 1898-1898

Mary V.BOYD McDONALD 1878-1960
Hugh N.BOYD d.Feb.15 1908-age 40yrs
Wm.E son/H.N.& M.V.BOYD Oct.17 1901-Feb.28 1902
Shelton A. son/H.N.& M.V.BOYD July 11 1903-June 16 1905

Henry Q.POWELL son/GEO.W.& Sarah C.POWELL June22 1896-Nov.7 1915
G.W.POWELL May 28 1856-Sept.4 1905
Wm.Newton son/S.C.& G.W.POWELL Nov.25 1888-Jan.10 1890
Mary A. wife/J.W.NORRELL May 8 1846-Dec.20 1900
Lula dau/J.& M.E.POWELL July 17 1886-May 11.1891
Thomas Jefferson RAWLS Feb.14 1863-Sept.24 1915
Georgie A. dau/S.C.& G.W.POWELL Oct.1 1890-Mar.5 1907
Ghita May dau./S.C.& G.W.POWELL Aug.12 1901-Jan 29 1907

Mrs.Conie SANDLING wife/W.F.SANDLING Au.g6 1890-Nov.16 1917
Ellen Katherine SANDLING Oct.26 1921-Oct.12 1923

Robert L.COOK Sept.6 1884-Mar.11 1908   WOW

B.Smith HODNETT June 7 1881-Sept.14 1906

O.E.CHEATHAM May 8 1871- Apr.23 1910
Ernest E. son/W.I.& O.E.CHEATHAM Apr.27 1907 Nov.1 1917

Eulon PORTER 1925-1943
C.F.PORTER 1885-1932
James PORTER 1914-1914

Andrew Harmon McDONALD 1868-1925
Jessie .McDONALD-Ms.cook 162 Depot Brig.Oct.1924
Jorah F. wife/A.H.McDONALD Dec.16 1868-Oct.3 1908

Charley H.CANNON Feb.24 1908 Age 60 yrs.
Argie CANNON 1850-1937

Bennie E.TURNER Ms.Pvt.3 Casual Co. Nov.14 1920
Father-John TURNER d.Apr.4 1908 age 85yrs.9mo.5days
Mother-Sarah wife/John TURNER d.Dec.8 1887 age 63

JN.N.HARLAN Aug.17 1850-Mar.29 1927

Katie Jo WILKES 1883-1936
Dave Lacy WILKES 1863-1947

Fath.John Clinton McDANIEL Aug.24 1886-Nov.5 1967
Moth.Mamie R.McDANIEL Feb.7 1894-Oct.17 1957

STRAIGHT BAYOU, SHARKEY CO., MS.
Julia Ann McDANIEL 1860-1936

Essie Pearl TURNER Aug.16 1872-Oct.22 1941 MOTHER
William Jasper TURNER 1867-1943-Mason   FATHER
Clara Mae TURNER RATLIFF Dec.31 1899-May 22 1961

Lilla M. wife/W.M.ATKINSON 1872-1933 MOTHER
Melisa B.EVANS Feb.17 1875-Sept.1 1959
J.W.EVANS 1861-1941   FATHER

Coallie E.SMITH Sept.16 1888-Oct.23 1972
W.H.SMITH May 31 1881-Feb.18 1936

John B.WILSON   1886-1936

The following two are side by side-surname spelled differently;
Gertrude WINDHAM 1873-1941
John C.WINDAM Nov.29 1867-Sept.29 1949

JOHNSON | Wiley B. Aug.31 1874-July 10 1937 FATHER
        | Alma H. Aug. 1 1880- Jan 22 1962

Wm.Jesse HODNETT 1867-1958
Sarah Powell HODNETT 1872-1954   MOTHER

HOOKER | James E. July 7 1881-Mar.22 1959-Mason   FATHER
       | Myrtle J. Feb.27 1902- May 20 1978 Eastern Star   MOTHER

Walter M.McDUFF Apr.2 1882-Sept.24 1960
Vencie M.McDUFF Jan 13 1889- June 16 1965

Mathew J.SIKES Apr.30 1877-Mar.18 1915   WOW
Ola King SIKES Jan.24 1885-Oct.11 1923

Lucy B.McNEIL Aug.6 1880-July 24 1958
John M.McNEIL Sept.20 1874-Dec.30 1951

Mary Elizabeth HOLLIS 1883-1946
Wm.E.HOLLIS 1877-1958

Lula DIFFEY Aug.12 1888-Nov.27 1956
Thomas M.DIFFEY May 2 1882-June 30 1947

Louise RAY 1856-1931
Jack RAY   1858-1934

Lance MERCHANT 1870-1957
Tennie Ratliff MERCHANT 1888-1938
Joseph O.TISDELL Dec.7 1882-Oct.30 1935
Stella Ratliff TISDELL Jan. 17 1887-Mar.20 1950
Oscar E.TISDELL Dec.7 1909-June 3 1963

Wm.R.King Apr.21 1878-Dec.14 1935

HALL | Joseph W. Dec.24 1880-Mar.14 1926
     | Lena Howell Sept.8 1882-Sept.16 1972

STRAIGHT BAYOU, SHARKEY CO., MS.

MOORE | Effie E. July2 1876-June 18 1949
      | James A. May 15 1851-Apr.19 1935

Jiff POOLE Jan.9 1884-May 9 1928
Lizzie POOLE Apr.9 1891-July 30 1929

W.R.KING Sr. Aug.9 1855-Oct.5 1934

Charley M.BATES 1887-1940

FAMILY NAMES ON "NEW"STONES NOT CATALOGED.

TOLAR	COURTNEY	SMITH
WILKES	ANDERSON	MATHIS
DONALD	LEWIS	ALLEN
YELVERTON	HUDGENS	LILLY
EVANS	WHITTINGTON	McNUT
PORTER	McCOY	SPEARS
JOHNSON	CATLEDGE	HUSSEY
McDUFF	PARISH	BUSBY
KING	MOORE	GREEN
GRIMM	MOUCHETT	GRANT
MERCHANT	CROTWELL	DIXON
McWILLIAMS	COVINGTON	SANDERS

RICHEY, SHARKEY CO., MS. COOK FAMILY CEMETERY-PRIVATE
Quadrant #29 at Richey-South east of Delta City. Fenced in-large plot-many fire ants-overgrown with vines & weeds. Could only find three stones, should be more

COOK | Mary Green Mar.25 1854-Jan.7 1920
     | James Monroe Feb.10 1852-Dec.19 1941
Waunell COOK Aug.16 1926-DEc.30 1928

FOLLOWING NAMES SUPPLIED BY COOK DECENDANTS TO W.E.PATTERSON OF DELTA CITY,MS.THEY WERE INTERRED HERE,MARKERS NO LONGER HERE.
James M.COOK & Mary Green COOK
Charles A.COOK
Louis COOK
Amanda JOHNSON
Wynell COOK-2yrs.old
Johnny & Julius JOHNSON
PATTRIDGE boy
Henry's son Boy COOK
Little girl-dau.of Charles COOK
J.F.HAWES son/4yrs.old
Clark COOK
Susan COOK-wife/Clark COOK
Albert FURNISS
Gladys JERIGAN & 2 children
James Louis COOK Jr.& baby son

ANGUILLA, SHARKEY CO., MS. FEB.20,1986-K.BRANTON-A.WADE

The cemetery is reached by following Deer Creek on the South east side westward, quarter of a mile. Known as THE ANGUILLA CEMETERY-THE UNION CEMETERY-and written in an arch in the lovely iron fence around the perimeter of the old part-GOLDEN LINK CEMETERY,1907. Many of the original stones are gone and there are a number of unmarked graves. Floods,and neglect in the early years are the reason for this. But now it is a well kept place and some families have replaced stones, or added names to other existing ones. We started cataloguing on the the North east corner,working South within the Chain link fence.

EWING | Milton Cyrus, May5 1880-Apr.19 1954---Father
      | Mabel Dixon,Dec.21 1880-Apr.29 1962---Mother

EWING | William Thomas July29 1918-Aug.17,1978
      | Elizabeth Martin May 7 1919-Living

MARTIN | Albert Edwin Mar.15 1850-Feb.18 1942
       | Mary Lavina Warren Dec.3,1854-Nov.14,1938

James W.MARTIN Nov.9 1875-June 22,1928
Mamie E.MARTIN May28 1876-July 12 1954
My Husband J.T.MARTIN Aug.19 1873-Oct.28 1937

Plot enclosed in a beautiful marble rail;
Harris Fields GREER-Oct.31 1905-Dec.25 1977
Lillie F.THOMASON July4 1888-Oct.9 1968
W.B.THOMASON Sr. Oct.14 1887- Nov.8 1966
Homer Cicero GREER Mar.9 1874-Dec.5 1958
Laura Fields GREER Feb.4 1876-Jan.15 1960
Fred Theo GREEN Sr. July 13 1885-Feb.9 1968
Hallie Fields GREEN Sept.4 1890-Mar.10 1976
OBELISK, ON FRONT AND BACK,TWO FOLLOWING NAMES:
Martha K. wife of H.J.FIELDS Nov.12,1849-Oct.7 1904
Harris J.Jr. son of H.J.& M.K.FIELDS Aug.4 1878-May 11 1903
Emma M. dau.of H.J.& Catherine Fields June11 1872-Oct.12 1886
LARGE MONUMENT-TWO NAMES AS FOLLOWS:
H.J.FIELDS- 1842-1922
His wife-Martha Katherine 1849-1904(**Martha K.is on two stones-one with her son,and one with her husband**)
Grover C.FIELDS Nov.17 1884-June 22 1938
Ruby Lynn Wray FIELDS Oct.3 1887-Aug.26 1977
Rebekah B.FIELDS Sept.18 1901-July 19 1984
Tom W.FIELDS Dec.14 1882-Nov.9 1935

Large enclosure-1grave-two stones,one a Confederate Marker
W.B.BARNARD Pvt. 28M Cav. CSA Jan 6 1914
W.B.BARNARD Nov.19 1846-Jan.6 1914
FOUR NAMES ON ONE STONE:
Dr.Joel C.HALL 1838-Nov.19 1920
Dr.Joel S.HALL Jan.13 1869-Nov.22 1955
Sarah L.B.HALL Mar.18 1842-Apr.22 1930
John W.HALL Feb.2 1870-July 15 1948

Henry Leon WARD 1911-1935
Louie Henry Ward 1885-1934
Hillary Lack Ward 1879-1927
FIVE BROKEN INITIALED FOOTSTONES PILED NEXT TO FENCE
GBH:Sarah L B: Joel C.: C E M :John W.

ANGUILLA, SHARKEY CO., MS. GOLDEN LINK CEMETERY 1907

Fred JONES Jan.25 1888-Aug.18 1928

ENCLOSED WITH MARBLE RAIL:
Merlyn E.HENRY-1899-1940
Samuel Rodney HENRY 1888-1949(under a bush)
Lou Teat HENRY wife of R.M.HENRY 1858-1941
Robert M.HENRY 1851-1922

Eola Sylvester CARNATHAN Mar.11 1867-Nov.25 1957
O.N.CARNATHAN Sr. Sept.9 1860-Feb.19 1913
Christine Craig CARNATHAN Dec.25,1890-Aug.20 1912
Sidney Rose CARNATHAN June 20 1911-Nov.20 1978
Oswald N.CARNATHAN-Ms.Pvt. US ARMY WWI-Oct.26 1899-Apr.20 1972

Robert L.COLE Dec.17 1873(all dates badly washed)Nov.9 1929
Robert L.COLE July 3 1901-Apr.26 1926
Willie C.COLE Ms.Corps 58 Inf.4 Div. Feb.13 1924
Willie C.COLE Dec.20 1896- Aug.16 1924
MOTHER-Wille COLE 1892-1924

Wm.RATLIFF,b.Wayne Co.,West Va.Jan.1,184_,d.Sharkey Co.Ms.
                                                  Feb.4,1925
John Whitney COOPER,Dec.12,1831-Mar.12,1936

Sammy B.,Son of S.B.& S.E.HENDRICKS,Apr.1,1880-July 28,1882
J.Leonard,Infant son of S.B.& S.E.HENDRICKS,Mar.6 1882-July 23
                                                          1882
Glyn Don B.,son of S.B.& S.E.HENDRICKS,Sept.11,1879-Drowned,
                                                  June 22,1886

Alma Maud HOOKER,May25,1938-May 14,1942

John W.LYLE,hus.of Mittie M.BODE 1861-1915,Footstone-J.W.L.
Mittie Bode LYLES 1875-1941
John W.LYLES,Jr. 1902-1955

Milton Ray STEWART Son of W.H.& Sallie Bode STEWART,Jan.26 1895
                                                  Oct.24 1918

W.H.STEWART Jan.11 1858-Apr.14,1924
Sallie Bode STEWART Feb.27,1869-Jane.1934
STEWART | Vernon Earl, July 17 1890-Nov.25 1968
        | Eury Mae,May 28 1895-May 1,1985

Martha Dunbar COMPTON d.Aug.9,1916

Anderson Mimms LEE June 22 1878-Nov.13 1922

M.A.HANSER 1876-1924

Nancie L.BARNES May 27 1838-Feb. 19 1916
Carrie E. wife of W.D.MARLER Feb.20,1860-May 14 1917
MARLER | Wm.David May 2 1857-Oct.7,1921, Father
       | James Thomas Jan2 1880-Aug.20 1940, Son

ANGUILLA, MS. SHARKEY CO., GOLDEN LINK CEMETERY 1907

STEVENS | Vivian, Sr. Feb.12 1893-Jan.27 1968
        | Leona R. June 6 1896-Mar.17 1963
Batton Lynell STEVENS Aug.11, 1917- Feb.27 1962
Elbert BABB Dec.27 1905-Aug.5 1914

Ina W. MARTAK 1898-1961
Clyde J. MARTAK 1894-1937

Ina Martak TULL Dec.7 1917-Mar.9 1962
Angeline BOYKIN 1844-1912
George W. BOYKIN 1847-1917
Adam K. MARTAK 1859-1935
Arletti B. MARTAK, 1868-1946
Duncan D. MULLINS Oct.14 1891-Mar.21 1952
Dora M. MULLINS Nov.14 1901-Mar.16 1982

John Hilbert DURST 1847-1922
Delia Sullivan DURST 1857-1934(two headstones-same info.)
James Hilbert DURST 1888-1937
Mary Ellen DURST 1892-1956
Robert Emmett DURST, Dist. Columbia, Yeoman 1cl, USNRF Oct.19 1939
ENCLOSED IN MARBLE RUNNERS-STEVENS:
Jesse A. STEVENS 1904-1943
Jesse Allen, son of Pierce & Jesse STEVENS, Feb.12 1955-May 7
                  1955, footstone JAS
Andrew Leveirn ROCHELLE Sept.4 1919-Dec.9, 1975

BATTON | Wiley Martin May 19 1909-Feb.11 1984
       | Bessie Martin Feb.25, 1903-----No date
Elton A. STEVENS, Sr. 1900-1945
Telly V. STEVENS Feb.9 1910-Sept.3 1960 Husband
Christine Lucille Dau. of F.O.& F.B. STEVENS Feb.19 1906-Mar.23
                                                              1907
Wm.B. son of F.O.& F.B. STEVENS Apr.15 1898-Mar.22 1899
Fannie Belle wife of F.O. STEVENS Aug.6 1884-Aug.25 1914
Ursie STEVENS d.Oct.15,1913(flat slab concrete-date scratched in)
Leohn, son of S.T. &E. STEVENS July 16 1907-Nov.20 1908
**THREE FLAT SLABS OF CONCRETE, ONE WITH NOTHING ON IT, ONE WITH
BABY & NO DATE, ONE WITH**
Nessie wife of T. STEVENS- no date
F.O. STEVENS 1872-1931
John O. STEVENS Oct.9 1841-Jan.6 1893
Joel A. STEVENS 1870-1959
Jimmie L. STEVENS 1886-1979
Oscar STEVENS Oct.14 1913---only date
Harvey Laurence STEVENS Sept.16 1898-Nov.4 1952
John Pierce STEVENS Oct.21 1938 Apr.12 1959
James Terrell STEVENS Apr.7 1897-Nov.23 1968
Harry Fuller STEVENS Ms.PFC Qrt.Mas.Corps WWI Apr.19 1892
                                                July 28 1962
Sarah Jane STEVENS Aug.15 1873-Oct.28 1959   Mother

STEVENS | Cullie STEVENS Age 62 d. June 15 1922   Husband
        | Eli H. STEVENS age 17 d June 15 1922   Son
H.G. STEVENS Nov.7 1819-Oct.3 1888
TWO NAMES ON I STONE:
Joel Ormand STEVENS Hus/M.F. STEVENS, Dec.11 1829-Nov.25 1891, Mason
Jno.B. STEVENS Oct.11 1859-Oct.5 1890

ANGUILLA,MS.SHARKEY CO.,GOLDEN LINK CEMETERY 1907

Capt.J.O.STEVENS d.Nov.25 1891,age 61 yr.11 mo. 25 days
Lizzie R.STEVENS July 1 1839 d.Apr.7 1901

STEVENS | Samuel T. 1867-1960
        | Eliz.A. 1873-1944

HICKMAN | James Louis Oct.26 1884-Oct.5 1954
        | Shellie Irene Dec.24 1890-Apr.12 1970
Geo.W.MARSH July 4 1848-Jan.27 1894   Mason
Broken stone;Atwo---Aug.4 1863-June 23 1899
James Robert BROOKS Mar.10,1875-Oct.12 1954
James Wilburn BROOKS Ms.Pvt.US Mar.Cps Sept.15 1909-Nov.6 1969
Dora BROOKS Feb.29 1875-Mar.21 1919   Mother
Inf.son/J.H.& R.H.WILLIAMS Apr.18,1910-Apr.20 1910

Eugene A.FLOWERS June 15 1905-Feb.8 1960

FLOWERS | Willie Earl Aug.24 1903-Sept.23 1967
        | Etta May Sanderford Oct.3 1909-Oct.8 1970

Lino L.CUISON-Tn.Pvt. US Army WWII Sept. 26 1899-May 3 1964

Sarah Frances WILLIAMS Oct.28 1854-Apr.13 1944
James C.WILLIAMS Sept.8 1881-Nov.24 1954
Eunice Pendarvis WILLIAMS July 30 1890-Mar.20 1971

Margaret Wadlington wife/Jas.A.DINKINS 1828-1911
James A.DINKINS Oct.20 1822-Nov.11 1898
Paul DINKINS 1865-1911

In memory of our Aunt-Josie PHELPS ANDERSON June 26 1869
                                                Aug.16 1946
Dr.Vida Odessa STEWART Apr.13 1884-June 27 1957
Georgia Lou STEWART Oct.31 1885-Mar.15 1966

H.S.HANNER,Jr.inf.son/Henry & Myrtle HANNER 1917
LARGE STONE FACE DOWN-WILL HAVE TO HAVE A STRONG BACK TO TURN IT OVER. THE FOOTSTONE INITIALS ARE W.H.B. WHICH I FEEL SURE IS W.H.BARNARD, SO I WILL ADD A FOOT NOTE TO THIS CEMETERY WITH THE FACTS WHEN I FIND A STRONG BACK!

Sallie J.RATLIFF Oct.16,1868-Sept.4 1910   Our mother
BROKEN STONE d.June----1920. Footstone B

Litic(g)hie ENGLAND Wife/R.O.ENGLAND May 12 1854-Jan.23 1923
John Powell ENGLAND son/R.O.& Lettetia"Lou"ENGLAND Aug.13 1882
                                                    May 19 1974
R.O.ENGLAND Sept.15 1842-May 13 1902

Bonnie A. son/S.O.& M.A.HURSE Aug.28 1889-June 3 1910

N.E.HESTER 1865-1938
Charles O.HESTER Sept.7 1869-Mar.19 1910
Dennis Hoyte HESTER 1895-1945
Ruby HESTER CAUTHEN 1897-1940

ANGUILLA, MS. SHARKEY CO., GOLDEN LINK CEMETERY 1907

Jessie Martin dau/JesseT.& Mamie E.MARTIN, May 17 1898-
July 9 1898   Sister
James Noel MARTIN son/Jesse T.& Mamie E.MARTIN Sept.6 1908
Oct.31 1908   Brother
Blanche MARTIN PERKINS dau/Jesse T.& Mamie E.MARTIN June 11 1895
Nov.27 1922   Sister
1sided wrought iron fence under tree,1grave,two broken ft.stones:
Martha A.TEAT wife/Thos A.HENRY Mar.30 1850-Sept.10 1898
Ft.Stones MCB: B

Wm.M.DOUGLASS Oct.7 1866-Feb.11 1906-Woodman of the World
MOVING W ON N FENCE LINE
Ft/St W.J.J.
Mary E.McMILLAN 1855-1905
Wm.J.LANG 1886-1916

LANG | Jemmie Ella Oct.7 1867-June 25 1962
     | Wm.Meriweather Aug.23 1860-Feb.22 1958

DRINKARD | Lillian Lang July 23 1888-Oct.2 1981
         | Rufus C. Oct.15 1874-July 5 1934
F.H.LANG Feb.14 1866-Dec.25 1908
Eveline P. wife/Robert LANG May 31 1836-d.Aug.11 1900
ENCLOSED IN MARBLE RUNNERS:
Wm.T.McKINNEY Feb.11 1890-June 16 1960
Marion McKINNEY Oct.29 1892-Dec.13 1899
W.C.H.McKINNEY Jan.9 1842-Feb.2 1938
Belle BAGGETT McKINNEY Aug.31 1865-May 4 1952

TALL OBELISK-Edward Virden son/A.A.& Rebecca SAUNDERS
May 8 1878-Jan 19 1899

Phillip Ray MARTIN,Nov.21 1924-Sept.13 1932,Our Darling Boy
Emma Simmons MILNER 1894-1966
Evelyn Simmons KIMBRO Sept.27 1914-Sept.25 1954--wife
Robert B.SIMMONS July 26 1890-Aug.2 1947
Arthur,son/J.H.& Annie SIMMONS,d.June 22 1891-age 14y.8m.22days

Mabel Robbie MILAM Jan.31 1905-Jan.7 1906
Johnnie Henry MILAM Nov.20 1908-Feb.6 1910
Lottie Dale MILAM Oct.14 1898-May 3 1915
G.K.GILLIAM Jan.4 1876-Aug.9 1903
O.R.DAVIDSON,Jr. 1920-1921
Ft/St.   BABY
Infant of J.T.&M.A.MILAM July 31 1897-Dec.12 1897
Jesse Thomas MILAM 1863-1916 Ft/St.FATHER
Ft./St. only J.T.F.
 M.L.COLLINS Dec.22 1866-Sept.11 1949 Ft/St.M.L.C
M.J.COLLINS Apr.8 1869-May 23 1934. Ft./St. M.J.C.
Walter Leslie MILAM 1892-1920-Ft/St WLM
Mary Annie MILAM 1871-1930-Ft/St MOTHER
J.T.FARRAR Oct.23 1860-Aug.18 1927
Howard B.FARRAR Ms.Pvt.U.S.Army Nov.18 1931
Horace C. son/J.T.& K.FARRAR Feb.11 1889-Feb.4 1910
Martha dau./J.T.& Kate FARRAR Nov.15 1908-May 14 1908
Mildred dau/J.T.& Kate K.FARRAR Mar.6 1911 June 8 1912
Julia Lee wife/R.L.MILAM May 2,1871-Aug.17 1918   Mother

ANGUILLA,MS. SHARKEY CO.,GOLDEN LINK CEMETERY 1907

Eliza J.McMILLAN 1830-1907-Ft/St EJM
Charlie Spencer JONES,Oct.6,1876-Dec.25 1952.Husband Ft/St CSJ
Mary Etta JONES Feb.9 1870-Jan 23 1956-wife Ft/st-MEJ
Martha C.BROWN 1851-1915 Ft/St MCB
James T.L.BROWN Aug.22 1844-Feb.4 1904-Mason
J.McMILLAN,beloved husbanb of E.J.McMILLAN,Feb.20 1816-Oct.28 1882-Mason
Minda, wife of J.R.DICKINSON,dau.of M.L.&M.J.COLLINS-Apr.4 1897-Oct.14 1927

Novella L.BARNES June 15 1877-Jan.17 1963-Mama
Wallace N.BARNES Dec.11 1873-May2 1925- Papa
Sarah J.,wife of E.F.BARNES-Died Nov.16 1874-aged 56 yrs.
Matilda, "   "   "   "   -Died July 20 1874-aged 56 yrs
¶We double checked the two above entries and it is as recorded on the head stones.
(broken stone) Mary I.,dau.of N.B.& M.J.SYLVESTER Mar.10 1868-J-- -- 1876
John.L.SYLVESTER Feb.10 1852-Apr.17 1877 Ft/St JLS
N.B.SYLVESTER Nov.9 1821-Jan.9 1903
Hattie SYLVESTER LOW Mar.28 1879-Mar.2 1907
Base stone with initials MGS no top
ONE LARGE STONE FACE DOWN.STRONG BACK NEEDED
Sarah E. wife of B.L.BARNES Mar.7 1850- June 20 1884
Oscar son of B.L.& Sarah E.BARNES Apr.10,1881-Dec.16 1881

S.L. wife of J.R.WEEKS Nov.5 1860-Dec.27 1879
PILE OF BROKEN FOOT STONES:SGB: M.B.: BWR: S.R.

On same stone | Benjamin W. ,Feb.22 187-(broken)-May30 187-
              | Sarah,Aug.27 1874-Children of Wm.& Maggie ROBERTS
Eli, son of B.S.& Sarah M.ROBERTS Oct.1 1865-Aug.8 1874(stone is grown into a crepe myrtle tree)

Clarence James RUTLEDGE Nov.7 1914-Feb.21 1961
LOOSE FT/STs. K.E.G.:E.W.
WRIGHT | Elizabeth dau.of J.W.& Theodocia E.,Nov.2 1877-Dec.2 1877
       | Theodocia Epperson wife of J.W.WRIGHT,Aug.16 1858-Nov.14 1877
MOVING WEST ON NORTH FENCE ABOUT MIDDLE
Katie Edna,dau.of J.M.& E.A.CLANCEY Nov.26 1877-Oct.13 1879

James Marvin COOPER Aug.18 1885-Feb.5 1949
Pearl H.COOPER Oct.1 1885- Jan.1 1977

Z.H.DENMAN Sept.15 1845- Apr.1,1877 Ft/St Z.H.D
In this plot are footstones and no headstones:W.D: S.I.D.:R.D.: R.D.: J.D.
BROKEN STONE-DOVE CARVING-CAN'T READ ANY OF IT-LOOKS OLD
DOUBLE STONE WITH 3 NAMES & DATES:
John W.DENMAN Jan.8 1821-Oct.1 1866(Earliest date we found)
Smith T.DENMAN Oct.24 1852-Oct.2 1873
Emma J.DENMAN Nov.11 1845-Sept.11 1872

ANGUILLA MS., SHARKEY CO., GOLDEN LINK CEMETERY 1907

Gilfey Nov.11 1872-Nov.22 1874/ag.2yr. | Inf.sons of E.F.& L.D.
Benney Jan.7 1875-Jan 14 1875 | ELLINGTON

Ohny son of J.M.BROWN
Cora D. wife of J.M.BROWN Died Oct.1 1871-age 21 yrs.
John M.BROWN Feb.15 1825 Apr.30 1901 Ft/st J.B.

ENCLOSED IN FENCE
Christian HANSER Feb.9 1847-Aug.2 1909,Age 62y,5m,24d-WOW
Martin HANSER Oct.5 1851-Aug.1 1873
BROKEN STONE LARGE-PARTLY UNDER FENCE-FACE DOWN
Ft/st.;A.E.H.: J.M.B.
ON WEST SIDE OF THIS FENCE LARGE DOUBLE STONE   FACE DOWN

Enclosed in Marble runners:
Brok.stone/F.C. SON of W.M.& H.F.MYERS Feb.26 1849-Nov.24 1903
Wm.MYERS Dec.26 1812-Dec.27 1877
Mary C. wife of Wm.MYERS Apr. 8 1833- Jan.25 1897   Ft/st M.C.M.
DOUBLE STONE-NO LAST NAME:
Kate May3 1852-Aug.-- 1860
Kate Sept.2 1860-Sept.8 1862
Robert S.MYERS Jan.4 1851-Sept.1 1916 Ft/st. R.S.M.
Brok.st. propped up in enclosure-H.T.BRANCH died Oct.27 1871-age
       55--not sure this belongs in this plot
Brok.Ft/st;E.B. one with no writing
George D.MYERS 1872-1923
Ella wife of R.E.G(C)ARY Nov.8 1852-May 16 18--maybe 77

Rowena West DINKINS Nov.10 1855-Mar.15 1920 MOTHER
Henry Lee DINKINS Dec.31 1862-Jan.4 1907-In loving memory of
                    my Husband
James L., son of H.L.& R.H.DINKINS Mar.10 1891-Sept.25 1898
Mary R.,dau.of H.L.& R.H.DINKINS Sept.26 1889-Feb.16 1890

Iva Allene BARNARD Nov.10 1913-Aug.21 1930
Emilius Glaze BARNARD Feb.15 1864-Feb.17 1938
Mary Josephine HENRY wife of Emilius Glaze BARNARD Dec.20 1877
                    Dec.25 1953
Aubrey Henry BARNARD Son of E.G.& M.J.BARNARD Nov.13 1904-Nov.
                    27 1905
Ora L.MARKETTE Mar.8 1845-Mar.20 1927
Willie B.Markette Jan 9 1867-Aug.22 1893
Mrs.Eliza BARNARD Sept.8 1835-Nov.11 1899 Age 55yr,2mo
H.C.BARNARD Died Mar.14 1871 Age 40yr,11mo& 4dys.
Henry W.BARNARD May 3 1897-Mar.21 1964-Here lies a gentle man
Brash BARNARD Dec.10 1865 May 3 1941   FATHER
Mae Markette BARNARD Jan.26 1875-Sept.15 1958
Clarence B.BARNARD Feb.12 1892-May 24 1974
Henry O'Rourke BARNARD Sept.24 1903-July 24 1981
Myrtle Barnard HOLMES Feb.3 1894---no other dates

Edmund P.OVERBY,Jr. Jan.1 1859-Mar.8 1874
Willie P.OVERBY Nov.24 1862-May 30 1879

Bailey J.CHANEY died Feb.6 1874-aged 55 years
Catherine A.CHANEY died May 20 1871-no other date

ANGUILLA MS.,SHARKEY CO.   GOLDEN LINK CEMETERY 1907

Cynthia A., wife of W.D.FERRISS bMay 2 1832-d.date in ground
George Guice son/W.D.& C.A.FERRISS b.June 15 1872-death dates
           on these two below ground & in Fire ants.
Mittie Anna ROGAN Dec.3 1879-Feb.21 1880
Frank Preston ROGAN Aug.29 1877-d. same day

SOUTH FENCE,STARTING IN THE MIDDLE,MOVING WEST ON EDGE
Francis Flowers MARTIN 1899-1940

FLOWERS | Wm.C. Jan 4 1876-Oct. 5 1922
        | Mary Dollie R. Oct.17 1883-Mar.16 1960

STEVENS | MOTHER- Ada, Aug.1 1906-Sept.7 1939
        | FATHER- Argyle G. Dec.28 1904-Nov.18 193-(broken off)

STEVENS | Douglas STEVENS Jr. Apr.14 1891-Jan.11 1939
        | Margie Cole STEVENS Dec.19 1898-Oct.29 1978
ANOTHER Douglas Jr. STONE-SAME INFORMATION
Jennie MacAdams STEVENS May 11 1846-Dec.13 1928
Douglas STEVENS Sr. Oct.30 1865-Sept.7 1951
Annie Cook STEVENS July 4 1880-Sept.16 1960
Barnard STEVENS Ms. PFC 187 ABN INF 11 ABN DIV.Korea PH July 5
                    1931-May 28 1951

Richard J.LEE Co C Powers Ms. Cav. CSA--And beside this stone
  is a double stone reading;
LEE | Richard Mar.9 1832- Oct.20 1912
    | Mary Ann Sept.11 1836-Oct.29 1892

Lois Lorraine CHILDRESS Jan.31 1911-Sept.27 1911

B.J.ANDERSON son/MR.&MRS.B.J.ANDERSON Jan.17 1917 Our darling boy
Grover ANDERSON Feb.6 1923-Feb.8 1923 | Twins-double stone
Clinton ANDERSON Feb.6 1923-Feb.7 1923 |

Grover A.ERVIN Sr. Ms.Cpl Btry C 140 Fld Arty WWI Dec.4 1892-
                    Jan.20 1966
Anna Olivia WILLIAMS Nov.9 1866-Dec.31 1958
Augusta L.ERVIN Aug.22 1856-Aug.31 1894

Milliam Sackstone MILAM July 5 1869-Jan.4 1914   WOW
Newton Jasper son/W.S.& Lula MILAM Sept.22 1897-Aug.20 1898
Ruby Christine DEVINE Apr.27 1918-Apr.24 1920

Era R.STEVENS Oct.27 1897-Feb.10 1958

Mary Louis POTTER Feb.15 1882-Feb.2 1949 MOTHER
John Ransom POTTER Sept.9 1879-Nov.24 1959 FATHER
Dalton POTTER Jan.25 1901-July 3 1974

Thomas Ray HARDEN Feb.7 1941-July 1 1973
John Willie HARDEN June 3 1876-May 22 1941
Willie Edgar HARDEN b.& d.Aug.18 1931

Ft/st-O.B.
Henry W.PIPPIN May 6 1889-Oct.12 1947
Eva Buford PIPPIN Nov.25 1893-May 26 1979

ANGUILLA MS., SHARKEY CO. GOLDEN LINK CEMETERY 1907

Mattie Lee BUFORD Nov.25 1905-Mar.25 1983
Olive R.HOWELL Nov.30 1898-Sept.16 1925
Willie May WINSTEAD May 18 1890-Apr.10 1909
BUFORD | Carey Bell Buford Feb.22 1865-Dec. 25 1906 MOTHER
       | James Arthur Buford Mar.15 1859-Sept.28 1948 FATHER
James F.PIPPIN Sept.28 1913-Apr. 24 1963

PRETTY IRON FENCE ENCLOSES 2GRAVES
Lucinda wife of Chris.HANSER June 27 1853-Jan.28 1905(He's buried
      on the north side of cem.in fenced in plot)
Effie Carey dau/G.C.& L.JOLLY June 27 1863-Oct.17 1891

3 infant sons of J.A.C.& M.E.SHRADER- no dates or names
Pile of stones behind above, 1 put together to read:
James son/S.OR J.L.& H.A.BOYKIN Mar.2__died Apr.19 187_

Hannah wife/H.PINFIELD May 16 1845-Oct.1 1903
Wm.H. son/H.& H.PINFIELD Apr.27 1872-July 18 1885
Jennie Dau./H.& H.PINFIELD Apr.5 1876-July 27 1888
Ft/st only H.H.

Fernando ROGERS July 22 1935-Aug.12 1948
Santiago son/Joe ROGERS Mar.10 1954-Dec.1 1954

FLEMING | Lillie Mae FLEMING Apr.20 1908-June 6 1949
        | James C.FLEMING June 15 1905-June 18 1980

J.D.MATHYS Dec.25 1866-Feb. 23 1906 WOW
Clara Alva inf.dau/W.T.& E.B.ELLIS May 10 1889-July 6 1889
Leah Ada   "   "   "   "   "   d & b Feb.6 1901
BLOCK OF CONCRETE-SCRATCHED IN TOP could be;
Velva ELLIS   14 mo.
TALL OBELISK-off its base,bottom buried in Fire Ant Hill:
Wm.T.ELLIS Sept.23 1858-_____
Ft/sts. W.D.M.: C.A._
BIG STONE WITH MOTHER AT BASE-NO NAME-WITH DATES 1862-1937
    and is next to Obelisk of Wm.T.Ellis.

J.T.ROSAMOND Nov.21 1864-May 4 1956
Jimmie K.ROSAMOND Feb.26 1881-Nov.18 1957 MOTHER

Lillie McKEE Jan.27 1912-May 2 1981 MOTHER

Rebecca Ann STEVENS Nov.3 1974-July 23 1982
"Stevie"Telly Vance STEVENS III Aug.28 1971-Jan 11 1980
   A carving of an angel and a boy at bat.

J.C.BATTON Sept.1854,-Dec. _1931
Ida Martin BATTON Sept.3 1879-Sept.6 1969
Irene BATTON 1904-1904
Leandell BATTON Jan.28 1897-Aug.25 1901
J.A.BATTON June 25 1859-Sept.10 1901
M.A.ODOM wife/J.C.BATTON Dec.3 1866-Mar.27 1901
Clara M.BATTON 1914-1918
Infant son/J.C.& Ida M.BATTON 1915

ANGUILLA,MS.,SHARKEY CO. GOLDEN LINK CEMETERY 1907

Mary C.BATTON Aug.12 1891-Sept.29 1892
C.E.BATTON Jan.15 1889-Oct.22 1890
W.A.BATTON Jan.9 1887-Oct.11 1888

Rosa A.ANDERSON Nov.21 1851-Mar.20 1929
J.H.ANDERSON June 15 1845-June 27 1921

ON THE WEST END HEAVY HEDGE ROW,SEVERAL VISIBLE BUT UNREACHABLE F
Emma Kay dau/J.W.& U.B.HOLENGER Sept.2 1900-June 29 1901
Inf.of J.W. & U.B HOLENGER May 8 1899-May 12 1899
J.W.HOLENGER Nov.1 1865-Dec.16 1931
Bertha HOLENGER Sept.2 1878-Jan.13 1961
Ft/st in hedge row--R.A.A.

PATTERSON | Wm.Edwin Aug.3 1883-Mar.26 1966
Beatrice England Apr. 12 1903-Mar.27 1976

ENGLAND | James M. Nov.26 1870-July 23 1950 DAD
Martha A. Aug.16 1880-Feb.5 1928 MOTHER

Lee Roy MILLER Jr. Aug.28 1947-June 10 1973 "Bubber"Ft/st LRM

John Artie DERRICK Apr.2 1885-Aug.10 1959 FATHER Ft/st J.A.D.
A.B.DERRICK Jr. Nov.30 1938-Aug.29 1957 SONNY Ft/st A.B.D.

Charles E.ALLEN 1901-1955

GRAHAM | George Guy Nov.7 1899-Oct.11 1959
Inez Stevens May 3 1900-Aug.16 1975
Hubbard T.TAYLOR Apr.10 1857-July 3 1883

Lonnie M.EMERSON July 10 1910-June 27 1912

BOBO | Johnnie H. Aug.27 1902- Aug.2 1966
Jeffie E. June 2 1894-Aug.15 1980
James H.DAVIS Ms.Pvt US Army WWII Feb.5 1905-July 24 1960
Wm.E.DAVIS Sept.24 1959-Oct.25 1984
MOVING EAST ALONG N FENCE FROM WEST END
John S.PERKINS Ms Wagonner Co G 4 Ammo Tn. WWI Jan 7 1892-Aug.
7 1954   PH
Elizabeth PERKINS Mar.26 1893-Nov.13 1981

(broken)E?M.STEVENS Apr. 19 1840-May 6 1889
Henry S.SHANNON Sept.24 1851-Aug.20 1902

Joe Mc.Govern MELTON Tec.5 US Army WWII July 15,1909-June 21 1982
Funeral Marker:Wm.H.Bobo Mar.12 1910-Dec.31 1982

Margaret A.F. wife/John DUE(C)DS May 8 1841-Apr.26 1881(first
    date and surname is good guess!

Mattie V. dau/N.B.& M.A.HULL b&d Feb.6 1884(grown into a bush)

Sam MARANTO Dec.27 1901-June 8 1953

HAKES | Dewitt Clinton 1860-19__ (no death date)
Nancy Maud   1885-1942

ANGUILLA MS. SHARKEY CO. GOLDEN LINK CEMETERY 1907

Walter P.GAVIN 1883-1936
Chas.E.GAVIN 1920-1934

UNCLE-Edgar E.TURNIPSEED Nov.25 1886-May 26 1936

Falcon O.STEVENS June 10 1908-Oct.10 1949

Leland Ray SAXON Jan.2 1945-Oct.10 1948
DADDY-Verdis Vernard SAXON July 15 1891-Sept.24 1952

WANKER | Minnie Hellen Nov.27 1896-Nov.29 1972   MAMA
WANKER | Orris Otto Dec.19 1885-Feb.13 1961   DADDY
Robert Wayne WANKER Feb.12 1958-Mar.9 1959
Jenniv DUNN May 29 1917-Feb.18 1936   SIS
Veril O.WANKER Ms.Pvt US Army WWII May 1 1928-May 16 1971

THE END OF Golden Link Cem. that is with in the fence.
Henry PARHAM was buried in this cemmetery as documented by his
    daughter, but no grave site found.
The following names are taken from the records of the Chapel
of the cross in Rolling Fork, as having been buried here and
no grave site found.
Thomas C.WATSON JR. Age 20,no date in rec.
James BARNES 10 months 1881
Earl BARNES 2½ yrs. Jan 10 1881
W.E.HARRIS buried Mar.18 1881
Saml.McKENZIE Buried Mar.19 1881
Thos.C.Watson buried 1887

KEllY FAMILY CEM. next door to 600 S.3rd Street in Rolling Fork,
   Sharkey Co.Ms.Mar. 6 1986-by Alice Wade
S/E SIDE
J.JENNINGS McCOMB-Nov.14 1899-Feb.2 1962   BROTHER
ELIJAH BLAND McCOMB Nov.9 1850-Aug.4 1934 FATHER
LEILA SHELBY McCOMB Feb.8 1875-Dec.7 1957 MOTHER
EMMA S.SHELBY Nov.30 1849-Nov.10,1883---Flat Stone
FLAT DOUBLE STONE-TOP BROKEN no SURNAME:
MOLLIE B. Jan.18 1872-Dec.18 1875
LULU MAIMAI Nov.5 1875-Dec.1 1875
W.B.KELLY Dec.7 1874-Apr.8 1924
OLIVER CLIFTON KELLY Mar.17 1886-Sept.2 1922
JOHN BUTLER KELLY son/JNO & E.B.KELLY,Dec.8 1884-Jan.24 1906
KATHERINE A.KELLY Jan.23 1882-Sept.4 1947"Mother of none-yet
         Mother to many"
W.B.McQUILLAN Oct.6 1824-Dec.23 1884
IRINE KELLY Mar.12 1909-May 9 1909 | Two crosses with info on the
No name-Mar.18 1925 | cross arms. Two graves
JANE M. dau./JNO.& E.B.KELLY Nov.13 1882-Dec.23 1882
MARY K.PRIDEMORE dau/J.E.BUTLER,Jan.28 1853-Dec.23 1882
EMILY A.BUTLER wife/R.S.WOODBURY Aug.29 1851-Sept.22 1882
JOHNNIE son/JNO.& E.B.KELLY Dec.29 1879-Sept 3 1882
CINTHY J. wife/J.E.BUTLER Sept.4 1835-May 17 1882
JOHN E.BUTLER Feb.8 1824-June 20 1900
NANNIE B.LUM wife/J.E.BUTLER d.May 22 1894

KELLY | ADA EULALIA May 25 1886-Mar.20 1981
      | ROBERT W. Feb.13 1877-Apr.7 1947

KELLY | JOHN Dec.19 1850-June 17 1934-died on Fathers day.Ft/st/J.K
      | EVANAH BELLE Oct.10 1855-May 2 1929-died on Mothers day.EBK
JOHN KELLY GILLILAND June 21 1908-July 10 1944-Ft/st/ J.K.G.
ROSALIE KELLY GILLILAND "Little Mama"Feb.11 1892-May 8 1967-RKG
THOMAS CLAUDE KELLY Feb.22 1889-Mar.15 1951
HALLIE FRANCIS KELLY Mar.26 1918-Apr.14 1981
ROBERT SMITH COLLINS Aug.1 1906-Feb.14 1960
DOUBLE HEADSTONE WITH LARGE STATUE OF MAN IN FLOWING ROBES-THIS
      IS THE GRAVE OF MS.GOV.F.L.WRIGHT-
FIELDING LEWIS WRIGHT May 16 1895-May 4 1856
Stone blank-wife living in 1986
**SPANISH FORT,SHARKEY CO.,MS.two graves on an embankment alleged
   to be the remains of the fort wall.Aug.1985.A.Wade-K.Branton**
CLARENCE MELVIN COGHLAN-1908-1910
H.L.COGHLAN-1865-1919

CARY, MS. METHODIST CHURCH CEMETERY.
Church and cemetery are on highway 61, middle of town. Fenced in side of Church. Recorded only tombs dated before 1912.
Copied by Alice Wade, Katherine Branton, April 1984

M.C.MARTIN, June 14,1851-Feb.15,1902(above ground Mausolem)
MARY L.wife of M.C.MARTIN, Mar.28,1854-June 25,1887
GUS L.son of M.C.& M.L.MARTIN, July 19,1884-Aug.9,1899--G.L.M.
LIZZIE MARTIN, wife of GEO.W.DAVIS, Nov.23,1872-Sept.21,1898--L.M.D.
"WALTER"--stone submerged in ground, couldn't read rest of it.
W.N.SAUNDERS, Aug.27,1863-July 4,1905. Woodsman of the World.
BERTHA BERRY, wife of J.F.WEIGANT-Feb.4,1879-Jan.18,1921
Mother-LUCY BOZEMAN, Aug.10,1842-Jan.19,1904
Mother-MARY M.GRAVES-Jan.10,1836-Jan.12,1909
WALLACE W.GRAVES, Oct.23,1831-Sept.28,1902
AULCIE daughter of J.W.& M--STEWART, b.1900-d.1902
CAPT.A.H.JOHNSTON, Aug.20,1833-Feb.5,1904"Rest soldier, rest, thy
    warfare is over."

HARVEY CEMETERY
   1 mile south of Rolling Fork, Ms. in a pasture on Mound Pltn on East bank of Deer Creek, across from the Mounds Cemetery. Trees grown up and around the 6 identifiable headstones. Possibly more here at one time. By A.Wade, K.Branton, April 1984
Small foot stone wedged in tree--M.L.H.
ROBERT EMMET HARVEY, Nov.22,1864-Nov.28,1887
MA-------ARVEY, Nov.11,1832-July 29,1893(Curved top broken off)
MARY LIZZIE HARVEY d.Mar.29,1860-aged 1 year.(believe the small
    footsone with M.L.H.belongs here)
LIZZIE LE HARVEY d.July 26,1855-age 3 years.(Two pieces that
    seemed to fit together)
EFFIE LE(corner broken off) d.Mar.3 1860(Bottom gone)
-ATE H.HARVEY d.Dec.18,185_, age 1 yr.(top corner missing and
    side of date broken off.

MOUNDS CEMETERY
SHARKEY COUNTY, ROLLING FORK, MS
COMPILED BY ALICE WADE
1983

Mounds cemetery was established as a public burial ground before 1891 on land donated by Dr. E.C.Clements. It is situated in Sharkey Co. Ms. ½ mile south of the city limits of Rolling Fork, on the west bank of Deer Creek. NW¼ of the NE¼ of Sec. 14, T 12, R 7 W, containing 2 acres in the original section.

Mounds Cemetery Association was formed June 29,1908, at which time the Methodist Episcopal Church South, of Rolling Fork, quit claimed a deed to the trustees, A.K.Barrier, R.S.Myers, W.H.Clements; recorded in Deed book U, page 135, Sharkey Co. Ms.

Maps of the cemetery plots and owners are on file at Carter Engineers of Rolling Fork and in the Chancery-Circuit Clerks office of Sharkey Co.

This is a listing from the <u>original part only</u>. The extreme South part is the new addition and is not in this compilation. The north eastern section contains the oldest burial sites, so I chose to start in this area.

Beginning east of the main entrance, I have recorded the plots numerically. Some of the outlines are not defined too well. Where I was not sure about a grave site I have make a note of it.**

The west side of the main entrance is laid out in an orderly manner, and I chose to record it in blocks instead of numerically, as will be explained before each section.

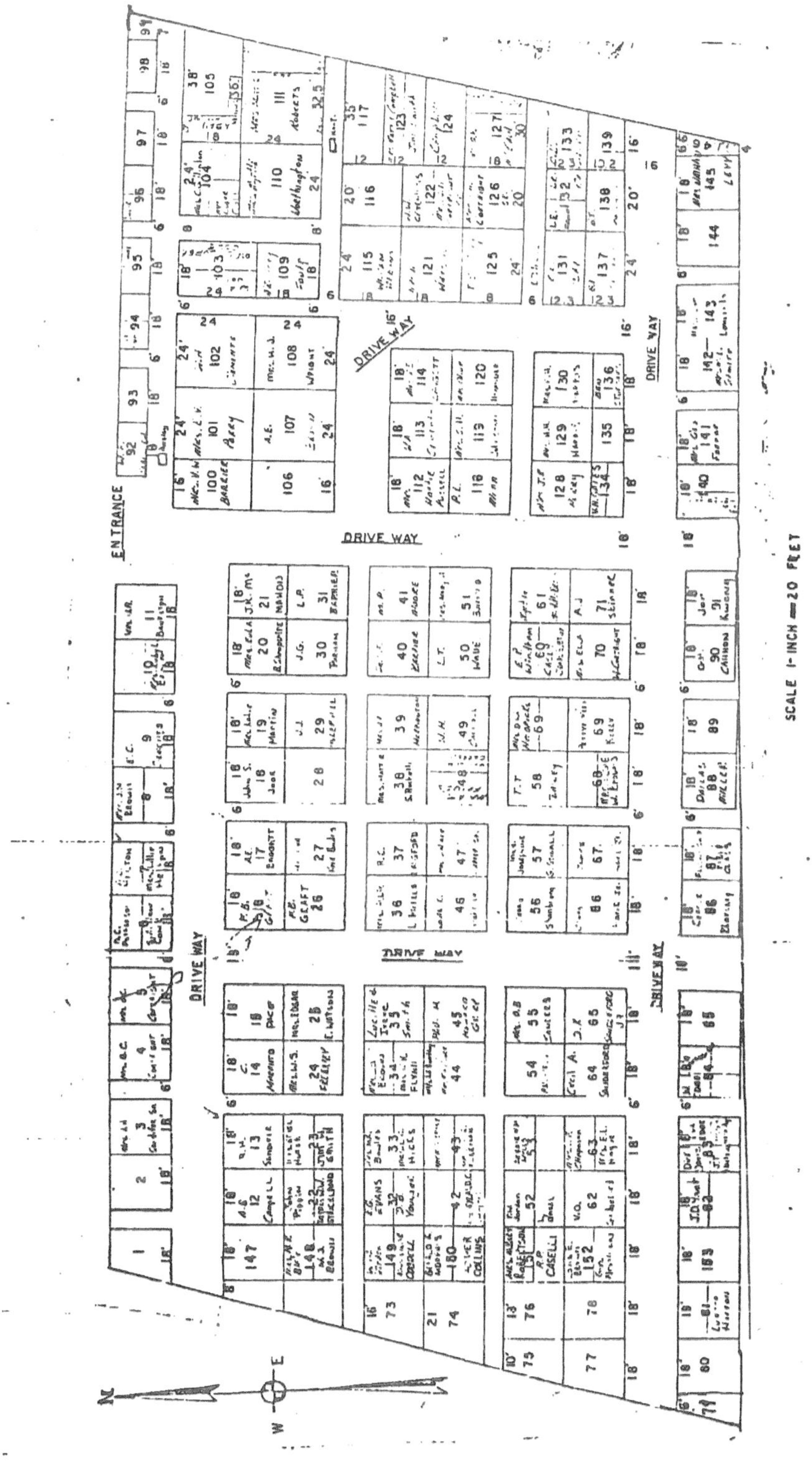
ENTRANCE
DRIVE WAY
DRIVE WAY
DRIVE WAY
DRIVE WAY
DRIVE WAY
SCALE 1-INCH = 20 FEET
N
E
W

BEGINNING EAST OF MAIN ENTRANCE

#92 W.B. BRADSHAW

    Joseph Bridgers June 9,1858-Nov.17,1907

    Enola Bradshaw dau. of W.B.& M.W.Bradshaw born in Ennis Tex. Sept.9,1902- died in Rolling Fork,Ms. Jan.4,1907

#93 VACANT

#94 W½ W.T.EVANS

#94 E½ VACANT

#95 W½ VACANT

#95 E½ BODIE--One grave--headstone broken, unreadable

#96 W½ BODIE

    Virgil Bodie June 23,1910-Mar.11,1936

#96 E½ VACANT

#97 E¼

    Albert M. Neal Oct.2,1892-Dec.17,1939. "Devoted Husband and Loving Father"

#97 W3/4 VACANT

#98 W½

    John Charles Son of J.E.& Ruby Bunting. Nov.10,1917 Feb.23,1923--"Darling we miss thee".

#98 E½ VACANT

#99

    Jennie K. wife of Dr.J.Bommer May 11,1869-May 11,1908

    "Beloved one Farewell". On the bottom of the stone-Katie.

***Between #92 & 100

    Flat stone, first name badly chipped, the best I could make it;

    Retler Presley June .,1884,-Nov.27,1920

#100 MRS. V.W.BARRIER

    Albert Kammeron Barrier July 11,1910-Dec.2,1947

    Warren on headstone, small foot stone V.W.B.Jr. Aug.17,1908- Aug.11,1929

    Leitha Carl Barrier June .0,1914--Sept.10,1914

    Margaret Ward May 29,1910-Aug.--1914

    Annette Loraine dau. of V.W.& A.A.Barrier, May 13,1912-Jan.28,1914

    Fannie Maud---------------------Gladys Earl

    Nov.8,1890-Oct.17,1891   Aug.27,1895-Aug.14,1905

        Children of A.K.& M.Z.Barrier

    Victor Warren Barrier-----------Ann Martak Barrier

    Mar.15,1887-Feb.12,1964   Sept.30,1891-----------

#100 cont.
> Jack William Hitchens Aug.23,1950-Oct.1,1950
> * One stone broken, top missing-no information

#101 MRS. E.V.PERRY
> N.T.Baggett July 31,1856-Nov.26,1904
> Annie Clements Baggett Nov.8,1865-Oct.6,1912
> William Clements Baggett Feb.22,1899-July 21,1964
> Greenfield Marion Baggett Oct.24,1852- Dec.16,1929
> Frances Baggett Perry Feb.8,1895-Jan.25,1977
> Earl Vincent Perry Oct.28,1889,-July 16,1981

#102 W.H.CLEMENTS
> Corinne Parham-wife of W.H.Clements Feb.22,1885-Aug.18
>   1952."Rest is thine and sweet remembrance ours"
> William Hardy Clements Sr. Aug.27,1873-July 25,1953
>   "Rest in Peace"
> Gertrude Parham-wife of W.H.Clements May 19,1883-Mar.19,1917
> Infant son of Corinne & W.H.Clements Apr.18,1926
> Jack Greenway Clements Nov.4,1906-Dec.4,1906
> Dr. Early Coleman Clements Aug.16,1828-Sept.27,1903
> Ann Foote Clements Dec.29,1838-Aug.31,1910

#103 W½ W.A.JOLLEY
> Mary Butts Jolley 1868-1923
> Walter A.Jolley 1854-1931
> Walter A.Jolley Jr. 1889-1951
> Stella W.Jolley 1892-1958
> Robert K.Shelby July 22,1863-Aug.27,1885
> Margaret Elizabeth Shelby Nov.28,1835-Sept.27,1894
> Evan B.Shelby Feb.2,1870-June 29,1906
> Rev. J.V.Penn Nov.10,1851-Aug.5,1897

#103 E½ MRS. LUPER COLE
#104 SW¼ MRS. LUPER COLE
> Lillian Caroline Cole 1938-1938

#104N½ MRS. C.G.HINTON
> Leona Graft Dau. of R.C.& L.G.Buck. Aug.8,1909-Aug.5,1910
> R.C.Buck Jan.21,1874-Aug.24,1921
> Bea Hinton, 1912-1982 "Suffer little children to come unto me"
> Dorothy Jean Hinton 1932-1932
> Dorothy Elizabeth Tinnin 1938-1940
> Christine Graft Hinton 1882-1964
> Noah Blanchard Hinton 1863-1923
> Wm. Lobdell Hinton Mar.25,1918-Sept.25,1918
> Jack Perry Hinton Sept.25,1915-Sept.16,1918

#104 SE¼   VACANT

#105 W¼ LABON RICHMOND
    Wm.L.Richmond 1879-1933 "Daddy" on top of stone

#105 SW MIDDLE-MRS. H.W.TURNER
    Frances Louise-dau. of Louis & Frances Turner.Apr.8,1930-
        July 29,1930
    H.Walter Turner--------------------Ada C.Turner
    Dec.5,1881-Feb.5,1967   May 4,1893---Living
    C.Lamar Turner Aug.23,1911-June 26,1930

#105 SE MIDDLE- E.L.TURNER
    Mike Curran Ellison Oct.4,1907-July 8 1976

#105 NE CORNER
    Marvin Barrett, Husband of Lera Gaston. July 4,1902-
    Sept.10,1943. Father of Louis Barrett."He was the sunshine
        in our home"

#105 WHAT IS LEFT IS VACANT

#106 N½ (MAP SHOWS VACANT. CONTAINS 3 GRAVES)
    Charles O. Walton Aug.28,1875-feb.14,1968
    Henry C.L.Taylor Apr.28,1890-Nov.26,1909
    Charles H.Walton Feb.22,1842-Oct.31,1906

#106 S½ VACANT

#107 A.E.BROWN
    Mayme B.Alexander Aug.9,1822-Feb.28,1965
    Leila B. Brown Mar.9,1859-Feb.--1948
    A.E.Brown Feb.28,1966-June 15,1918
    Mrs. A.A.Glisson July 1,1865-Feb.11,1911

#108 MRS. H.J.WRIGHT
    Lloyd Earl Dowdy July 28,1893-Apr.10,1936
    Lewis Wright Dowdy Apr.28,1903-Apr.1,1980
    Fannie Clements Wright July 21,1870-June 20,1957
    Henry James Wright Feb.22,1860-Oct.10,1938
    Early Clements Wright Oct.11,1898,Aug.20,1938

#109 MR. SHELBY FOOTE
    Shelby Dade Foote 1891-1922
    H.L.Foote Jan.24,1856-July 18,1915
    Katie Shelby Foote 1865-1928
    Baby

#110 MRS. MYRTLE WORTHINGTON
    Elizabeth Acee Sullivan Nov.9,1857-July 7,1927 "Mother'
    John W.Jr. son of John & Myrtle Baggett Oct.15,1906-Mar.2,1907

#110 cont.
- John W. Baggett Sr. Jan.16,1898-June 6,1912
- Myrtle Sullivan Worthington May 28,1891-Feb.2,1967

#111 W3/4 MRS. MATTIE ROBERTS
- Benj. Roberts Nov.30,1826--May 30,1895
- Sarah M. Dingee-wife of Benj. Roberts, Mar.30,1827-Jan.22,1891 "Our Mother"
- Georgie Lee Roberts Dec.22,1890-Oct.16,1892."A bird on earth, transported to Paradise"
- Chrispen Ruth-Wife of W.B.Roberts,Jan.9,1896-Dec.18,1926
- W.B.Roberts 1895-1931
- Julius S.-Son of Wm. & Mattie Roberts. Aug.6,1893-Nov.15,1903
- Mattie Roberts 1870-1952 "Mother"
- ** Gladys Horton 1901-1918 (This is not exactly in #111,nor the Turner plot of #105

#111 E¼ VACANT

#112 MRS. HATTIE RUSSELL
- Mary Louise-Dau. of T.G.&.H.Russell July 13,1906-June 10,1907
- Hattie Sims Russell ------------------Thomas Gray Russell
- July 31,1882-July 9,1954   Nov.11,1879-July 4,1947
- M.Russell---------------------------Nannie E.Roach(wife)
- June 1,1850-Oct.17,1925-Mason   May 1,1849-Oct.11,1920
- ** IN NW CORNER OF LOT #112 SMALL STONE, ALMOST IN DRIVEWAY
- Leroy Campbell son of E.L.& E.R.Passmore.Aug.14,1905-Apr.9,1907

#113 W.A.CROCKETT
- Ellen Moss Campbell 1882-1930
- Thomas W. Campbell-----------------Augusta Emily Campbell
- Mar.4,1844-Aug.1,1921   Feb.28,1851-July 27,1907
- Richard Clifton Platt Oct.8,1860-Sept.28,1924
- William Andrew Crockett---------Mary Alice(Nee Campbell)
- July 31,1861-Feb.13,1947   Dec.27,1874-June 7,1945
-     Husband   Wife

#114 MRS. A.E.BAGGETT
- Alleyne E. Baggett----------------Elizabeth W. Baggett
- Jan.27,1893-Sept.17,1970   Apr.2,1903-Living June 1983
- George William West Jr. May 8,1907-Jan.23,1908
- Alice Baggett West- Died Apr.2,1903
- George W.West Nov.5,1869-Mar.28,1918 (Woodsman of the World Knights of Pythias, Mason, Flt.)
- Mrs. E.S.West wife of Geo.W.West Oct.5,1838-Mar.24,1914
- Charles I. West Died Nov.11,1936

#115 WM. GIBBONS

    Sarah Jane wife of Lewis Jones Oct.18,1836-Oct.31,1920

    Lewis Jones Nov.3,1863-Oct.23,1950 "Brother"

    Mary E. Gibbons Jan.31 ,1832-July 6,1903

    Enola Montgomery Gibbons Sept.1,1877-Oct.2,1906

    D.Carroll son of Wm.& Enola Gibbons Nov.2,1903-Aug.5,1905

    Harry Hart " " " " "   Sept.2,1898-Aug.6,1905

    Mary E. Gibbons Mar.22,1874-Aug.14,1955

    Wm. Gibbons Oct.16,1867-Sept.8,1956

#116 MAP SHOWS VACANT. 2 GRAVES SEEM TO BE ON WEST END OR BETWEEN #116 and #110

    Kate S. Baggett-----------------John R. Baggett

    1871-1932   1848-1901

    Lena Montgomery-------------D. Hugh Montgomery

    1851-1907   1840-1902

****THESE TWO GRAVES ARE EITHER IN E#116 OR W #117

    Ruth Farrar Dau. of J.T.& Kate Farrar. July 30,1902-July 8,1903

    Louis Farrar Son "   "   "   "   " July 2,1900-Oct.28,1901

****FLAT STONE BETWEEN #111 & #117 , COULD BE IN N W SIDE OF #117

    Bettie-wife of Thomas Kent. Nov.25,1843-Apr.30,1900

#117 MAP SHOWS VACANT. SEE ABOVE * ITEMS.

#118 P.L. MANN

    Leon E. Mann-- -------------William M. Mann

    Oct.9,1874-July 19,1944   Nov.8,1844-Nov.26,1926

        Son   Father

#119 MRS. S.H. JOHNSTON

    Joseph Walker Johnston Feb.24,1849-Aug.13,1909

#120 MRS. OLIVE ALEXANDER

    Olive Alexander Aug.25,1875-June 16,1950

    Samuel Bryce Alexander d. June 17,1889 age 55 years

    Amy Olive Alexander d. Nov.12,1908 age 65 years

    **THE ABOVE TWO NAMES ARE ON SAME HEADSTONE, SUGGESTING TO ME REMOVAL FROM ORIGINAL BURIAL SITE.

    Samuel Bryce Alexander 1934 (only date)

  ** ON WEST ½ OF ALEXANDERS #120, LARGE DOUBLE STONE WITH ONLY THE NAME BARNARD. IN FRONT, TWO SMALL FLAT STONES-ONE J.L.B THE OTHER S.A.B. NO DATES. BELIEVE THIS IS JOSEPH L. BARNARD AND SARA ALEXANDER BARNARD.

#121 MRS. A. WATSON

    A double head stone; tall slender column, names on opposite sides;

#121 cont. on double stone
    Mary L. Dau. of Thomas C.& Mary P.Watson.Feb.1855-Jan.19,1897
    Joseph Son of   "   "   "   " Oct.24,1849,Dec.7,1909
    Annie Elizabeth Watson Aug.16,1851-Aug.12,1943
    Harry Gordon Carpenter Feb.9,1890-Oct.11,1970
    Fannie Watson is also buried in this plot, but stone was destroyed during the 1927 flood.

#122 N½ W.W.CATCHINGS
    Warrene Kirkland, Dec.28,1894-Nov.20,1957."No pain, no greif, no anxious fear, can reach our beloved sleeping here"
    Howard Phipps Kirkland June 9,1882-Aug.4,1953
    Allie Mae Catchings wife of G.O.Couvillon Sept.11,1898-Mar.19,1920
    Rosa S. Cathings "Mother"Jan.17,1876-Feb.27,1947

#122 S½ (SEE #126-MRS. J.H. CORTRIGHT SR.)

#123 N½ MRS. MATTIE CAMPBELL
    Caro Bogard Buckley Apr.18,1930-Apr.12,1983
    Dorothy F. Bogard Feb.3,1896-Apr.17,1977
    Daniel A. Bogard June 11,1896-Feb.4,1966
    Miller M. Bogard Jan.6,1894-Mar.13,1956

#123 S½ Jim Smith

#124 CAMPBELL
    W.H.Campbell 1847-1920
    Mattie Bogard Campbell 1866--1935

#125 D.C.CASEY
    D.C.Casey Oct.1845- May 20,1914
    Cornelia E. Casey Apr.26,1846-Oct.25,1920
    Charlotte Womack Pace Aug.12,1906-Apr.25,1965
    Courtney Culpepper Pace June 3,1904-Jan.24,1979
    Robert B.Womack Sept.7,1877-Nov.1,1910
    Laura Cornelia Cortright Oct.20,1882-Dec.7,1918

#126 & #122 S½ MRS.J.H.CORTRIGHT SR.
    Edward Payson Cortright Jan.25,1861.D.date sunk in ground
    Willie son of J.H.& C.P.Cortright July 16,1889-age 1yr. 4 mo..16days."Such is the kingdom of Heaven"
    Tecumseh Blaine Cortright Apr.26,1890-Sept.26,1953
    James H. Cortright Jr. Feb.9,1883-Nov.27,1946
    Ray Hamberlin Cortright July 31,1902-Sept.1980
    Clementine Cortright Apr.3,1863-Dec.27,1924
    James Henry Cortright Nov.6,1848-May 9,1923
    Louise V. Cortright 1895-1983

#127 W 3/4 MRS. G.B.McCAUL
   Addie Watt McCaul 1868-1928
   G.B.McCaul 1862-1921

#127 E ¼ A.J.BAGGETT
   Jack M. Baggett Aug.9,1923-Jan.13,1983
   A.J.Baggett June 5,1896-July 8,1960
   Mildred McCaul Baggett Aug.26,1900-Apr.21,1957

#128 MRS. J.R.PERRY
   W.T.Baskin Aug.14,1847-Feb.8,1925. Woodman of the World
   Hattie Cornelia Baskin 1865-1930
   Dr.Joe Reid Perry-- ----------Willie Earle Baskin Perry
   1878-1959   1885-1980
   Dick Perry son of Mr.& Mrs.J.B.Green 1936-1939
   Earl Baskin Perry---------------Miriam McClellan Perry
   Aug.9,1915-Apr.5,1981   Sept.11,1916-Living June 1983
   Joe Reid Perry Jr. 1915-1977

#129 & #130 MRS. H.H.HARRIS
   George Carroll Harris S.T.D.-D.D. Feb.6,1836-"Entered into rest"
      July 2,1911."Right dear in the sight of the Lord is the death
      of his Saints".
   Helen Scrymgeour Johnstone Harris May 21,1839-Nov.19,1917
   **ON EXTREME WEST SIDE OF #130,BESIDE A LARGE MAGNOLIA TREE IS:
   George Carroll Harris Jr. 1867-1927 Mason
   William James Hibbler Jan.24,1872-Nov.16,1918

#131 C.E.DAY
   Walter Brown Jan.26,1860=May 7,1919 "in memory of our Brother"
   W.D.Brown Mar.4,1833-Mar.2,1918
   Alice V. wife of W.D.Brown Feb.14,1842-Mar.16,1917
   W.R.Harper M.D. Jan.26,1862-Aug.11,1911
   Estelle B. wife of W.R.Harper Dec.1,1862-Oct.5,1955
   Cary Emerson Day- ---------------- ---Garnett H.Day
   Jan.15,1891-Dec/8,1976   Jan.21,1890-Dec.25,1976

**** BETWEEN #131 DAY & #125 CASEY
   Joseph A. Thomas June 15,1856-June 30,1903

#132 W ½ L.E.MANN

#132 E½ & #133 DR. C.D.CRAWFORD
   Mary Ella Crawford Jan.24,1921-June 25,1926
   Maggie O.Crawford---------------Claude D. Crawford
   Jan.18,1899-Living June '83   Apr.20,1892-June 17,1980

#134 N½ V.N.GATES vacant
#134 S½ MAP SHOWS VACANT. TWO GRAVES IN S E CORNER
    Hattie Sanford wife of R.L.Burch Oct.2,1854-Mar.21,1915
    Charley Conrad Sanford July 26,1863-May 26,1912 "Our Brother"
#135 VACANT
#136 BEN STURGIS
    Emm Luhm Sturgis Nov.4,1877-Apr.19,1970
    Jacob Benjamin Sturgis Mar.15,1855-Feb.12,1910
#137 B.T.ORENDORF
    Louis Munsey Elliott Apr.12,1881-Apr.10,1946
    Mary Orendorf Elliott Nov.30,1882-Jan.8,1970
#138 B.T.ORENDORF
    T.T.Orendorf--------------------G.G.Orendorf
    1847-1902   1843-1913
    Alice E. Orendorf (Goldie) Feb.27,1899-Mar.13,1973
    Mary Hopkins Bell Aug.2,1838- Aug.19,1912
#139 SW CORNER:1 GRAVE ONLY (W.S.Ferguson Jr.)
    Marion Roan 1884-1927
***OLD MAPS SHOW A DRIVEWAY SOUTH #134,BUT WHEN THE NEW PART WAS
    ADDED THE DRIVEWAY WAS CHANGED TO SOUTH OF #140
#140 W½ D.W.HENDRICKS
    Watt-Oct.2,1924 | on same stone
    Mary-Jan.15,1928! Infants of D.W.& E.P.Hendricks
    William Madison Peeler-----------Sorintha Winters Peeler
    Aug.3,1857-July 2,1947   Mar.8,1868-May 20,1934
    Maudie Uzzle July 21,1895-Mar.6,1911
    Viola Uzzle Aug.7,1911-Jan.10,1928
#140 E½ VACANT
#141 MRS. GEO. FARRAR(MRS. CLARENCE L. HAZELWOOD)
    Lee Jean and Lee Dean Hazelwood Nov.6,1923-June 9,1924
    Marie A. Hazelwood----------------C.L.Hazelwood
    Feb.6,1897-Oct.27,1964   Nov.26,1893-Jan.24,1983
    George Cohron Farrar Dec.16,1916-May 13,1966
#142 S½ MRS.M.L.SCHMITZ
    Daniel K. Sandeford Dec.4,1874-Dec.3,1958
    Melvin L. Schmitz Mar.17,1900-Dec.26,1946
#142 N½ VACANT
#143 MRS.JOE LOMBARDO
    Joseph Verderemo July 11,1877-Nay 11,1913
    Jimmie Colletta, July 18,1903-June 26,1940
    Annie Lombardo----------------Joseph Lombardo
    May 14,1880-Jan.13,1953   Nov.2,1874-Mar.21.1952

#144 MAP SHOWS VACANT BUT WEST½ CONTAINS GRAVES

 Susie Elizabeth daughter of Mr.&Mrs.J.W.Holloway Sept.23,1889
  Mar.18,1925 "Our loved One"
 Infant son of T.A.& Nona Heath Jr. Sept.22,1918
 Pvt.J.H.Holloway son of MR.& MRS.J.W.Holloway "FOR WORLD LIBERTY"
  Mar.2,1893-Jan.8,1919 "Our Darling Son.He died that we Might Live"
 J.W.Holloway Mar.1,1863-Mar.26,1923
 Laura Zeigler Holloway-"Mother" Oct.31,1864-Oct.28,1952

#145 MRS. NATHAN LEVY VACANT

#146 N.LEVY (HARRY B. BUTLER)
 Hiram P.Butler-------------------Lee C.Butler
 1910-1935   1915-1937
 Sadie Vibell Feb.4,1897-Jan.21,1909
 H.J.Butler Jan.25,1859-Apr.21,1928
 Eddie P. Butler Apr.5,1870=Jan.21,1949

** THE NEXT 7 PLOTS UP TO #153 ARE IN THE EXTREME WEST SIDE OF
  THE CEMETERY AND WILL BE INCORPORATED IN THE WEST SIDE LISTINGS.

** WEST OF THE MAIN ENTRANCE DRIVEWAY IS A SINGLE ROW OF
  PLOTS BORDERING THE BLACKTOP ROAD. STARTING WEST OF ENTRANCE:

#11 MRS. J.R.BANKSTON-One large stone linking 4 graves.
 East side J.R.Bankston   &wife   Leoda Reneau
  Died July 3,1943- Reunited Died Sept.10,1957
 West side, C.W.Reneau   & wife   Theodosia Hickman
  D.Mar.21,1932   D. Feb.1,1930
 Small foot stones-Father   Mother
 William Frank Martak Apr.11,1893-Apr.13,1933

#10 MRS. RUBY L. BROWN S½

#10 N½ VACANT

#9   E.C.CLEMENTS

#8   N½ MRS. J.M.BROWN
 Alma K.Brown(Mother)---------------James M.Brown(Father)
 Mar.29,1892-Jan.8,1970   Mar.19,1869-Apr.19,1937

#8   S½ VACANT

#7   S½ LILLIE HELTON
 Garland W. Helton   Feb.28,1913-Sept.26,1942

#7   N½ A.J.HELTON (R.L.BURFORD JR.)
 Robert Lee Burford "Father" May 30,1876-Feb.5,1937

#6   IS SPLIT E & W INSTEAD OF N & S AS PER MAP

#6 E½ O.C.PATTERSON
    Oscar C. Patterson-----------------Eula Newcomb Patterson
    July 14,1898-May 12,1968   Aug.1,1890-Dec.6,1945
    Woodrow Patterson Sept.11,1924-Jan.29,1943

#6 W½ S.A.NEWCOMB
    Dora Moore Newcomb Sept.10,1875-Dec.22,1955
    Samuel A.Newcomb Dec.22,1870-June 27,1952
    Vernon Ray Newcomb Mar.13,1920-May 5,1943

#4 & #5 MRS. G.C.CORTRIGHT
    George Curtis Cortright Feb.28,1881-Nov.27,1945

#3 MRS.J.H.SANDIFER
    Joel H.Sandifer------------------Florence Sandifer
    July 9,1877-Feb.4,1946   Jan.28,1879-Oct.18,1961
    Mr..J.H..Sandifer Sept.22,1905,Oct.16,1982-77 years.Metal Marker

#2 VACANT

#1 IN WEST CORNER
    Joseph Brashear McPherson--Miss. 2nd Lt. 155 Inf. 39 Div.
        Nov.23,1929

**THE SECTION WEST OF ENTRANCE IS IN BLOCKS OF 4 PLOTS EACH TO THE NEXT DRIVEWAY WEST, EXCEPT FOR A SINGLE LINE ON THE SOUTH END SHOWN ON MAP ACROSS A DRIVE WHICH HAS BEEN CHANGED TO SOUTH OF THIS SINGLE LINE. I HAVE RECORDED IN BLOCKS,

#21-20-30-31

#21 J.R.McMAHON
    Baby-Robert Estes son of R.E.&A.McM. Matthews June 16,1927
        Aug.25,1927
    Huldah Sept.16,1932
    Joseph Dec.30,1942 | Infants of Carl & Huldah Day
    Thomas R. McMahon Jan.3,1903-Sept.5,1975
    John L.McMahon 1858-1896
    Thomas McMahon June 25,1866-Mar.19,1944
    Huldah Parham McMahon Aug.8,1880=Aug.25,1962

#20 N½ MRS. EULA B. SHROPSHIRE
    Edwin Demar Shropshire------------Elizabeth C.Clements
    May 29,1907-Sept.11,1972   Sept.16,1908-Apr.2,1984
    Eula B. Hatchett Oct.28,1887-Dec.19,1973
    Doss Shropshire Mar.25,1876--Jan.13,1929
    Augusta Shropshire 1849-1940

#20 S½ MRS. W.P.CARROLL

#30 J.G.PARHAM
    Junius Greenway Parham -- -----------Alice Gertrude Parham
    1853-1937   1857-1939

#30 cont.
    Junius Parham McMahon Jan.26,1901-Jan.30,1980

#31 L.P.BARRIER
    B. Alvis Stafford, M.D. Nov.30,1892--Jan.26,1961
    Alice B. Stafford Jan.5,1896-Nov.10,1955
    Leonard Paul Barrier July 17,1891-Sept.28,1930
    John Paul Grice Mar.27,1919-Mar.20,1977

#40-41-50-51

#40 DR. L.F.BARRIER
    Albert Kelly Barrier M.D.---------Margaret Warren Barrier
    Dec.6,1859-Nay 31,1939   Jan.17,1860-Jan.22,1944

#41 M.P. MOORE
    Marvin Pierce Moore-------------Annie Gale Sparks Moore
    1882-1928   1882-1962

#51 MRS. MARY A . BUNTING
    Edwin T.Garrett Feb.2,1883-June 14,1948
    Izola B. Garrett July 8,1893-Oct.14,1957
    Mary A.Bunting Dec.27,1870-Nov.8,1969
    Chas. I. Bunting Aug.9,1873-Jan.4,1932
    Evelyn J. Bunting Jan.18,1930-Nov.4,1936

#5o L.T. WADE (ORIGINALLY MRS. MABEL PERKINS)

#60-61-70-71

#60S½ (reverse on Map)E.P.WINDHAM
    Thomas Eugene Windham--------------Nancy Ellen Windham
    Mar.4,1881-Aug.17,1948   Feb.23,1884-June 24,1966

#60 N½ CASEY JONES et ux
    Sammy- son of Sam & Maxine Smithhart Oct.22,1946-Apr.18,1960

#61 MYRTLE MIDDLEBROOK(MRS. MAMIE MIDDLEBROOK)
    Myrtle Lillian Middlebrook-----Ethel May Middlebrook
    Feb.1,1908=July 4,1979   July 14,1898-Sept.25,1982
    John T.Middlebrook---------Mamie R. Middlebrook
    1866-1927   1869-1944

#71 A.J.SKINNER
    Alonzo Asa Skinner 1874-1930. Mason
    Lolah Belle Skinner 1884-1929 Eastern Star

#70 MRS. ELLA CORTRIGHT
    Ira Sherman Cortright Sept.16,1885=Aug.30,1954
    Buford Lee Williams June 17,1866-Aug.17,1934 "Father"
    Amanda Taylor Williams Nov.8,1867-Nov.17,1938 "Mother"

#90 G.H.CANNON (DRIVEWAY MOVED TO SOUTH OF THIS SINGLE ROW)
    Kathleen Partridge May 17,1950-May 20,1950
    George Henry Cannon------------Susan Frances Cannon
    1869-1935"Father"   1866-1954 "Mother"

#91 JOE KWONG
    Jim Kwong Feb.22,1928- Age 10 mos.
    Joe Kwong June 2,1932-age 69 yrs. Born Canton, China

#89 VACANT

#88 DALLAS MILLER
    Charley E.Dunbar-------- ------Catherine E. Dunbar
    1890-1935   1899--1958
    Lavera Miller Hayes May 29,1942-Sept.12,1962

#69-68-59-58

#69 PETTY E.MEEK KELLY
    Petty E.Meek Kelly Feb.27,1900=May 22,1962
    Lizzie Y. Meek----------------James Edward Meek
    July 27,1872-July 14,1932   July 20,1872-Oct.10,1939

#68 S½ MRS. ELSIE BROWN
    Argyle L.Brown----------------Elsie Williams Brown
    Apr.21,1876-Nov.24,1949   Jan.31,1877-Oct.1,1950

#68 N½ VACANT

#58 T.T.BAILEY (MRS.LOLA BAILEY)
    Truman T. Bailey Nov.24,1898-Aug.6,1943
    Lola S. Bailey Feb.14,1902-Dec.22,1949

#59 N½ MRS. D.W.HENDRICKS
    Daniel Watts Hendricks-----------Emma Peeler Hendricks
    May 14,1874 Yazoo Co.   Oct.31,1890 Arrala Co.
    May 2,1952 Warren Co.   Nov.10,1979
    Earle Winters Peeler Atta.Co. Apr.20,1892-War.Co. May 20,1952

#49-48-39-38

#49 W.H.CARROLL
    M.C."Cotton"Thomas---------------Floye Carroll Thomas
    July 31,1906-Oct.20,1977   May 10,1911-Living

#48 E½ MRS. W.H.CARROLL
    Dorothy Cady Carroll Nov.15,1913-Aug.25,1976
    William Holmes Carroll June 14,1873-June 14,1935
    Floy Butler Carroll Jan.1,1887-Sept.19,1941

#48 W½ MRS.A.J.FRANCIS
    Alexander Tribble Francis Apr.27,1883-Dec.10,1943
    Sybil Clements Francis Oct.27,1879-May 16,1948

#38 MRS. HATTIE S. ROCHELLE
   Chas. A. Rochelle-------------Hattie A. Rochelle
   1882-1942   Aug.18,1889-Apr.23,1982

#39 J.P. HERRINGTON
   Lilla Martin Herrington Feb.15,1886-June 21,1973
   James Robert Herrington Jan.19,1884-Jan.24,1931

#29-28-19-18

#29 J.J. UNDERHILL
   Georgie L. Baggett Sept.14,1866-June11,1937
   Georgia Catchings, wife of J.J.Underhill Sept.11,1900-Dec.9,1930

#28 MAP SHOWS VACANT----CONTAINS TWO GRAVES
   Albert McArthur Jones----------Mary Stillman Jones(DAR AShmead
   Mar.12,1870-Jan.4,1936   Jan.15,1871-Dec.7,1939   Chpt.)

#19 MRS. KATIE MARTIN
   Lewis Earnest Martin 1881--1930
   Katie Joor Martin July 10,1884-Nov.8,1975

**#18 J.S. JOOR
   John Shelby Joor Jr. Jan.22,1881-Mar.25,1965
   Lady Walker Joor Sept.10,1885-Aug.7,1940
   Baby
   M.W. Waddill died Mar.9,1934
   Berta Waddill   ⎰ Double small stone like 2 tablets
   Fairy Lee Joor   ⎱   No dates
   "Mother" Kate W. Joor 1855=1922
   John Shelby Joor 1845-1917

#17-27-26-16

#17 A.E. BAGGETT(L.M. JACOBS)
   Thomas Burrage Baggett Sept.1,1904-Aug.14,1946
   Susan G. Baggett 1887-1948
   Edgar Madison Baggett Jr. Mar.9,1890-Apr.16,1948

#27 MRS. EVA K. BOWLES
   Theodore S. Bowles Oct.19,1912-Oct.7,1968 "Son"
   Eva K. Bowles Oct.16,1876-June 22,1964 "Mother"
   Dolores Olga Bowles June 30,1915-Jan.20,1964 "Daughter"
   David Oscar Bowles July 4,1868-Apr.10,1939 "Father"

#26 F.B. GRAFT
   F. and Sarah Graft Aug.16,1893-Sept.19,1893
   Fredrick B. Graft 1840-1932
   Sarah F. Graft 1862-1941

#16 F.B. GRAFT
   Frederick Bernard Graft Mar.1,1885-June 2,1955
   Floyd Bogard Graft Sept.11,189- -Oct.19,1939
   Lillian E. Graft Jan.10,1890-July 17,1973

** Some of the stones in #18 were originally in the garden of
   J.S. Joors home on Race Street, according to the Episcopal
   Chapel of the Cross records. A.C.W.

#36-46-47-37

#36 MRS. ALLIE L. RICKELS
   Frank Liddell Rickels July 24,1900-May 18,1944
#46 L.E.ROCHELLE
   Baby Rochelle--Nov.10,1945
#47 MRS. W. CARTER SR.
   Wallace Carter June6,1887,-Nov.8,1943
   Yolande Louise Clark Carter Oct.23,1895-Oct.19,1968
#37 R.C.LANGFORD
   Robert Clark Langford June 19,1880-July 3,1967
   Mary Scudder Langford Feb.5,1895-Feb.13,1950
#57-56-66-67
#57 MRS. JOSEPHINE G. STIGALL
   James Millard Stigall 1904-1944
#56 FRANK SHARBROUGH (MRS. GEORGIE S.)
   "Mother" Mary R. Shepherd Sept.9,1879-Nov.24,1945
   Wm.H.Gray Jan.23,1909-Oct.8,1975
   Frank B. Sharbrough Feb.18,1892-Nay 20,1947
#66 & 67 JAMES HAND JR. on line between plots,large double headstone
                    Hand
   James,Jr. 30 July 1893   Theresa M. 30 Nov.1898
            3 Sept.1978   16,Nov.1975
#86 CEACLE BLAKNEY across old driveway
   James P. Blakney Nov.11,1908-July 1,1949
   Hugh I. Blakney Jan.29,1885-May 19,1957
   Janie C. Blakney June 12,1903-May12,1976
#87 FELLOWSHIP BIBLE CLASS
                    Cottle
   James D. Sr.   Janie Mae
   Sept.18,1897-Nov.1,1980   June 28,1917-Jan.20,1946
* On this lot,a very old stone. No inscription. Definitely markes a grave
#85 VACANT
#84 NE¼ GRACE BRADSHAW
                  Bradshaw
   Jesse Franklin   Grace Dulaney
   Oct.20,1896-Nar.13,1960   July 18,1898-Sept.30,1979
#84 NW¼ E.W.EDGE
   Lee Allen Childress Mar.7,1905-Mar.9,1976
                  Childress
   Frank A. 1875-1960   Susie E. 1886-1970
#84 SE¼ and SW¼ VACANT

#65-64-54-55
#65 D.K. SANDEFORD JR.

Sanderford

Dan	Mattie
Oct.1,1914-Feb.28,1973	Dec.3,1914------------

In Memory of our Son D.K.Sanderford 3rd. June 27,1934-July 31,1951

#64 CECIL A. SANDEFORD

Juanita Lee Donald Sept.13,1929-Oct.18,1966
Cecil Andrew Sanderford Jan.29,1952-Feb.2,1952
Juawice Lee Sanderford Oct.4,1930-Jan.29,1952

#54 A.M.KIRBY

Johnson,"Dusty" #10 Mar.3,1959-Aug.23,1981 "Our son and our brother, we miss you"
Edith G. Kirby 1915-1969

#55 MRS.O.B.SANDERS

Mother	BODIE	Sonny
Dora K.Schlottman		Clarence Bodie Jr.
Aug.10,1913-Nov.3,1980		Dec.14,1930-June 23,1951

Sons,John and Sonny Bodie on the mothers stone.

#45-44-34-35
#45 PAUL H. & HOWARD GRICE

Rev. Paul H. Grice	Eloise Brinson Grice
May 16,1888-May 1,1950	Sept.2,1889-Feb.21,1955
Rev. John Howard Grice	Maude Gunn Grice
Oct.25,1877-Aug.22,1952	Jan.1,1880-Oct.17,1969

#44 S½ M.P.MOORE   VACANT
#44 N½ MRS. J.E.BUNTING

Ruby White Bunting Nov.5,1896-Aug.25,1965
John Edwin Bunting Dec.26,1950-Apr.7,1955 "Son"

#34 S½ W.K.FLYNN

Wm. Kelvie Flynn Jan.26,1907-Oct.21,1956

#34 N½ W.O.BROWN(NOBLIN)

Brown

Wm.Orla	Mary Noblin
Apr.1,1904-Nov.11,1980	July 7,1913-------------

Noblin

Father-Frank	Mother-Aletha Hamilton
June 12,1872-Sept.5,1963	Oct.2,1878-Nov.7,1956

#35 LUCILLE SMITH & IRENE CLEGG SMITH

    Charles Russell Smith Oct.16,1901-Jan.24,1949

Smith

Fentress W.	Lucille P.
June 22,1910,Oct.10,1975	Oct.10,1910----Living

    Amelia Anne Schmidt June 1,1971-Feb.9,1972

#25-24-14-15

#25 MRS. EDGAR E.WATSON

Watson

Edgar Eugene	Purity Batte
Sept.9,1885-Apr.10,1947	May 12,1884-Dec.15,1967

#24 MRS. W.S. FREENEY

Dunaway

Jabus Brown	Emma Boyd
Mar.11,1879, feb.14,1958	June 21,1883-July 18,1969

Burney

Joe L.	Naomi D.
Sept.17,1904-Nov.11,1967	Aug.9,1913----Living

    Wm.S. Freeney "Father"Sept.11,1913-Mar.12,1970

    Jimmy Carl Freeney Dec.6,1952-Dec.8,1952

#14 C.MARANTO(MRS. JOSEPHINE MARANTO HAMSON)

    Sam Paul Maranto July 24,1907-Apr.4,1974

Maranto

Charles Maranto	Rosalie M.Maranto
June 7,1874-Sept.3,1950	Jan.1,1887-Feb.6,1968
" Father	"Mother"

#15 PACE-VACANT

*THIS LINE IN BLOCKS OF 6 STARTING NORTH DRIVEWAY WORKING W & S

#13-12-147-148-22-23

#13 R.H.SANDIFER

    John Bucklen Burns Jr.Jan.1,1926-Nay 18,1961

Sandifer

Harriet Rosa	Robert Horace
May22,1907-June 4,1966	Oct.6,1903-May 18,1969

    Charles Amos Reynolds Sept.5,1879-Sept.21,1946 "Precious in the sight of the lord, is the death of his Saints."

#12 A.P.CAMPBELL

    Albert Pintard Campbell Mar.17,1879-Apr.30,1952

    Ophelia Price Aug.14,1910-July 1,1980

    Adolphus Price Mar.17,1898-Sept.18,1966

    Virgil Eugene Maxwell Feb.14,1870-May 4,1958

#12 cont. A.P.Campbell
    Emily Ella Maxwell July 26,1877-Jan.10,1947
#147 **VERY LARGE SOLID CONCRETE TOP SLAB ON BRICK---INITIALS
    L.B.M.---NO OTHER INFORMATION.
#148 N½ MRS. M.R.BLAIR
    Mrs. Marjorie R. Blair Oct.13,1917-July 25,1975
    Lucian Gunn Blair Miss. Pvt. 370 Field Artillery BN World War 11
        Sept.24,1904-Apr.5,1964
#148 S½ W.O.BROWN
    Sam Kirkley 1896-1967 | Double
    Ada Kirkley 1901------ |
#22 S½ DR. & MR.W.W.STRICKLAND
    Warren W. Strickland Miss. Pvt. U.S.Army WW1. Mar.1,1899-
        Aug.25,1963
    Wade H. Strickland Miss. Cpl.U.S.Marine Corp.Res. Aug.25,1930-
        Jan.4,1960
#22 N½ JOHN PIPPIN
    John Wesley Pippin,Sr. Sept.15,1884-Dec.19,1959 "Daddy"
#23N½ MRS. RONIE HURST
    Ronie Hurst Feb.2,1896-Feb.2,1957
#23S½ JIM H. SMITH--VACANT
#33-32-149-150-42-43
#33 S½ MRS. L.C.HICKS (originally L.P.Barrier)
    Leonard Carradine Hicks Feb.4,1897-Feb.20,1959
#33 N½ MRS. M.K. BOWLS
    Thomas J.Rawls "Brother" Nov.23,1903-May 21,1959
#32 N½ E.G.EVANS
    Edgar G. Evans Mar.30,1882-May 17,1960
    Willie Causey Evans Jan.29,1880-May 21,1973
#32 S½ D.B.YOUNGER
    Exa C. Younger 1900-1968
    Barney P. Younger 1902-1961
#149 N ½ W.M.VIRDEN-Vacant
#149 S.½ MISS VIRGIE COGDELL
    Virginia Catherine Cogdell Mar.18,1896-Mar.9,1979
    Vaughn D. Cogdell 1907-1975
#150 G.A.MORPHIS N½
    Rex Morphis Dec. 9,1906-Feb.12,1961 "Daddy"
    Rosalie C. Morphis Apr.11,1908-Mar.28,1963 "Mother"
    Rex Morphis Jr. Mar.12,1931-May 2,1970 "Beloved Brother"

#150 S½ HOMER COLLINS

              Collins

   Mother   Son

   Homer C. McCain   Ike Jarred Collins

   July 23, 1977   July 19,1933,Aug.26,1965

#42 S½ MRS. RYLAND C.SHROPSHIRE

   Ryland C. Shropshire Nov.1,1912-May 29,1961

#42 N½ VACANT

#42 N½ NICK CHERONES

   "Mom" Lillian Cash 1881-1961

   Nicholas J. Cherones Pvt. U.S.Army W.W.I June 20,1888-Feb.20,1980

#43 S½ W.E.FLEEMAN

   William Earl Fleeman Sr. Apr.12,1896-June 2,1965

**#53-52-151-152-62-63

#53 N½ BESSIE M. WELLS

   Virgil Monroe Wells Dec.31,1893-July 29,1959

#53 S½ VACANT

#52 N½ T.W.JORDAN

   Mildred F. Jordan July 22,1908-Jan.15,1963

#52S½ L.O'NEAL

   Alice F. O'Neal Dec.25,1886-May 19,1963

#151 N½ ALBERT ROBERTSON

   Angela Michelle dau. of Dot and W.T.Robertson. b & d Aug.28,1969

        "O Son who diedst for us, Behold we bring our child to

            thee"

   Albert T. Robertson 1912-1966

   Lessie F. Robertson Burton 1916-1977

#151 S½ R.P.CASELLI

   Sandra Caselli Hunter Apr.15,1943-Mar.11,1966

#152 S½ GUS NEWMAN

     Father   Newman   Mother

   Gustave Earnest,Sr.   Bennie Mae Maxwell

   July 31,1897-Sept.4,1976   Mar.25,1897-Oct.23,1966

  * L NA Jean Newman Dec.11,1929-Apr.5,1930

#62 V.O.SANDEFORD

   Bertha G. Hanna Oct.15,1913-Jan.14,1964

#152 N½LOUIS E. BROWN

   J.P.Busby Sr. Mar.4,1904-Aug.9,1966

   Polly K. Busby Jan.23,1896-Aug.24,1973

  *L NA -EXACTLY AS ON THE STONE.

63 N ½ MRS. J.F.CHAPMAN

Chapman

James F.	Nonnie V.
May 30,1892-Sept.26,1963	Jan.2,1903-Aug.1,1977

James F. Chapman Miss.Sgt. Co.D 155 Inf.W.W.I-May 30,1892-Sept.26,1963

*This is not an error-two stones for James F. Chapman

Baby- David C.Cole-1959-1959

#63S½ MRS. E.L.HOGUE

Evelyn Grace Hogue Moore Oct.28,1940-Sept.6,1976

Ethel Lloyd Hogue Oct.16,1911-May 19,1960

83 NE¼ E.W.EDGE

Edge

E.W. Phil	Susie C.
Dec.23,,1906-----------	Jan.4,1907-Feb.8,1981

#83 SE¼ ROBERT PARTRIDGE

Robert T. Partridge Sept.4,1905- Sept.18,1957

Mrs. Hattie Partridge 1908-1977

#83 NW¼ DICK DAVIS

Mother	Davis	Father
Elsie Crow		James Harrison
Oct.1891----------		Apr.28,1887-Jan.22,1958

#83 SW¼ J.T.BLACKBURN

Blank	John Thomas Blackburn
(double stone)	Jan.28,1906-Apr.13,1957

#82 N½ J.D.YOUNT_VACANT

#82 S½ Mapshows vacant-one grave Wilson Adams----No dates

#15.3 VACANT

****Beginning with #81 on south west edge of original section and running north next to church are a number of graves that do not exactly follow a pattern. I have placed them in a numbered plot as closely as possible for ease of locating them.

#81S½ LUETTA HINTON

Luella Hinton Jan.22,1865-Mar.18,1946

Percilla Daniels May 30,1863-June 25,1949

#81 N½

Steven Lee Heigle b & d June 15,1966.Son of Mr.&Mrs. Roger Heigle

Roger Dale Dennis Feb.3,1961-Dec.14,1964

#80 & #79 --a jungle of trees and vines

#78 S½
    Laura Lee Guthrie Sept.6,1966-Sept.27,1966 | Same headstone
    Infant Boy Tesch Sept.13,1966 b & d
    Robert Arrow Whitt b.6/18/73-d.6/18/73. (assume to mean 1973--
        this was painted with black paint ona rock)

#77 ALMOST IN THE HEDGE ROW
    Leona Uzzle Feb.9,1905-Sept.13,1936

                Edleston

    Betty E.   George C.
    Apr.22,1885-Mar.3,1948   July 13,1886-May 26,1963
    "Tho lost to sight-to memory dear"

#76 VACANT

#75 VACANT MOSTLY IN HEDGE ROW

#74 A NUMBER OF METAL MARKERS TOO WEATHERED TO READ. EVIDENCES OF SITES

#73
    Mary C. Willhite Jan.30,1903-Nov.6,1980
    John Stephens Mar.18,1903-Sept.6,1959 "Daddy"
    3 unmarked graves in this plot

***UNMUMBERED PLOT WEST OF #148
    Mary E. Pierce 1868-1943
    Ethel Jewell Jobe May 5,1918-June 2,1966-Mother
    Shirley Wayne Jobe July 10,1938, Dec.8,1968-Father

INDEX

¶ Alphabetized given names, except in the Census & Cemetery records. The **single black numbers** indicate surnames only, from page 110 through 183. The page could have multiple lisings of a surname.

A

AARON-**116**
A.L.39;Fannie 28,38;M.R. 38;Wolf 28,38 72;Zariffa 38
ABBEYS-R.I.A.16
ABBOT-J.D. 78;W.R.44
ABNER-Warren 68
ABY-Leila Alice 21
ACHE-OCHE-Alex 59
ADAMS-**115,130,143,182**-
A.77;A.J.98;Caroline 5;Daniel 62; Daniel A.5;Delia 57;Frances 59;Jno.73; Lila 5;Mabel(Nobel)5;Mary Ella 5; Osey 64.
ADDISON-W.J.51,78
ADEN-H.B.41,82;Willie C. 82
ADER-Mrs.103
AGEE-Sandy 59
AIKEN-Geo.R.46;James E.46;Nannie B.46; Wm.M.46
ALCORN-Gov.91
ALDRIDGE-**116**
A.D.27,63;Alta R.27
ALEXANDER-**126,127,166,168**
Amy O. 34,100;Bryce 90;Doc.67;Henry M. 12;I.P.31;J.R.88;S.B. 31,33,34,37.
ALFORD-Stewart Floyd 19
ALLEN-**135,148,158**
Maggie 73;Mattie 80;Nathan 78;R.A.26, 31;W.G.7,13.
ALLSIP(ALLSIS)-ALLSOP
Emma 64
ALSTON
Arcola 6,22;Hall 6;Jennie Foote 21; Malvina 21;Naomi 6;Naomi A. 23;Percy Gaines 6,23;P.G.6;Philip 23;Philip J.6; Willie A. 23
AMES-Gov.A.29
ANDERSON-**120,124,126,129,145,148,152, 156,158;**-Alvernon Keep 23;Dan.73;D.N. 27;Dot 22;Frank Hill 22,23;Frank W.2,3 5,7,27,53;Lindsey 68;Maggie 72,109; Mose 55,68;N.R.27,31,50,61,78;Sarah W. 27;T.J.78,109;Walton 53;W.S.11,50.
ANDREWS-G.D.14
ANTHONY-**134**
R.A.78
ARCHER-Carrie 60;Dr.Jos.F.77;Mary 65; Rev.Stephenson 60,77,103;Stephen 66.
ARMSTEAD-ORNSTEAD-Roxie 59;Susan 62.
ARMSTRONG-A.J.5
ARNETTE-**110**

ARNOLD-Mary 28;Wash.28,58,62;W.A.78
ATKINSON-**147**-Eliza 102.
AUSTIN-Hannibal 78;Ida 65.

B

BABB-**150**
BACON-W.O. 7
BAGGETT-**117,118,165,166,167,168,170,176**
Alice 70,85,87,89;Chas.Ellis 37,42; Dolly 72,94;F.M. 37,42;Frances 93;Frank 37,42
G.M.41,42,45,54,58,70,78,89,93,100; Isaac P.37,42;Jno.87;Jno.R.65,74,78,93; Mrs.Marion 72;N.T.35,42,49,50,69,70,74, 78,70,82,85,91,108;Tom 94;W.E.31.
BAILEY-**125,127,175**-Mrs.Bettie 44;W.S.44
BAKER-Easter 32;Edw.78;Edgar W.49;Fannie 58;J.H.67;Jos.15;Lucia 89;Lucy 15; Mariah 65;P.H.3;Rich.(Dick)65,68;Wm.58; W.M.32
BALDWIN-BALDON-Andrew 60;Ibbie 66;Sarah 51;Sila 51,54,55,56.
BALL-Col.29
BALLARD-Benj.28;Emma 65;Jerry 56;Wm.64.
BALLINGER-**127**
BALLINGTON-**125**
BANKS-**113**-Carrie S.11;E.R.62;Haywood 78; James 53,MillieC.47;O.R.4,11;Sam'l 57.
BANKSTRON-**172**-Rich.22.
BANUM-**133**
BAREFIELD-Marion 36
BARDSDALE-Henry 59
BARNARD-**114,120,121,149,152,155,168;**
D.B.46;Ellen Watson 104,107;Emilius G. 78;Eudora J.46;Ida 91,95,96;Jos.L.61,64; Lady 88,91,95;Lizzie West 107;Mrs.W.B. (Henrie)76,100;Mrs.Will 72,85;Sarah Louise 107;W.B.31,40,56,78,98,100,103, 107;Wm.Bailey 107;W.H.28,34,35,36,40,43 46,66,73,78,85,93,107;W.T. 53,54,56, 59,60,63,72,78,107.
BARNER-John Drew 23
BARNES-**126,134,150,154,159**-B.L.60,85; Earl 107;Jas.107;O.F.33.
BARNEY-**122**
BARRETT-**166**
BARRIER-**162,164,174,180**
BARTLETT-Mrs.W.L.97,103;Nelson 97; Vincent R.52;Wallace 52.
BASKET-Mr.96
BASKIN-**170**

BLACK NUMBERS INDICATE SURNAME ONLY IN CENSUS & CEMETERY RECORDS

BASS-Chas.D. 107;Matt 64
BATES-**140,148;**Spenser 57
BATTAILE-C.M.78;Jennie 70
BATTLE-Arthur 58;Hanah 61
BATTON-**151,157,158;**Charity 67; J.A. 78,106;J.C.78
BAUGH-Harry 13
BAUM-J.F.36
BAUSWELL-B.J.10
BAY-**126**
BAYAFOURS-**129**
BEARD-Benj.J. 5
BECK-R.F. 83
BEDWELL-Adeline 53
BEIDENHORN-H.H. 28
BELKNAP-Jennett L. 12
BELLAR-**136**
BELL(E)-**111,117,124,129,171;**Chas.63; Geo.68;James S.6,38;Jim 67;Jno.63; Mariah 27,62;Mary H.71;Matilda 66;Mr. 70;Simon 27,55,56,57,62,64,66.
BELLSINGER-Christian A.5;Sarah 5
BENNETT-E.T.78;M.G.78;Ruby E.23 Sandy 78
BENSON-Henry Wade 19;John Porter 19
BENTLY-**124**
BERESFORD-Mrs.W.F. 46
BERNSTEIN-Ike 89
BERRY-**161**
BETTS-Egbert M.109;Virginia B.109; ---109
BIRDSONG-F. 18
BISSELL-J.W. 27
BLACK-**116;**Jake 29;Jane 66;Kansas 62; Rev.M.M. 23,24
BLACKBURN-**182**
BLAIR-**180;**Weston 54
BLAKE-**126;**E.C.105
BLAKNEY-**177**
BLAND-Mrs.E. 14;W.O. 49
BLUE-Gen.66
BLUM-**116,126;**Chas.N.43;S.H.74,78,90, 92;M.A.92;Mrs.R.92;Sara 71
BOBO-**158**
BODAY-**126**
BODIE-BODE-**164,178;**Mattie 71; Mittie 102
BOGARD-**169**
BOHAN-**125**
BOLLING-Albert L.12;Chas.H.12;Chester A.12;James G.12
BOLTON-**111,126;**Edmond 61,Thos.J.Jr.2
BOMMER-**164;**Dr.J.C.93
BONDLESS-Wm.67
BONHAM-Isaac 30
BONNAR-Ella 32;Hattie 23

BOOKER-Ambrose 57,58;Elvira 18;Frank 18; Hattie 18;Isaac 53;Laura 18;Mary 18
BOOTH(e)-James 53,57;H.78,85;Mrs.H.H. 85,99,104
BORODOFSKY-Israel 89;Louis 101
BOUSHILL-**125**
BOWEN-D.56
BOWERS-**138;**louis 13
BOWIE-Dock 62,64;Elder 53,55,Eliza 63
BOWLS-BOWLES-**176,180**
BOWMAN-Izora 24;Robt.24
BOYD-**146,179;**Kennedy 59;Parlee 53
BOY(a)KIN-**119,130,133,141,142,143,145, 151,157;**A.G. 43,47,48,65,66,69,78; A.M.48,77;Cinda 60;Clyde 102;D.P.78; E.C.64;Fielding B.47,48,78;G.W.58;J.M. 48;Joanna 56;Lena 47;Melvin 47,48; Mitchell 47,48
BOZE-Sallie 56
BOZEMAN-**161;**M.51;S.J.91
BRABHAM-W.C.78
BRABSTON-J.H.93
BRACEY-**138**
BRADFORD-**121;**Fannie 53;J.C.61;T.C.63, 65,66,67
BRADSHAW-**164,177**
BRANCH-**119-155**
BRANDINGAX-Wilson 57
BRANDON-Mrs.Leanora 4
BRANSFORD-Jno.L.74
BRANTLY-**129;**B.J. 59
BRAZIER-Mrs.Jas.D. 71
BRAZIL-Albert 8;Jos.8;L.T.78;Mary Magdalen 8;Patsey 8
BREARD-Chas.A.70,78,89,109;C.W.92 Jno.89;Josephine 109;Madelain 109; Ray 89
BREEKEN-**110**
BREHM-**138;**Alma 18;Anna 4;Anna E.23; Bessie 18;Etta 4,23;Gertrude 23;Jno.4; Jno.H.4,18;Liddy 4;Lidia 22,23;Lizzy 4; Magdalene 4;Maggie L.23;Nannie T.18; Rebecca 4,22;Susan 4;Wilbur 18;Wm.4
BREWER-**113;**Brewer 41;Wm.27
BRICKELL-**123**
BRIDGERS-**164;**Albert 36;E.P.60;E.T.36, 63;Wm.36
BRIDGES-**115,127,131;**Carrie M.108;J.M.88
BRIGHT-J.M.78
BRITTON-**118;**Abbie 60;J.A.56;Laura N.44, 45,75,77;Louis 75;Mrs.Fannie A.44,75,76; Mrs.T.A.32;Mrs.Wm.72;Sarah 60;Wm.32,42, 44,45,76,78,84;Wm.Jr.43,44,75
BRONSON-Lee 55
BROOKE-BROOKS-**120,141,152;**Abby 16; Alberta 14;Brederick 59;Eliz.55,108; F.P.P.78;Fred 108;Jno.F.108;Kittie 14; Lydia Martha 21;Mrs.Walker 95

BLACK NUMBERS INDICATE SURNAMES ONLY IN CENSUS & CEMETERY RECORDS

BROUGHAL-Daniel 62
BROWDER-Mollie 57
BROWN-**111,112,117,119,120,123,126, 127,140,144,154,155,166,170,172,175, 178,180,181;**-Adam 58;A.E.78,93; Alice V.27,32;Anna R.107;Annie 60; Argyle 70;Daniel 49;D.H.78;Estelle 107;Etter 50;Hulda 61;Isiah 61;Jno.W 50;Jordan 65;J.T.L.50,78;Mrs.Prentiss 88,99;Perlie 50;Pricilla 61;Rev.T.W. 22,23,24;Tolbert 55;W.D.27,30,41,45, 47,55,78,88,99,107,109;W.H.15
BROWNLEY-**125**
BROWNSON-Walter 68
BRUCE-J.C.74,75;Josie P.75;P.P.75, 78;R.M.78.
BRUMFIELD-Willie 79
BRU(a)ZELIUS-J.K.58
BRYAN-Annie V. 103;E.J. 15;Flora B.15
BRYANT-**133,137;**J.A.83;Laura Bell 83
BUCK-**126,165**
BUCKALOO-Sue E.22
BUCKINGHAM-James 57,104;Lizzie 104
BUCKLEY-**169**
BUCKNER-Isabella 53
BUFORD-**157**
BULLIKEN-**128**
BUNN-Alex.6,8,15;Georgie 15;Sarah A. 15
BUNTING-**164,174,178**
BURCH-**171**
BURFORD-**172**
BURKS-Susan 54
BURNEY-**179**
BURNS-Annie 60;Mrs.M.B.1;Nellie 60 Rita 68
BURTEN-BURTON-**110,181;**G.W.28;N.H.10; Sam 66
BURR-Annie 16;Mary Jane 16
BURRUS-John V.16
BUSBY-**148,181**
BUSH-**112**
BUSTER-Mrs.87;Therese 88
BUTLER-**117,136,160,172;**Eugene T.78; Geo.W.59,78;J.E.37,39,50,71,78,81,96 102,106;Julia 14
BUTTS-**114;**Edw.S.4
BYAS-BIAS-James 53,54,56,62,67,68
BYERLEY-Company 73;Edw.38,49;Frank 49,78,80,86;Miss 99;Mollie 49
BYRAM-Brook 78
BYRD-BIRD-Clarissa 59;Kirby 71; Rueben 31;Victoria 61
BYSON-**122**

C

CAGE-**141;**Cassandra 59;Mr.95;W.C.28
CAHILL-KAHILL-Emma 65;Mattie 64
CAHOUN-J.H.18
CALAWAY-Wilst 57
CALDWELL-Elzy 59;J.R.60,62,78;H.R.54, 56,57,58,59
CAMERON-A.P.97;Capt.79;Jno.R.34,104; Mabel 69;Malcolm 42,77,78,92,93,96,97; Mattie R.96;Mrs.88,90;Mrs.Hattie 69; Mrs.Jno.R.89
CAMMACK-Ella 80;Rev.J.G.101
CAMPBELL-**167,169,179,180;**Ellen 86; Loudoun 86;Mrs.T.W.86,99,106;T.W.96,104
CANADA-Albert 45
CANNON-**146,175**
CANNY-Milly 55
* CANOVAN-Jno.47;Mrs.Bridgett M.47; Patrick 47
CARLILE-CARLISLE-CARLYLE-**128,132;**Emma G.23;Florence 24;Hays 24;John 24;Louise 56;Mary E.24;Susan G.24
CARNATHAN-**143,144,150;**O.H.78;---76
CARPENTER-**112,169**
CARR-Mary 34;Mrs.R.K.47;R.K.78;Sebon 61,68
CARRINGTON-Issabela 68;James 53
CARROLL-**130,173,175;**A.W.78;Chas.55
CARSON-**112;**Catherine 63;Chas.55;Jno.53
CARTER-**110,111,177;**Edmond 56,59,68;G.W. 14;Henry 60,68;Mary 60;Walter 62
CARY-CAREY-**155;**James 57
CASEY-**116,169;**Cornelia 69,88;D.C.26,29,38, 43,74,78,90,92,96,101;Eliza 69;J.T.29, 90;L.C.R.38,109;Mrs.D.C.69
CASH-**181**-Thos.55
CASSELI-**181**-Mary P.P.50,96;Renato P.50, 96;Rinalin P.50
CATCHINGS-**169,176;**Oliver 85;T.C.85; Warren 22;Wm.Warren 16,19
CATLEDGE-**148**
CAUTHEN-**152**
CAYGLE-**142**
CHAFFEE-Chris.Jr.28;Jno.28;Wm.H.28
CHAISING-**127**
Chamberlin-Isaac 61
CHAMBERS-Jos.54
CAMBESS-**129**
CHAMPION-**118,127,134;**Dr.70;Dr.W.M.43, 74,78;G.M.39,78;Mrs.70;Mrs.Hope H.40,43
CHAMPLIAN-CHAMLIN-Isaac 56,57,58; Matilda 57
CHANDLER-**115**
CHANEY-**114,142,155;**Dr.75;Holcomb D.16; Jno.F.31,64;Martha A.43;M.J.31;Wm.J.32, 36;Wm.I.45,78,90
CHASE- **111**-Aaron 57,66,68;N.C.78

* CAPERTON:E.M.80;MRS.JENNIE M.75,80

BLACK NUMBERS INDICATE SURNAMES ONLY IN CENSUS & CEMETERY RECORDS

CHAVIS-Jordan 62
CHEATHAM-**146**
CHELF-CREFT-Lizzie 54;---52
CHERONES-**181**
CHEW-Augustine 57
CHILDERS-**121,122,124**
CHILDRESS-**156,177;**Luther 39
CHILDS-Wm.60
CHISHOLM-**127;**Annie 103;Jno.71,78; Nancy V. 87
CHRISTESON-Ellen 58
CHRISTIAN-CHRISTIANSON-Joe 34
Christmas-Geo.Wash.108
CHOCK-Alfred 47;America 47;Eugene 47;Gracy Ann 47;James 47;Jordan 47 Jos.47;Millie 47;Percy 47;Sadie 47; William 47
CLANCY-**154;**Jno.H.68
CLARK(E)-**111,116,139;**Alin 34;Amaline 39;Catherine34;Cherry 39;Edw.D.35; Eugene 26,30,33,35,53,54,56,57,61,62, 63;G.A.39;Geo.39,62;Green 64;Jane 34; Jno.Wesley 53;J.R.97;Leigh 35,67; Lotta 68;Lyle 33;Mary 107,108;Mrs. Eliza Leigh 35;Mrs.Jas.R.90;Pearl Leigh 35;S.Jackson 35,79;S.S.78; Thos.54;Wm.34,53,78
CLARY-**128**
CLAYTON-Friday 55,56
CLEMENTS-**162,165,172,173**-Anna 64; Annie 55,71,75,82;Clements & Wright 41;Dr.E.C.26,43,77,78,82,88,89; Eliza P.68;Fannie 71;Mrs.E.C.(Ann Foote)26,43,83,99,100,104 Sybil May(Sunshine)43,90,99;W.H. 43,50,70,76,90,96,97,102;---85
CLINKSCALES-**139**
CLOUD-**139**-M.R.78
CLYCE-Thos.C.81
COALTER-COULTER-COLTER-**131-133;** W.A.58
COATS-B.F.54
COBB-Gustus 67
COBBLER-Lizzie 45
COGDELL-**180**
COGHLAN-**160**
COHN-**110,125;**Esther 65;R.28
COKER-Alice E.47;Chas.108;Jessu 108; J.H.64;Jno.107;Marion B.47;Maud M.47; Mrs.99;Mrs.Maud 95;Nancy Ann 107;Wm.108
COLBERT-**143,144**
COLE-**125,131,150,165,182;**C.C.78;Chas. A.63
COLLETTA-**171**
COLLIER-R.J.65
COLNELL-**135**

COLSEN-**142**
COLUMBUS-Joe 60
COMMER-Isom 67
COMMODORE-**136;**Jandy 63;Wm.45
COMPTON-**150**
CONES-Flixie 68
CONGO-Susan 20
CONLEY-Emily 65;Geo.58
CONNELL-**120;**W.A.50,78
COOK-**132,146,148;**A.H.54;Annie 102; J.H.42,78,105;Judge H.F.92;Miss 95
COSBY-Annie 35;Dan 35,36;Dan Jr.35;Ella 35;Ennis 66;Martha 35;Sam 35
COSTLEY-Ira 51
COTTER-**136**
COTTLE-**177;**Jas.81
COTTON-**135;**Ben 36;Jeff 36
COURTNEY-**148**
COURTS-Mrs.W.E.76;W.E.78,86
COUVILLON-**169**
COVINGTON-**123,148;**Mala 65
COWARD-**120**
COWART-**144**
CRAIG-Caroline 60;Eli 60,78
CRANE-**119;**N.C.57
CRAWFORD-**170;**Thos.54,57
CRAWLEY-J.N.81
CREATH-Ida 66;J.H.46
CRENSHAW-**115;**Jno.W.34;Mary 34;Tinsey 38
CRIPPEN-E.L. 46
CRISLER-Annie I.24;Jno.Wesley 24; Rev.John W.24
CROCKETT-**167;**C.W.78,98;Chas.88;Dora 88, 98;Mrs.C.W.100;Mrs.M.H.44;W.A.42,50,78, 86,88,98
CROTHERS-Dr.Victor M.19;Philip H.19
CROTWELL-**148**
CROUCH-Jno.H.46
CROW-**182**
CRUMP-Anthony 56;Dr.R.C.50;R.P.47,78; Wm.63,68
CUISON-**152**
CUNNINGHAM-Jason 58
CURNETT-**143**
CURPHEY-Edith 100

D
DAIRY-Elvira 66
DAMRON-W.53
DANDRIDGE-Susan 55
DANIELS-Alex 65;Angeline 60;Nancy 67; Rita 54;Winnie 65
DANS-**135**
DANSLER-London 55
DARBY-Mary Ella 85,102;Mrs.S.L.102
DARDEN-Company 93,99;Dr.G.T.78,81;H.A.93

BLACK NUMBERS INDICATE SURNAMES ONLY IN CENSUS & CEMETERY RECORDS

DARNELL-125
DAUGHERTY-O.R.6
DAVENPORT-**120,145;**Caroline 62
DAVIDSON-**153**
DAVIS-**158,161;**Alice 6;Bessie 81;Chas. S.72;C.L.102;Griselly 54;H.H.8,84; Irene 93,96;Jas.58,61,65,67,68;J.G. 56,60,62,63,64,66,78;Louis 67;Maggie 53;Mariah 62;Martin 65;Mattie 22; Nathan B.66;Nellie 62;Rich.63; Sarah 54
DAWSON-Rev.W.54,56,64;S.R.61,68;W.D. 78;W.P.86,90;Zeke 66,68.
DAY-**170,173,182;**Alice o.62;Mrs.98; Pricilla 6;Thos.57
DeBERRY-Jennie M.80
DECELL-Beatrice 108;Geo.108;Jas.108; Jno.108;Lula 108
DEDMAN-DEDMON-R.78;T.Frank 45
DeMARCO-Prosper 32
DEMENT-Abner 38
DENAS-Martha 66
DENAY-Adele 53
DENMAN-**142,154;**A.L.90;A.R.77,102; Jno.C.43,66,77,84;Lizzie 43;Lovie 95;Mrs.A.R.93,95;Mrs.J.C.76;Mrs.R.L. 77
DENNIS-**182**
DENNY-Monroe 68
DePERRIN-Mary 81;Mrs.E.O.81
DERRICK-**158**
DEVINE-**156**
DEWEES-DUEWESE-**115;**Eliza A.64;Jas.M. F.109;Marg.109;T.B.109
DIAMOND-**130**
DICKENS-E.B.16
DICKERSON-**112**
DICKINSON-**154**
DIFFEY-**147**
DIGGS-C.W.4,8,15;Emily 15;Ida S.15; J.J.4;John 18
DILL-Emma 62
DINKINS-**152,155;**E.D.42,43,78;H.L.78, 90,94;J.A.74,75,78,79;Jno.F.70,80; Lalah 88;Lola 69;Mrs.85,87;Paul 78; R.T.7,81;---72
DIOMINE-**123**
DIXON-DISON-**125,129,148;**Minus 55; Monroe 61,66;Peter 56
DODGE-Dr.Jno.L. 81
DODY-**123**
DOLL-Jno.53
DONALD-**148,178;**Adine 59;Emeline 61
DONALDSON-Althea L.12;James 12
DONAVAN-**126**
DONERT-**136**
DOOLEY-W.V.36

DORSEY-Augustus 78;Daisy Bell 102;Dr. Geo.B. 102;Geo.54;Geo.H.102;Mary 16; Mrs.Josie 13
DORSON-S.R.68;W.D.64;
DOSIER-Abram 62
DOUGLAS(s)-**153**-Abraham 41;Geo.q.41;Jno. T.41;Joe 67;Leroy 67;Lucy 41;Spivey 41
DOWELL-**118**
DOWDY-**166**
DOVER-**124;**Calvin 68;Carrie 68;Fred 54; Mary 65;Max 99;Miriam 95;Selma 95;Simon 27,32,36,47,78,95
DRAYTON-Wm.67
DRINKARD-**153**
DRUMNIGHT-**133**
DUANE-A.A.41,51,78
DUCKET-Nancy 57
DUEDS-DUECDS-**158**
DUESE-Alma L.98,103
DUESTER-**124;** E.35,36
DUDLEY-**118;**Marg.J.E.87;O.F. 38
DUKE-**131,133;**Eliz.102;Esther J.108;Jos. 61;J.W.27,78,102;Katie 77,108;Lizzie Ray 108;T.J.67
DULANEY-**177;**Georgianna 19;L.C.11,12,75, 87,96;Mrs.L.C.92
DUNAWAY-**179**
DUNBAR-**175;**James T.13;W.O.105
DUNCAN-**110,115;**Katie 81;Mrs.91;Steven B. 3;Thos.59,60;Wm.56
DUNN-**159;**Henry 58
DUNNING-Mrs.49
DURMAN-Eliza 16
DURST-**139,151;**John 50,78;John H.50; Mollie 60
DUTY-Mrs. 81

E
EARLEY-**113**
EARVINE-Annie 50
EASTERLING-, ---4
EATON-Flenoy 65;Fradonia 68
EDGE-**182**
EDLESTON-**183**
EDMONDSON-EDMONSON-J.C.78;York 65
EDWARDS-Edwin W.12;Laura 59;Mary 81 Sallie 58
EGGLESTON-Geo.W.78,95
EICHELBERGER-Geo.Fred.19;Willie F.19
ELLERBY-Col.57
ELLISON-ELISON-**111,166;**W.P.36
ELLINGTON-**131,135,139,155;**B.F.38;C.D. 84;Clare D.108;Cora 108;Jno.C.108; Minnie 65;Mrs.L.D.38
ELLIOT(t)-**131,144,171;**Emily 22;S.C.4; W.W.16
ELLIS-**129,157;**Isaiah 60;Katie 71; Meleinda 54;Melissa J.26;Rev.102;W.H. 26;W.T.78

BLACK NUMBERS INDICATE SURNAME ONLY IN CENSUS & CEMETERY RECORDS

ELLZEY-**114;**W.J.38
ELSESSER-Lilly M.103
EMBREE-Celete 20
EMERY-EMORY-Julia 59;Peter 55,56
EMLEN-Jennie 63
EMMERSON-**158;**Catherine 34
EMMITH-**114**
ENGLAND-**152,158;**R.O.78
EPPERSON-**135,141;**Robt.E.64
EPPS-J.H. 54
ERVIN-**156;**A.L.78;Miss Lou 22;Sam 67
ERWIN-J.C. 3
ESTMAN-E.C.31
EUSTIS-Alex 61
EVANS-**134,141,147,148,164,180;**Geo.55; Martha 59;Minerva 54;Willard 30
EVERT-Sophia 6
EVERETT-Delia 65
EVERHART-Altha 6;Annie 6;Eddie 6; Ellen 6;Geo.6;Ira 6;Isaac 6;Jacob 6; Jonathan 6;Jos.6;Lizzie 6;Lucy 6; Willie 6
EVERIDGE-B.J.78
EWING-**149**
EZELL(e)-**112,133,140;**Benj.F.56

F
FAIRCHILDS-Chas.57;Nannie E.20
FAIRFAX-Easter 53
FARISH-FARRISH-**137;**Dr.Robt.Davis 4, 19;Duncan 84;H.P.19;J.D.19;Kate M.F. 109;Stephen P.19;Thos.H.109;W.D.109; Wm.S.4,19,84
FARMER-Sam 79;W.C.72,78,79
FARR-**124;**David D.73,90,92,93,94,102; Mrs.Ella 30;Ora Mann 106
FARRAR-FARROW-**144,153,168,171;**Albert 60;Hanah 62;H.C.47;J.T.78
FARRIS-**131**
FEATHERTON-FEATHERSTEN-Rev.F.M.22,23 56
FERBY-Haywood 59
FERGUSON-FERGUESON-**139;**Alean H.49; Andrew 62;Easter R.12;Jennie 68;May 89;Parker 49;Richmond 63;S.W.70; Thaddeus C.S.49;Wm.12
FERRIS(s)-**113,156**
FIELDER-**115**
FIELD(s)-**149;**Chas.58;Grover 98;H.J. 44,68,69,72,73,78,94,95,96,100,101; Jesse 77,87;Laura 77,88,95,96,98; Margie(Mattie)88,95,96,98;Mrs.H.J. 90,97;Tom 96
FINCH-H.J.4
FINGER-**136**

FISHER-Chas.H.27,41,68,78,100,104; Peter 58,65;Rose 27,65;Sam'l 58,61,64; Wm.57
FITLER-**138;**C.A.13
FITZ-Elize Columbia 11;Emma F.11;Jno.Wm. 11;Oliver Cornell 11;Robt.Wm.11
FITZERALD-W.F.27
FLAKE-Dr.John 98;H.L.98,99
FLANAGAN-R.E.75,78;Mrs.Robt.91
FLANERS-**133**
FLEEMAN-**181**
FLEMING-**157-**Chas 37;Grace 37;Harriet 37; James G.37
FLORIDA-John 15
FLOYD-**131;**A.G.36,42,61,67,70,72,73,78; A.J.78;Henry 31,56
FLOWERS-**152,156;**Walter C. 3
FLYNN-**178**
FOE-Adaline 15;Arthur W.15;Henry 15; Isaac 15;Louella 15
FOLK(e)S-F.M.19;Nora E.23;Mayfield H.23; T.M.27;Wm.23
FONTAINE-Mary Agnes 107;Lamar 107
FOOTE-**114,166;**Ann 104;Geo.70;Judge H.W. 26,71,83,104;H.L.38,41,42,69,70,73,78,79 83,85,86,87,101,104,107;Mary S.26;Mrs.H.L. 85,87,89,99,100;Ms.100;Robt.70;Thos.83; W.H.26
FORD-Dave 62;Edna 16;E.W.78;Harriet 64; Henry 57;Wm.61
FOREMAN-A.H.51;D.J.78;L.W.51
FOSTER-Jno.M.44;Lewis 78;Mrs.Mattie D. 13,14;Nancy 62;N.E.14;R.E.14;Rev.Jas.107, 108;Thomas R.4
FOWLER-Ebenezer 6;Sallie 4;Sanders 6,15; Sarah 6,15;
FOX-A.36;E.T.R.10;Jim 65
FRAIRSON-Henrietta 63
FRANCIS-**175**
FRAZIER-FRAZER-Anderson. 55;Dave 45,64; Mrs.Emma 30
FREEMAN-T.T.78
FREENEY-**179**
FRENCH-Aaron 3
FRIEDBORG-I.15
FRIEND-Felix 62
FRY-**132**
FULGER-**135**
FULTON-**140-**Nelson 28
FUQUAY-Geneva 24;Mrs.Mollie 23,24;Pearl 24;Wm.24
FURL-**111**
FURNCHESS-Mary 57
FURNISS-**148**
FURR-**140**

BLACK NUMBERS INDICATE SURNAME ONLY IN CENSUS & CEMETERY RECORDS

G

GAITHER-E.H.52
GALCERAN-Mrs.D.100
GALES-GAYLES-Adeline 30;Beady 30;
Edie 60;Johnson 78;Otis E.78;Peter
26,66;Stephen 34;Tyler 30,60,62,66;
Wesley 30
GAMBILL-**128**
GANT-Geo.60;Louis 59
GARDNER-Clara 56;Julia Ann 59;
Mary 9
GARRETT-**174**;David 64;Rena 22
GARY-GEARY-**155**;D.W.17
GASSETT-**134**
GATES-**171**
GAWLEY-Belle 22,23
GAUNT-Charity 58
GAVIN-**159**
GEE-Arhie 58;Noah 59
GEORGE-AlonzoPhelps 50;Henry 80;
Nannie P.50;Peter 50,80
GEWIN-W.T.78
GEY-Din 40
GIBBON(s)-**113,168**;Mary E.32,45;Wm.30,
32,41,45,68,75,78,108;Wm.Jr.45,108
GIBBS-Ann 57;Emma 51;Ida 62;Marg.63;
Mary 58;Matilda 55;Thos.51
GIBSON-**114,118,136**;Albert C.107;Alex.
64;America 57;Callie Lou 107;Grace M.
17;Hattie L.107;J.C.66;Marg.Eliz.107;
Melinda 67;Minda 64;R.E.107;Sib 53;
Tilda 55;T.M.69;W.W.107
GILBERT-Store 6
GILKEY-Ada Louise 23
GILL-**130,145**
GILLIAM-**153**
GILLILAND-**160**;J.D.69
GILMAN-**114**
GILMORE-**129**
GINKHAM-Betsy 15
GLASS-Edw.103;Murton 61
GLAUTON-Isaac 68
GLENN-Jane M.34;Monroe 39,64
GLISSON-**166**;Pattie 95
GLOVER-Hon.A.Y.91;Mrs.88,100
GOLDEN-**116**;W.T.78
GOODLOE-Calvin 35;Claude 102;Julie
102;Nicholas 35,36;Rosa 35;Wash.55
GOODMAN-**113**;Dr.B.31,32,36,38,41,42,
49,73,78,81,100,109;Dr.H.S.106;Dr.
Samp 91;Jonas 84;Mrs.85,89,99,109;
Mrs.H.S.106;Rexel 109;Robbie 100;
Wm.84,86
GOODWIN-Erma 10;Ethel10;Jno.L.10;
Lelia Legayette 10;Leon 10
GORDON-Jno.60,68;Levi 3
GORMAN-**121**;B.J.59

GRAFT-**176**;Bernhard(Bernard)92,96;
Christine 96;Frederick 36,37,42,71,75,78
92,103;Mrs.Fred.98
GRAHAM-**158**;Dollie 61;Katie 54
GRAM-Henry 47
GRAMLING-GRAMLAIN-**130**;A.D.9,24;Adam D.Jr
9,24;Callie Jones 9;Ell 22;Emma 9;Katie
Eudora 9,23;Maggie R.9;Mary E.23;Oscar
22;R.O.9;Thomas Jeff.23;Vida I.9,23
GRANGER-**124**
GRANT-**129,148**;James 9;John 9;Lawrence H.
9;Lenora 9;Mrs.Annas 9;Rev.60;Thos.65,66,
67;Thos.J.9
GRAVES-**161**;Ula 22
GRAY-**177**;Agnes 109;Dilla 67;Hollis 58;
Jas.W.109;J.C.78;J.P.60;Mary R.109;Mrs.
Lizzie 46;M.T.78;Wm.61
GREEN-**119,127,148,149,170**;A.L.67;Annie
C.2;Annie E.14;Ashbell 12;Dr.Wm.A.14;
Francis 11,14;Francis Jr.14;Henry 11;
Jno.71;Jno.Wm.67;Julia E.14;Lucy 64;
Lucy A.2;Lyla 4;Matilda 14;McKinley 14;
Oscar P.2;R.D.6;Sarah E.2;Viola 14.
GREENSHIP-Hannah 57
GREENWALL-**112**;Kitty 57;S.G.107
GREER-GREAR-**133,149**;H.P.92;Julia 53
GREY-Clara 54
GRICE-**128,174,178**;Bethinia 67
GRIFFIN(g)-**111**;Alex 61;Clara 22;Dan 60;
Dot 24;Geo 54;J.E.75,78,81;Jno.15,16,22,
24,60;Jno.Wesley 7,24;Rebecca 54;Rev.W.T.
22,23,24;Thos.B.24;Walker 53;Walter 58;
Wm.A.24;Wm.15,24
GRIFFITH-**114,121**
GRIGG-Rich.4
GRIMM-**148**
GULLIE-Aaron 51
GUNDY-Amanda 41;Lloyd 41,53,61;Manah 41;
Napoleon 41;Pearly 41;Riley L.41;Sargent
41;Stella 41.
GUNN-John 20;Rev.Elmer C.20
GUTH-Mary 9
GUTHRIE-**183**
GWIN-S.34

H

HAKES-**158**
HALBERT-F.M.6
HALEY-**130**
HALL-**119,141,147,149**;Dr.J.C.31,32,69,74,
78,90,107,108;Jno.108;Joel B.108;J.R.78,
89;Mrs.77;Sarah L.91,107,108
HALSELL-W.W.41
HAM-Lee 71
HAMBERLIN-Dr.S.T.86,91,109;Fred W.107;
M.49,73,76,78,85,91;Mrs.S.T.89,109;
S.L.78

BLACK NUMBERS INDICATE SURNAME ONLY IN CENSUS & CEMETERY RECORDS

HAMILTON-**178**;C.H.64;Chas.59;Janes S. 28;Mrs.Emma 10;R.J.38
HAMMERS-**127,128**
HAMMETT-**141**
HAMPSEY-**142,143**
HAMPTON-Chas.H.61;Elijah 57;Geo.73; Gen.Wade 88
HAMSON-**179**
HAND-**177**
HANDY-M.T.13
HANEY-Mr.100
HANNA-**181**
HANNER-**152**
HANSBERRY-Rich.64
HANSER-**150,155,157**
HARBER-**134**
HARDEN-**156**
HARDENSTEIN-A.D.36;Earnest 36
HARDING-Henry 62;P.M.87
HARLAN-**146**
HARMON-Jessee Banks 109
HARPER-**139,170**;Dr.W.R.6,40,41,45,71, 75,78,86,100,104,107,109;Garnet Rivers 109;Jos.56,57;Mrs.85,89; Mrs.W.R.100,109
HARRELL-**116**;J.P.34;Mattie 34;Minnie 71
HARRIS-**119,120,123,131,159,170**;
Agnes 59;Anderson 59;Celia 62;Fannie 22;Frank 66;Geo.C.25,32,43,44,45,72, 77,94,107,108,109;Geo.C.Jr.32,44,45, 72,78,79,91,95,96;Gen.Nathan H.19, 21;Jas.66;J.E.22;Jno.W.18;Joab 60; J.R.2;Helen 74;Helen L.J.25,72; Henry 67;H.J.22,23;Lawrence 108; Martha 53;Maymie 77;Mrs.Geo.C.74,92; Mrs.Geo.C.Jr.93;Mrs.Mary 2;Patience 35,39;R.C.67;Richmond 55;Rosina Johnston 21;Sarah J.18;Wash.58;W.E. 107;Wiley 60;Wm.Henry 39;Wm.61; W.M.11
HARRISON-**113,115**-Wm.S.30
HARSH-**116,136**;Eliza 59;F.65,66; Jno.33,35,37,39,61,62,63,64,77
HART-David 4,9,10;Mrs.Annie S. 8
HARTFIELD-Isham 8
HARVEY-**161**;Doc 58;Eva 40,43,70; Evan J.43;Julia 40,43;Martha J.40, 43,75,79;Robt.Emmet 40,43;T.H.78
HARWELL-Mrs.D.R.11
HARWOOD-S.B. 3
HATCHETT-**173**;Caroline S.34
HAUSER-HOUSER-**118,124,127**;Chris 54,80;Geo.55,56
HAWES-**148**
HAWKINS-**112,113**;Amanda 56;G.S.78; Lewis 61,64;Mary 55;Toney 53,59, 62,66

HAYDEN-G.C. 89
HAY(s)-HAYES-**138,175**;Alfred 57;Jack 1; Jack P.8,80,84;Judge 84;L.H.8;Mrs.E.E.8; Thos.W.8;W.E.33
HAZELWOOD-**171**
HAZLIP-Alice 19;Jno.Kirkland 16,20; Sam'l W.20
HEAD-J.C.13
HEARD-W.A.4
HEARN-HERN-C.E.91;S.46;Rev.W.C.42
HEATH-**137,172**;Annie 24;Dr.T.A.13,14,24; James P.8,10,13,17,22,23;Jno.13;Jno.W.7 12,13,24,75;Lou 17;Mary 24;T.A.Jr.24
HEBB-Bertha 51
HEIGLE-**132**
HEIMAN-L.5,10;Hirsh 10
HELMICH-**125**
HEMMINGWAY-W.S.35
HEMPHILL-**112,145**
HENDERSON-Daniel 59,64,67
HENDRICKS-**150,171,175**;Byron 40;Jno.W. 40,41,78;Mrs.S.E.40;Sam'l D.40
HENLEY-Floyd Rufus 23;Nettie G.23;Ollie Virginia 23
HENNESSEY-Dennis M.17
HENRY-**121,128,150,153,155**;Annie 103; Celia 54;Inee 56;R.M.78
HELMETT-**119**
HELTON-**172**
HERMAN-**116**; ---33
HERRINGTON-**176**
HERRON-**141**
HERZOG-Isaac 15;Simon 6
HESTER-**152**;Mrs. 100
HIBBLER-**170**;W.J.97
HICKMAN-**115,120,124,152,172**;Frank 58; Geo.B.78,107;Mary Louisa 107;Rowena West 108
HICKS-**110,140,180**;Elmira 59;Mrs.13; Nancy 66;Wm.P.7
HICKSON-HIXEN-**115**;Dr.W.H.35,36,37; Mrs.Laura S. 36
HIGGINS-**119**;Issa.5;Joel G.2;Randall G.2;Sara E.2;Westley 78
HIGHLAND-Jas.8;L.H.15;S.H.8,18
HIGHTOWER-Rinda 57
HILL-**133,140**;Amanda 53;Burrell 8;Chas. 67;Emma 61;Eva 23;Francis 9,10;Geo.55, 71,74,77;Georgianna N. 8;Hattie 18; H.E.95,96,105;Henderson 18;Jackson 57, 58,59;Jas.58;J.R.34;Juliann 66;Lizzie 22;Mrs.89;Mrs.E.C.22;Mrs.H.W.93;Nathan 56;S.A.31;W.H.66;Whitman 58,59,64
HILLIARD-Henry 53;Maj.19;Thos.62,78
HINDON-Josephine 54
HINDSMAN-Kye 53,54
HINES-Elbert 66;Lucy 15

BLACK NUMBERS INDICATE SURNAME ONLY IN CENSUS & CEMETERY RECORDS

HINTON-**165,182;**Chas.L.109;Daisy 109; Eugene F.109;Lucy Ann 55;N.B.86
HIRSH-Frank 72,78,93;Joseph 13,50
HITCHENS-**165**
HODGES-Lydia 35
HODGSON-Eliz.Irving 4
HODNETT-**146,147**
HOGAN-Mrs.M.J.106
HOGG-**118,125;**Alonzo 55;H.M.55,78; Issa 55;Jos.56
HOGIN-Alex A.83;Jno.E.83;Mrs.Pearl 79;S.H.73;Thurla 83
HOGUE-**182**
HOLBERG-R.E.14
HOLDER-W.E.47
HOLDERAFT-**113**
HOLENGER-**158**
HOLLAND-**112**
HOLLIDAY-Mary Ellen 68
HOLLIMAN-Rev.T.B.80
HOLLINGSWORTH-;--33,44;Glen 96;G.W.36;J.C.46,51;Jim 41;J.L.66;J.M.69,78
HOLLIS-**147**
HOLLOWAY-**146,172**
HOLLY-HOLLEY-W.M.8,22
HOLMES-**155;**Dan 18;Marg.Hughes 18
HOOD-**122,133;**Clifton R.88;G.W.66; Mollie D.76;Mrs.Emma Nelson 1;Will 51
HOOKER-**124,147,150**
HOPKINS-John 51,66;Lumford 59
HOPSON-**144**
HORD-**134**
HORTON-**167**
HOSE-Elisa 62
HOUSE-T.P.74
HOUSTON-HUSTON-Dena 65;Geo.18;R.W.78 Squire 78;Stewart 54,78
HOWARD-;--71;A.G.78;Chas.57;Geo.W.53 Polly 58
HOWE-**136**
HOWELL-**157**
HOWY-Aurora 19
HUBBELL-Mary 70
HUDDLESTON-Ned.57,68;Wm.27
HUDGENS-**148**
HUDSON-Edw.60;Eliz.26,27;John 26,27; Matt 65
HUGGINS-James S.12
HUGHES-A.D.3;Anderson 54;Archie 109; Jos.J.109;Lita 97;Martha 56;Mary 109 Mary Lilia 109;Mrs. 93,97;M.W.47
HULL-**119,158;**N.B.66
HUMPHREYS-Steve 54
HUNNICUTT-Rev.W.L.C.23
HUNT-**110,112;**Abijah 30,32,33,38,49, 69;A.C.81;Anna B.30,32,33,49;Dunbar 6,49;Felix 64;Geo.F.30,32,33;James 32,33 49;M.33;Mrs.A.87;Nancy 61;Omer 14,64,78; Vida 30,32,33
HUNTER-**181**
HURD-J.H.41
HURST-HURSE-**152,180**
HUSSEY-**148**-S.L.31
HUTCHINS-Laura 21
HYAM-Hannah S.16;L.H.16

I
IMONT-Mollie 60
INGERSOLL-Chas.J.4;Wm.K.4
INGRAM-INGRAHAM-L.W.37,40,68,78
INSLEE-E.A.78
IRBY-Jas.Jackson 49;Jas.J.Jr.49;Jno.R.M. 49;Sanders 49;Virginia R.49;Wm.R.49
IRVING-David 4;Jane 4;J.C.3;Jno.4;Rebecca 4;Wm.4
ISAAC-**136**
ISBELL-R.S.23
ISHMAEL-Blanton 68
ISIAH-R.P. 64,78

J
Jackson-Albert 55;Anderson 60,61,68; Chas.59,62;David 53;Flora 60;Geo.54,56; Hester 61;Jno.65,68;J.W.78;Liza 60;Mrs. C.L.11;Pauline 10;Sallie 57;Thos.64; West 55;Wm.64
JACOBS-**176**
JAMES-**114;**Alice 34;Allen 34;H.50; Rhoda 61;Rosa 61
JAMISON-M.C.49
JANIC-A.T.5
JAYS-Mrs.S.H.22
JEANS-Josephine 57
JEFFERIES-Martha Rowena 46;M.L.78;Moses 46;Walter Lee 46
JEFFERSON-Charlotte 67
JEFFORDS-C.S.3
JENKINS-**114-**Emma 61;Jerry 78;Harriett 66 Mose 55;Rich.68
JERIGAN-**148**
JOBE-**183**
JOEL-Adolph 31
JOHNSON-**128,142,147,148;**Adeline 61;A.H. 61;Angeline 66;B.E.78;Botley 67;Cal 86; C.H.12;Col.38;D.67;Dave 56;Dinah 66;Edie 60;Ella 66,Ellen67;Eliz.60;Elvira 61; Essex 61;Fannie 61;Francis 53;Fred 60; Grace Ann 66;Hester 59;Isaac 66;Jacob 10 Joanna 58;John 56,66;Jos.60;Katie 68; Lindsey 54,57;Lizzie 68;Ned 53;Pierce 65 P.H.53;S.A.78;Sam 62;Susan 61;Thos.67; Vicey 66;Willis 71;Wm.56,59,68

BLACK NUMBERS INDICATE SURNAME ONLY IN CENSUS & CEMETERY RECORDS

JOHNSTON-**168**;A.H.49;Edgar 96;Gen.
Jos.E.20;J.W.97,98;Miss 93,99;Mrs.
Alice L.73,76;Mrs.J.W.93,96;Sam 98.
JOHNSTONE-Helen 76;Mrs.Marg.L.25
JOLLY-JOLLEY-**121,157,165**;Marguerite 109;Mrs.Lucinda 80;Mrs.W.A.85,99,109
JONES-**111,122,126,135,141,142,144, 150,154,168,174,176**;Adeline 54;A.E.78;Benj.78;Catherine 67;Charlotte 60 Drayton 46;Dr.Walter 68;Ed 61;Emily 56;Fannie 59;Frank 78;Geo.55,56,58, 60,61,62,63,65,78;Glen 64;G.W.78; Hilliard 62;Issabella 55;Jeff 66; Jonas 67;Kansas T.7;Lalla Brooks 95; L.G.58;Martha 46;Mary 55,65;Mollie 56,67;Mrs.M.B.14;Rachel 67;Rev.J.A.B. 23,71;Rev.J.W.56,64,68,80;Rich.78; Sam'l L.10;Wm.57;W.R.16.
JOOR-**117,176;**Jno.S.28,32,33,34,35,36 37,39,50,53,59,68,69,78,85;Jno.S.Jr. 95,99;Katie 87,99;Mrs.J.S.85,99,105; Mrs.K.W.42,108.
JORDAN-**181;**E.M.13,22
JOSHUA-E.W.78
JOU-Lee 40

K
KADI KIN-123
KAGLER-S.T.69,78
KAIN-H.H.27
KALFUS-Geo.64
KANE-**110**
KAUFMAN-W.M.12
KEENE-Rev.F.M.80,82
KEEP-Annie Lum 2;Caroline M.2;Chas. 2;Col.H.V.2,20;Oliver H.2,20; Sally B.2
KEHO-P.M.31
KEIGHEE-Katherine 51
KEISER-T.F.31
KEITH-Jos.33
KELLER-**110**
KELLOGG-John Blake 13;Mason Bartett 4,9,13
KELLY-**115,117,160,175**;Claude 50;Cliff 50;Evanah Belle 50;Geo.50;Jno.Butler 50;Jno.39,50,78,96,106;Judy 55;Kate 50;Mary 57;Nannie 50;Rosa 50;Sylvia 30,55
KEMP-Moses 65
KENT-**168;**Mrs.B.39;Mrs.T.J.106; T.J.39,50,78,97,106
KERNAGHAN-Henry 64
KESTENBAUM-**137**
KETCHERSIDE-**136;**J.A.58
KETTLEMAN-Annie 51;Frank46,51;Ida 51 Jessie 51;Lillie 51;Lucy 51;Selma 51 Tony51;Will 51

KEY-Alice 59
KILKEY-Mrs.N.L.22
KILLIAN-Max 11;Mrs.Marg.11;V.A.16
KIMBRO-**153**
KING-**147,148;**(E)Manuel 56,57,61,66,67; Francis 67;Mitchell 64
KIRBY-**178**
KIRKLAND-**169;**Howard P.23;J.R.83;Martha 20;Norman 23
KIRKLEY-**180**
KLAUS-David 42;Edw.42,78,85,100;Klaus Bros.73;Lena S.42;Mrs.Babetta 42
KLEIMAN-Louis 16
KLINE-KLEIN-Ben 78;Geo.M.30;Henry 89
KNAPPER-NAPPER-Daniel 49;J.D.47;Jno.49, 53,54,55,57,60,64,68;Lucy Ann 47
KNIGHT-**110**
KNUCKLES-Mattie 57
KRESS-Geo.C.30
KUPPENHEIMER-Mrs.Belle 86
KWONG-**175**
KYLE-**135**

L
LACHS-S.W.7;W.6,8
LACY-LACEY-**121;**B.F.14,18;Jas.56;Mr.19
LAIRD-**117**
LAKE-**136**
LAMB-Lallie 81;Lowry 81
LAMBERTSON-R.T.78
LAMON-E.B.4,20
LANCASTER-Sophia 6;Wm.55
LANCHESTER-Wm.60
LANDAU-M.D.87
LANE-G.F.78;Mahala 35;Mr.80;Mrs.Mollie 84;Sarah 62;Stephen 35,62
LANG-**141,153;**Lotta 52;Will 70,76
LANGFORD-**177;**Annie 74;Gertrude 19;Mrs. Geo.N.74;Sidney W.69,74,76,78;Walter H. 109
LANKSTON-Charity 61
LANIER-**122**
LATIMER-**129**
LAUGHLIN-Larry 55
LAWSON-**120,136;**Daniel 62;Easter 63;Mrs. Louisa 14;Wm.31,33,64
LAWYER-Cyrus 33,42;Minna 41
LEANETT-**121**
LEDBETTER-R.T.88,89,90,94
LEE-**121,150,156;**Chas.59,67;Ed 63;Flora B. 14;Gen.20;Jas.39,66,67;Jno.60;Joan 50; Mary Ann 50;Mary L.59;Mattie M.7;Rich.39 50,78;Sallie 66;Sam 40;S.W.73
LEECH-**113**
LEIGH-**116**
LEMLE-Julius 42
LENNOX-Henrietta A.12;Jas.12;Jennet 12

BLACK NUMBERS INDICATE SURNAME ONLY IN CENSUS & CEMETERY RECORDS

LESSER-F.N.8
LESTER-Emanuel 59
LEWIS-**131,139,148;**Anthony 62;Autrey 68;Ben 56,61;Edith 27;Henry 27;Jno. 60;Jno.Henry 61;Manerva 66;Taylor 66
LEVY-**172**
LIGHTNER-Jas.68
LIGHT(S)-Dorcas 11;Eliz.11;Martha 11 Rial 11
LILLY-**148;**Emmanuel 57
LINDSEY-Jack 56;Jas.47,78
LINGY-**123**
LINK-**133**
LINTON-Robt.61;R.W.49
LIPPITT-C.T.32
LIPSCOMB-W.L.76
LISBORG-W.A.49
LITTLE-Rev.D.A. 24
LIVERSINGER-**125**
LIVINGSTON-LEVINGSTON-**135;**J.P.56
LLOYD-L.A.57
LOCKETT-C.S.78
LOCKMAN-Mashoek 61,62
LOCKRIDGE-**145**
LOGAN-**135;**Howell 107
LOMBARDO-**171**
LONG-**112,133;**Edw.62;Jas.A.78;J.W.78;W.D.50
LOPER-**130**
LOPEZ-**140**
LORENZEN-Chris.70,78,84,89,94;C.W.84
LOUIS-Emma 64
LOVE-Col.84;Emma J.26;Flora 56;Robt.H.26,35;Thos.J.35
LOWE-;----76
LOWRY-Dr.Jno.75;Gov.81
LUCAS-Isidore 12,13;Isidore Jr.13
LUCKETT-Rich.60
LUM-LUMM-LUHM-**138,160;**Julia 98;Mrs.Ann 2
LUSK-**141;**Linnie C.81;Lydia 47
LUSTON-Emanuel 60;Sarah 60
LYLERLY-Irene 81
LYLES-**150;**J.W.102
LYNCH-Jas.C.7;Jas.Percy 7,8;Mattie F.7;Mollie 64;Robt.Ray 7,8;Ruby 7,8;T.J.8

M
MACK-Amanda 57
MAHAFFEY-**120;**W.B.78
MAITLAND-Alex 12;Eliz.S.12;Mary Currie 12;Robt.L.12
MAKES-Jack 60
MALLET(T)-**127;**Bettie C.59;Carrie E.63;Geo.108;Jas.B.108;Jos.Geo.108;Irene W.108;Robt.M.108;W.H.87;Winnifred 108.
MALONE-Annie 58;Moses 58
MANGUM-W.W.74,78
MANN-**168,170;**Anna 107,109;Corinne 72,107,109;Josie 93,93,102;L.E.93,93,102;Mrs.Robt.90,92;Nina 102;Ora 89,92,93,102,109;P.L.11,13;R.A.72;Ruby 88;W.M.43,92,93,94,102,107,109
MARANTO-**158,179**
MANOR-**133,142-**J.T.74,76,77,78;Lizzie 56
MARCIERS-MAIRCIER-Moses 58
MARION-Mrs.Barney 87,96
MARKETTE-**155;**Claudia J.46;Mrs.Ora 47;Willie Eliza 46;Wm.46
MARLER-**150**
MARR-**129**
MARRIOT-Mrs.Francis 91
MARSH-March-**123,152;**G.W.65;J.10
MARSHALL-A.E.47;Alverman Maria 26;Estelle B.47;Frederick 68;H.J.47;Jas.T.25,26,27,;Jennie 61;Millie 59;Miss 94
MARSTON-**129**
MARTAK-**143,151,172;**A.K.47,48,74,78
MARTIN-**114,149,153,156,161,176;**Geo.65;Gus 104;Henry N.28;Mary F.28;Maud 90;M.C.31,65,78,90,92,104,109;Minnie 109;Mrs.M.C.79,104;Peter 54;Rose 64;W.T.78
MARTLEY-Lucy 58
MASON-Alex 18;Allen 62;J.W.16;Liza 53 Rueben 65
MASSIE-Mary 81
MATHEWS-MATTHEWS-**173;**Chas.60;Lenzy 78;Sam'l 2.
MATHYS-MATHIS-**148,157;**Peter 80
MATT-Mattie 65
MATTELL(E)-**108,119,127**
MATTEN-Rittie 45
MAURY-Dillie F. 2
MAXEY-Viney 10;Walter 10;Walter S.10
MAXWELL-**179,180,181;**Elias 65;Jno.39;Lamar 106;R.G.31;R.Y.58;Sallie 83;Tobe 106
MAYER-David 5;Emil 5,10,15,16;Henry L.2,8,28
MAYFIELD-Florence 22;James L.3
MAYHAW-**124**
MAY(S)-A.H.26;Jno.S.107;Pat.55,58,62
MEACHAM-Adam 68;Orville 2
MEEK-**175;**J.E.50,95;May 76;Mrs.J.E.86,95
MELMORE-**110**
MELTON-**158;**Caroline 58,65;Green 58
MELVILLE-Green 57
MERCHANT-**147,148**
MERRETT-T.J.78
MER(R)IDITH-Wm.31,67

BLACK NUMBERS INDICATE SURNAME ONLY IN CENSUS & CEMETERY RECORDS

MHOON-Ellen 44;Foster 44;Jas.A.44; Jas.44;Junius 44,78;Mary 44;Mrs. Marie A.44;Robt.B.44;Stanley 44; W.J.44.
MICAM-Adam 59;
MICKEY-Ann 56;Carrie 5£;D.M.55,56,60 61,63,68,78;Henry 51;Henry M.51; Mina Kemp 51;Susan 51
MIDDLEBROOK-**174**
MILAM-**153,156**
MILES-Bettie 106;C.C.41;Earnest 57; Dent 106,O.C.78;Warner 54
MILLER-**113,124,158,175**;Andy 78;Anna Choplain 23;Annette 45;Ary 58;B.N. 4,6;Dr.A.36,38,43,50,74,78,86;Earl 22,23;Eol Vandorn 23;Jno.10;Mary 9, 64;Mollie 18;Otho Singleton 23;Roman 9;T.M(orW.)25,26;Wm.C.23;W.W.72
MILLS-T.D.7;---52
MILNER -**153**
MILTON -**136**
MINOR-Ann 3;Polly 3,4;Robert 3,4
MITCHELL-**123**;Adam 56;Chas.55;Green 56,61;Joe 8;Rueben 68;R.W.61,62; Wm.58
MIZELL-Jno.T.33,63
MOBLEY-Judge P.8
MOCLEY-Nancy 53
MOLLISON-Ida W.7;Robt.7;Tommy 3; W.E.6,7,13
MONROE-Jefferson 55
MONTGOMERY-**112,168**;A.J.109;Arthur J. 109;Chas.62,99;D.H.70,99;Edmund 53; Howard L.109;Nola 89,96;S.A.109
MOODY-Denis 53,54,55,59
MOORE-**112,132,133,147,148,174,178**; Alex 10;Anita 51;Bacon 51;Blanton 106;Brayer 52;Bowman 52;B.R.30,51,78 C.11;Capt.33;Chastine 11;Corinne 11; Daniel 51;Daniel L.51,73,85,94,95; Daniel L.Jr.51;D.B.92,94;D.E.86;Dr. J.H.51;Harry 51,52;Jas.C.37;Jas.H. 30,51,52;Jas.H.Jr.51,52;Jno.B.51; L.A.31;M.92;Mack 51;Marg.A.11;Mary Bacon 51,86;Mattie H.33;Minnie B.51; Mrs.90;Mrs.D.B.87,88,92;Mrs.E.M.107; Rev.M.H.22,23,24;Thos.51;T.S.46;Virginia 51;Wm.D.51;W.W.30,56,91,97
MOORMAN-H.66;July 63
MORDECA(I)-Ruffian 66;Sam 57,66
MORELAND-Maria 54;Patterson 53,78
MORGAN-W.T.4
MORGANSTERN-Alfred J.50,51
MORPHIS-**180**
MORRIS-Napoleon 64
MORRISON-Annie 17;Beatrice 17;Chris 17;Eliz.17;Grace 17;Jno.17;Jno.W.17; Osceola 17;Wm.C.17

MORSE-Esther 51
MOSBY-Mrs.Sallie 89
MOSELEY-E.78;Mrs.85;Nelson 65;R.J.78
---76
MOTIN-**111**
MOTT-**123**
MOUCHETTE-**148**
MOULTRIE -Ed 12
MULLEN-MULLINS-**134,151**;Mrs.89
MULLER-Wm.34
MURPHEY-Isaac 59
MURRAY-MURRIE-**111,112,119**;Chas.55;Emma 58;Dr.T.J.33;Jas.43;J.B.63,78
MURTON-MERTON-Isaiah 64
MYERS-MYRES-**120,155,162**;Alice Maud 31, 93,100;Annie 76;Chas.54;Emma 6;F.C.31,33 78,104;Geo.D.31;Henrietta F.W.31;Jerry 71;Joel 6;Lucy 31;Mary C.31;M.C.109;Mrs. 98;Mrs.Wm.93;Robt.65;R.S.31,42,47,78,93

Mc
McALPINE-**112;**J.T.63;R.E.78
McAMERAN-**121**
McBRIDE-Joe 68
McCAIN-McCANN-**181**;Eliza 16;K.D.51;Robt.16
McCALEB-**115;**J.M.30,35,84;Lillie 51;Mary 51;Thos.D.84;W.D.84
McCALL-G.B.93
McCARTHEY-M.E.67
McCARTNEY-Ollie 81
McCARY-**118**
McCAUL-**170;**Tom 77;Geo.97;Mildred 97
McCLENDON-**113**
McCOMB-**160;**E.B.40,71,73;Evan S.107; Sam'l 40,41
McCORMICK-H.W.51
McCOY-**148;**Guy 57;H.B.78
McCRAW-**132**
McCUE-Jno.Howard 23;Jno.W.22
McCULLUM-Mack 68
McELOWN-**119**
McELROY-Julia 58;Rosa 67
McENESRY-Thos.78
McEVINS-Thos.37
McEVOY-**113**
McDANIEL-**146,147;**Mrs.Eliza 84
McDONALD-**146;**D.32;Frank67
McDOUGALL-**122;**Jno.A.36
McDOWELL-W.H.34;W.W.4
McDUFF-**147,148**
McDUFFEY-Parret 61
McGEHEE-Curtis R.24;Eunice E.J.24;J.9,24 J.A.16;Joanna G.24;Justin W.24;Kate C.21
McGERKIN-Mrs.22
McGINNIS-Annie 27;Chris.27;Eliz.27;Jas. 27;Mary Jane 27
McGOWN-McKEOWN-Rev.M.103

BLACK NUMBERS INDICATE SURNAME ONLY IN CENSUS & CEMETERY RECORDS

McGRANGER-**135**
McGUIRE=Rev.W.C.77,107,108,109
McINTYRE-Catherine 55
McKEE-**157**
McKINNEY-**124,153;**Marion 105;Mrs.W.C.
H.72,86,94,95,96,105;W.C.H.27,28,30,
31,36,42,66,69,72,78,95,99,105;
Willie 95
McKINS(Z)IE(Y)-McKINZU-**120,122,159;**
Eva Eliz.108;H.R.(or K.)64,78,106,
108,109;Louis K.109;Sam'l A.107,109
McLARREN-**134**
McLAURIN-**110,116;**--33,38,85;A.G.71;
Annie 76;Ansolom Joe 71;Dr.Albert 90
Gov.90,91,104;H.J.39,73,95,104;J.H.
73,80;Mrs.85;Mrs.H.J.87,88,89,91,92,
95;R.L.41,42,78,84;Sylvester 104;
Wallace 104;Walter 39,71,104;W.K.41,
82
McLEAN-Capt.Geo.P.21
McLEMOREChas.58
McLEOD-Lumbr.Mill 93;Mrs.106
McLOYD-**129**
McMAHON-**120,173,174;**Mrs.Thos.88,89,
92,99;Thos.71,73,74,76,77,78,86,92,
99,109
McMILLEN-McMILLAN-**125,153,154**
McNEELY-Mrs.J.King 1
McNEIL-**147**
McNUT-**148**
McPHERSON-McFEARSON-**173;**Albert 54,68
Harrison 54
McQUAID-**137**
McQUILLAN-**117,160;**Martha A.C.43;
Wm.B.35,55,57,58,64
McRANIE- D.W.78
McRAVEN-Annie E.14
McWILLIAMS-**148**
McYOUNG-Jno.14;Hannah 14

N
NAPOLEON-Sophia 65
NASH-Catherine 14;Cornelius 14;
Eugenia 14;Gus 14;Hagan 2;Hester 16;
Joe 14;Joseph 14;Katie 14;Leah 14;
Marg.14;Nellie 14;Travis Jr.4.
NATHAN-Alick 61
NATHANIEL-David 60
NEAL-**142,164;**A.L.39,50,78,85,99,100,
102
NEFF-**142**
NEILAND-Harriett T.37
NELSON-**123,135;**Elena H.(Emma)1;Eunice
R. 1;Francis S.1;Howard J.1,2;Jas.1;
H.H.14;Jno.W.1;Lulu L.1,2;Manie 1;
Mary L.S.1;Sam'l 1,2;Sam'l Jr.1,2;
Tom 1;Thos.1;Thos.C.1;Wm.P.1
NESMITH-Cornelius Robinson 20;Early
20

NEWCOMB-**173**
NEWMAN-**181**
NEWTON-Alma 100;Emmett 100;Gen.A.E.100
NICHOLAS-Susan 63
NICHOLS-**136;**Albert R.10;Adeline 42,43;
Harry 42,43;Jas.3,49,59;Jennie 24;Jos.24
Rena 42,43;Walter 24
NICHOLSON-**120;**Lena 77;Lizzie 45;L.M.77;
Louis 69;Meta 75,84
NICKERSON-Allen 33
NIXON-**120**
NOBLE-Allen Jr.8
NOBLIN-**178**
NORMAN-Gabriel 53;Peter 67
NORRELL-**146**
NOVELL-**129**
NUGENT-Annie 94,96
NUNNELLI-NUNNALLEE-Beauregard W.14;Hardy
H.14;H.H.7,14;Maggie L.14;Marg.E.14;
Nashti R.14

O
ODOM-**123,157**
OHLEYER-E.H.81;Lottie 81;Mrs.Jno.81
OIVES-S.V.83
OLIN-A.S.13
OLIVER-Gabriel 66,67;Melia 55
O'NEAL-**123,130,145,181;**Ellen 66;Hubert
14;Jinnie 14;Kitty 14;Lucy 58
O'NEIL-Mollie 56
ORENDORF(F)-**117,119,171;**Mary 91;Mrs.Alice
6;T.J.33,34,35,36,38,58,60;T.T.27,28,33,
35,37,38,39,78,79,81,83;W.A.38,56,78,81,
83
ORMAND-M.85
ORR-**136**
OSTROFFSKY-OSTROFFISKY-**110;**E.73;Fannie
28;J.27,78;Jake 65;S.78;Store 6
OTEY-Peter J.49;W.H.49
OTTO-**120;**Jno.57;Mrs.John 97,100
OVERBY-OVERBA(E)Y-**139,155;**J.A.57
OWENS-**111,124;**Mrs.Sarah 93;Thos.62

P
PACE-**169**
PAGE-**128**
PALMER-Lucy 58
PARHAM-**124,159,165,173;**Corinne 86,87,90,
95,98;Gertrude 85,88,90,95,96,98;H.G.27,
78;Hulda 99;J.G.39,54,58,72,78,89,99,100;
Lucia 77;Mrs.J.G.76,77,90,99;Mrs.Mary 89;
Wm.61
PARKER-B.J.78;Co.Noah 29;Hiram 53;Jno.65
Leanna 26;Martha Evans 30;Miss 95;Nat.W.
26,30,45,49,59,61;Rebecca 56;R.W.56;
Sally 56;Virgil 57
PARKS-**119,120;**Lizzie 61;R.60;Rich.65;S.D
57;T.G.27,57

BLACK NUMBERS INDICATE SURNAME ONLY IN CENSUS & CEMETERY RECORDS

PARLEE-112
PAR(R)ISH-**112,128,148;**Annie 35;Jno.
35,55;K.N.78;---76
PARSONS-**118;**Chas.Carroll 32;M.L.B.32
PASCO-Martin 65
PASSMORE-**167;**E.L.100
PATTERSON-**158,173;**Andrew 57;Brimmage
35,78;Gracie 49;Jane 66;Lucinda 49;
Wash.58
PATTON----26
PAT(T)RIDGE-**148,175,182;**Hyman 61
PATTY-Mrs.71,98;Mrs.Robt.C.26,98;
R.C.86;Robt.103
PAYNE-Bell 51;Beverly 56;Bob 61;
Mrs.M.E.91,92;Richmond 54;Willie
D. 73,80
PEARL-**118;**Ben 47,73,78
PECK-D.F.3
PEELER-**171;175**
PEGRAM-G.G.36
PEMBERTON-**128;**Fannie 33;Maj.H.M.89;
M.H.33,36,41,98,99
PENDERGAST-M.C.28
PENDEROIS-PENDO(A)RVIS-**122,123,125;**
M.E.67;Tom 65
PENN-**165**
PENNY-PENNEY-Jos.78;Rev.J.H.67,68
PENWRIGHT-Jas.53,71
PEPPARD-W.J.77
PEPPER-D.G.26
PERCY-Leroy 76;Hon.W.C.25
PERKINS-**125,153,158,174;**Austin 66;
C.H.51;J.L.22;Lou 57
PERRIN-W.H.83
PERRY-PARRY-**165,170;**Edmund 53;Edw.53
54,55;Dr.V.M.22
PETERS-Geo.27
PET(T)IT-D.R.25,27
PETTWAY-Celia 55;Rich.1
PEYTON-Della 24;Gertrude 23;Idella
Gert.24;Livingston 5,6,8,9,15,21,22,
24;Lydia 24;Malvina 21;Marie Gert.20
22;Murray M.10,11,21;Shirley 24;
Susan Eliz.24
PHARR-**137**
PHELPS-**126,136;**Dr.A.J.50,66,72,78,80;
Ellen Bodley 50;Henry V.50,78;Hon.
W.G.5,25,60;Mamie 80;Mary B.V.50;
Mary P.72,80;Mrs.94,96
PHILIPS-PHILLIPPS-Airy 66;Capt.Mose
21;Charlie 67;Chatman 58;H.W.73,74,
78;Mamie Lee 23;Mary 56
PHIPPS-R.B.10,16
PICARD-H.53,57,60
PICKEL-J.W.78
PIERCE-**183;**Evana 55;F.G.83;Floyd 83;
Jno.53;Margy 59;Mrs.72

PIGGS-120
PINDELL-H.C.25;Mrs.25
PINFIELD-**157;**H.78;Wm.74
PINKARD-Susan 61
PINTARD-Chanc.42;Claude 49
PIOIMAN-**132**
PIPPIN-**156,157,180**
PIT(T(MAN-Byron Lera 23;H.H.5,6,
Kizziah 5;Mrs.24
PITTS-A.B.35;Sophy 4
PLANTATIONS
Annandale 25;Anna Vista 8;Anguilla 35;
Arcadia 14;Baconia 45,85,95;BenLomond
3,4;Bradford & Elliston 8,80;Cameron 30;
Chicorea 74;Clements Pl.85;Clover Hill
5,14,17;Cottage Home 11;Council Bend 41,
45,73,91;Dahomey 87;Danover 31,74;Dudley
Place 87;Eagle Eye 6;Eaglenest 6;Egypt
30,34;Ellwood 4;Esperanza 13;Fairfield
13;Forked Deer 80,92,100;Georgiana 30,
32,49,73;Glen Annie(Anna)2,20;Gwin Place
90;Hall Place 85;Hardee 73;Helens Place
25;Holly Ridge 4;Homochito 10;Hopedale
13;Lakeside 13;Lexington Place 76;Mary
Leah 2;Meta 76;Mount Holly 87;Muscadine
7;Nitta Yuma 26;Oak Grove 80;Oakley 83;
Old Auburn 80;Onley 8;Patmos 90;Promised
Land 4,15;Reveland 92;Reserve 16;Rifes
16;Sandy Bayou 92;Shiloh 101;Tillman Pl.
30;Valewood 15;Vickland 25,42;WadeLawn 5;
Watsonia 76,91,93,97,99,106;Weeping Will-
ow 26,34,79,93,97;Woodlawn 6;
PLATT-**135,167;**Nannie E.106;R.C.99
PLEASANTS-Jas.20
POINDEXTER-Geo.53
POOLE-**148**
PORTER-**146,148;**Dr.Wm.O.109;Mrs.109;
Mrs.J.E.80
POSTELL-Capt.E.C.76
POSTON-**141**
POTITE-Benj.65
POTTER-**156;**Alice 45;Anthoney 45;Geo.45;
Henrietta 34,45;Lewis 45;Nelson 34,45;
Wesley 45
POWELL-**113,116,123,146;**Corine 102;Geo.60
65,67;Judge 58,59;H.J.78,102;L.M.45;Mary
61;Mary Louise 16;Mrs.J.E.105;Rea 96,103
POWER(S)**113-**Caroline H.19;Col.S.B.106;
Katherine Maude 19;Maj.S.F.21;Rosina J.H
21;Stephen Francis 21
PRADER-Ben 58
PRATT-Louis 67;Wm.H.28
PRESTLEY-**164;**Jas.44
PRESTON-Cornelius 67;H.C.7;Mary Eliz.5;
Misses 100;Zenas 5
PRICE-**144,179;**Julia 66;Julius 78;Lucy 10
T.H.78;Thos.66;Wm.10

BLACK NUMBERS INDICATE SURNAME ONLY IN CENSUS & CEMETERY RECORDS

PRIDMORE-**115,160**;Edw.50
PURCELL-**111**
PURDY-Juanita H.80
PURNELL-Ed.T.12;Henry P.12;Jno.
H.12;Millard R.12;O.12;Wm.8,12;Wm.R.
12
PURVIS -**117**;P.G.59
PUTNELL-**121**

Q
QUIELLEN-**111**

R
RAGAN-**130**
RAINEY-**140**
RANDLE-Ritchie 53
RANKINS-Owen 61
RANOR-**123**
RANSOM-**129**
RATCLIFF-Ernest 69;Nat 69,80
RATLIFF-**147,150,152;**D.78;F.L.78
RAWLS-**146**
RAY-**147**
REDDY-T.G.4,7;T.Y.6
REDMOND-REDMAN-Emma 90;Jas.R.107;J.M.
78;Mrs.J.M.93;Rich.6
REED-**132**;Alvina 60;Edmond 68;Hiram
55;Louisa 68;Minnie 64;Sam 68
REEVELY-REAVLY-Adeline 68;Alice 26;
Emaline 26;Marshall 105;Sam'l 26,66;
Thos.58,67
RENEAU-**172**
RESTER-J.J.40
REYNOLDS-RENALDS-**119,120,179;**Frances
J.57;Georgina 60;J.H.103
RHODES-Murphy 59;Willie B.W.41
RICE-Katie 24;Mrs.M.B.24
RICHARDSON-**115,141**;Alex.45;Edmund 26
Elijah 68;Fannie May 81;Henrietta 16
Henry 45,56;Henry Jr.45;Jas.16,78;
Jas.S.75,87;Jno.P.75;Martha 45;R.C.8
R.E.78
RICHMOND-**166**
RICKARD-**124**
RICKELS-**177**
RICKS-Family 84
RIDLEY-Geo.53;Susan 63
RIFE-Thos.C.16;W.W.16
RIGSBY-Wm.55
RILEY -**130**
RINE-Matilda 34
RITCHIE-**127**
RITTER-Jas.H.74;Mary K.S.74,77,105;
RIVERS-Pink 54
ROACH-**167**;Nailor 86
ROAN-**139,171**;Lulu 64;Rich.54
ROBERSON-Jack 66
  *ERROR-double entry

ROBERT(S)-**116,126,154,167**;Benj.78,98;
Clemantina 66;Dr.J.C.22;E.D.50,95;Geo-
rgie 84;Jno.Q.41,78,84;Mrs.Jno.Q.71,84;
Mrs.Wm.73;N.J.80;Wm.28,78,80;---79
ROBERTSON-**118,181;**Annie 61;Eliza 66;Ella
C.27;Frank 65;Jas.27;Ida W.83;J.H.27,28,
31,57,61;Lou 65;Lula C.27,108;Rev.Ira.B.
72,80,82
ROBINSON-**130,134;**Adeline 68;Adolphus 12;
Alex 65;Allen 68;Ed.12;F.R.78;Frank 54;
Geo.15;Harry 12,61;Ida 71;Jno.61,66;Joe
58;Kitty 12;Mattie 55;Ned 41;Penny 58;
Rev.H.W.81;Roxanna 58;Sam 57
ROCHEL-ROCHELLE-**151,176,177;**Mary Ione 17
ROCHESTER-Olivia 51
RODICALS-J.F.50
ROGAN-**114,134,156;**C.W.42,78;Henry 99;Irby
89,105,106,108;L.W.53,54,55,57,58,66,68,
78,99,108;Mrs.L.W.89,108;Will 99;Wm.B.108
ROGERS-**131,144,157**;Ananias 55;Dr.P.S.78,
81;J.M.78;Jno.A.78;Vertena 57
ROOT-J.L.3,41,75
ROSAMOND-**157**
ROSE-Emanul 3;Henry 3,4;
*ROSEBROUGH-R.L.4ROSEN-**120;**Augustus 39,50
59;Easter 56;Jno.39;Mary 39;Rich.39
ROSS-**135**;Geo.65;Jno.78
ROUSSEAU-**141**
ROWE-Mahulda 56
ROWELL-**121**
ROWLAND-D.R.W.109;Nannebelle 109;
Sarah R.109
ROYAL-C.C.77
RUSH-Wm.53
RUSHING-**118;**Alfred 71;Lizzie 58;W.H.
39,41,45,78
RUSS-Stephen Myer 24
RUSSELL-**144,167**;catherine 53;David 38,
64;Jos.38;Laura Cornelia 38;M.85,100;
Mrs.Laura 38;Rev.E.61
RUSSIN-James 53
RUTHERFORD -**129**
RUTLEDGE-**154;**Brown 58

S
SAM--Os 57
SAMPLE-Lucy 67
SAMUEL-Cyrus 49
SANDEFORD-**171,178,181**
SANDER(S)-SAUNDER(S)-**111,119,120,122,148
153,161,178;**A.A.78;E.V.104,105;Hamilton
55;Jack 61;J.J.64,78,101,105;M.99,102;
Mary Frances 50;Mary W.C.50;May 68;Mr.&
Mrs.77;N.H.78;Sadie 74;Sallie 104;Walton
50;W.R.64
SANDERSON-**110**
SANDIFER-**179**

BLACK NUMBERS INDICATE SURNAME ONLY IN CENSUS & CEMETERY RECORDS

SANDLIN-**146**
SANFORD-**171;**C.C.16
SASSAMAN-**128**
SAVAGE-**130;**W.E.78
SAXON-**159**
SCHMIDT-SCHMITZ-**171,179;**Mrs.Alice M. 79,90
SCHOALIN-Jos.59
SCHOLOTTMAN-**178**
SCOFIELD-D.L.65
SCOTT-**110,144;**Chas.73;Col.Jno.S.21; Eliz.M.5;Flora 62;Frank C.12;Henrietta 59;Henry 57;Henry P.4,6,7,11, 12,14;Jessie 58;Martha E.5;Matilda 14;Millie 64;Miss P.108;Nancy P.11, 12,13;Purnill 108;Sam'l 5;Sara A.5; Willis H.12;---108
SCREWS-J.N.78
SCRUGGS-James 10
SCUDDER-Celete 24;C.I.24;E.N.4,5,6,9 23,24;Dr.W.H.9,11,16,19,20,22,24; Fayssoux 24;Gert.24;James B.20;Mary Eliz.24;Monita 24;Sarah 24;Seymoura 24;W.H.Jr.20,24;W.W.16
SEALS-Perry 61
SEARLE-Dan 30;Mrs.99
SEARS-Peter 43
SEESTRONG-Carrie 54
SELBY-Mrs.Robt.95;Rev.Robt.92,101,103
SHACKLEFORD-W.P.86
SHADRACK-SHADDRICK-**114;**Malicia 63
SHANNON-**116,158;**Bettie C.33;B.H.89; Burleigh 40,102;Burrus 85;Carrie 92; Carrie Irene 40,87;H.E.32,33,39,40, 59,71,78,87;Mrs.H.E.79,90;Mrs.Burrus 87;M.Y.70,72,78,84;Susan 39;W.W.33
SHARBROUGH-**177;**J.W.78,91,92;
SHELBY-**113,115,117,160,165;**A.C.30,32 Creath 33;Emily M.32;Evan B.30,32,37 58,87,107;Flournoy 31;Mary Butts 107 Mary C.107;Mary Kate 108;Molly K.32, 37,105;Mrs.Emily 70,109;Mrs.Mary E. 107;R.P.32;Thos.J.32,37
SHELDEN-Cyrus 58
SHELTON-**116,119,132;**E.A.38;Elsinore 109;F.E.38;Lulu 62;Mrs.Mary E.38; Mrs.S.V.83;Mrs.T.P.83;Rev.J.H.22,83; S.F.38,39,60,65;T.P.38,83;W.H.36, 38,39;
SHEPPARD-**140,177**
SHIELDS-Dr.Bisland 5;Minell E.5; Miss M.L.5;Mrs.M.L.5;P.R.Jr.5; R.B.15;W.B.4,5
SHLENKER-Isaac 42
SHOEMAKER-Nancy 20
SHORT-Ima May 23

SHRADER-**120,132,139,157;**Ellen I.57; Henry 62;J.A.C.28,55,61,62,68,71,74,78, 91;J.H.55;M.T.62;Sam.H.59,71,78;W.H.56, 78,79;W.P.71,78
SHROPSHIRE-**173,181**
SHULTS-Mrs.Jack 19
SHUMPORT-**126**
SKINNER-**174**
SKIPPER-Rev.V.D.22,23,24
SLATER-Chas.T.6;Emma 6;John D.6
SLAUGHTER-F.R.78
SIBLEY-**137;**C.G.78;Rife 16
SIDNEY-Emanuel 61;L.E.67,68,78
SIKES-**147**
SIMILTON-Francis 60;Isaac 54;Silas 55
SIMMONS-**117,129,153;**Sydney 18
SIM(M)S-**116;**A.B.85;"Bunnie"103;Capt.Thos 102;Julia 102;Minnie 108;Mrs.T.E.96; T.E.102,104;Thos.108
SIMPSON-Flora Bell 89
SIMRALL-G.H.14
SINAI-**120;**B.33,66,93;Esther 71;Jos. 103;Julius 33,36,44,45,78,87,93,103; Mose 74,78,93,103
SINGLETON-Mollie 68
SIRRONIA-Lulu 13
SMALL-Fannie 53;Jno.61
SMART-Mollie 60;Mrs.M.C.13
SMEDLEY-Marg.53
SMILEY-Jas.32
SMITH-**122,128,133,137,143,144,147,148, 169,179,180;**A.10;Aaron 54;Alfred 67;Allie Mae 23;America 56;Anna Marg.8;Annie L.K. 2;Capt.19;Capt.Bill 99;C.B.22,23,24;C.E. 78;Celeste F.53;Chris.W.25,26;Clarisa Ann 55;Eliza.14;Fannie 65;Fred.A.20; Gilliam M.20;Harriet 57;Harrison 53; Hattie 62;Henri G.56;Ione A.17;Isaac L. 20;Jas.47,57;Jerry 67;Jno.53,62;Jos.58; Lawrence 17;Lee A.17;Leon T.11;Lou 17; Lurena 22;Mahala 62;Marg.Inex 17;Marg.S. 17;Marshall R.20;Mary 58,62;Millie 55; Mrs.Frank 24;Nathan 54,62;Nellie M.23; O.P.24;Preston 17;Preston H.8;R.M.3,5, 7,8,9,11,12,15,17,22,24,73,79;R.M.Jr.22; Rosa Lee 22;Sarah 64;S.Eunice 24;Stephen 3;Sydney I.22,23;Walter Hazel 20;Walter J.22;Wash.27,53,56;W.H.16;W.M.7;Wm.58; Yeomans 7
SMITHHART-**174;**G.W.7;Ida 7;O.C.1;O.E.7; Olive Ennis 7;Sam Dunbar 7;Wm.O.7
SOMERS-Benj.53
SORRELL-Tillman 80
SOULES-Louis 60
SPEARMAN-SPIERMON-Carrie 68;Ella 68; Jennie 55;Judge 55,63

BLACK NUMBERS INDICATE SURNAME ONLY IN CENSUS & CEMETERY RECORDS

SPEARS-**148**
SPELLER-Robt.58
SPENCE-David E.49
SPENCER-Mrs.107;
SPIARS-Idella G.22;Jas.21;Lydia M.9, 21;M.M.9,21
SPRIG(GS)-**114;**Banks 34;Elias 53,55, 57,64;Flora 59;Merridy 63;Sylvia 34
SPROULA-Rev.H.F.105
SPURLOCK-Cegis(?)24;Jas.W.23,24; Mrs.Fannie C.23
SPURMAN-Lena 68
STACY-**129**
STADSKER-H.H.38;L.J.38
STAFFER-**131**
STAFFORD-**174**
STANDARD-**115;**Alice 36;Mrs.Laura 36; Walter 36,37
STANDIFER-**173;**W.S.78
STANTON-Annie 2;Fannie 2;Sam 2
STAPLE-Emily 58
STARLING-**135**
STAUB-C.A.56
STEEL-Henry 39
STEGALL-STIGALL-**177;**G.E.103;Mrs.Alma 96,98
STEPHENS-**183**
STERN-STEARN-**124;**Cecile 15,16,18;Ella 5;Hannah 5,15,16;Henry 5;Henry Jake 15,16,18;Jos.14,15;Paulina 5;R.5;Roa 15;Sam 15,16;Simon 5;Solomon 15,16,18
STEVENS-**112,114,122,130,140,151,152, 156,157,158,159;**Alice G.54;Douglas 40,78,102;Edwin 49;Emaline E.43;F.O. 43;F.L.67,68;Georgiana 60;Henry 49; H.G.33,40,62,63,66,67;J.A.43;Jno.40; Jno.H.49;Jno.O.30,43,78;Joel O.43,80 83,84;Lou 72;L.R.40;Mary E.49;Maude E.43;Mrs.80;Mrs.Belle 81;Mrs.Jennie 83;Mrs.L.R.85,97,100;S.E.50;S.T.43; Prentiss 83;P.W.43;W.C.49
STEVENSON-Mrs.W.E.85,88,89,92; Sargent 86;W.E.86,94
STEWART-**117,150,152,161;**G.Y.33,34,36 58,59,64;J.D.34,36;Thos.W.14;W.H.78
STILES-Alice P.18;E.W.18
STINSON-Albert 62;Mary 55
STOCKNER-E.2,3
STRACHAN-David 14,15;Jane 14;Robt.14
STRATTON-Mrs.R.E.100;R.E.94
STRICKLAND-**180**
STRINGEY-**120**
STRINGFELLOW-**127,132,142,143**
STOKES-Ed 66;Macklin 11;Mrs.Laura 46
STORY-Rev.G.T.84
STOUT-A.J.13;Isidore Lucas 13;Lulu Sirronia 13
STOVALL-Col.76

STOWER-J.H.3
STOWLES-Dora 60;Minnie 60
STUART-**137;**Mrs.Gen.F.E.B. 1
STUBBLEFIELD-**122;**Bill 32;Jno.W.32,60
STUBBS-Amanda 96;Jack 96
STURGIS-**115,171;**Ben 85;J.B.78;Mrs.Ben 98;Mrs.J.B.89
SUGG-Aby Duncan 21;Harry Lee 21;Lucius D.21;Mary 22;Sam'l H.21
SUGGAR-S.S.78
SULLIVAN-**166**
SUM-**132**
SUMMERS-**139**
SUTIN-Crecy 67
SWAN-Geo.F.30
SWANSON-Giles 62
SWAYZE-W.G.85
SWEENEY-SWIN(N)EY-Ellen 59;Mrs.Biddie 56
SWINT-Pope 78
SYLVESTER-**134,143,144,154;**Jas.55;N.B.78; W.C.78

T
TACKETT-**140**
TAYLOR-**122,123,124,158,166;**Annie 61; Bessie 87,98;C.C.24;Dorothy C.24;Dr.J.T. 87,98;Ella 22;Frank 54,103;Gertie 72,73, 102;Jane 66;J.F.43,78;Jno.30,58,64;Lt. Gen.Rich.19;M.C.28;Penny 68;Penny R.30
TEA-Esan 58
TEAT-**153**
TEIFER-Bettie 67
TELLIS-Rachel 53
TERMANT(TENANT)-Lem 59
TERRILL-**128,129**
TESCH-**183**
THAMES-Viola 14
THOMAS-**129,170,175;**Chas.61,66;Henderson 10;Isaac 61;James 60;Jane Lights 11;Jesse 60;Jos.41;Kansas 7;Leannah 7;Scott 7; Sistella 7
THOMASON-**149;**Mary Anne 58
THOMPSON-**110,127,132;**Amy 68;Carrie 65; Ead 58;Ellen 97;Emma 62;Eliza 67;Herbert 66;J.A.61;Julian 102;Levi 54;Lucy 67;Mita 97;Mrs.Herbert 76;Mrs.Sarah 59,97;Sadie 72,103;Smith 45;Virginia 60;Willis 45
THORNELL-O.46
THORNTON-C.78;Geo.61,67;Jno.67
TIFFORD-**122**
TILLMAN-H.W.22
TINNIN-**167**
TISDELL-**147;**B.F.81
TODD-**136**
TOLAR-**148**
TONNAR-**138;**B.6;J.P.6,79
TOOMBS-**138**
TOWNS-Ellen 57

BLACK NUMBERS INDICATE SURNAME ONLY IN CENSUS & CEMETERY RECORDS

TOWNSEND-Caroline 58;Dave 65;Jno.7
TOY-**137**
TREVILLION-Martha Rozena 20
TRIBBLE-Mrs.1
TRIM-**142**;P.R.10;T.F.78
TRUCKS-Abner 34;Ellen 35;Josiah 35
TRUNDLE-John G.27
TUCKER-**141**;Enoch 28,30;Isaac 28;
Jennie 54;Nancy 26;Sally 55
TULL-**151**
TUNSELL-**130**
TURNBULL-Mr.& Mrs.108
TURNER-**134,141,146,147,166**;Henry 28,
65;Jacob 28,34;J.M.67;Jno.80;Lizzie
28,34;Lucinda 68;Stewart 62
TURNIPSEED-**159**

U
UNDERHILL-**176**;Georgie L.42,90;Georgia
Waddell 108;Jeff.Jr.42,70;J.J.42;
Mrs.105;Mrs.Georgie 74,75,98,99
UTZ-Lovell 3;W.H.3
UZZLE-**171,183**

V
VALENTINE-Austin 59;Elzie 64;Macon
65;Malcum 67;Nancy 53
VALLEAN-**113**
VANDENANBORG-John 22
VANDENING-Rochus 22
VANHOOK-Rev.H.M.85,102
VANVE(A)COVEN-**129**;Frank 62
VAUGHN-Jno.S.49;Mrs.F.B.5
VERDEREMO-**171**
VERNELL-**140**
VIBELL-**172**
VICK-Burwell 72;H.G.25;J.W.35;Kate
90;Maj.Henry 84;Newitt 72,84;N.J.
89,90,95
VICTORY-Daniel 68
VINCENT-Mrs.M.A.64
VIRDEN-**180**
VIVENS-Maria 58
VOLLAR-W.J.17
VOORHIS-Abigail 6

W
WACHENHEIM-;----33
WADE-Alice Gray 16;Chas.16;Geo.16;
Jas.H.54,55;Jane 16;Louise Hoyt 16;
L.T.16;L.T.Jr.16;W.R.16
WADDI(e)LL-**118,176**;A.C.46;Andy 105;
Dr.A.M.31,57,105,108;Geo.68;Katie E.
59;Maj.Geo.C.105;Mary 105,108;Mollie
C.35;Mrs.A.C.37,91,108;Mrs.Berta 99
WAGGE(o)NER-Emma 70;Green89;Mrs.Will
70;Willie 89

WALKE-J.P.35,83
WALKER-**115,121,123**;Anthony 16,64,66;
C.D.14;Damon 56;Dennis 64;Ellen 16;Fannie
14;Frank 78;Henrietta 16;Isaac 16;Jno.16;
Josephine 16;Mrs.85;Mrs.Emma F.11;Mrs.
W.F.88,91,95,100,109;Patsy 60;Ruth 16,28
29;W.F.70,78,109;W.F.Jr.109;Wm.59
WALKINS-Edgar P.26;Granbery M.26
WALLACE-Levi 63
WALTERS-**144**
WALTON-**124,166**;C.H.47,50,72,78,80,85,86;
Minnie 85;Theodore 85
WANDELL-Mrs.Hattie 85,89
WANKER-**159**
WARBURTON-Rich.6
WARD-**149,164**;Mary Malinda Jane 22;Thos.B
33;T.J.59,60
WARE-**129**;Eli 55
WARNER-A.30
WARREN-**129**;B.B.14;Emma 74;H.7;Rosa 58
WASHINGTON-**111**;Adaline 54;Allen 62;Alonzo
53;Ann 53;Col.Harry 84;Emma 53;Jerry 58;
Jeyy 67;Judge 71;Winnie 14
WATKINS-Altimore 67;G.M.26,27;Mary 58;
Spencer 26;Wm.67
WATSON-**110,112,115,127,128,142,143,159,
168,169,179**;B.H.68;Calvin 59,64;C.L.51;
Elbert 60;Ellen 61;Fannie 56,76,108;Isone
15;J.C.45,78;J.J.78;Joe 66;Mary 107,108;
Mr.97;Pompey 12;Sallie 66;Sam'l F.12;
Sarah 68;T.C.31,107;T.C.Jr.107,108
WATTS-Jno.31;Mary L.39;N.W.39;S.W.83
WEBB-Bettie 35;J.E.78;Thos.58
WEBSTER-Daniel 62
WEEDIN-Harriet 10,11
WEEKS-WEAKS-**128,135,143,154**;Annie 55;
J.R.60,78
WEIGANT-**161**
WELL(S)-**135,181**;Alice 61;David 61;Jas.J.
31,55;Jno.59,65,66;Lizzie Ann 61;Sam'l W.
31,43;Thos.61
WELSH-Marg.53
WESLEY-James B. 57,59
WEST-**110,167**;Geo.86,94,97,99,102;J.M.54;
Laura D.80;Mary J.60;Mrs.E.S.94;Sallie
107
WESTCOTT-W.F.6,8
WESTON-Martha 59
WHEAT-Mary Ann 54;Sarah 66
WHEATLEY-Sallie 64
WHEELER-**131,142,144**;A.S.56;Emma 56;
Mary 53;Nancy 53
WHILDEN-Mary M.52
WHILHITE-**183**
WHITE-**137,138,140**;C.L.78;Easter 62;Freeman F.21;Grant 52;Henry 39;Hilliard 55,
66;Kate C.M.21;Marshall 21

BLACK NUMBERS INDICATE SURNAME ONLY IN CENSUS & CEMETERY RECORDS

WHITEHEAD-Catharine T.12;Isaac 62; Mrs.Irene 13;Sarah 62
WHITEN-**112**
WHITING-Ella 68
WHITSON-**143**
WHITT-**183**
WHITTERKER-Delest 57
WHITTINGTON-**148**
WIGGINS-**125,131,134,143;**Belle 60; Mary George 19;R.G.78
WILBUR-T.32
WILDY-Fannie 62;Isaac 62
WILKERSON-A.J.3;---95
WILKES-**146,148;**Mary 53
WILKINS-Susan Ann 53
WILLARD-Maj.89
WILLIAMS-**115,124,128,129,130,135,136 145,152,156,174;**A.J.43,69,78;Alis 65 Amy 61;Andrew 78;Angeline 30,67; Annie 56,61;Anthony 49;Attie 22,80; Augusta 98;Bill 65,66;Calvin 56;Cap 59;Chas.29,30,49,55;Chas.W.59; Colbert 78;Colin 53;Cornelia 54;Edie 67;Edith 59;Eliz.54,56;Elliott 54; Emma 42,43;Francis 57,Frank 60;Geo. 56,60,67;Harriet 57;Henrietta 31; Henry 54,68;Jerry 53;Jim 65;J.J.7; Jno.30,59,;Jno.L.63,65;Jno.W.81; Josephine 16;Lewis 3;Lincoln 108; Martha 64;Mary A.(Marg.)31,107;Mattie 47;Mrs.90;Oliver 66;P.78;Penny 66; Peter 16;Polly Minor 4;Preston 42,43 49;RachelDover 30;Rev.F.M.22,23,24, 37,80;Robert 57,60,61;Rueben 60;S.A. 78;Sampson L.30,31;Warner 68;Wash 57; Winnie 65;W.H.58,61,62,63,64,65,66, 67,68
WILLIS-**132,135;**Aislee 53;Bannister 71;Benson 45;Charlotte 56;Dempsey 45; Dennis 45;Ellen 54;Eliza 45;Geo.A.56 Geo.M.45;Henrietta 45;Jno.42,79,84, 86,96;Kyle 60;Meta N.42,75,79,84,95; Mrs.Fannie(Mrs.Ed.)10;Nettie Anne 57 St.John 42,75,84,96;Wesley 68
WILMAN-Mrs.Emma N.1
WILSON-**124,139,147;**Atwood 104;Bash 61;Clara 64;C.M.22;E.A.7;Elijah 59; Levi 54;L.H.53,54;Morris 61
WILTSE-W.37
WIMS-Lewis 56
WINDHAM-**147,174**
WINGATE-C.J.59,107
WINKLEY-Geo.67
WINN-WYNN-Agnis 67;Alfred 60,65;Amanda 55;Delia 67,Pearline 66
WINSLOW-Eliz.May(Maysie)3;Dr.Rich.C. 3;Rich.P.3;Sallie P.3
WINSTEAD-**157**
WINSTON-Angeline 68
WINTER(S)-Annie Laurie 22;Family 84; ----94
WISE-Father 106;Frank 78
WIXON-Ella 51;Ida 51
WOLFE-B.H.97
WOMACK-**114,144,169**
WONG-Lee 40
WOOD-Edgar Jr.31;Wm.10;W.S.8
WOODCOCK-**112**
WOODBERRY(bury)-**160;**R.S.6
WOODMAN-**115**
WOODRUFF-John 55,56
WOODRY-**137;**Eunice 22;Susan E.23
WOODWARD-**112,114**
WOOLFOLK-Chas.108;J.Marshall 106; Mrs.Emaline 55
WORCHESTER-**141**
WORTH-Andrew 30
WORTHINGTON-**166;**Geo.3;---15
WRIGHT-RIGHT-**112,118,134,135,154,160,166** A.L.65;Allen98;David 54;Henry 58,65;H.J. 50,69,74,77,78,88,91;Ida 27;Jno.W.59; Mary E.34;Mollie 64;R.L.54,55,56,57,61, 62,78,79;Spencer 58;W.B.63;W.R.66
WYLEY-Peter 7

Y
YANCY-Mrs.Rocena 86
YARATSKY-**116**
YATES-Alex 62
YELVERTON-**148**
YERGER-Capt.W.S.21
YOUNG-**128;**Alex 56;Dave 63;Dennis 63;Edmond 60;Grant 18;Nicholas 15;Sarah Fowler 6,15;Virginia 53
YOUNGER-**180**
YOUNT-**182**

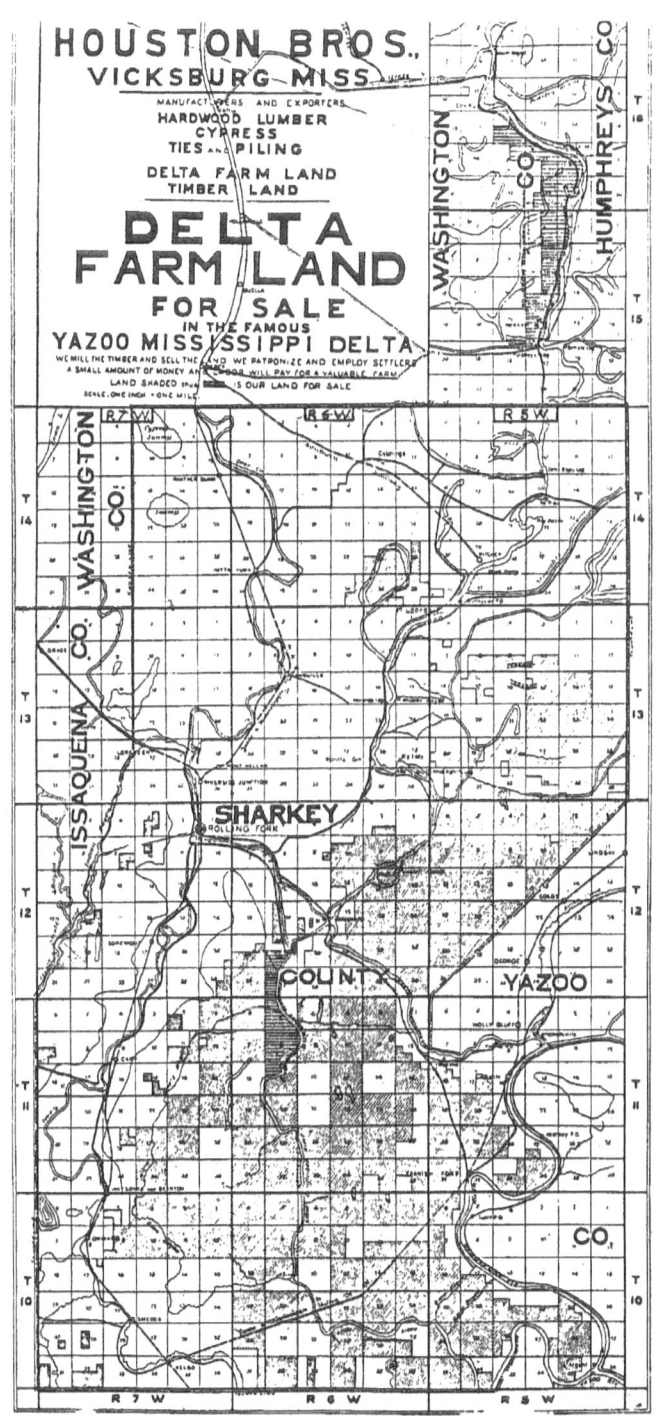

www.ingramcontent.com/pod-product-compliance
Lightning Source LLC
Chambersburg PA
CBHW030227100526
44585CB00012BA/336